Leonard Hill, ⬚⬚⬚⬚⬚⬚⬚⬚⬚⬚⬚⬚⬚⬚⬚⬚⬚⬚ n
Southampton ⬚⬚⬚⬚⬚⬚⬚⬚⬚⬚⬚⬚⬚⬚⬚⬚⬚⬚ n
teaching, he ⬚⬚⬚⬚⬚⬚⬚⬚⬚⬚⬚⬚⬚⬚⬚⬚⬚⬚ d
the results of ⬚⬚⬚⬚⬚⬚⬚⬚⬚⬚⬚⬚⬚⬚⬚⬚⬚ d
in the summer ⬚⬚⬚⬚⬚⬚ M000118645 ⬚

Among the tributes to Benny Hill, on his death in April 1992:

'Without a doubt he was a master comic and one of the funniest men to grace the stage and mug the television screen. He made bawdy an art form for everyone to enjoy. I'm saddened by his passing, but so is the world. He made us all laugh, and all the laughs were big.'   BOB HOPE

'He was one of our greatest exports. He had great comic inventiveness and was master of the visual joke.'

ERNIE WISE

'He was the personification of everything we ever enjoyed of Blackpool seaside postcards.'   DEREK NIMMO

'Benny's comedy found a warm welcome with millions of viewers throughout the world because he was a great clown in the classic sense . . . a professional and thorough genius and also a very kind man.'

RICHARD DUNN, *Chief Executive Thames TV*

'Benny's humour was like Chaplin's. It was body language. No words spoken but the whole world laughed.'   FREDDIE STARR

'Benny Hill was that rare breed – a funny man . . . He is one of those comics who will be more highly regarded after his death than when he was alive. The criticism of his humour as sexist and old-fashioned will pass, and he will be restored to the platform where he should be.'

PHILIP JONES, *director of light entertainment for Thames Television 1968–88*

like his younger brother Benny, grew up in
in the 1920s and 1930s. After retiring from
wrote many plays for children and publishes
his researches on early reading habits. He die
of 1960.

LEONARD HILL

Saucy Boy

The Life Story of Benny Hill

OLD CAPULET (TO TYBALT):
Am I the master here or you? . . .
Go to, go to;
You are a saucy boy.

Romeo and Juliet, act I, scene v

Grafton
An Imprint of HarperCollinsPublishers

To Margaret With Love

Grafton
An Imprint of HarperCollins*Publishers*
77–85 Fulham Palace Road,
Hammersmith, London W6 8JB

Published by Grafton 1992
9 8 7 6 5 4 3 2 1

First published in Great Britain by
GraftonBooks 1990

A CIP catalogue record for this book
is available from the British Library

ISBN 0-586-20521-7

Printed in Great Britain by
HarperCollinsManufacturing Glasgow

Set in Palatino

Contents

Acknowledgements

I thank all those people who, by agreeing to talk to me, have made a contribution to the life story of Benny Hill. Their names are to be found in the following pages. My gratitude is also tendered to the undermentioned for the considerable help they have given me: Jack Breckon, Thames Television; Melanie Louis, Thames Taffner; Nancy Allen, Thames Taffner Marketing and Merchandising Co.; Eddie Pedder, *TV Times*; James Moir, BBC; Ann Rosenberg, BBC; Irene Gray, Richard Stone Partnership; Juliet Simpkins, Madame Tussaud's; James Poteat, Television Information Office, New York; Dana Rogers, Museum of Broadcasting, New York; Leslie Gardner, Artellus Limited; Richard Johnson, GraftonBooks; Shenagh Richardson, London researcher; Peter Nissen, New York researcher; Florence Jaques; Tilly Underwood; Harold Tilley; Gordon Russell; Helen McIntyre; Caroline Oakley; and Karen Game.

Finally, I must offer my profound thanks to my brother, Benny Hill, for allowing me to make public matters that he has spent a lifetime assiduously keeping private. He has accepted this uncalled-for imposition with his usual courtesy, generosity and good humour.

Leonard Hill

Illustration Acknowledgements

Benny as cockney comedian *Norman Page*
Scene from *Light Up the Sky (British Film Institute)*
Benny and Michael Caine in *The Italian Job (Kobal Collection)*
Scene from *Chitty Chitty Bang Bang (British Film Institute)*
Scene from Schweppes advertisement *Cadbury Schweppes plc*
Benny with stooge Jackie Wright *Thames TV*
Stuntman Ken Sedd *Ken Sedd*
With Dennis Kirkland at Madame Tussaud's *Thames TV*
Benny in circus sketch *Rex Features*
Shaking hands with Prince Philip *Thames TV*
Benny's team as the Crook Report © *Sun Newspapers/ Rex Features*

All other photographs are from the author's collection

1

Baptism of Fire

The slim, fair-haired lad stood under an oil lamp in a medieval dungeon and pattered away to sixty human bundles huddled together in the darkness. It was one night during the 1940 blitz on Southampton and the boy was more afraid of the audience than the German bombs which were dropping all around. He had never performed to a crowd of strangers before. Benny Hill was undergoing his baptism of fire.

'Don't worry, Mrs Woman,' he cried, as the thunder of nearby explosions rolled on. 'It's only the bums upstairs takin' out the furniture!' A stick of bombs walked slowly across the town towards them. 'Look on the bright side, chums. If you get a crater in the garden, boast about it! Tell the neighbours you're having a swimming pool!' The sudden deep roar of an exploding land-mine made the floor shudder. The boy felt it in the soles of his feet and sensed the fear in his audience. Even behind stone walls twelve feet thick, no one felt safe. Right. No more bomb jokes. He changed his tack. 'I'm fed up with this corned beef, aren't you?' he asked. 'My Dad said, "I don't know what you're grumbling about. We had it in the last war." "I know," I said, "but it was fresh then!" What about the rationing lark, then, Mrs Woman? Isn't it a carry-on? Up in Scotland they can only get whale meat. That's right. Nothing but whale meat. My cousin up there reckons he's had so much whale meat that every time he coughs, a fountain shoots out the top of 'is 'ead!' The boy was not getting many laughs but he was giving the shelterers something else to think about.

I had done my stint in the vault under Catchcold Tower on the old town walls a week before – fifteen minutes of ancient jokes leavened by a few original wheezes and rewarded by an enthusiastic round of coughing. Now it was my brother's turn. I had introduced him with a few ridiculously improbable prophecies (which have all come true) and, wearing our young sister's tiny brown bowler, he had walked into a circle of yellow light.

At last he began to warm to the task. Raising his voice above the cacophony of explosions and ack-ack fire, he was rapping out the funnies better than ever. I felt proud of him. After all, at the age of sixteen, he was tackling a difficult audience, with a lot on its collective mind. The prospect had daunted me, and I was two years older. Now here he was, getting titters if not laughs. I could see occasional smiles on faces in the patch of light. It was quite an achievement under the circumstances. At the end of his set, there was scattered applause. I clapped heartily to keep it going.

'They're using their hands to hold on to their blankets, Alfie,' I said.

Several well-wrapped punters came up to thank my brother as we put on our overcoats. I could see that he was gratified by the courtesy. He nodded and smiled. Turning to me, he said, 'Let's see what's happened to the town.' We both wanted to go, although the all-clear had not yet sounded. Fear is infectious in air-raid shelters. Get out in the open and it vanishes. At least, that was our experience at the time. Despite the pleas of a couple of blanketed citizens, we lifted our bicycles through a hatchway in the great oak door and wheeled them on to the esplanade that had once been the harbour wall.

We felt the cold night air on our faces and heard the heavy drone of a German bomber fleet overhead. Searchlights swept a sky rosy with the glow of huge fires. Now and then they stopped to pick out a particular plane for the attention of the guns. However, although the coastal batteries made a lot of noise, they seemed unable to prevent the raiders doing exactly as they wished. In the lower air, a myriad sparks floated like fireflies around the turrets of the Catchcold Tower. As we clambered on to our bikes, Alfie pointed back towards the estuary. Above the Old Walls, flames were waving like flags. They were rising from a spot close by the memorial to the Pilgrim Fathers. I wondered if the tall monument was still there.

It was not a time to stand and stare. We cycled off northwards with all speed, swerving to avoid the rubble and debris in our way. Where the road was clear, I moved alongside Alfie to congratulate him on his performance.

'I wasn't that good,' he said. 'I couldn't get their interest.'

'Don't give me that,' I retorted. 'Did you see that bald fellow in the front? He was there last week – and I couldn't get him to crack his face, even without an air-raid. But you got a giggle out of him. And with the bombs dropping.'

'I don't look at individuals,' Alfie said.

'Well, I was watching him. And if you can get laughs from a stoneface like that, you can get 'em from anybody.'

In Hill Lane a fire-engine with its hoses and gear was straddled right across the road. We had seen the fire half a mile away. A large Edwardian house had suffered

a direct hit. Firemen were busy, working by the light of
the flames. We approached, pushing our bikes.

'What the hell do you think you're on?' an angry
air-raid warden shouted.

'Can we help?' I asked.

'Get off the bloody street,' he answered, beside himself with rage at our foolishness. 'Take cover!'

'Come on,' I said to Alfie. We put our bikes on
our shoulders, kept away from the firemen and tiptoed over the pipes and bricks until the road was
clear.

Then we cycled away up the slope and raced round
into Wilton Road. By this time, the Luftwaffe had
settled down to do a thorough, methodical job of
destruction. They were dropping flares that lit the
wide expanse of the school playing-fields with an
eerie green light. Drifts of smoke from burning houses
added to the semblance of a sinister Whitechapel
fog. We were not impressed. The dreadful thump
of bombs dropping did not bother us much, either.
Both the Hill boys were in a state of euphoria. The
danger and excitement of the air-raid had got to us.
Alfie was now convinced that his debut had been a
triumph.

Adrenalin coursing through our veins, we swung
our bikes back and forth across the road, shouting
our challenges to the gods.

'Buck Benny Rides Again!' Alfie cried, quoting the
title of a recent film.

'Lucky Lenny Rides Again!' I countered. He topped
me with 'Buck Benny Hill Rides Again!' unknowingly
anticipating his future professional name. We began to
sing at the tops of our voices. Occasionally, a policeman or warden would bellow at us and we would put
on a spurt.

Once, our noisy progress out of town was interrupted by the sibilant sound of a bomb falling immediately above us. It was hissing its unmistakably hostile intent. 'Geddown!' I shouted. We swerved together like cornering speedway riders and laid the bikes down, as we had done a hundred times before, threw ourselves into the gutter and lay flat. At that moment, the bomb landed a garden away, exploding with such a blast that it not only deafened us but threatened to split our eardrums. It blew many tons of earth into the air, pelting us with clods that seemed to continue falling for ever. Our overcoats saved us from the worst bruises.

At last, thinking it was safe, we stood up. A final tardy sod dropped nearby. 'It should have hit me on the head,' said Alfie. 'Chaplin would have done it that way.' I laughed – not only at the picture he suggested, but at my brother's insatiable lust to make comedy out of every experience. We brushed ourselves down and rode on, unshaken. I knew we would shake later. At last we reached Winchester Road and waved goodbye. I turned left for the family bungalow at the edge of the New Forest and Alfie turned right for his lodgings in Eastleigh. After that evening we never shared the same stage again.

Full of ourselves, we had passed Number 164 Wilton Road, the semi-detached house where we Hill boys had spent most of our infancy, with scarcely a glance. Neither of us was born there. Alfie first saw the light of day in a flat above a lamp shop in Bernard Street, Southampton. The lamp shop was close to the docks and a few doors from the cattle market. Thus, when young Alfie was born on 21 January 1924, he was informed by the sounds around him – the lowing of cows from the cattle pounds and the occasional basso-profundo fart of a liner's horn that rattled the window above his cot. These were the dissonant notes, the charivari, which greeted his arrival. No wonder he became a clown.

Our father Alfred and grandfather Henry had been clowns, at least for part of their careers. Their days in the circus were often recalled by our father when Alfie was young. To amuse his sons, Dad would make himself up as a clown and walk upstairs on his hands. Then he would dress us up in similar style. That was one side of his personality: there was another side.

'In every human being there is a Lear and a Fool,' wrote Cyril Connolly. The Lear in our father was a large, noisy, irascible man who believed that the Fates conspired against him. He was right – they did. Born into a raggle-taggle family on the run from a posse of creditors, he joined the circus as a child, became a cheapjack as an adolescent and a soldier as a young man. He was bombed in Ireland, gassed in France and taken prisoner in Belgium.

Upon his return to Southampton in 1919, he was offered a partnership in a tiny shop selling surgical and rubber goods. When my grandfather refused him the relatively small loan needed, my father became the sole employee of the firm. On the strength of his prospects, he married a rosy innocent, Helen, who promptly produced two sons to whom she transferred a good deal of her affection. Meanwhile the rubber goods business took off and eventually made my father's employer, his former prospective partner, a millionaire. These experiences induced in my father a profound scepticism, if not cynicism. He believed that the institutions of the State, the Church, the Law, the Army, were all fraudulent, but that political action was unlikely to improve things. His philosophy is best summed up by the boxing referee's dictum – 'Protect yourself at all times!'

Our mother, on the other hand, rarely revealed her opinions about anything except the most immediate domestic matters. And in these she always got her way. Mum came from a home where money was scarce. It was kept 'respectable' largely by the efforts of her mother in the teeth of her father's easy-going ways. When Mum grew up, she went to work in the offices of the huge Rolling Mills in Southampton. At that time she was a lovely, milky young woman with a sweet smile and the kind of healthy glow on her that you cannot get out of a pot. She was much taken with our father at a dance, but when she met his family she was unimpressed by their bohemian lifestyle. Mum determined to do better for him, married him and kept her promise. She was always a conscientious and hardworking wife. Her greatest satisfactions, however, were obtained in the company and care of her children.

On the day of Alfie's birth, my mother sent me to a kindly aunt's house to stay overnight. When my aunt returned me to my parents the day after, I found them much relieved that their second child was strong and healthy, without the serious digestive problems that had marred my first year. Alfie was a beautiful, cuddly baby and no trouble at all. Even his conception had banished his mother's previous post-natal depression caused by my birth and early illness. Within a few weeks of his arrival Mum had scooped up both her little ones and deposited us in the new nest at Wilton Road. It was a raw and sparsely furnished home at first, but we soon wore it into a kind of simple comfort. Before long, Alfie was crawling all over the kitchen floor – except that he did not crawl but, half-sitting, dragged one leg beneath him. The constant friction of the side of his calf on the linoleum created a painful grey ulcer which could not be cured until he was toddling.

That kitchen was a magical place for a small child to play. Most mornings a small wood fire was burning in the slow, black glowback iron range. Often the early sunlight streamed through the marbled glass panel of the garden door, making miraculous patterns on a chair or table. After Dad had left for work, Alfie and I would sit at the table, each with a pudding basin of sugared bread cubes sinking in a lake of warm milk. As we took breakfast, Mum would sit with us and read something from *Bubbles Annual* or some other Christmas book for children. Benny can remember many of the stories to this day. He still thinks the giant in 'Pompety Finds a Needle' the most terrifying character in fiction. And, at the drop of a hat, he will recite a ballad beginning,

> I'll tell you a story
> If you don't make a noise.
> Mustapha and Hassan
> Are two little boys.
> They both live in Egypt,
> The sun there is hot.
> Mustapha's a good boy,
> But Hassan is not.

It was one of Alfie's party pieces as a small child. It has been one of his party pieces ever since. He has altered the words a little now and again of course.

Benny's first memory is of the expectant excitement of a Christmas Eve, the pair of us in our double bed unable to sleep. A few hours later he was overjoyed to find a blue and yellow wooden engine at the bottom of the bed. I was given a red and green wheelbarrow of similar make. These gifts were not only expressions of love but signs of equal regard. Our parents went to great lengths to give us parity of treatment. In disputed claims I was expected to divide; Alfie to take first pick. All these efforts at fairness, however, did not stop us grumbling at every turn.

My first memory of Alfie is when he was two and with the family at the silent pictures (before they were called 'movies'). These occasions were quite informal, as a good deal of chatter went on. Alfie was standing on his father's knees with Dad's bowler hat swaying on his head. When the lovers on the screen kissed, Alfie pointed at them and cried, 'Ooh, look! Mummy and Daddy!' This brought the house down. It was the first laugh he ever got from a large audience.

By the time Alfie was toddling, we were both sturdy, tow-haired youngsters with huge red apple cheeks. If we were not flying red flags, our mother knew at once we were poorly. She fussed over us, enjoying our utter dependence upon her. Sometimes she liked to play a game in which she hid in the house or garden, listening to our cries and waiting patiently for one of her toddler sons to find her.

When putting us to bed, Mum would insist that we lay straight on our backs, so that she could throw a sheet completely over us. We remained still, staring up at the vault of white, hot breath tickling our lips. The soft covering was soon pulled tight, then Mum would put on the blankets and make the bed as if there was no one in it. After a minute or two, the blankets above us at the head of the bed would be folded back one by one. Only the sheet remained over our faces. We were always good boys and trusted our mother. The ritual ended with her pulling back the sheet to reveal her two fair-haired sons, looking up at her with bright blue eyes. That moment was her reward. I think she was intoxicated by her love and her power over us.

Mum liked nothing better than working at her domestic chores in the back garden with her boys playing
round her feet. She would be turning the stiff great
wheel of the mangle by the house, pegging out clothes
on the line, chopping wood for the voracious kitchen-
stove, seated peeling potatoes or shelling peas into a
bowl in her lap – sometimes all in the one morning.

The garden, originally a bare rectangular strip of
earth, had been seeded into a grassy patch that scarcely
warranted the name of 'lawn'. It sloped up to a steep
bank, topped by thick bushes and large oak trees.
This was the edge of an adjoining field that looked
down upon us, and gave us a sense of being in the
country. Benny remembers with pleasure the annual
pageant when the shouts of the ploughman announced
the approach of two splendid chestnut shire-horses,
brasses rattling and gleaming through the leaves. They
turned at the end of our garden, their huge heads
nodding above the bushes, nostrils blowing out great
clouds of breath. Round they went, the tackle slapping
and creaking, the ploughman urging them on with
affectionate curses – and we would run to see them
before their empire faded.

Alfie was often taken in his push-chair to play on
the nearby common, a square mile of wooded parkland surrounded by a sod wall. As well as copses,
the park contained three lakes, half a dozen football
pitches, a vestigial race-course where cattle grazed,
a public house and a horse pound. Children, cows,
horses, dogs, swans, Muscovy ducks, red squirrels
and multi-coloured soccer players all helped to make
it an enchanted country. It is one to which Benny has
returned many times in his lifetime. When he was old
enough to walk there, he would hold his mother's hand
and rub his face against her fur cuff. 'Lovely Mummy,'

he used to say, as he looked up at her. Once on the common, he was most solicitous for his mother's safety, in a manner remarkable for a child of his age. He would help her across ditches and remove brambles from her way. In return, she gave him free rein, providing sandwiches for him to eat or throw to the swans and squirrels. Mum would sit on a seat by the lake for ages, while we boys and our imaginations ran riot.

Mum was easy about the functions of the body, too. She encouraged us to pee without restraint, whenever we felt like it. One afternoon she was chatting to a neighbour by the shops in Wilton Road. Alfie was in the push-chair. I was making an interesting puddle in the gutter nearby, when a bigger boy on a bicycle pulled up alongside to watch the performance. Then he asked the way to Shirley Road. I was leaking and directing at the same time when he interrupted me. It seemed that I had misheard him. 'Don't you know that's rude?' he asked, pointing. I did not. Suddenly I felt how Adam must have felt when he took the first bite of the apple. I blushed and mumbled and put it away. 'Your face and my arse would make a good pair,' observed the boy triumphantly as he rode off.

Benny believes his mother was right and the world was wrong. I am inclined to agree with him. But he was also caught out once by her easy-going sanity. When he started infants' school, Mum told him, as she had told me: 'If it's wet on the way home from school, don't be afraid to shelter under the nearest porch. Just open the gate, walk up the path and wait under cover until the rain stops. The people won't mind.' So he did. When it rained, the tubby little five-year-old opened the nearest gate, walked up the path and waited under the porch. Immediately a top window opened and a woman leaned out. 'Little boy!' she shouted. 'Little boy!'

'Yes?'

'Don't stand there. Go away. Go away at once!'

'Why?'

'Go away. We've got pneumonia in the house! Go away!'

Alfie slunk out into the rain and arrived home soaking wet. 'Fancy turfing a child out into a downpour like that!' Mum said. 'The poor little nipper might have caught his death of cold. He could have died of pneumonia!'

Mum was broadminded enough not to interfere in my brother's first serious affair. It began when I started school at five. Alfie looked around for a new playmate and found that he was strangely attracted to a pretty neighbour of his own age. Her name was Peggy Bell (all little girls were called Peggy, Betty or Molly in those days). Her mother allowed Alfie to visit at any time of the day. In a tiny tent at the bottom of her garden Peggy introduced him to the delights of love. He remembers it well. She had bobbed golden hair and smelt of biscuits. Alfie was entranced by her beauty. He would lie alongside her in the tent, clutching her plump body, stroking her hair and kissing the sweaty bridge of her nose.

That year the field beyond the gardens lay fallow. Under the summer sun, it was a paradise of lush grass, wild flowers and butterflies. Alfie and Peggy played there for hours, hunting butterflies, gathering daisies, smelling poppies, dancing, singing, shouting, chasing, embracing, and rolling in the grass, with nothing to mar their joy. One afternoon, they wandered hand-in-hand into the common. They were astonished to find the park full of teenage scholars on their way home. The paths were bright with school uniforms of different colours. There was laughter, horseplay and dalliance. Alfie and

Peggy stared fascinated as the boys and girls paired off and disappeared into the bushes. Life, it seemed, had its compensations for everyone.

My education, too, had begun. After three months' attendance at the infants' school, I was able to impress my extended family at a crowded Christmas party. Alfie was trying to tell the company something. No one was paying much attention. Alfie tried again. His comment seemed familiar to me. 'What is the boy on about?' demanded my father irritably. 'I think he is saying "Fuck it!"' I volunteered helpfully. There was sudden, total silence. The revellers froze.

I was completely innocent, only repeating what I had heard in the playground. I did not know what the adults knew. But they were certainly paying attention now. The spell was broken by my father. 'To bed!' he roared. 'To bed! How dare you? To bed! And no Christmas tea for you, my lad!' I was ushered tear-stained upstairs, and left alone to contemplate the rank injustice of the world. Later, my mother sneaked up with tea and sympathy. I even had a slice of Christmas cake.

Every Saturday, Mum took us to visit her mother, Grandma Cave, who lived in a road of little old semi-detached houses that had closed ranks to look like a terrace. I did not realize how cramped Grandma's house was until I walked into the empty shell of it many years later during the blitz. One could hardly walk around it inside, the place was so small. It was then open to the street and sky, having been damaged by a bomb. But we boys saw it in the early days. Grandma Cave's tiny parlour was an Aladdin's cave. Unlike our own rather bleak front room, it was warm, cosy and crammed with treasures.

As soon as we opened the parlour door, the rings

and tassels of its wine-red velvet curtain made voluptuous clicking and swishing noises. Our eyes were
caught immediately by the heavy bronze statuette of
St George and the Dragon on the mantelpiece. This
was the kind of art we boys really appreciated. Of
course, the dragon was rather small, but the length
of George's sword made up for that. At any moment
he was about to skewer the dragon like a round of
beef. It was some years before we were tall enough
to confirm that George's improbable sword could be
unscrewed and that the point was sharp enough to
draw blood from a youthful finger. Once inside the
minute museum, we were surrounded by buffets and
whatnots full of knick-knacks and bric-à-brac. On
the shelves stood glass animals, copper bowls, leop-
ard shells, souvenirs of Le Havre, ivory elephants,
chiming clocks, silver baby boots, small porcelain
vases, fairground prizes, framed snapshots, Japanese
saucers, marble paper-weights, china dogs, brass
bells, ebony deer, pottery figurines, Chinese fans
and presents from Southsea. Years later, our cousins
told us smugly that they were privileged to examine
gems we had never seen. The Hill brothers had, it
appears, so Gothic a reputation that before each invasion Grandma removed all her valuable ornaments to
places of safety.

In the spaces between the buffets and whatnots stood
a very prickly horse-hair sofa (a torment for boys in
short trousers), a noisy, extrovert grandfather clock
and a stuffed jay under glass that stared bitterly at a
live jay in a cage across the room. The birds were both
victims of Grandpa's widgie, a countryman's catapult.
Ancestors gazed sternly down at us from photographs
all around the walls. In summer, the tiny grate under
the mantelpiece was furnished with a brown pot of

dried wild flowers, bulrushes and tall grasses; on winter evenings we would watch pictures in the fire while Grandpa read his pink *Football Echo* with its esoteric front-page cartoon.

In the centre of the window-space, on a tall table, stood the aspidistra, as it did in every other window of the street. Grandma would stand beside this unprepossessing plant, looking through the lace curtains at the passing show of sweet and sour women who were her neighbours. 'Mrs Copplestone commences to look old,' she would announce, with satisfaction.

Sometimes Grandma, our mother, and her sister, Auntie Louie, would go shopping for the afternoon. Grandpa, a kindly, long-suffering man, would take charge of his four grandsons. He gave us the run of the ground floor and garden, keeping an indulgent eye on his charges until it was time to prepare the tea for eight. This was something of a ritual. We boys gathered round as he took a long, razor-sharp knife and, globular cob-loaf against his stomach, cut towards himself. His spellbound audience felt sure that the knife would slip and disembowel him. But it never did. He always produced perfect, thin slices, on which he trowelled butter without stint.

Grandpa was held in awe because we had all seen the photograph of him in a menacing stance as an amateur boxer – a beetle-browed, stocky middleweight. Later I learned that he had a reputation around town as a man, who, as they say, 'could look after himself'. He was by trade a carpenter and joiner. When we were young, he used his skills to make us a splendid set of wooden bricks. Benny reminded me how the bricks, being of various shapes and woods, could be used to make all kinds of structures. Grandpa was always a generous man. When Alfie and I were still

small enough to fit into one pram, he was chided by
Grandma for giving us pennies as we said goodbye to
him. Though he knew we threw them into the street,
he continued to press the coins upon us at every
opportunity.

When he was short of employment, Grandpa would
work as an odd-job man at a local department store or
office. But he was always a countryman at heart, hap-
piest when tickling a trout, snaring a rabbit or downing
a pheasant with his widgie. He was an excellent horse-
man. When he was four, Grandpa's father had lifted him
into the saddle and ordered, 'Learn to ride – or fall off!'
He learned to ride.

Our Great-grandfather Cave had died before my birth
so that Alfie and I had never seen him. We had been told
that he was a Jerseyman who had brought his bride to
England from the island off the coast of France. They
had settled down to farm a smallholding at Netley
Marsh in the New Forest. After a few profitable years,
they moved into Southampton and opened a green-
grocer's and pork-butcher's shop in St Mark's Terrace,
Six Dials. However, Great-grandfather was no businessman and, as the pork-butchery enterprise failed, he
went to work as a docker. Great-grandmother Cave
continued to preside over the greengrocery. She did
not leave the shop for forty years, inviting the world
to visit her. The shop in St Mark's Terrace became a
popular meeting-place, but never made much money.
Great-grandmother Cave had a habit of giving away
her fruit to needy children. Seated at the counter and
never seen without a snood to keep her hair tidy, she
became a well-known character in the St Mary's district. As children, we heard affectionate tales about
the friendly countrywoman, but had arrived too late
to meet her.

Grandma Cave (whose maiden name was Sims), on the other hand, enjoyed going out, and when on a shopping trip, or some such, took great care to look smart. She knew about clothes. As a young mother, Grandma had worked long hours sewing garments to help provide for her children. She was interested in fashion, but always adopted the style of a previous era. When her daughters were wearing cloche hats, short skirts and cloaks, Grandma wore a dark bombazine suit with a long skirt and a great hat listing under a huge bunch of red cherries. Sometimes her chapeau would support a nesting pheasant with a tail-feather that curved away into the distance behind her. Alfie was making fun of the still life on Grandma's hats at a very early age.

When out on parade with Grandma Cave, 'stopping to speak' was an important part of the excursion. Although death, illness and the price of fish were usually dealt with, the staple topic of conversation among her acquaintances was their neighbours. Surprisingly, morals were rarely in question. There was tacit agreement about that subject. The general view of relations between the sexes was best expressed by one of Benny's characters: 'I don't approve of that sort of thing before marriage – and I'm not too sure about it afterwards!' There appeared to be no dissent in practice to this philosophy. No, it was not sex, but a fondness for gin that was the universal weakness. And how excruciating when it was discovered! 'I knew she kep' it!' they would declare, with wicked glee. 'I knew she kep' it!' The pursed lips, the folded arms heaving up the indignant bosom, the righteous shake of the head – sixty years later, Benny can reproduce them with breathtaking fidelity.

Benny inherited his talent for mimicry from his mother's sister Louise, or Auntie Louie, as we called her. She was a lively, high-spirited and musical girl, who at an early age was repeating not only the cheapjack patter but the style of delivery she heard at the fairs on the common. Her father made her a set of wooden rings so that she could imitate the gypsies and didicois who ran the Hoopla! stalls. Unfortunately for him, Louise insisted that he played the part of the punters. She expected him, in various guises, to lose money at her parlour stall. Grandpa Cave, kindly man that he was, meekly obliged.

Louie's favourite cheapjack was a black man who had a pitch in Kingsland Square market. She learned his spiel and shocked her mother once when she came out with: 'Why don't you pawn your face and lose the ticket!' Not the sort of comment a nice girl would make! But she was irrepressible. When her Grandfather Cave heard Louie's whistling as she cleaned his kitchen he chided her with:

> A whistling woman and a crowing hen
> is neither good to God nor men!

That would not stop Louise. She whistled all the louder.

What we boys loved about Auntie Louie was not only her sunny disposition but her infectious laugh. She had this great gusher of laughter inside her and when she began to tell you a funny story you could feel the pressure building up. She would start to gabble in a vain struggle to get to the punch line before the merriment erupted from her. She rarely succeeded. Half-way through the story she would burst into peals of laughter at the thought of the ending. She would go weak at the knees and fall about, tears streaming down her apple cheeks. Her audience would be mystified as to the cause of the hilarity, but her laughter was so infectious that in no time at all you would be hooting along with her. She laughed with every fibre of her being. Every part of her had a good time. And you had a good time too. The punch line did not matter. She had the power to evoke gales of laughter by the sheer dynamism of her personality.

Like her sister Helen, Louise kept up-to-date with all the latest songs and show-business gossip. She loved the music-hall and longed to become a professional singer. The performers at Sunday-afternoon concerts taught her a great deal; she was a regular attender and watched every move. By the time she was fifteen she had a mature, robust voice, so resonant that it could be given free rein only in the lavatory on the outside wall of her home. In the tiny cubicle, her voice was allowed to exercise its full range and power.

One day Helen was in the garden when she was accosted over the fence.

'Who was that lady with the lovely voice I heard singing in your house?' asked the neighbour.

To her credit, Helen replied, 'That was no lady. That was our Louie!'

When Louise sang in public at the Coliseum, Southampton, her big voice echoed round the dome to remarkable effect. As she walked off to appreciative applause and shouts of 'Encore', the director cried, 'Louise, you takes the cake!' It is clear that she could have had a successful career on the stage, but, like so many women of her generation, she gave it all up for marriage – and in her case a home in Kent. A home so far away meant that the Hill boys never saw enough of her.

When Alfie and I were young, Grandma Cave already had commitments that, in her mind, were as important as those to her husband and children. Those obligations were to her aged parents, who lived in the tiny bedsit above the parlour. Like many of her generation, she took filial responsibility very seriously. She therefore, in her own phrase, 'waited hand and foot' upon our great-grandparents, whom Alfie and I called Grandpa and Grandma Sims. The fact that Grandma Sims had always been 'delicate' and had therefore abdicated her menial responsibilities for her own mother did not deter Grandma Cave in the zealous discharge of her daughterly duties.

Alfie, while still small, grew fond of Grandma Sims, a quiet, gentle creature, whose bone structure bore witness to an early loveliness. It was said that, when courting her, Grandpa Sims saw her every weekend one summer. Each Saturday he walked from Southampton to Wimborne, where she lived, and each Sunday he walked back: thirty-nine miles each way.

During his courtship, Grandpa Sims was a railway policeman in Southampton Docks. Later he joined the Metropolitan Police Force in London and was involved in the hunt for Jack the Ripper. His great-grandsons were most disappointed not only that he had been unsuccessful but that he had no clue as to the identity of the fiend. We cheered up when he described how, one foggy night, he nearly lost his life in a murderous mêlée with footpads down a back alley in Limehouse. He restored his credibility by modestly admitting that he had arrested one of the thugs and helped to bring the others to book.

On Saturday evenings we were expected to visit our great-grandparents upstairs. The forbidding chamber had a strange perfume. We left the cheery yellow glow of the parlour's gaslight for the darting shadows of the candlelit stairs and then the corner light of Grandpa Sims's oil lamp. Neither Benny nor I can remember visiting the top front room together. One was always the lone child in there. It could be a fascinating experience. Grandpa Sims was a spellbinder – a spare figure, pushing ninety, but a clean old man. There is a race of men, English, French, German, Polish, Russian, who are all tall, fair, bony, with grey eyes, a spot of colour high on each cheekbone and a glowing complexion. Perhaps they are throwbacks to the original Vikings.

The old man certainly descended like Thor upon Alfie one afternoon. The Hill boys were eating jam sandwiches in Grandma Cave's minute kitchen at the end of the narrow downstairs corridor, when the kitchen door burst open and there stood this avenging god from Asgard, quivering with rage from head to foot. Close white hair framing his bony head, grizzled moustache bristling, eyes darting lightning glances, the old man thundered his threats to destroy the evil five-year-old, my brother. In his hands he held the symbols of Alfie's wickedness – a cut-throat razor and bunch of newspaper shavings.

The child had been left alone in the top bedsit for a few minutes and had taken the chance to experiment with Grandpa Sims's dearest treasure – his set of seven lethally sharp razors, each handle labelled with its appropriate day. Alfie had hidden the evidence of his misdeed, but not well enough. Now Viking justice was to be administered. Grandpa Sims put down the razor and shavings and unbuckled his leather belt. Eyes and jammy mouth wide open, Alfie stared in disbelief. He slowly lowered the sandwich that he had been supporting in mid-air. Sensing the danger to her offspring,

our gentle Mum was galvanized into action. She leapt
to her feet and placed herself between old man and
infant, feet astride and arms flung out wide in the
approved Mary Pickford manner. Offering her grandfather apologies, excuses, threats and bribes in short
order, Mum managed slowly to placate the disgruntled
giant. He continued to chastise the accursed boy with
blunt upbraidings and his bitter scoffs. But at last he
turned and, muttering his disapproval, trundled back
to Asgard.

Grandpa Sims never forgave Alfie, whom he saw, no
doubt, as an evil dwarf, the spawn of Loki. He liked
talking to me, as I never reminded him that he was
repeating himself. Every time I visited his eyrie, he
pointed out the steel engraving of Wellington greeting
Blücher on the field of Waterloo and explained that
the Prussian general had arrived too late to affect the
outcome of the battle. It irked him that Blücher's tardy
arrival might detract some credit from Wellington. A
typically underhand Prussian ploy, he thought. And as
for Bonaparte, Grandpa Sims was the only man I have
ever met who tended a flame of hatred for the little
Corsican. He was convinced that Napoleon was the
Devil incarnate. But then, Grandpa Sims died before
the twentieth-century tyrants made their challenges for
the title.

Alfie was much affected by the death of Grandma
Sims, who slipped away without fuss in 1929. He felt he
had lost a friend. Grandpa Sims, on the other hand, was
an unconscionable time a-dying. Alfie was expected, as
I was, to visit his great-grandfather while the old man
slept. The poor little lad sat alone at the foot of the
bed looking up the black tunnels of Grandpa Sims's
nostrils and listening to the deep, pumping rattle of his
snoring. The light of a single flickering candle threw

shadows which mocked the boy, gesticulating at him from the walls. He was terrified. But he continued, as I did, to sit with the ancient Viking until he died, at last, in 1930.

2

The Man Who Fell Out
of the Balloon

'He's a comic genius,' said Phyllis Diller. She paused.
'He was hurt as a child, wasn't he?' went on America's First Lady of Comedy. It was an assertion, not a
question. 'That's right,' I said. 'You see,' she explained,
'the hurt is the grit in the oyster. It has created the
pearl of his comedy.' Another assertion. 'Yes,' I said.
A wise woman; wise enough to play the fool. She had
seen the truth without having met my brother. They
had corresponded by postcard for years, but she had
spoken to him only on the telephone. Nevertheless, she
understood.

Benny's father was a Cockney, born within the sound
of Bow Bells. But only just – at Leytonstone in north
London. Not that one could tell from his accent. He
claimed to have visited every county in England and
lived in most of them. His speech, therefore, sounded
like a flat, earthy version of Standard English. If 'It
is impossible for an Englishman to open his mouth,
without making some other Englishman despise him',
as Shaw suggested, our father was the exception. His
speech would provoke no one. Nor would he despise
the sounds of another Englishman. He delighted in
his country's oral riches and could imitate a score of
local accents. Like Shaw's own Professor Higgins, Dad
would startle newcomers by pinpointing their upbringing from the clues in their speech. 'Have you seen

the Stump lately?' he would enquire of an astonished Lincolnshireman, or say to a Yorkshireman, 'Ah'll lehk thee at dominaws, if tha's a mind.' This wealth of experience was acquired because he spent his childhood and youth on the move.

During the early years, his poverty-stricken parents, Henry and Sophie, were continually uprooting and resettling their family in vain attempts to escape the debt collectors. Dad's parents were poverty-stricken because they had married against the wishes of the elders of the two families concerned. Very young and headstrong, the pair were disappointed in their expectations of a dowry. Love will find a way, they thought. It did – but not a way of feeding the children that love usually engendered in those days.

Both Henry and Sophie, who later insisted on our calling them G. P. and Nana, had comfortable, middle-class backgrounds. Henry was left an orphan at six, and had been brought up in Yorkshire and sent to public school by an uncle who was financing Henry's medical training at the time of the precipitate wedding. Sophie's people owned the Enfield Dairy Company, which consisted of a cattle farm and a tiled dairy-shop in Shoe Lane near Fleet Street, London.

Nana once told me that, at the age of sixteen, on her wedding night, she began to weep at the loss of her parents, family, friends, servants and home. When she confessed to her eighteen-year-old husband, he was mystified. 'But now you have me!' he answered reassuringly.

Henry was not quite enough, as they were both unused to the ways of the world. Hard times ensued. Their first baby, Marie, died, aged three, in a fire. Their second child, Rose, was rescued by a benevolent aunt, who brought up the girl independently. By this time,

Henry was desperately trying to scratch a living as an entertainer. Dressed as a clown, he worked 'ponging buffers' (performing dogs) at street corners and tavern doors. Sophie was pressed into service as a singing assistant. The third child, Leonard, was soon being trained in circus arts. He was adored and admired by the next arrival, Alfred, Benny's father. The two boys bore the brunt of the daily struggle. Even as infants, they were often hungry and neglected. Alfred, as a baby, was once badly cut by an open milk tin dropped into his cot.

Dad told us that in the years of cross-country flight he and his brother had attended many village schools. As strangers, they were always picked on. The brothers soon discovered that the first confrontation with the local children was crucial, usually at morning break in the playground. Len had devised a technique to deal with it. Males of most species indulge in a ritualistic foreplay before fighting each other (it gets the adrenalin flowing). With boys (and men) there is pushing with chest and shoulders that leads to shoving with hands and arms before the fisticuffs. Len had seen the build-up of aggression before. When approached by the school bully, he would back off, keeping his hands to his sides. Encouraged by Len's apparent submission, the bully would advance and push again. Len would lower his head, look at the ground and turn away, moving his feet apart. Then, quite without warning he would swing back again, using every ounce of leverage to deliver a tremendous right-hand punch smack on the bully's nose. The effect was devastating. For a few seconds, the adversary would be paralysed; the blood would spurt from the wound; when the bully saw the red stuff fear and pain hit him together; tears would flow; his breathing would be difficult, his clothes ruined. He was destroyed. This impressive lesson would not be lost on the rest of the village children. The Hill offspring could walk in peace for a few weeks.

Leonard and Alfred were followed into the cot by William and Ernest and finally by Violet and Cecilia. According to my father his brothers and sisters were always the most ragged in the school. That did not prevent Henry Hawthorn Hill, their father, lining them up on parade before school every morning. He told them that they were a cut above the village kids. Benny remembers that even in his day, 'G. P. and Nana subtly suggested that, as a Hill, you were a member of a natural élite.'

Dad looked back with bitterness to his infant days of deprivation and squalor. Clearing up after the dogs sickened him and he remembered with rancour the occasion when he was given the top of his father's boiled egg for his birthday. He vowed his own children would never go hungry – and we never did.

Life improved for a short while when Henry was left a legacy. However, he was persuaded to invest the small fortune in a pickle factory, which promptly went bankrupt. Alfred left home at the age of ten to join Fossett's circus. The Fossetts expected him to lend a hand in all departments – and learn fast. The dark-haired, brown-eyed lad helped to pitch and strike the Big Top, feed and muck out the animals, 'bottle' (take money) at the entrance, cook for the performers, and, joy of joys, make up his face and perform. He was a useful circus hand as he had an affection for, and a rapport with, the animals. His favourite was Queenie, the leader of the cow elephants. He admired her. Her drunken Irish trainer often slept in the straw underneath her, but she took the greatest care never to tread or piss

on him. Queenie, in her finery, always led the parade
through the streets of the small towns they visited.
Once Dad saw Queenie embarrassed by a small child
who was marching in front. She knew that the child
was holding up the parade, so she lifted the little girl
carefully with her trunk and deposited her gently on
the pavement.

Alfred also enjoyed grooming Ahmed, a magnificent
but vicious black stallion. Ahmed caused a commotion
once, by kicking down his stall and stoving in the ribs of
a neighbouring mare. He was immediately pardoned as
he was a valuable attraction in the circus programme.
The day came when the boy, as a diminutive Bow
Street runner, performed in the ring with the stallion
starring as Black Bess in the Fossett version of 'Dick
Turpin's Ride to York'. Thomas Hardy had seen the act
some years earlier and describes it thus in *Far From the
Madding Crowd*:

> . . . the play began, and at the appointed time,
> Black Bess leaped into the grassy circle amid
> the plaudits of the spectators. At the turnpike
> scene, where Bess and Turpin are hotly pursued at
> midnight by the officers, and the half-awake gate-
> keeper in his tasselled nightcap denies that any
> horseman has passed, Coggan uttered a broad-
> chested 'Well done!' which could be heard all
> over the fair above the bleating, and Poorgrass
> smiled delightedly with a nice sense of dramatic
> contrast between our hero, who coolly leaps the
> gate, and halting justice in the form of his enemies,
> who must needs pull up cumbersomely and wait
> to be let through. At the death of Tom King, he
> could not refrain from seizing Coggan by the
> hand, and whispering, with tears in his eyes, 'Of

course he's not really shot, Jan – only seemingly!'
And when the last scene came on, and the body
of the gallant and faithful Bess had to be carried
out on a shutter by twelve volunteers from among
the spectators, nothing could restrain Poorgrass
from lending a hand, exclaiming as he asked Jan
to join him, ' 'Twill be something to tell of at
Warren's in future years, Jan, and hand down
to our children.' For many a year in Wethbury,
Joseph told with the air of a man who had had
experiences in his time, that he touched with his
own hand the hoof of Bess as she lay upon the
board upon his shoulder. If, as some thinkers hold,
immortality consists in being enshrined in others'
memories, then did Black Bess become immortal
that day if she had never done so before.

Circus life was tough, and Alfred had to look after
himself. When he was attacked by an older hand,
he seized a kettle of boiling water from the camp
fire and flung it at his assailant. Unfortunately, the
handle caught his fingers and he scalded his own
arm. However, continued treatment by the beautiful
auburn-haired Emma Fossett made up for his momen-
tary chagrin.

Alfred picked up the joeys (clown's antics), learned
to tumble and trained as an acrobat. He described himself wryly as 'the weakest strong-man in the business',
but even as a growing lad was able to carry three others
in a pyramid. At sixteen he struck out on his own, as
a cheapjack, like Autolycus in *The Winter's Tale*. He
sold clip-on bow-ties at fairs and chocolate to Welsh
troops stationed on Salisbury Plain. His mother worried
about him, but was reassured to see him bang together
the heads of a couple of stallholders who were giving

him trouble. In later years, when he was a respectable shopkeeper, he told Alfie and me of the activities of race-course gangs, which made us suspect he must have been a participant in these adventures. However, he never admitted to more than a passing acquaintance with the many Runyonesque characters involved.

A reluctant hero, Alfred was called up into the army when the Great War broke out in 1914, and sent to Ireland. He liked the Irish and disapproved of what he was doing there, but not enough to desert. He was slightly injured when his barracks was bombed but bore the perpetrators no ill-will. The strangest story that he told of this excursion was that, thirty years later, an unknown Irishwoman walked into his shop and recognized him. She had last seen him, she said, among a hundred soldiers marching in ranks of four through her village. The troops, he remarked, had not stopped there, even for a drink of water. The tale did not surprise us. He was a man of immense charisma.

After a short leave, our father was sent to France. The years there and in his Belgian prisoner-of-war camp were seared into his memory. On the Western Front, for long, long periods without leave, always hungry, sometimes starving, ever fearful, watchful, alert, using every sense, gift and skill to survive, like a hunted animal, seeing his comrades, their replacements and then their replacements die, he lived so intensely at so primal a level that, I believe, he saw the rest of his life as through a glass darkly.

Somehow, through it all, he kept cheerful. 'Gilbert the Filbert', they called him, 'The Colonel of the Nuts', after a popular song of the time. He was well liked by his mates, as he was, like Autolycus, a 'snapper-up of unconsidered trifles'. His eyes were everywhere. Nothing edible was safe from him. No mushroom, onion or greenstuff poking its head above the earth in a neglected corner of the field. No ill-guarded tin of bully beef or sack of rice. Officers' private stores provided many a useful addition to the meals he cooked his comrades. With side-dishes by Gilbert the Filbert, their diet was sparse but at least it was varied.

Dad was in the Machine Gun Corps and told us how one day his group were driven mad by thirst. At night-fall, when he could stand it no longer, he abandoned his customary caution and climbed over the parapet and under the wire to drink water from a shell crater. Taking care to make no noise, he crawled in the moonlight to the edge of the nearest man-made lake and bent to slake his thirst. He was about to suck in a lethal draught when he saw, just under the surface, the eyes of a white-faced corpse staring into his. He changed his mind at once and scuttled back to his lines. A rare lapse. On another occasion Alfred's athleticism saved his life. After a successful German advance, his machine gun group was over-run. The front-line trench was full of Jerries. Dad heard only the angry words, 'Mein Bruder!' behind him, and leapt, in one bound, up on to the rampart. Before making off, he saw the German bayonet meant for him stuck into the trench wall.

However, his survival skills came into their own when he was taken prisoner. Though many of his fellow-prisoners died of malnutrition, Dad never blamed the Germans for starving them. He knew that the civilians were starving too. Soon after being captured, the British prisoners were paraded in a courtyard. A German officer went down the ranks picking out the tall men, who were marshalled against the opposite wall. They quaked, thinking they were to be shot. But our father spoke Yiddish and so was able to understand the officer's orders. Dad was not picked, but immediately the officer had passed him by he walked smartly over to join the chosen few. No one noticed his ruse. A minute later, the tall men were marched off to harvest potatoes in the field. By the end of the day, all the prisoners had potatoes stashed about their persons. They were marched back to the courtyard and lined up in a single rank. A search of each man then began at one end of the rank. Immediately, potatoes began to tumble from bulky uniforms into an open drain behind them. Everybody was jettisoning their ballast. Except Dad. '*Pissen?*' he asked of the sergeant in charge. The Kraut nodded. Dad made his way to the latrine. When the search had passed his space, he returned to it still in possession of his life-supporting spuds. That night he ate while dozens did not.

Dad saved his own life by the opposite process soon after. The prisoners were unloading bottles of schnapps from barges. Alfred nipped round and warned them all not to drink the stuff on an empty stomach. 'It will kill you!' he told them. It did: three of them. Dad swapped his bottles for food from a German guard. Alfie and I often laughed at Dad's account of his prison capers that came unstuck. Once he stole a loaf from a bakery and stuffed it up his front. However it was still hot and blistered his belly. Another time, he poured dried peas into his boots. On the march home the peas packed down like a Chinese torture until the pressure made his toes bleed.

But our father's most inventive effort was conceived when he learned that barrels of jam were stacked in a locked wooden shed in the yard where the prisoners worked. He tore a long tin binding strip from a broken box, put the ends together and squeezed the two sides tight. Then, after several scouting forays, he removed a large knot from the shed wall and used his tin prong

to widen a crack in the nearest jam barrel. When he
had opened it up, he was able to use the double-sided
spatula to penetrate the interior of the barrel. Jam was
held in the space between the two sides of the instrument so that it could be withdrawn. And withdraw it
he did. Again and again. He and his fellow-workers
gorged on jam. In a couple of days, the barrel was
methodically ravished of its sweet cargo.

Alfie and I never doubted the veracity of our father's
accounts of his adventures. We had seen proof of his
quick intelligence, courage and practical expertise,
and called him 'The Captain' in recognition of them.
In his yarns, he often presented himself as a fool when
things had gone wrong. Furthermore, he would occasionally recount incidents in which he appeared in a
bad light, as if inviting the criticisms we dared not
enunciate.

When the Great War ended in 1918, our father was
released from prison camp in Liège. A seven-stone
matchstick-man, he returned to England convinced
that he and millions like him had been the victims
of a gigantic con-trick. He was a very angry young
man, long before it became the fashion. He fumed
against the Establishment before it was so called and
against anyone within earshot who had not shared his
experiences. Civilians he regarded as accomplices in a
criminal conspiracy. He had no respect for the army,
either, taking the German view that British troops were
'lions led by donkeys'. Professions and institutions were
held in contempt, including the most plausible, the
Salvation Army, of which his experiences, like George
Orwell's, had engendered a particular distrust.

At that time he was ill, exhausted, undernourished,
poverty-stricken and unemployed. He got very little help from anybody; his countrym⸱⸱ ⸱ app⸱

ungrateful for his sacrifices, were indifferent to his plight. Throughout his beloved England, sin continued, disgrace abounded. Selfishness, hypocrisy and greed were everywhere. All his prison skills would be needed to survive.

A friend of earlier days, Jack Stanley, gave Alfred hope. Jack's father had made a fortune as a cheapjack in the United States. The old man had perpetrated the saddest, most reprehensible and hilarious scam ever conceived. He sold bottles of coloured water to huge crowds of blacks all over the South, claiming the contents would lighten their skin. They believed him because the man who handed them the bottles was a black man with a totally white skin. Old Man Stanley was using an African albino.

Some of the ill-gotten fortune had been used to purchase a small chemist's shop in Canal Walk, a 'colourful' precinct built over an unfinished and abandoned canal running down to Southampton Water. When Old Man Stanley died and left it to him, Jack offered Dad a partnership in the business. They decided to make the back of the establishment a store to supply mail order clients in the new, shadowy birth control business. The shop itself would concentrate on surgical appliances to give it credibility. In the event, Alfred was unable to raise sufficient capital and he entered the small organization as manager. However, it was his drive that lifted the store-shop enterprise into orbit to boldly go where no other local emporium had been before. He took care of every aspect of it, in the process training himself to be a first-rate surgical appliance fitter.

The proprietorial pair's cheapjack background made them brilliant entrepreneurs. It was not long before their enamelled advertisements for rubber goods were adding an educational dimension to the illustrated walls of gentlemen's urinals all over the south of England. They maintained high standards in other aspects of the business, too. They spent long hours inventing the most impressive and distinguished names for their birth-control products, suppositories and various ointments which they bought in bulk whenever possible. The reassuring labels were always embossed in silver and gold. Dad admitted that the packaging usually cost them more than the contents.

They were innovative in other ways too. Long before it became general practice, they introduced the modern improvement of packaging products in sets, so that in order to obtain the single item required the customer has to buy half a dozen. They were assisted, of course, by the mealy-mouthed ignorance of their clientele. Although only the occasional customer was brave enough to enter the shop, sacks of letters stuffed with cheques and postal orders arrived for the store every morning. Mining the deep vein of English hypocrisy, the creative friends built up a huge 'under plain cover' mail order trade. Envious bank managers told them they had the most lucrative business in Southampton. The bankers did not know the half of it.

Jack Stanley had a serious heart condition, for which the prognosis was not encouraging. When it became clear that the business was thriving he made his will, with a more than generous provision for his associate. Already on commission as manager, Alfred felt the future was assured and looked round for a wife. He had already noticed Helen a number of times when they passed each other on their way to work in the morning. He told a friend, 'That's the girl for me!' and introduced himself to her at a dance. The courtship was short – they were married on Helen's

birthday, 20 June 1920, at the local register office. The
bridegroom's father Henry held a watching brief for
the Hills and Helen's mother Alice represented the
Caves. After a modest ceremony, the quartet returned
to Grandma Cave's house for sherry and sandwiches.
Young Mr and Mrs Hill were soon on their way for a
honeymoon in London, where Alfred left his bride's
side only to buy a packet of cigarettes. In that minute
outside the tobacconist's, Helen was 'buzzed' of her
gold necklace. Alfred was furious with himself as he
was streetwise enough to have prevented the loss.

Back in Southampton, they set themselves up in
a flat over a lamp shop in Bernard Street. Eighteen months later their firstborn, named Leonard after
Alfred's beloved brother, arrived in a local nursing-
home at Portswood – a great disappointment from
the start. I was so ugly and sickly that I startled
visitors into frankness. 'Couldn't you do better than
that?' asked Louie of her pretty sister. 'He looks like
a pet monkey!' said a friend of the family.

My parents must have taken the comments to heart.
They practised so hard that two years later they produced the perfect child, who was called Alfred Hawthorn, after his father.

One of the noises of the charivari that greeted Alfie's
entry into the circus of the world was the sound
of his father's bass-baritone voice. Dad rarely lowered it for anyone and spoke with such intensity and
resonance that he always sounded angry through the
bedroom floor.

Every evening the Captain turned the corner in Wilton Road at twenty past seven. Helen was always
waiting at the window. She would have already cooked
the supper, tidied away all the toys and sewing, laid the
table and decorated it with a vase of flowers. By the

time the Captain had washed his hands, his meal was on the table. Helen and the boys would join him for dinner. Slowly the food would relax him. There was little formality at the table because Dad had no time for it. However, he knew the conventions and could play the charades of correct arrangement and proper form when required. He had worked in the kitchens and dining rooms of manor houses and hotels in his early days.

On one occasion our spontaneity caused Alfie some embarrassment. At the age of five he was invited by a Catholic family to a birthday party. When all the children were seated at the feast, Alfie tucked in and was well into a large salmon sandwich when he was rebuked by the hostess for not waiting for Grace. Alfie felt that if Grace had been invited to tea, she should have been there on time.

After dinner, in the days before the wireless, we all listened to the gramophone in the front room while Dad read his newspaper. The records had been brought over from New York by the crews of the great transatlantic liners. Thus, in the mid-twenties, the Hill toddlers were familiar with the voices of Fanny Brice, Whispering Jack Smith and the Two Black Crows and sang the latest hits from the Great White Way. As a change, Dad would sometimes play his one-string fiddle. The original was a horned, deep purple, mahogany job with which he became infatuated. However, in time, he tired of it and made another of white wood, which he varnished yellow; it lacked the dark good looks of his first love, but the cheap blonde appealed to him. He would play, 'A Little Love, a Little Kiss' on it while Alfie sang the lyrics. Sometimes we all joined in. The Hills were alive with the sound of music, you might say.

When visitors came they were usually sung at by a

tiny performer. We boys were made up, dressed up, and
stood up in a corner to entertain. 'One of my earliest
memories,' says Benny, 'is of Mum and Dad making me
a clown suit out of an old pair of pyjamas and shaping
a felt hat for me by steaming it and pushing a broom
handle into it.' He sang songs and recited rhymes,
bullying his audience into complete silence and full
attention. If their eyes closed or flickered away for a
moment, he would stop, come out of character, and
say accusingly, 'You're not watching me!' Nobody
slept while he was on. At a remarkably early age
he committed to memory, and repeated exactly, the
jokes that his mother read to him out of the newspaper
or comic. I can still hear, in memory, his little treble
voice trilling the punch line of one story: ' "Ever since
it was a wheelbarrow!" was the humorous reply!'

The Captain had a way with animals. He saw in
each creature a victim of circumstance, like himself.
He sympathized with them and offered his friendship.
The first pet that the Captain installed at home was a
marmoset, now the merest wisp in Benny's memory.
The tiny, bushy-tailed monkey was very appealing and
very active in many ways. He was into everything –
metaphorically, practically and sexually. Mum did not
approve, and, despite Dad's pleas, the velvety manikin
had to pack his cheeks and leave.

The Captain then conceived the notion that the
family could produce its own milk and cut out the mid-
dlemen who were costing him so much. We boys were
soon welcoming Daisy, a nannygoat, into our garden
playground. Sure enough, the nanny delivered prodi-
gious quantities of milk, and brown fibre buttons that
fascinated little Alfie. Unfortunately, Mum never mastered the knack of milking Daisy. That meant intimate
attention by Dad, who quite enjoyed the experience.

However, his ministrations were required on a regular basis, which affected his social life and thus his vital private business interests. Reluctantly, we bade farewell to Daisy.

One afternoon, Mum arrived home from a shopping expedition, making an entrance like a mugger's victim in a Benny Hill sketch – hat askew, coat half off, stockings torn, fruit rolling out of her bag. She had been attacked by a mad dog in a nearby street. When Dad arrived he was given the details. 'What breed of dog was it?' he asked. Mum did not know – but it was very large and fierce. The Captain was off like a shot to sort out the owner. 'Take care!' was Mum's advice. We boys waited expectantly for him to return torn and bleeding. He was soon back, the recipient of sincerest apologies, solicitous enquiries and a five-pound note. 'What about the mad dog?' asked Mum. 'He's not a mad dog!' scoffed Dad. 'He's a pussy-cat. An Airedale. Licking my face in no time.' The Captain really had extraordinary confidence with animals. Benny tells the story of how, as a lad, he was crossing a warehouse yard with his father when a large black guard dog raced out of nowhere, barking, showing its large teeth and coming straight for them. Benny was backing away, about to run for it when he saw his father bend over and place his fist a few inches from the ground. 'Go on, if you're so keen. Take a bite,' said Dad to the hell-hound. Benny says: 'The dog put on the brakes and skidded to a halt, looking at the fist. Its expression changed from insane hatred to bafflement. Then it licked the fist and began wagging its tail. Dad patted it and we walked on.'

Dad could be an abrasive young man. His father often counselled the soft answer that turneth away wrath, reminding his son that 'Honey catches more flies than vinegar'. But the Captain was not always difficult. He would talk most amicably to anyone from whom he could learn. A feature of our walks with him was the frequent stops to chat with workmen. Whether in the town or country, whatever the work, Dad would not stop asking questions until he was sure he could do the job as well as his informant. Consequently, the chats were usually friendly but lengthy interrogations. Adults who might be accompanying us would lose patience and walk on. Dad was unconcerned. As long as he had added to his store of knowledge and competence, he was satisfied. His quest would continue wherever he might be – quizzing a head gardener, an electrician, a garage mechanic, or a chef, depending on the circumstances. Most of his interviewees were flattered that so obviously intelligent and well-informed a man should be interested in what they were doing. They realized later, perhaps, that by the time he had finished with them he was, in the army phrase, 'as wise as what they was'. There were very few tasks, therefore, about the house and garden that were beyond him.

Remembering his own childhood, Dad made continuous efforts to be a good father – and succeeded most of the time. He was a born story-teller, an amusing companion and a mine of fascinating information that he had picked up in his travels. He went to considerable lengths to please his two sons. From the first, he played with us a great deal and took us for walks on the common and into the country. He taught us to move through a wood without a sound. We went round the town with him and into the homes of his Jewish friends. He regularly bought us toys and liked to surprise us with novelties. Benny remembers to this day the deep-sea diver who could be manipulated up and down a bottle by thumb pressure and the tiny Japanese garden that burst into life under water. And many more.

One example of the Captain's thoughtfulness was our introduction to the dirt track. When Alfie was four, Dad took us both to see the legendary American speedway rider Sprouts Elder, in Southampton. Standing at the first bend of the track in the first race, we were covered by ash – and loved it. We were thrilled by the baptism of cinders, the roar of the engines and the smell of the crowd. We could not wait to see the star turn taking the first corner. In the interval, Alfie piped up, 'When's Brussels Sprouts comin' on then, Dad?' The spectators roared with laughter at the funny little nipper who was out long after his bedtime. Sprouts did not disappoint us. Alfie and I talked about the races all the way home. Next day Dad brought home coloured oil-cloth and two bowler hats. With Mum's help, he fashioned riders' tunics for us each, complete with numbers. The bowler brims were cut away and authentic-looking speedway helmets created. Mum fitted them so that when we next raced our trikes round the garden, Alfie wore the red kit and I the blue. They were elegant outfits: we never saw anything nearly so smart in the shops.

Dad's efforts were not always so successful. He once brought us home a large blue and green box kite. At the weekend, Alfie and I scampered alongside him as he carried it on to the common. We went up to the open Racecourse Rise, where the wind blew free. I walked away with the huge construction dwarfing me: Dad unwound the string. Once I threw the splendid flier into the air, the wind took her and she sailed away. Up she went, while Dad played out more and more line. She was a beauty, swinging round and round above the town. 'Let's have a go, Dad,' I cried. 'My turn first,' said Alfie. 'Just a minute,' replied Dad. He explained that he could not hand over the line until he had mastered all the kite's tricks. So we kids waited.

And waited. Every now and again we asked to hold the line, but it was never the opportune moment. We watched the kite and longed to hold her. To no avail. At last, we wandered away and played games of chase in the bushes. When Dad was ready to hand over, we were too far away to hear his calls. He wound in the kite and came to find us, rebuking our impatience.

That fiasco with the kite was played out several times. I think that in the end both boys were permitted the experience of holding the kite-line. But it was too little and too late. Years later, Mum told me that Dad had been disappointed that we had shown so little interest in the kite.

Alfie suffered by being the younger. Or did I suffer by being the older? Certainly when Dad failed after making great efforts to teach me some skill, he made little effort with Alfie. The cycling lessons, for example. When I was seven, Dad bought me a brand-new bicycle. Not a child's fairy cycle, a first-class sit-up-and-beg machine, a little big so that I could grow into it. Then for my first lesson, he took me out on to the quiet suburban roads. At least they were quiet until he arrived. The poor man did try. He explained, he instructed, he guided, he advised. I fell off the machine. He held me on. I fell off. He pushed the seat. I fell off. He began to sweat. I fell off. He cursed. I fell off. He shouted. I fell off. At last, at the end of our respective tethers, we pushed the bike home. Dad did not give up. He tried once more, I'll give him that. But it was no use – the more he insisted, the more nervous I became. So Dad sold the bike and Alfie never had his chance. Two years later I taught myself to ride on Auntie Lena's bicycle while on holiday at Eastleigh near Southampton. Dad was not there to see me.

Much the same results were achieved when Dad

taught us to swim. Alfie, now six years old, got rather more attention on this week's course at Ryde in the Isle of Wight. The beach there is very wide and slopes gradually. Every day, Dad marched us in our little swimming togs over the sand and out to sea. He insisted on the water being up to Alfie's neck, so we waded out for quite some time. When we halted, Dad demonstrated a stroke and bade us imitate it. We did – and slowly sank to the ocean floor. Dad pulled us both up by the hair and showed us again. The same descent occurred. We repeated this four or five times. Then Dad led us back and marched us up the beach again. We undertook this exercise most mornings. By the end of the week, Alfie and I had swallowed a great deal of salt water.

As Benny says, 'The Captain was a larger-than-life personality, very much in command. He'd never wait until you'd finished speaking if he had something to say.' He would frequently interrupt others and, sometimes when a joke was being told, he would jump right in on the punch line to cut the laughter dead. It was a galling experience for the teller. Dad did not suffer fools gladly. Or in silence. He would express his feelings very eloquently. At length. When, years later, I encountered dyspeptic sergeants and sergeant-majors during five years' army service as a private soldier, their imprecations left me unmoved. I was well used to beratement. I had a long history of castigation by a master of invective.

Visitors to our home have told me since that they were astonished at the tedious jobs the Hill boys were given at an early age. While still quite small, Alfie was expected to keep the gravel path clear of weeds. He tried at first, but, when Dad caught him playing with the little stones, Alfie looked for a way out. He began to act dumb. This was his first ploy in the struggle to

resolve his relationship with his father, to deal with
oppressive paternal domination. Knowing the Captain's
likely reaction, Alfie would simulate incomprehension
and ineptitude. He became a very slow worker. When
given a task, he fumbled it. Faced with his son's dilatory
incompetence, the Captain would lose patience. 'Give
it here,' he would grumble. 'You've got no bloody idea,
you bloody idiot! Let me do it. God Almighty! You're
like the man who fell out of the balloon – you're not
in it!' This last phrase was race-course parlance. The
Captain used it constantly. 'You're not in it' means 'not
in the race – at the back of the field – a loser'.

Afraid to confront our father about his eccentricities,
we would complain to Mum. She always encouraged us
to accept them. 'It's only your father's way,' she would
say. 'He doesn't mean any harm by it.' Only once did I
ever hear her mention his jealousy of his sons to him –
and then in regretful rather than reproachful terms.

Mum was always calm and equable. Auntie Lena can
testify to that. She was helping her sister in our kitchen
once when Dad stormed in, looking for 'a clean white
cloth'. He often needed one, as he refused to use an oily
rag to clean his tools. He rummaged in the drawers,
cursing, while Mum was occupied at the stove. The
Captain became more and more exasperated as the prize
continued to elude him. He slammed cupboard doors,
rattled the cutlery drawer and buzzed about like a bee
in a bottle. 'I don't know why this place is always like
a dog's breakfast,' he bellowed. 'Can't find a bloody
thing! It costs me enough to keep the bloody place
going. You'd think I could get a clean white cloth
once in a while. That's not too much to ask, is it? God
damn and blast it! Where do you keep the cloths?'

Mum looked up from her pans and said sweetly,
without any hint of sarcasm: 'Are you looking for

something, darling?' Then she found and handed him his cloth. Dad took it and, as he passed Lena on the way out, he said *sotto voce*, 'She won't answer back. You can't quarrel with her.' God knows, he tried.

When I was in my thirties, I came back to look after the family home while my parents visited Australia for six months. One summer evening, I was working in the small front garden when a neighbour I had not met for years came across to chat. 'I'm so glad to see you doing well,' he said. 'Alfie, too. You a schoolmaster and Alfie a success on the telly. I must say I'm amazed that you've both turned out to be such a credit to your parents. I never expected that. Your father used to shout so loudly that the whole street could hear him. We tried not to listen but he made so much racket it penetrated closed doors and windows. Many a time, I've got as far as the front door to come across the road to stop it. But my wife would stand between me and the door and tell me that it was nothing to do with us. It will pass, she used to say. She always held me back.'

The Captain's irritability and impulsive nature led him into situations that were the stuff of legend. He appears as the central character in a host of anecdotes savoured by a circle far wider than the extended family. One tale told by our Auntie Lena is of a Sunday long ago when she, her sister Kath and their dog accompanied our family on a picnic by the river. Outings were *de rigueur* on fine summer Sundays, because the Captain took every opportunity to show off his splendid picnic box. This contained all the impedimenta needed and could be transformed into a table. Unfortunately, the Captain had made it so heavy that only he could carry it. Consequently, as there was no family car, picnics were characterized by displays of his filthy temper. This particularly warm Sunday was no exception. Matters

were not helped by the ladies' indecision as to where
to make camp. At last, the Captain flung down the
box and stamped away up the river bank to fish. He
returned two hours later with no catch, dejected and
thirsty. In response to his request, the ladies told him
that there was nothing to drink. The last of the lemonade had gone. They had given it to the dog. 'You
gave my lemonade to the dog?' roared the Captain,
incredulous. 'Well, he panted so,' said Auntie Lena.
'The poor little thing was so hot.'

'If he was so hot,' bellowed my father, 'why didn't
you cool the bloody thing off?' At which he seized the
bewildered creature and threw it in the river.

Our cousin Billy tells his picnic story of the hornets
at Netley Abbey, on Southampton Water. The same age
as Alfie, he joined our family on this outing, and was
much impressed by the picnic box and the feast that
was laid out on the grass. The meal had only just begun
when the jolly party was attacked by a hornet. Alfie
leapt up and ran with a large crust liberally buttered
and strawberry-jammed. Down to the beach he raced,
followed by the hornet, with the family tagging along
behind. Round and round the beach he stumbled,
trying to keep the hornet at bay. 'Stand still!' roared
the Captain. 'Stand still. And throw the crust away!'
But Alfie had no intention of giving up his prize. The
Captain explained to the others what a serious matter
this was. A sting from the hornet and the boy might die
in agony. 'Throw it away!' he begged. But Alfie would
not. He managed to take the occasional bite out of
the loaded crust and kept on the move. The Captain,
tottering down towards his stricken son, explained to
him that the local hornets were the most deadly in
the country. Billy gained the distinct impression that
they were a species of lethal insect dive-bomber. Alfie

took no notice of his father, beating off the hornet and gobbling down the rest of the crust. He wiped his mouth at last and the hornet flew off in disgust. The Captain's words, however, were not lost on Billy. He still has nightmares about hornets. And he has never been back to Netley Abbey.

A picnic might occasionally be a moveable feast celebrated by the entire Hill extended family – a couple of dozen people, counting camp followers. As no Hill ever possessed a motor car, this was sometimes difficult to organize. So, from time to time, we Hills descended on Auntie Lena, who kept open house at Eastleigh. One of the attractions for the children, besides her generous hospitality and refreshing informality, was the fact that Lena and her brood lived opposite Fleming Park, a large area of greensward suitable for ball games. This fact did not escape the Captain's notice, especially as he had a secret delusion that he was a dead ringer for Babe Ruth, the baseball player. He attempted to clothe this insanity in some verisimilitude by purchasing a baseball cap and making himself a baseball bat. I write 'himself' advisedly as the finished article was too long and heavy for any child to wield.

On certain summer Sundays in the early thirties, a lucky local might have seen the Captain, splendid in cap and bat, marching into Fleming Park, trailing crowds of glorified ball-boys – the Hill family at play. Only the very young, the ancient and those preparing tea were excused (and what competition there was for those few places!). Everyone else knew what was expected of them. There were no teams. The object of the game was to hit the ball with the bat – or, more precisely, for the Captain to hit the ball with the bat. He took up his stance and the score of fielders spread out, one or two of the more unsociable hiking beyond hailing distance. I always began the pitching, largely because the Captain was more comfortable cursing me than more distant members of the family.

Here I have to explain to baseball aficionados that in the Captain's version of the game the function of the pitcher was to provide balls that the batsman could hit EASILY. 'Hip and shoulder!' Dad would roar (meaning – 'Pitch them between my hip and shoulder'). Then he smote them hip and thigh. Ball after ball was whacked into one or other of the park's four corners. It was quite an active game for all concerned, as the fielders had to run to pick up the ball but could rarely reach the pitcher with a return throw. The ladies and younger children would have to run the two hundred yards to give the ball back to me – and then run back to their positions. The Captain would be fuming at the delay, but the fielder had a healthy glow on her face after returning the ball. Needless to say, there were no bases as this was scarcely a competitive game.

It was understood that if anyone was fortunate enough to catch the ball (a consummation devoutly to be wish'd), the Captain would be out. I do not remember that ever occurring. Uncle Ernie, who had bad feet and walked like a duck, once had a real chance. The hard ball was hurtling towards him out of the sky. He paddled backwards, fell over and was nearly hit by it. He claimed the sun got in his eyes. It was a feeble excuse and we never forgave him.

Sometimes the Captain would clout the ball with such effect that it landed in the adjoining pasture. Finding it necessitated organizing a field trip that would also return with interesting specimens of wild flowers, feathers or birds' nests. The serious business would be resumed until I threw a stinger that caught the Captain in the belly. I swear I never did this deliberately. But the profanity this provoked would be the signal for a change of pitcher. Tom Wooldridge usually took the ball from me. He was a young man so madly in love with Lena's younger sister Kathleen that he would go to any lengths to ingratiate himself with the family.

Tom, of course, took the greatest care not to hit the Captain in the belly. He would pitch until his right arm was aching. 'Just one or two more, Tom,' the Captain would shout. Somehow, despite the enormous arcs in every direction described by the ball, Dad was never satisfied. 'Just one good hit, Tom. That's all I want. Just one good hit.' Towards the end of an hour at the bat, the Captain would grow tired. Tom was exhausted as, encouraged by the Captain's cries, he politely ran every time to accept the ball back from the ladies.

At last, Dad had had enough. Babe Ruth would retire. The Captain, to his credit, never took the bat with him. He dropped it on the grass, to be fought over by the children, who could not use it. Dad would wander over to the pavilion and sit down, and was presently joined gratefully by his brother Ernie. Officially the game continued, but with the Captain absent the heart went out of things. One or two uncles would try a hit or two in a desultory way. The ladies would seek the shade in groups; the children, hot and sticky, would quarrel. Everyone was glad when it was time to return for tea.

Auntie Lena once told me of the time that Dad took a dozen children of the family for ice-cream. They were in a tiny seaside resort and had difficulty finding an ice-cream shop. After much searching, they discovered Leoni's and Dad ushered the kids up a flight of stairs into the cool parlour. Once he had assembled the expectant throng the Captain discovered that the crafty Italians offered no half-portions for children. He

trumpeted his disgust, about-turned, and led the horde
on a noisy, reluctant, interminable descent. The way
Auntie Lena told it, the long drag downstairs made
Napoleon's Retreat from Moscow look like a New
Year party.

Another outing often scuppered by the Captain's
touchiness was the family's weekly trip to the movies.
Dad frequently found the cinema management wanting and the arrangements, in many instances, deeply
disappointing. The auditorium was too hot, the seats
were too close to the screen, members of the family
were unable to sit together, etc. The Captain would
storm out, thundering his disapproval to the audience,
while the family trailed shame-faced behind. 'Bloody
liberty-takers!' he would rage at the manager as he
demanded his money back. If he brought the family
late to the last show, he would expect the projectionist
to stay behind to screen the portion of the programme
we had missed. And always he complained about being
overcharged. But then, most monetary transactions
were painful to him. He found the whole financial system profoundly unjust. The Captain was not a radical;
he just could not approve of a society in which total
strangers were constantly making money out of him.

3

Lies About Us in
our Infancy

Benny cannot remember a time when he was not sexually aware. He appears to have skipped 'latency', as
the Freudians call the period when young boys have no
interest in females. Attending Shirley Infants' School in
Wilton Road for the first time at the age of five, he was
delighted to find large numbers of girls held captive
there. His affection for them knew no bounds. The
headmistress attempted to circumscribe it. She sum-
moned his mother. Mum was unconcerned. She felt
that such interest as Alfie showed in the young doxies
was quite natural and indicated a robust constitution
rather than a sinister deviation. However, like the good
mother she was, she advised her son not to be so free
with his kisses. She, of course, was largely responsible
for his extrovert behaviour. When we were infants, she
lavished her considerable maternal charms on her two
sons with such abandon that neither of us has ever had
the slightest difficulty in recognizing the opposite sex.

The gossip about Alfie did his reputation no harm.
He told me that the girls would gather round him in
the playground –

> Alfie Hill
> Took a pill
> On the top of the Shirley Hill.
> Shirley Hill began to shake and
> Gave poor Alf the belly-ache!

The Infants' was at the bottom of the totem pole that was Shirley School. Similar totems are to be found all over the country – Victorian piles for the education of children segregated by age and sex. A floor above the Infants' was the Big Girls'; above that the top floor, housing the Big Boys'. Each of the departments was so rigidly isolated that it was not possible to ascend from one to another without returning to the playground and re-entering the building at the appropriate door. One of the two separate playgrounds was used by both Infants and Big Girls. Alfie's experiences there prompted his lifelong testimony in praise of older women. A Big Girl took an interest in him. Among the fascinating things that his mature sweetheart, Molly, showed him was the way to 'trammy up'. For this game, Alfie stood next to her. They held hands behind their backs, left to left, right to right. Both right knees were raised. At a signal from Molly both right feet stamped down to begin a high-stepping trot in unison, that took the prancing pair in a circle round the playground. With their sweaty palms clasped behind them, they were performing a kind of cake-walk *à deux*. Years later, Alfie realized that, although in his childhood the local trams were electric carriages on lines, the first trams had been drawn by pairs of horses – the 'trammy up' game was a folk memory of the early days of local public transport.

Alfie really fell for Molly. She knocked him clean off his feet when fighting over him with another Big Girl. Alfie hit his head on the stony playground and passed out. When he came to he was sitting, head in arms, at his desk, a placatory sweet already in his mouth. His mother came to take him home, but he never mentioned Molly to anyone.

Alfie's possessive sweetheart was responsible for his

being caned. She urged him to take part in a high-pee competition with three other boys. Perhaps she wanted to find out if the rumours were true. Among the Big Girls it was said that Fire Drill was unnecessary. If the school was on fire, Alfie would piss on it and put it out.

At the Wall Game, Alfie had just cleared the sprinkler bar when his final spurt was interrupted by the teacher on playground duty. The water sportsmen were hauled before the headmistress, who donned the dreaded rubber apron while hearing evidence of their excessive competitive spirit. No Freemason ever had a more lively sense of the significance of the apron as symbol than the children at Shirley Infants'. Like the axe-man's black hood, it appeared only at times of execution. Seen by miscreants alone, it was whispered about by all. To some it suggested a headmistressy fear of being spattered by bodily fluids in particularly energetic exercises in rehabilitation. Alfie found that he was grateful for it at the time. He allowed the cane's descent to slide off his hand and hit the apron with an almighty thwack, thus giving the impression that he had sustained a severe injury rather than a light sting on the hand. After punishment, Alfie left the study overjoyed at outwitting the system. Several decades later, it dawned on him that his headmistress had deliberately contrived the effect.

While at Infants' School Alfie conducted the traditional experiment of pushing a marble up his nose. Unsuccessful attempts by teachers to dislodge it led the young scientist to believe that it would be a permanent installation. When the school doctor arrived, he pushed the marble even higher up the tube and caught it with two fingers at the back of Alfie's throat. The lad was astonished. One moment the huge globe had been trapped in his nose, the next, it was coming out of his mouth. Benny says that no conjuring trick he has seen since has ever amazed him more.

One day, Alfie ran out of the school gate and, as the newspapers say, 'collided with a motor-car'. I have always felt that colliding with a motor-car is likely to have much the same effect as colliding with a bullet. Fortunately, this was not so in Alfie's case. The collision occurred in the days before the automobile had developed such an appetite for human flesh. The Morris Cowley, going about its business at a civilized pace (about sixteen miles an hour), braked and gently nudged the side of Alfie's knee. He fell over but was unhurt until Mum discovered the tyre-mark later that evening at bath-time. She, of course, was horrified and called at once for the Captain's opinion. A great deal of noise ensued, best described in a theatrical phrase that G. P. often used, later taken up as a catch-phrase by the great comedian Sid Field – 'What a perFORMance!' As with some of the most distinguished dramas, the last act was apparent from the opening lines. After an hour, it was generally agreed that no real harm had been done and no one was to be pursued. Alfie was then allowed to go to bed.

One afternoon, Alfie was squeaking away with his crayon on his very own slate when the headmistress entered the classroom and called for attention. She told the children that a nasty, dangerous man was in the district. They were to talk to no strange men in the street on the way home from school. Alfie had a pretty good idea of what nasty, dangerous men looked like. He had seen them in the films and comics. They were large men, with heavy black eyebrows and huge walrus moustaches.

After school that day, Alfie was with a few school-friends and nearly home when the group was approached by a small, thin, boyish man. He said he had lost his daughter on the way from school and would somebody help him find her. He looked so worried that Alfie had not the heart to say no. Besides, the little man did not look the slightest bit nasty or dangerous. He declined the help of another boy but accepted Alfie's offer to accompany him in his search. The pair set off up Wilton Road towards the school. Then the worried father turned a corner to the left and began to trot. Alfie trotted, too. Turning left again, and left again, they soon found themselves in The Swamp, an area of derelict ground used as an unofficial tip. Hidden from the road by a ridge and surrounded on three sides by the backs of houses, it was rarely visited. Its principal unattraction was a poisonous central pond, surrounded by a grassy bog. This had the reputation of being a hotbed of scarlet fever, diphtheria, and the many diseases that haunted the twenties.

The little man led Alfie to a dry piece of ground, turned and faced him. Alfie pointed. 'That's my house – just over there,' he explained. A hundred yards away stood 164 Wilton Road. The boyish face looked perplexed. Then the man sighed and said, 'Well, she's not here,' and brushed past Alfie on the way out. They parted at the entry to The Swamp.

Alfie was sorry he had not been able to help more and hoped that his new friend would find his daughter waiting for him at home. He said so at dinner and began to tell of his adventure. To his surprise, for a few moments the family was actually listening to him. But for a few moments only. There was a sudden explosion of questions, threats, recriminations, weeping and gnashing of teeth. No one had the time or appetite for dinner. If Alfie's brush with the Morris had inspired a performance, the assistance he gave to the little man produced an opera. The long duet of his father and mother over the matter taught Alfie one lesson. Whatever happens, don't tell your parents!

Not all Alfie's interesting experiences were connected with school. He spent most spare daylight time playing within half a mile of the house. Not only was the common within easy reach, but there were plenty of sequestered plots and building sites to interest him. Partly built houses were exciting places to play. The smells of wood, bricks and paint were everywhere. There were stories, among our friends, of children who had fallen between beams and broken their limbs below. It was whispered that one boy slipped into a lime pit and was never seen again.

An overgrown corner, in which a steel crane nested, was Alfie's favourite playground. The structure had fallen and been entwined by weeds. It set his imagination alight – serving at times as a galleon, a bomber, an airship or a submarine. We would clamber about it while Alfie barked his orders. He liked dressing up to play his part even then. Once he fell on his sword in a distinctly un-Roman way when, as Julius Caesar, he climbed up the crane with a tea-cosy on his head. The tea-cosy slipped over his eyes, Julius Caesar slipped off the beam and the wooden shaft slipped through his cheek and down his throat. We managed to pull it out immediately. With the liberal application of zinc ointment, and without a single stitch, the wound soon healed perfectly.

At about this time Alfie was being taught to read by his teacher at school and his father at home. He was not making much progress, but once the Captain gave up on him he began to improve. Two activities helped.

One was Alfie's hobby of collecting car numbers. On Saturday mornings in the summer he would sit for hours on the pavement opposite and take down the letters and numbers on the identification plate of each car that passed. In 1930 they did not pass that often: there was plenty of time to look at the list in the notebook. Alfie noticed that some of the letters made short words. Other groups could be made into words with the addition of another letter. As he waited for the next car, he became familiar with many short words.

The other influence was his mother's interest. Most evenings Mum would read to us from an ancient children's annual or that week's favourite comic paper. In either case, the stories had no literary merit, a fact that troubled the Captain whenever he was running out of subjects to grumble about. Strangely enough, the quality of the writing seemed almost irrelevant. Some of the hack stories heard then have a resonance in Benny's memory as powerful as the classic tales read much later. We boys were much taken by two serial tales that appeared back-to-back in a comic paper long since forgotten. One of these interminable yarns was a saga of conflict between the Saxons and Danes, the other an epic of the struggle for the north-eastern woods between the early American colonists and the Red Indians. Both stories relied heavily on lurid descriptions of battles over cabins and barns. Flaming arrows were much in evidence. It was a long time before Mum's avid audience realized that the two entertainments were really the same story.

Sitting close to Mum, and peeping at the print, we both gained the practice needed to make sense of the marks on the page. One Sunday morning, when Mum and Dad were resting late, Alfie slipped into their bed between them. Dad had his *Sunday Express* with the

front page in view. Alfie looked at the headline. 'King's
Life in Grave Danger,' he read out loud. Dad was mystified. Where had the bloody idiot learned to read?

About this time, the Hill brothers were taken to the
theatre for the first time. Sitting in the front row of the
circle, Alfie was entranced by the apparent opulence
of the local Hippodrome. Only in later years was he
shown the squalid dilapidation hidden from public
gaze. At his initiation into the delights of the drama,
the entertainment on stage was a farce from London.
The play came as no surprise to Alfie. He recognized
the situation at once. It was all too familiar – the loud
voices, the running about, the slammed doors, the
wise-cracking men and the over-painted women, the
laughter, the emotion, the excitement. It was a scene
Alfie knew well. He had been to Jewish homes before.

On Sundays the gentle pace of life came to a full stop.
For everybody. It was not that the Hill family went to
church or kept any kind of religious observance. We
were all agnostics, some more resolute than others.
No, it was simply that, by universal acquiescence,
Sunday was the day when all shops shut, sports and
entertainments were curtailed, and banished from the
wireless programmes was any item likely to induce a
smile. It was the one day of the week when the Captain
was ever-present in the family. He therefore dictated
its pattern – early newspaper, tea and biscuits in bed,
in which we boys shared; three hours' gardening and
odd jobs, in which we also shared; a hot bath for
the Captain, while we swept up, cleaned, oiled and
put away the tools and equipment he had strewn all
over the house and garden; a huge dinner in the early
afternoon (Mum's Yorkshire pudding still eulogized to
this day by privileged members of the extended family);
post-prandial kip; Sunday walk; high tea, graced by

Mum's home-made cake; musical or social evening; early bed for boys.

On holidays or when visitors came, the Sunday walk might take place in the morning. The small party would traverse the common to the Bassett Hotel, at its northern edge. Benny still recalls the smell of beer and cheese biscuits in its lounge. After refreshment the Captain always inspected the animals in the hotel's garden zoo. Visitors chortled when he announced that he was going to talk to his simple friends, but they came away marvelling at the way the blue-nosed mandrill, the baboon and others responded to his enquiries. The hotel displayed a stuffed bear, once an inmate of the zoo, which had escaped on to the common and been shot for its presumption. The impotent monster cued the Captain into his lecture on the treacherous ursine character. 'Never trust a bear!' he would tell his guests. They must have been impressed for I never heard of one who disobeyed him in that particular.

My brother remembers those family walks on the common. 'Dad was so funny,' says Benny. 'When his feet hurt, he would say, "Let's have a rest!" then he would remonstrate before I said a word. "No, no! Come on, my son, your mother's feet are hurting!" Mum would say, "No, I'm all right, dear. I don't want to sit down." Dad would insist, "No, no, my dear. I know your feet are hurting. You have a nice rest. I know you need one. You sit down. Don't worry about us. We'll be all right." He would never admit that he was the one who needed to sit down.'

One Sunday the family party passed a group of boys and girls playing kiss-chase in the bushes. They were so full of laughter and excitement and joy that Alfie ached to join them. He asked his mother how old they were. 'Sixteen, I would think,' she replied. For years afterwards, before he went to sleep, Alfie dreamed of the day when he would reach the magic age of sixteen and be able to play kiss-chase for ever among the common's bosky glades.

At the age of seven, Alfie joined me in the Big Boys'. He found a playground very different from that of the Infants' – one in which there was a great deal of ritual aggression. Alfie soon learned to curse and swagger like the rest of us, to call everyone 'nipper' with the all-important glottal stop, 'ni'er', to speak only in questions – 'Oo wants to know? Wot's it to ya? Iz zat so? Oo sez?' He was soon marching round the yard with a mob of his new mates shouting and singing:

> We are the Shirley Boys
> We mind our manners, we spend our tanners,
> We are respected wherever we go.
> Walking down the Shirley Hill
> Wiv a fag stump in our mouf
> You should hear Old Baldie shout
> Put that bloody fag stump out!
> We are the Shirley Boys!

(Old Baldie was the headmaster.)

Alfie obviously found the Big Boys' as educational as I had before him. Within the first week he was regaling me with a local joke old enough to be respectable.

> Teacher: Where have you been?
> Boy Latecomer: Up Shirley Hill.
> Teacher: Who are you?
> Girl Latecomer: Shirley Hill!

The common unit of currency among the boys was

the cigarette card, which was the lowest stake accepted in the casino of the playground. Gambling went on all the time, before school, every playtime, lunchtime, after school and on the way home. Many lads had their own pitch in the yard, where they organized games of chance based on covering cigarette cards or flicking cards to knock down others which stood against the wall. There were of course seasonal pastimes like conkers, dibs or marbles, but none of these ever entirely usurped the central role of card gambling.

Alfie was most adept at the card games and kept busy, building up complete sets of cards that could be sold for a few pence in small, dark shops around Canal Walk. He went into the entertainment business too, by making a peepshow in a boot-box. It was rather like a Pollock's Toy Theatre. You paid a cigarette card and looked through a window in the end of the contraption to see a three-dimensional arrangement of cut-out characters against a coloured background lit by a skylight of tinted, transparent paper. Alfie's peepshow was a scene from *Treasure Island* and very popular.

Unfortunately, despite all our efforts to conform, he and I were never fully accepted, as we longed to be, into the rough working-class camaraderie of the playground. Our petit-bourgeois background was clear for all to see. We stood out like foreigners in the Cultural Revolution. We were branded. It was our haircuts that gave us away. We wore short hair, but it was trimmed. Nearly everyone else had endured a no-nonsense all-over crop with the clippers, leaving a small horizontal fringe on the forehead. The Hill boys had not been initiated. Our capital crime set us apart.

Other errors must be confessed. There was the matter of Alfie's appearance in his first school cricket match held at The Wreck (Shirley Recreation Ground), an

immense sunken pie-dish lined with grass. Mum had
made him a pair of white shorts for the occasion, which
she attended as sole spectator. When it was Alfie's turn
to bat, he came to the wicket with no pads or gloves but
otherwise immaculate – fair hair, blue eyes, red-apple
cheeks, white shirt, white shorts, white socks, sandals
– the only boy there in whites. His mother was proud
of him. The proletariat was not impressed.

'Oo do you fink you are – a bleedin' Royal Cricketer?'
scowled the bowler. He would have mentioned Little
Lord Fauntleroy, had he ever heard of him. Still, 'Royal
Cricketer' was good enough. The band of shabby field-
ers took it up. 'Thass what 'e is – a bleedin' Royal
Cricketer!'

The bowler ran up for the first ball. He hurled it
straight at the white shirt. Alfie lifted his bat to fend it
off and jumped away. The ball hit neither bat nor body
but flew past into the distance. Every ball was delivered
the same way – the ruffian aiming for Alfie's ribs, Alfie
aiming to avoid that painful eventuality. In the process,
the ball once accidentally struck his narrow shield of a
bat and raced away to the boundary. The sixth delivery
snicked off the willow to spreadeagle the stumps. Alfie
was out, had scored four runs and was still rib-sound.
Only Mum clapped his return to the imaginary pavilion.
In relief, probably.

Alfie was competitive at that age and enjoyed playing
cards with his father and me. Mum would sometimes
join in to make up a foursome. One of the joys of the
Captain's misspent youth had been night-long card
games. He taught us whist, poker, brag, clubyos, crib-
bage and many others. Alfie learnt fast but rarely
beat Dad. The Captain would remember every card
laid down, and mentally forecast the play as it progressed. Alfie learned to do that too. Consequently,

when he began to play with Auntie Kate's friends, he cleaned up.

Auntie Kate was Grandpa Cave's sister, though you would never have thought so from her long, plain face, tall figure and saintly disposition. She lived in the most cramped conditions you ever saw. Imagine a tiny upstairs bedroom in an old terrace of little houses. Fill the bedroom with a bed, so that a person can only just squeeze in through the door. Now fill the two feet of space between that side of the bed and the wall with all the necessities to sustain life and make it comfortable and useful. Her window looked out over Hoglands Park and, in the summer, we would sit there eating jelly and cake, watching the cricketers making white patterns on the lush green grass.

Auntie Kate attended to people. She listened and she helped, all through her life even when she was working full-time as a cashier in a butcher's shop. She always had something for you, sometimes even the clothes off her back. In consequence, if people had a little something to spare, they would 'give it to Miss Cave', confident that she would know where it would do most good. She never kept anything for herself. If you gave her a present, no matter how personal, she gave it away. It was always sweets for the children, curtains for the old lady, a bob or two for the old man. 'Miss Cave' was known and loved all over the St Mary's district.

During our weekly visit to Auntie Kate, we boys were expected to pay our respects to the other elderly occupants of the house. No doubt Auntie, knowing their loneliness, wanted to share her company with them as she shared everything else. The formal visits led to Alfie's participation in a weekly poker game. The players included Mrs Bosey, a bird-like noblewoman who had fallen on hard times. Her powdered,

alabaster profile lent a touch of class to the proceedings which were often held up as she was stone
deaf. Mr Herbert was clearly an unfrocked clergyman,
well-spoken, apologetic and furtive. We boys were fascinated by the pungent, bag-like contraption which
hung down inside his trousers. The fourth member of
this ill-assorted quartet was a marooned bo'sun, Mr
Lewis, full of strange oaths and bearded like the pard.
One of his curses, 'Ach y fi!', was adopted by Alfie
who discovered only recently from Dylan Thomas's
Under Milk Wood that it is a Welsh expression of
disgust. The reason for Mr Lewis's continual use of
it is now clear. Alfie won too many tricks, and too
many halfpennies. Luckily for his slower opponents,
the weekly game lasted no longer than an hour.

Alfie's favourite among Auntie Kate's visitors was Mrs
Scruggs, whom he teased into Joycean monologues. On
different occasions, she boasted of her 'lovely garding,
full of melligolds and coronations', recommended 'a
fillum, where that Charles Laughton was cap'n of a
tarpeder', and announced that her nephew was 'in
horse piddle with his adeloids and tonstils'. Alfie never
forgot Mrs Scruggs's revision of the English language
and once wrote a monologue on the sights of London
in Scruggsian terms. The itinerary included, as I recall,
Horse Carts' Parade, Convent Garden, Marble Arse,
The Natural Gallery, Gilder's Groin and The Houses
of Polo Mint.

No sooner the word than the blow. Mrs Scruggs
defined it and immediately Alfie realized it. He went
into 'horse piddle with his adeloids and tonstils'. Mum
had remarked for some time that Alfie was breathing through his mouth. The doctor recommended
removing the impediments in the air passage. An
hour after the operation Alfie was astonished to find

that a taxi-driver was carrying him up the path to 164 Wilton Road.

In addition to his unremarkable physical difficulties at this time, Alfie showed signs of psychological tension. He began to bite his fingernails raw. This worried his parents, who saw it as a distressing and disreputable habit, unaware of its emotional implications. They regularly dipped his fingers into a wormwood solution, hoping the bitter taste would deter him from chewing his nails and the skin around them. It did not.

Another sign of Alfie's insecurity was a new self-consciousness. His eyes began to water when he was the centre of attention. It began as a natural reflex to sunlight in the eyes. Dad was a keen photographer and insisted on taking snapshots of the family with us all smiling into the sun over his shoulder. When the print came back, the pose was less than perfect. Alfie had been snapped rubbing his eyes. 'You've ruined the bloody picture!' Dad would explode. Sometimes Alfie would be caught screwing up his eyes. His father was not encouraged by this reaction. 'What's the matter with the boy?' he would ask. It was clear that Alfie was no longer enjoying his performances in the corner, either. Pressed into entertaining, he would turn away from his audience, eyes streaming, fists in eye-sockets.

This must have been a stressful period for him. How could he come to terms with a father so unpredictable – caring, interested and affectionate one minute, yet critical, dismissive and furious the next? Years later I recognized Cyril Connolly's description of his first meeting with Ernest Hemingway: 'The animal warmth of the bear-like hug was overwhelming, but one was aware that the bear had claws.' My attitude towards Alfie was ambivalent too – often hostile and quarrelsome, at other times friendly and affectionate. I enjoyed our games together. Alfie was an inventive and resilient playmate. He enjoyed my company in return, especially when I read to him in bed or made up stories for him. Alfie must have felt he was losing the sibling struggle. I was the firstborn, two years older and stronger. Although I never noticed any difference between Mum's treatment of my brother and me, the Captain's occasional grumble that 'She thinks the sun shines out of Len's jacksie' could not have reassured him.

Alfie was always a loveable and a loving child, yet we often quarrelled. Our cousin, Lena's boy Chris, who visited us frequently, was the ubiquitous peacemaker. An amiable, dark-haired lad of Alfie's age, he would push between us to talk calmly and sensibly. Sometimes to his cost. Mum hit upon the strategy of placing Chris between her quarrelsome pair in the middle of our double bed. Upon waking up in the morning, Alfie and I would fight across his body. Chris remembers that he often got punched in the ears from both sides at once – as he says, 'A case of "Good morning, earache" in stereo!'

Another preoccupation that no doubt also disturbed Alfie at this time was the need to change schools. Dad was negotiating for a prettier semi-detached house in a more central district of Southampton. We boys were overjoyed to learn that the new house in Westrow Gardens was near to the county cricket ground, the speedway and greyhound track, the ice rink and the Dell football ground. However, our new address would have meant a walk of nearly two miles to and from Shirley School. Another school, Western, which had an excellent reputation, was considerably closer. Many of its pupils won scholarships (free places) to the local grammar schools. The headmaster of Western welcomed the prospect of two more possible scholarship winners, but Old Baldie accepted the loss of his token petit-bourgeoisie with little grace.

While the family awaited the completion of contracts and the consequent move in 1931, Alfie was given the job of clearing the new garden of rubble and stones. Every day after school, he walked over to the pristine semi, gathered broken bricks and stones in a bucket and emptied them in a corner of the garden to form the hard-core base for a wooden shed. It was a tiring task, but Alfie found he quite enjoyed it. He liked the smell of the fresh paintwork, the springtime song of the blackbirds in the neighbouring trees, the peace and the absence of tension. Sometimes, when he had finished his stint, he would sit against a wall for a few minutes and doze in the late afternoon, before returning home for dinner.

4

Dis Must Be De Place!

As far as the family was concerned, the new house in Westrow Gardens was all things to all men. To Mum, it meant release from the tyranny of the huge, black kitchen range, a beast that had to be fed into grudging compliance. Now she had a gas stove that obeyed her with the subservience of a batman. All around her were bright, airy rooms, waiting like tidy-boxes to be filled with toys. Mum had a wonderful time playing with the furniture. The Captain, as he often reminded us, had more important things to attend to. Such as the garden. He had, at the front and rear of the house, two plots of virgin soil to upturn. And there was the rates campaign, of course. As he had no car, Dad threatened to tear down the garage rather than pay rates on it. His appearance before them so frightened the members of the tribunal that they let him get away with it. Needless to say, he then proceeded to put another floor in the garage and stuff it to the gunwales.

Alfie and I found our new home a convenient base, as we soon discovered secret entrances into the nearby cricket ground, speedway and greyhound track and ice rink. We never managed to crack the Dell football ground although Alfie got in once on an old age pensioner's ticket and I saw a cup match disguised as a ladies' lavatory attendant. We boys appreciated our base's position, close to the common, yet within easy distance of the cinemas and shops. It meant that we could meet Dad in one of the parks on summer evenings after work. He always brought a large bag of sweets, which we would munch while we played ball games. When the Captain grew weary, he sat on the bench and chatted to Mum under the loaded blossom of the trees until it was time to go.

Those parks! How we loved those splendid parks. Particularly in spring. Southampton has always been a remarkably verdant city. It has no clear border with the countryside, greenery extending far along the central ridge. Alfie, Chris and I once walked the length of the town, downhill all the way, four miles under trees or on grass – from Lords Wood at its northern edge, through the sports centre, into the common and across to the Avenue, two miles of ancient trees that led straight down the spine of the watershed to the parks, named after great men of the city – Isaac Watts, author of hymns, Alderman Andrews, master coach-builder, and Lord Palmerston, Queen Victoria's Prime Minister; on through Houndwell Park and past the cricket pitches of Hoglands to end up in the shadow of the towering liners by the dock gates at Queen's Park. The three of us have visited many places, as individuals, since, but not one of us has ever been able to walk across a city, as we did in Southampton, to the sound of birdsong all the way.

Occasionally, that summer of 1932, Dad joined us on the pier, where Mum had taken us directly from school. It had plenty to interest a couple of lads. We would wander along the jetties, where the fishermen dropped their lines, to appraise their catch – a bass, an eel or a crab big enough to take home – and examine minutely the panorama of the waterfront for clues to the disposition of the liners, freighters and other vessels. Alfie had a small brass telescope that he used to check on the names, ports of origin, nationalities, signs, numbers, flags and arrangements of the ships in the docks or on Southampton Water. He kept me in line by refusing to allow me to use it, as he did with all his attractive possessions. 'Not without my permission!' he would say firmly. I had to behave myself if I wanted to spy on the flotilla of assorted craft around Southampton Pier. Top of Alfie's list of attractions were the pinball and other machines. He was the only person I ever knew who always made a profit on them – even though it was usually in halfpennies. The amount did not appear to justify the effort. His systems always involved a great deal of calculation and waiting for others to feed in the money that Alfie took out.

Mum usually sat in a deckchair, by the bandstand, to watch the dancing. I was too shy to chance my arm, but Alfie would find a young partner and waltz or foxtrot her round the floor. He was quite the expert gigolo although he had never taken lessons. As always, his natural gifts came to his aid – an ability to learn quickly plus an innate sense of rhythm. Alfie was very democratic in his choice of partner, which was always the most appropriate female there. However, if there were no young girls, he would make do with a more mature woman. He did not let his lack of height trouble him, but appeared to have no objection to placing his right hand on a well-rounded buttock and his nose in a large bosom. When the Captain arrived, he would sometimes dance with Mum. Dad never partnered anyone else. I am sure he never looked at another woman in his whole married life.

The new school was as welcoming as the new house. Alfie and I were reassured to find trimmed haircuts in the majority. We were accepted immediately and soon we each made our own friends. The establishment was businesslike and well organized, keeping the pupils interested and at full stretch. It was easy to see why

Western had a reputation for winning scholarships. Alfie began to blossom under the new regime, bringing home excellent reports. The headmaster, however, was eccentric. He loved music and was quite prepared to interrupt an arithmetic lesson to teach the class a new song if he had just received the music for it. On one occasion he punished Alfie for the single spelling error 'butterflys', by sending him in disgrace to Standard One (the bottom class) for a fortnight. Alfie shrugged off the humiliation and determined not to make such careless mistakes in the future.

Most afternoons the Hill boys used to postpone the return home to play in the alleys near the school. Gangs of our new friends would race through the narrow channels of a grid of lanes, hiding and chasing. The conditions were unpromising, but our imaginations furnished the excitement. Some of the streets were so quiet that we could play football in them. Alfie was taking part in a game when he booted the ball through a front-room window. Only one boy hared up the street out of trouble. All the others stuck by Alfie as he knocked on the door to apologize and promise to make amends. The footballers eventually collected enough money to pay for a new window.

From the first Alfie had applied himself diligently to his studies at Western, fairly galloping to top of the class. His success gained him general praise, halting his father's criticism and providing the model for me rather than the other way round. Some of his deeper anxieties were allayed. New-found confidence induced him to play the fool at home. 'I began,' says Benny, 'to lark around a bit.' His was the obliquest of challenges to paternal authority, perhaps only a bid to replace his father as centre of attention.

Alfie had plenty of targets for his fooling. The parrot

had a high priority. Laura, a splendid Amazon Green, had been brought home by the Captain as part payment in some arcane exchange. She was a handsome bird with touches of red, blue and yellow about her. The Captain was very proud of Laura. Unfortunately, she was noisy, smelly and had disgusting habits. If she disturbed the Captain's evening, he shut her up by closing the curtains around her cage. However, those at home during the day were forbidden to do this and had to endure the parrot's cries of 'Who's that?' and 'Is that the milkman?' It taxed even Alfie's wit to find fresh rejoinders to the unchanging questions.

We boys took turns to give Laura a bath at regular weekends, a treat for her but an ordeal for the lad in charge. While her cage was scrubbed in the garden, the bird was shut in the kitchen to be sponged down later. Occasionally, other members of the household forgot that psittacine ablutions were under way and opened the door to the hall. Sure enough, Laura would twinkle-toe it through the gap, waddling faster than a champion walker. Then it would be lunges and crashes, cries and whispers, Laurel and Hardy until the naughty bird was back in her cage. Only once, the door to the garden was opened without due care and a sunburst of colours exploded into the wild blue yonder. In seconds an unfamiliar beauty glided among the trees of the adjoining nursing-home. Alfie was over the fence in a trice, calling 'Laura' like a forlorn lover. She led him a dance all over the park. He trampled through the flower-beds and tripped over the stone lawn-edging in his eagerness to catch her. At last the flyaway disappeared into a bush near the great house. Under the eyes of the matron, the nurses, and the patients, Alfie slowly approached the hiding-place. He was hot, tired and mucky. 'It's all right,

Laura,' he called, reassuringly. 'It's all going to be all right.'

'Who's that?' she replied from the depths of the bush. 'Is that the milkman?'

One evening we heard a squawk and a thud from the draped cage. When the curtains were opened, there, on the floor, was a very dead parrot indeed. In due course, Laura was buried, with full avian honours, in the back garden. There remained the disposal of her beautiful brass cage. Alfie offered to remove it. Dad agreed in return for a halt in Alfie's interminable parrot imitations.

The cage was so large and heavy that a boy alone could not carry it. The help of good old, reliable Chris was called in. He and Alfie carried it between them to a second-hand shop called Clack and Back's, in Shirley. The dealer there offered them sixpence for it. 'I'm not taking sixpence,' grumbled Alfie. 'We'll try Orchard Lane.' Manhandling the cage on to a tramcar, the pair took the two-mile ride that cost Chris twopence to East Street and struggled from dealer to dealer along Orchard Lane. Not one would give them more than fourpence for the treasure. It was sixpence or nothing. So back they went to Clack and Back's, this time on foot, still staggering under the huge cage. When the young comedians finally arrived at the second-hand shop, they were grateful for the sixpence. Chris was given his twopence back and a penny ice-cream for his trouble.

Alfie was developing the acumen he had shown at Shirley School. His circle of friends were the sons of local shopkeepers. The shopkeepers did a little private business with the Captain; their sons did a little private business with Alfie. The lads were into foreign coins, second-hand toys, marbles, cigarette card sets, rags,

bottles and *bona fide* autographs. Such items could be
sold in grubby downtown lock-ups and second-hand
shops. The sharpest of the young dealers was Sammy
Burns, a freckled redhead, who had the innate advantage of a Jewish mother and a Scots father. Sammy had
many knock-down drag-out business struggles with
Alfie, whose ace-in-the-hole was his secret trade in
horse-manure. Alfie was the only boy to recognize
the commercial potential of this despised commodity.
With bucket and shovel he would follow the milk-carts
for miles.

Alfie once parlayed a cigarette card by way of a
Dinky racing-car, exchanged for a pull-along wooden
yacht, swapped for a broken magic lantern, traded
for a cricket bat, into a half-crown. The half-crown
(two shillings and sixpence, or twelve-and-a-half pence
in today's parlance) was paid for the cricket bat by
a second-hand dealer in Canal Walk. 'My education
began when the dealer promptly put the bat in the window after chalking it at three shillings and sixpence,'
says Benny. 'It had taken me a month of effort to get
the two and six. Now the dealer was getting three and
six with no trouble at all!'

Close and parallel to Canal Walk was Orchard Lane,
which, besides its second-hand shops, boasted four
fish-and-chip shops. When Alfie was negotiating sales
with the dealers, Chris was despatched to check on the
nippers leaving each of the shops with a penny cone
of chips. It was his critical responsibility to estimate
which shop was offering the most chips for a penny.
Once the deal was struck, tuppence of the proceeds
could not have been spent with more careful consideration than on those two heaped cones of chips.

The Birmingham City football team that played a cup
game at the Dell in 1935 had two big stars – Harry Hibbs,

the England goalkeeper, and Joe Bradford, a midfield schemer. After the game, Alfie was among the crowd of boys waiting in the club car-park for the players to leave. As a stocky man came out of the players' door, cries of 'It's Joe Bradford!' were heard. Autograph books were shoved under the chunky fellow's nose.

'I'm not Joe Bradford!' he protested.

'Oh yes you are,' shouted the lads.

'I tell you I'm not! I've just been on a job!'

'Joe Bradford! There's only one Joe Bradford!' chanted the crowd of boys.

'I tell you, I'm not Joe Bradford. I've just been mending the pipes!'

'Come on, Joe, sign the books!' cried the autograph hunters.

They flocked round him so that the poor man could not move. In the end, he signed every book, 'Joe Bradford'. Including Alfie's. Then the rest of the Birmingham team emerged and were mobbed on their way to the coach. They pushed a path through the clamorous throng and climbed aboard. So did Alfie. Only just in time. The door slammed shut and the coach pulled out of the car-park. As they went through the gates, Alfie looked back and saw the stocky fellow getting into a van marked, 'Ted Burrows, Plumber'. Alfie was not disappointed, for a few minutes later he had captured the signatures of the real Joe Bradford, Harry Hibbs and the rest of the Birmingham team. By the time he had been up and down the aisle, they were three miles outside of Southampton. The long walk home was a march of triumph.

On a one-day holiday from school, Alfie joined Mike, a classmate, for ball games on the common. When they met, Alfie was surprised to find Mike's mother and father present. It was an ordinary working day.

After a few strenuous tussles, Mike's dad bought the
boys an ice-cream each from a mobile cart. When they
approached the mother, she looked hard at her husband
and said: 'I didn't know you had money for ice-creams.'
Alfie realized with a sinking feeling that Mike's father
was unemployed. Many of his classmates came from
homes where the father was unemployed.

Alfie was conscious that, although there was no
luxury at home, he was relatively privileged. His family
had a holiday every year, for example. True, it was only a
week spent at a seaside resort no more than thirty miles
away, but it was still a holiday.

Every year, the Hill family would take a train or
ferry to Southsea, Bournemouth, or Ryde on the Isle
of Wight. We spent our week at a cheap guest-house,
but never returned to it for a second year. I suppose that
the Captain was looking for a better deal. Wherever we
were, Alfie's clowning made all the difference. If the
weather was poor, his high spirits made it bearable; if
sunny, hilarious.

We stayed at some strange establishments. Dad booked
us into a large, dark, rambling place one year. It was on
the top of the hill behind Ryde – a real Charles Addams
house. Everything creaked and rattled in the wind. The
woman who ran it resembled Norman Bates's mother
in *Psycho*. You remember her – grey hair in a bun at the
back, grey shawl, thin woman, cadaverous looks.

Alfie will never forget the first evening meal. The Hill
family, the only guests, had assembled in the echoing
dining-room when Mrs Bates appeared, shawl about
her shoulders.

'You like me?' she asked.

No, not a lot, but we did not care to say so.

'You would like some "you like me"?' she queried.
We looked blank.

'You like me, crab?' she enquired, looking at Alfie.

She left the room. Alfie and I were convulsed at this encounter. Our shoulders shook with silent laughter. We dared not look at each other.

Mrs Bates returned with a tin, which she held up for our inspection. It bore the legend – 'U Like Me Crab'. It became clear that she was offering us the contents for our dinner. It looked a remarkably small tin to share among four people, but we faked enthusiasm for it.

After Mrs Bates had taken the U Like Me Crab back to the kitchen, Alfie grabbed the antimacassar from an easy chair, threw it over his shoulders and bleated, 'You Like Me?' in imitation of Mrs Bates. 'Would You Like Me?', clutching his shawl he came to each of us in turn. Mum and I were in hysterics. Even the Captain could scarcely suppress a smile. 'You like me, crab?' went on Alfie. 'Would you like crab like me? You look like you like You Like Me Crab. Like me, you look like crab – ' Suddenly Mrs Bates appeared behind him. Alfie guessed she was there, stopped his fooling, and under her disapproving gaze returned the antimacassar.

Mrs Bates served the tinned crab with a huge tureen of steaming peas. We were about to sit down when Alfie noticed that the peas were moving. They were full of maggots.

'Look!' cried Alfie. 'Every pea has its own driver!'

The tureen was returned and Alfie deputed in future to assist Mrs Bates in the preparation of the evening meal. Despite his efforts, there was little improvement. We ate out a good deal after that.

Every summer holiday was given its catch-phrase. Alfie would pick one of the cheapjack cries heard on the promenade, reproduce the nasal delivery exactly and work it to death. It might be the fruit-seller's pitch, 'Apples, onchess and pinanas!', the tiny casino's, 'Eye

shades are free!', or even the darts stallholder's, 'It may
be your lucky day today!' Alfie would squeeze the
catch-phrase into every conversation. It never failed
to evoke a chuckle, from me at least. He would deliberately question figures of authority – policemen, clergy-
men and commissionaires – then slip in the deadly
phrase. They were mystified when I suddenly guf-
fawed. The catch-phrase tradition went into the family
folklore. We would remember that the holiday was
Bournemouth '33 because that was the year Alfie was
croaking, 'Don't forget your weekly "Woman"!'

Alfie was also learning his comedy tricks from other
sources. On the beach at Bournemouth was a pierrot
show that starred Willie Cave. He was the first stage
comedian we boys had ever seen and we thought him
the funniest man in the world. He was on stage most
of the time, and if the show was slowing down he had
a trick of backing into the piano so that the corner
caught his bum. He would leap away, with a very
disapproving look on his face. We thought the gag,
in the phrase of the time, 'the cat's pyjamas'. For a
while Alfie used it constantly. What am I saying? He
is still using it, to this day.

In the Willie Cave Show was a pierrette who won
Alfie's heart. He could not see her figure because she
wore the loose white pyjamas with black pom-poms
that they all wore. But oh! her fabulous face! She wore
entirely orange make-up – orange eye-shadow, orange
cheeks and orange lips. Alfie was stunned by this exotic
creature and watched her every show whenever he
could. The next year Alfie learned something of the
female form divine when we watched an exhibition of
the League of Health and Beauty on the promenade
lawns at Ryde. It was one of those androgynous displays of military precision, so popular all over Europe

in the thirties. There was also plenty of Health and Beauty on show. The Leaguers were marched about, lined up in rows and ranks and went through their exercises in unison under the eagle eye of a female sergeant-major.

'I reckon Miss Bossy Boots would be more at home in The League of Wealth and Duty,' commented Alfie. Miss Bossy Boots made our day when she hit herself on the nose with an Indian club.

Ryde was the setting, that year, for the children's sandcastle competition, organized by a national newspaper. Dad suggested that Alfie should model a whale in the sand to illustrate the slogan 'A Whale of a Paper!' with the words picked out in small stones. Alfie agreed, found his square on the beach among a hundred others and set to with bucket and spade.

Unfortunately, he had given little thought to his contribution so that his whale just lay there stranded on the beach. It was a smooth hill of sand with no colour or texture. Alfie would have achieved the same effect if he had buried his father on his back in the sand. In the next square, a little girl was working on an elaborate bas-relief with seaweed, shells, stones, clays, and sands of all colours. She told Alfie proudly that her daddy had driven her to Alum Bay and all over the island to gather the materials for her work of art. At the end of the morning, Alfie's pretty neighbour won first prize.

'The point is,' says Benny, 'that I tried everything I knew to persuade her to give me some of her trimmings. She had plenty. I smiled, I flattered her, I gave her sweets, I made her laugh, but she wouldn't even give me a single shell. I got nothing. The story of my life!'

As was her wont, Auntie Kate helped to cheer up

Alfie the very next day. Just before we had come to Ryde on holiday, she had been rash enough to praise Alfie's singing.

'A musician could do a great deal with him,' she opined. Alfie overheard the remark, and as was his wont, misunderstood it. He thought she made mention of a 'magician'. Immediately, he saw himself as a kind of singing sorcerer's apprentice. A glittering stage career, perhaps. It only remained for him to be discovered. Suddenly, he was vocalizing at every street corner. You never heard such a happy wanderer. Not so much melodious as loud. His parents were resigned to his insanity and accepted that he was now into the next stage of juvenile dementia.

So there he was, digging away on Ryde Beach, and singing loud enough to make the angels weep. A party of young people stopped to listen. They were impressed by the sheer volume of sound.

'Can you sing "April Showers"?' asked a bright young thing. Alfie not only could sing it, but would throw in the Al Jolson gestures and perform it in blackface if she would lend him her mascara for a moment. He proceeded to give it the deep diaphragm and telescopic arms. The lyrics had scarcely been chewed when he was handed a hat with more pennies in it than he could count at a glance.

When Mum saw his ill-gotten gains she ordered him to return the lolly. The young people refused to take it back and insisted that Alfie had earned it. He was reluctantly prevailed upon to keep the money – so reluctant that he could not stop smiling. Those eleven pence made up the payment for his first professional performance.

During the next summer holiday, in Bournemouth, Alfie once more demonstrated his faltering grasp on reality. Our vacation was much enlivened by the presence of Chris, whose family had recently moved to the Hampshire resort. We three boys were playing our version of cricket in a quiet park. Alfie was bowling to Chris. As wicket-keeper, I noticed that every time the bowler's arm came over, he shouted the same unintelligible phrase. Was it a prayer? or one of Mr Lewis's strange oaths? At last I asked him.

'I'm shouting, "Body Adore"!' Alfie called back.

'Body Adore? What's that?'

'You know – it's in all the papers – Body Adore!'

'What's he talking about, Chris?'

'Search me,' said Chris.

Then it came to me. The summer newspapers were full of the cricket scandal of 'body-line' bowling. The Australians had accused the English player Harold Larwood of bowling at their bodies, not the stumps. Alfie had experienced a modicum of that in his school games in The Wreck. In the same newspapers, Lifebuoy Soap had launched a huge campaign on the need to prevent Body Odour. Of course, Alfie had muddled up 'body-line' with 'body odour'! Body Adore, indeed! I teased poor Alfie about that for weeks.

Another press stunt was the *News Chronicle*'s Lobby Lud visit. 'Lobby Lud will be coming to your favourite seaside resort to add to the holiday atmosphere of gaiety and fun!' the newspaper claimed. Lobby Lud was a mystery man who would hand over a five-pound note if correctly challenged by someone carrying the latest *News Chronicle*.

When he came to Bournemouth that year, Alfie was waiting for him at the station. The young detective recognized the mystery man from his photograph, and sure enough the stranger followed the printed itinerary. Alfie was concerned about challenging too soon. He wanted more confirmation of his suspicions. The mystery man entered a pub and Alfie hung about outside for half an hour, then the stranger moved on, keeping strictly to his timetable, as laid down in the *News Chronicle*.

At last Alfie was quite sure. He would challenge Lobby Lud at the first opportunity. However, there was a serious difficulty. Had he the bottle? Alfie fluffed a couple of chances. He swallowed the anchor. Oh, dear. Would he ever be able to pluck up the nerve to make the challenge correctly? Alfie stuck to the trail. Lobby Lud made his way to the sea front. Alfie followed. The mystery man strolled along the promenade. Then, suddenly, he nipped into a bathing tent. Crafty beggar! He could not be seen in there. Right, thought Alfie, gotcha! Alfie took a deep breath, marched up to the tent and pushed his way in.

'You are Lobby Lud,' he stated firmly, 'and I am a reader – '

The stranger stood, stark naked.

'Get out of here!' he shouted in a rage.

' – of the *Nude Chronicle* and I claim – ' went on Alfie.

The mystery man had lost a good deal of his mystery.

'Get away! How dare you!' he yelled, white all over, except for his red face.

' – the prize of five pounds!' said Alfie.

Appendages swinging, the naked ape leapt at Alfie and threw him out of the tent.

'Get out of here, you saucy boy!' he cried. As Alfie sprawled in the sand, he thought: 'He can't be Lobby Lud. He's not adding to the holiday atmosphere of gaiety and fun!'

The day before we came home, Alfie fell off a small roundabout in a children's playground and broke a bone in his foot. Mum read to him for hours to take his mind off the pain. Back in Southampton he was given a crutch to help him get about. How Alfie loved that simple support, which enabled him, at the drop of an aitch, to go into his Long John Silver characterization (Wallace Beery film version); his only regret was that Laura had not lived long enough to play Cap'n Flint opposite him.

Upon his return from Bournemouth, Alfie began to watch over the ripening chestnuts on the sweet chestnut tree next door. Two great branches, full of spiky pouches, hung over our fence. Every year when the pouches fell softly on to our lawn, Alfie culled the plumper nuts, peeled them and teased me by eating them very slowly in my view over the following weeks. As they were only a handful of leathery scraps in the first place, this exercise required a steely determination on his part. I had no such determination, was too lazy to collect the nuts in the first place and used force to grab one when the opportunity occurred. At which, Alfie would yell, 'Mum! he's taking my chestnuts!' From another room would come the reflex, 'Len! leave his chestnuts alone!' and I would be foiled again. Alfie would say, 'If you really want a chestnut, then – ' and reel off a list of demands like the Versailles Treaty.

One morning, Alfie was galvanized into excited action by the sight, from the bedroom window, of a fall of large, dark chestnuts on our lawn. He could not collect them quickly enough, scrambling round in his pyjamas to gather this unexpected harvest. He had always known his faith in the tree would be rewarded one day. And here it was. Dreams can come true, it can happen to you, if you're young in heart. Had

Alfie stopped to think for a moment, he would have noticed that few of these nuts were in pouches. Each of them was suspiciously solitary. They were also plump, swarthy and obviously Italian. The caper had Dad's signature written all over it, but I never let on.

The dodge was so successful that, believe it or not, Dad pulled it again a couple of months later in Lords Wood. It was there that, every season, we visited one or two walnut trees to see what they had put forth. This time – lo and behold! – Alfie found a pound of remarkably clean walnuts nestling against the trunks. He appeared to believe the discovery fortuitous. Perhaps, as long as he was copping the nuts, he took a genuinely agnostic view of the provider.

It went against the Captain's inclination, of course, to do good by stealth. He certainly relished receiving the credit for his many acts of genuine generosity. When he brought anything of interest home, which he did frequently, it was understood as a matter of course that the item was of rare quality, redolent of privilege and difficult to obtain. 'You can't get 'em, you know,' he would say, meaning that only a man of his special gifts could lay hands on such a treasure. When he came home one evening with a brand-new radio set, he praised it in such extravagant terms that Alfie received the impression that we were honoured to hear from it programmes denied to *hoi polloi*. Consequently, when next day his teacher asked for volunteers to tell a joke, Alfie leapt up to regale his classmates with a jest he had heard on the radio, confident that it would be new to them. Imagine his humiliation when he was shouted down by all those who had heard it the previous evening.

One day, Alfie met a boy who was earning sixpence every Sunday by singing in the choir at our

local church, St Mark's. It sounded like an attractive opportunity, especially when the boy told him
that the young singers were shortly to be taken on
an outing by paddle-steamer to the Isle of Wight.
Alfie, who had never set foot inside any church, let
alone St Mark's, managed to persuade his father, who
harboured a deep suspicion of all organized religion,
to grant his assent to the application. Once accepted,
Alfie then required his mother to buy him a white collar
and surplice. These accoutrements cost her so much
that even with the payments at sixpence a week, the
family never broke even on the deal. For Alfie stayed
with the choir only until the outing to the Isle of
Wight. Southampton Water was choppy that day and
Alfie was sick all the way there and back again. His
prayers were not answered and he never set foot in St
Mark's again.

At about that time, one of the cigarette companies
produced a beautiful set of cards in full colour of the
head and shoulders of famous cricketers. The Hill boys
had on their visits to the county ground seen many of
the heroes depicted. These cards were so attractive that
Alfie was collecting them not for business purposes but
for himself. He made special efforts to complete a set
– raiding waste-bins, checking cigarette packets in
every gutter, accosting smokers and laying out good
money for rare cards. He had not quite achieved a
full set when I was told at school that I had won a
scholarship to Taunton's, a well-regarded Southampton
grammar school. When I relayed the good news to Alfie
in the playground, he whipped the rubber band from
his treasured cricketer cards and threw them up in
a great fluttering cloud. Our schoolmates scrambled
for them. He was so happy for me that he danced a
celebratory jig as the cards fell like snow around him.

I have never forgotten that marvellous, spontaneous gesture of affection.

Soon after that, in 1933, Alfie observed that his mother was getting fatter.

'I'm going to have a baby,' explained Mum. And presently she went into a local nursing-home for a fortnight. Although we saw her occasionally in the evenings, Alfie missed her at home. Lunch in Grandma Cave's kitchen was fun, but dinner with Dad was a bleak experience. Normally a stickler for clean tablecloths and polished silver, the Captain now insisted on our eating on newspapers with a minimum of cutlery and crockery. Alfie and I looked after ourselves and were relieved, astonished and delighted when at last Mum brought home our tiny sister, Diana.

Everybody adored the baby. Alfie redoubled his business efforts and had no sooner garnered a few pence than he spent them on rattles and toys for the new arrival. He also placed a pottery piggy bank in the hall at home to nudge visitors and the rest of the family into contributions for a fund for Diana. His concern for his baby sister was not one of the 'seven-day wonders' for which the Captain chided him. Alfie always made special efforts for Diana. So did Dad, who never directed his criticisms at her.

When I left Western in 1933 to take up my free place at the grammar school, Alfie was expected to apply himself to the same end. My impression was that my parents considered him brighter than their firstborn, thus adding to his anxiety about the result. Despite the time he devoted to his commercial interests, he responded to the constant urging from all sides by working very hard at his studies.

The school staff were encouraging and most of the pupils supportive. However, there remained a menace in the playground. He was Jackie Belper, a large, fat bully, who had perfected the trick of creeping up behind his victim and jumping on an unsuspecting back, landing with arms round neck and such a quantity of dead weight that the poor bearer bent at the knees and sank beneath it to the ground. When, at last, Belper released his victim, he would offer to shake hands. If given an opportunity, the menace would enclose fingers and knuckles in his massive mitt and crush them until they squeaked.

Alfie had always kept one eye on Jackie Belper and so had escaped his destructive embrace. However, one playtime in his last year at Western, Alfie noticed a look of alarm in the eyes of a prospective client. Knowing that his own machinations would scarcely induce terror he immediately bent forward, making a horizontal back. Arms were already round his throat and served to pull Jumping Jackie right over the top of Alfie in a somersault that sent the fat bully clattering to the ground. Belper fell with such momentum that the wind was smacked out of his body, leaving him bruised and dazed. He staggered to his feet, seeking vengeance. Alfie was saved by the bell – the handbell that sounded the end of playtime. He had never heard a sweeter sound. The last period at Western School that afternoon buzzed with whispers of The Big Fight. After school, Jackie Belper was going to beat seven colours of the proverbial out of Alfie Hill. Nobody wanted to miss that.

When Alfie came out into the playground after school, a crowd of excited schoolboys was there to greet him. They cheered when they saw him, in celebration, Alfie thought, of the fact that he was doing the fighting – not them. Jackie Belper followed, the lads cheered and began to move off. Alfie called for

them to stop and explained that if they stayed together
as a mob they would attract the attention of the police.
They would need to go to the fight venue in pairs. He
suggested that they all meet later in Hill Lane Cemetery.
It would be quiet in there and away from prying eyes. It
was an outlandish suggestion and much further away
than the boys had expected, but the prospect sounded
exciting. A fight in a cemetery! Great! It was agreed.
The keen ones hurried ahead.

On the way there, Alfie moved alongside Jackie
Belper. 'Can I have a word in private, Jackie?' asked
Alfie. The fat boy, who had been rather puzzled by the
turn of events, agreed. He could not quite understand
why he was not already tying Hill's arms round Hill's
neck – or why it was necessary to walk so far to do
it. Perhaps his enemy would explain.

'I'm a bit worried,' said Alfie. 'Are you planning to
wrestle Cumberland style or Cornish or in the Greco-
Roman tradition?' he asked.

'Wah?' replied Belper.

'It's important that we settle this, Jackie.'

'Whaddya mean?' asked Jackie.

'Well, if we're not wrestling in the same style, somebody's going to get badly hurt. You see, if you're using
the Cornish style and I'm using Greco-Roman, there
could be a nasty accident.'

'You don't say,' said Jackie.

'Oh, yes. I broke a boy's arm up at Shirley. I didn't
mean to, but he should have said he was wrestling
Cumberland style. I was using Greco-Roman, you see.
So I don't want all that fuss again.'

'No, you wouldn't,' agreed Jackie.

'I don't mind breaking your finger, or crushing your
toes, but I wouldn't want to do you a permanent
injury.'

'No, I can see that,' said the fat boy.

Jackie began to think hard about that cataclysmic fall in the playground. This lad knew something he did not. He made up his mind quickly.

'Crikey,' said the fat boy. 'My Mum'll kill me! I'm supposed to be over me Auntie Clara's by now. Toodle-oo!' And he was off down a side street.

Alfie called to some of the accompanying crowd, who gathered round him.

'Jackie's called off the fight,' he explained. 'Someone must have told him about the boy I injured in a fight at Shirley School.'

There was no one to throw up cigarette cards in Alfie's honour when he was told that he had won a scholarship to Taunton's in 1935. He had been on tenterhooks for weeks and now he sat in his classroom and hugged the good news to himself. Would it never be time to go home? At last it was, and he raced along the pavements to tell an adoring family of his triumph. Except that there was no adoring family when he arrived home. No one was in that afternoon. The house was locked. Alfie sat in the back garden and wept. By the time the rest of the family returned, he was totally deflated.

5

White, Black and Blue

'I don't mean the adjective. I want the noun. What is "shoddy"?' the schoolmaster asked the class. Alfie put up his hand.

'Shoddy is cloth made up of shredded woollen rags,' he answered.

'At last!' sighed the schoolmaster. 'And what is your name?'

'Alfred Hill, sir.'

'Well, Alfred Hill, you appear to be the only boy in the school who is familiar with that particular common noun.'

'I got a million of 'em,' muttered Alfie *sotto voce*. It was his first encounter with Dr Horace King, head of the English department at Taunton's, a Shakespearian scholar who later became a Labour MP for Southampton, Speaker of the House of Commons and, finally, Lord Maybray-King. Dr King was to play a significant part in Alfie's choice of career. Soon after this classroom interchange, a curious incident brought them closer together.

One day, Alfie, in his obligatory school uniform of badged blazer with white, black and blue cap, was approached in the town by an elderly gentleman who looked like a Victorian actor-manager. The stranger's voluminous black cape and flowing white locks were crowned by a wide-brimmed black hat. This Professor of Literature (for so he described himself) asked Alfie to deliver a manuscript to Dr King. He could not trust it to the post, he said, and arranged to hand over the papers to Alfie under a particular tree on the common. At this meeting, the Professor revealed that inside the envelope was a recent find, a letter from Shakespeare to the Earl of Southampton. It proved beyond doubt that Shakespeare, not Bacon, wrote the entire canon.

The old pedagogue was exultant at the prospect of his spectacular triumph. He chuckled. 'I know that Dr King will give this the most rigorous examination,' he confided. 'Ask him if he agrees that the signature is genuine. Or does he really believe that William S. S. stands for the Steamship "William"?' The Professor cackled happily at his own joke and handed over the letter. Alfie was thrilled to be part of what he took to be the literary discovery of the century. He carried the precious manuscript to Dr King, who questioned him closely about his role in the affair. The Shakespearian scholar promptly returned the treasure with a covering note. When Alfie passed on the package, under the tree, the snowy-haired sage was astonished to read Dr King's polite but brief rejection of his thesis.

'I might have known,' grumbled the Professor. 'Dr King cannot give an independent opinion. I've suspected it for a long time. He's under the spell of Black Magicians. They've held one of their covens and put the influence on him. He's just a tool of the Evil Ones. They're everywhere. You can always tell them, my boy. They have red curtains at their windows.' The old man grasped Alfie by the arm, leaned forward and whispered urgently: 'If you see the red curtain always cross yourself and walk away quickly.' Alfie freed himself and backed off, slowly. 'When I'm in bed, at night,' muttered the Professor, 'I can hear them. I hear the witches talking at night as they fly over my house . . . '

Taunton's School was not, on the whole, conducive to fantasy. Its outside appearance was deceptive. The front elevation was that of a town hall in a particularly sleepy market-town. A pleasant two-storey building of yellowed brick, it faced a great wood of bushy-topped trees at the edge of the common. To the rear a single structure of low wooden workshops overlooked a playing-field that would accommodate two games of cricket or football according to season. The whole comprised a remarkably efficient educational establishment.

Alfie should have thrived there. He did not. The reasons for his relative failure were complex. I think he was floundering at first, unsure of his role in the family. Diana, always called Babe, had taken over the mantle of the indulged youngest child; meanwhile, I had already established myself as a high-profile achiever in school, a position Alfie felt he could never challenge. Tooling along in the Lower B forms, he was not stimulated by the higher expectations I responded to in the Upper As. Alfie was bored. He hated maths and was uninterested in biology, chemistry and physics (latent heat was a mystery to him – although he claims he has mastered it well enough to be able to cool his coffee in a variety of interesting ways). Alfie could not cope with grammar of any kind. Despite that weakness Mr Robinson, his French teacher, praised his excellent accent. 'Merci, mon vieux,' replied Alfie in a perfect French sing-song that owed more to Maurice Chevalier, probably, than Mr Robinson. He produced some interesting, original essays. When set the task of writing scenes from *The Merchant of Venice* in another form, he thought of it in simple verse and looked to Molière for inspiration. He remembers a couple of scraps from the playlet:

Antonio (to Shylock): Hello, pigdog, wipe your shoes.
I want some dough.
It's not for booze!

And he had to find a part for his favourite pin-up of the time, Mae West.

> Mae West: I'll overthrow the dirty beast,
> Not as Mae West, but as June East!

Alfie, as my younger brother, followed me into the house named after a former master, Henry Darwin, son of the great naturalist. I played cricket, soccer and won medals at athletics for the house. Alfie did not. Old schoolfriends recall with some hilarity how Alfie's well-developed posterior slowed him down in the sports races. And as for his prowess at soccer! Jacques Tati must surely have pinched his 'Continental Goalkeeper' stage act from my brother. You never saw such drama as when Alfie kept goal. He was always on the move between the posts, pacing up and down, reacting to the play, jumping about in anticipation, bullying his defence, pointing to danger spots, racing out to clear, diving at feet, hurling himself into the mud and leaping up to punch over the bar with all the grace of the hippos' underwater ballet. And if he took a knock, it had a dying fall all right. What a perFORMance! He would collapse in such agony that nervous Catholics would be persuaded to send for the priest.

According to his art master, Alan Whitney, Alfie produced creative work that showed imagination and possessed a poetic quality. His efforts revealed the cast of his mind even then. When set 'The City of Dreadful Night' as a subject, Alfie's painting made Hogarth look like Beatrix Potter. However, among the scenes of degradation in and around a saloon he managed to include can-can dancers.

Mr Whitney appreciated Alfie's wit and was amused by a rather personal reference. Asked by the art master to draw a human limb, my brother chose to depict a female leg. Knowing that his young teacher was keen on his skating partner, Alfie added a skating skirt to the thigh. Underneath it he wrote 'La belle jambe sans merci'. When he saw it, Mr Whitney laughed and, showing it to the class, commented: 'I have often wondered how humour relates to Art. This afternoon we have an interesting example.'

Benny was reminded of that afternoon years later when, at rehearsal, he was shown the sculpted bust of a nun. 'It was a primitive head made in plaster of Paris,' he says. 'Connie Georges, a lovely lady on the show, brought the piece to me and asked me what I thought of it. The head was absolutely superb. I was knocked out by its beauty and said so. When I asked her who the sculptor was, she said, "Look at the base." I turned the bust over, and there, on the tiny pedestal, were the initials A. H. I was the sculptor! It was my piece of work, carved in my first year at Taunton's! Mr Whitney had always prized it and loaned it to Connie to show me!'

Taunton's laid great store upon the performing arts. There were trips to the theatre, regular visits by professional companies presenting Shakespeare, ample opportunities to take part in the yearly drama festival, when each form offered a short play in competition, the house concert, the sixth-form concert, and the annual production of Gilbert and Sullivan or some other light opera, a miracle of organization that engaged the talents of hundreds. I took my chances and am best remembered for my rumbustious interpretation of Sir Toby Belch in scenes from *Twelfth Night*. One might have thought that in such a creative environment Alfie's extraordinary acting ability would have shone. It did not. He gave his tutors no inkling of his gift.

Alfie appeared only once on the stage at Taunton's School, playing a rabbit in the trial scene in *Alice in Wonderland*. All that he had to do was waggle his ears and say, ' 'Ere, 'ere!', a pun that should have appealed to him. It did not. Alfie was unhappy. He looked at the floor, hunched up his shoulders, turned away from the audience, would not look up at the light, would not speak up. After gabbling his two words, he was removed from the court and from the stage. He deserved to be.

The astonishing irony is that, by this time, Alfie's domestic performances were brilliant. He was establishing a role as family clown. This enabled him to express, in an acceptable form, his feelings about a family structure that he found repressive. He could do this because he was irresistibly funny. Although it sometimes had an edge, his banter always raised a laugh. Even his father was moved to smile. On one occasion, I met him in the hall, wiping the tears of laughter from his eyes. The Captain had left the room so that he should not be observed. 'The fool is making his mother laugh again,' he muttered gruffly as he passed.

Alfie's burlesques went, as the music-hall impressionists used to say, 'Something Like This'. On the Freemasons' lodge night the Captain would come downstairs in evening dress. Putting on his white silk scarf and wide-brimmed hat, he would assess his image in the mirror. What he saw there was Warner Brothers gangster. Alfie would improvise on the resemblance. He might pretend to frisk his father as he helped him into his tight-fitting black overcoat.

'Not packing a rod tonight, Pops?' he would drawl. Or he might lean against the doorpost and spin a coin in the George Raft manner. Then 'Don't take any wooden nickels', as he showed the Captain out, and 'Run for it, Rocky. I'll cover you!' as his father walked down the path. Before the door closed he would shout, 'Come and get me, copper!' – or he would pretend his father had shot him and go into his big Cagney death scene – 'The dirty rat!' – clasping his hand to his heart, teetering around the hall, up the stairs and down again, into the front room and out, milking every gesture, until at long last he died and lay still. On another lodge night, the Captain would be cast as a great musician on his way to a concert, which would give Alfie the chance to conduct an imaginary orchestra or play a silent violin solo.

Not only would Alfie play the fool in the classical manner, improvising a commentary on contretemps as they occurred, but he also provided regular entertainments. These usually took place in the living room and would be based on recent radio programmes and films. He would stand in a corner and reproduce what he had seen and heard. If he could not remember the performance entirely, he would ad lib so well that his ideas were often funnier than the original. Over the years, Alfie must have imitated more than a hundred performers. Comedians were well to the fore. From the radio, the young entertainer would present echoes of Stainless Steven's punctuated prose, Claude Dampier's idiotic drawl and Horace Kenney's nervous comments. He would sing like Louis Armstrong or Harry Roy, offer instant opinions in Bernard Shaw's soft Irish brogue or H. G. Wells's bird-like twitter. Alfie would recall any kind of sports commentary, including sound effects: not only people but birds, animals, trains and racing cars. His radio country walk where golf balls hit the animals with noisy results was hilarious.

A visual approach and physical skills were required

to impersonate film stars. Alfie had been shuffling like Chaplin since he was three and now copied every idiosyncratic walk. He danced in different styles and mimicked gestures and mannerisms. He pulled out his ears to croon like Bing Crosby, stuck out his bottom lip for Maurice Chevalier, bit it for James Cagney and widened his mouth for Edward G. Robinson.

When he first saw Claude Rains, Alfie was so taken by the star's unusual smile that he cut a top set of similar teeth out of orange peel and, showing the white side, placed them carefully in his mouth. After pencilling on a thin moustache, he became a junior version of Rains. When the actor's voice came out of his mouth the effect was startling.

For his sketches of Mae West, Alfie raided his mother's wardrobe and dressing-table so often that Dad finally bought him an actor's make-up box. After that, there was no holding the budding Proteus. When our parents went out, nobody's clothes were safe. He tried on the lot. He would be a pirate one day, an old man the next, a *grande dame* on another, a gypsy next time, and so on. Alfie was fascinated by the possibility of total transformation. He still is.

Many subjects for Alfie's flippant observations were provided by the Captain's insistence on doing things his way. Not only Dad's preparation for lodge night but his whole attitude to Freemasonry, for example. He took it so seriously. There surely can never have been another member of that organization who called on its tradition of brotherly support so assiduously. The Captain never paid more than wholesale price for anything. If he did not know a Freemason who would supply his need as a favour, he would enlist the help of one of his Jewish friends, all of whom appeared to be under some ancient obligation.

Each autumn a local men's outfitters held a sale of school uniforms, caps and every other article of clothing a young scholar might require. The evening before the sale, the Hill family would descend on the shop and take their pick. In an eerie, deserted emporium, by the light of a single bulb, I would be kitted out, cap-à-pie, in baggy new clothes, large enough to provide for a year's growth.

'What the well-dressed swot is wearing,' Alfie would mock, knowing that he would be handed most of my cast-offs. Sometimes he would be mollified by the purchase of a pristine cap or scarf of his very own. When the bill was settled, it became clear that the Captain had not only been given the advantage of first choice and sale prices, but that he had negotiated a whacking discount on top of that.

These private initiatives sometimes led to embarrassment. One evening, a small, rather furtive gentleman came to see Dad who was upstairs in the bath. Mum called the Captain, ushered the visitor in to the front room and brought him a cup of tea. She thoughtfully provided a slice of her Madeira cake, too. The stranger had not given his name but Mum thought she recognized him.

'Are you one of the Crookes?' she asked, pleasantly. The poor man choked on his cake and coughed crumbs all over the carpet. He was in a bad way. I had never known Mum's Madeira cake to have that effect before.

The Captain's interest in Freemasonry was attested by a picture in his office, behind the surgical appliance shop. It was an eighteenth-century print, depicting the plight of a buxom young chambermaid who had attempted to eavesdrop on a meeting of Freemasons. The floor of the loft had given way beneath her so that she was represented as stuck half-way through the ceiling and vulnerable to physical abuse from below.

As it was the only item to decorate the sombre oak panelling of the office, the print drew Alfie's attention when he arrived every Saturday with his father's lunch. The food had been cooked and prepared by Mum, placed between two blistering dishes, carefully wrapped in napkins and tucked into a basket. Immediately it was ready, Alfie had set off post-haste, walking the two miles to deliver the food still piping hot. Of course, if the Captain had been prepared to shut up shop for half an hour, the gourmet gallop would have been unnecessary. He could have blown out his kite for a shilling, three doors away, at his friend Tommy White's restaurant.

The small office was redolent of leather armchairs and Jack Stanley's expensive cigars, an aroma that, to this day, Benny associates with luxury. After lunch there were a number of interesting possibilities. The pair of them might play clubyos, a Jewish card game in which each picture card has its own name. The prospect of winning a little money was exciting, but opposite the Captain it was problematical. Losing was more likely. On the other hand, Dad might get out the pint tumbler and send Alfie a few yards to Donnarumma's for a glass of ice-cream. Old Man Donnarumma had a tub of the heavenly sweet made from his family's secret recipe. Only privileged customers received a tumbler of that nectar. 'Tell them it's for Mr Hill,' Dad would insist. On the way there, Alfie once saw the ladies from rival dress-shops playing tug-of-war with a prospective customer. It was said that, in the Canal Walk shops, if a woman tried on a dress she did not get her own clothes back until she had bought another outfit.

On another day, the Captain might say, 'You look

a mess. Go and get a proper haircut,' and send Alfie across to the barber-shop. On the way back, if he had won at clubyos, Alfie might buy himself a small harmonica or a jew's harp at the music shop.

'You can't play that, you bloody idiot,' Dad would say, taking the instrument from him. 'Here, like this!' If the Captain sent him a few shops away to the fishing-tackle store for hook, line or sinker, Alfie knew that a trip on the Hythe Ferry was in the offing. The Captain would soon be buying ragworm and baiting hooks for a Sunday's fishing from the long Hythe Pier. His two sons would accompany him with lines of their own.

It could be a very pleasant and instructive summer's day. Dad would lean against the pier rail and tell us of his adventures during the war or of the elaborate schemes of confidence tricksters about which he was remarkably well-informed. In the long hours during which we waited for a bite, the Captain taught us grafters' slang, a mixture of Yiddish, Romany, rhyming slang and Parlary (which Dad called bastard Italian). He was also fluent in Retchtub's Kaycab Jeenals (butcher's back-slang) and cant (the secret language of the under-world). Dad would salt his speech with occasional German or dog-Latin words, American slang or archaic phrases such as, 'I've got an eye like a stinkin' eel!' or 'That's the jolly hammer!' He once described himself, in youth, as 'the little bird that flew from spike to spike' (doss house or workhouse). He never employed what he would regard as the fouler obscenities now in general use. If angry with another man, he would be more likely to call him a 'louse-bound, pox-ridden toe-rag'.

It was the possibility of secret communication in public places that excited us lads. Dad showed us the sign language of the underworld, for example, laying the finger alongside the nose to indicate the presence of a 'nosey' (usually a nark, or detective), or feeling one's collar, a sardonic reference to the chance of being 'collared' or arrested. To shut us up quickly Dad would cough and say 'fishbone!' or 'nanty palardi' (Parlary for the Italian, 'Niente parlare'). We boys exercised our new knowledge by making rude remarks in back-slang about fellow-passengers on buses and trains. 'Vatch a kool of the taf deelo woc in the renrock' – 'Have a look at the fat old cow in the corner!' or 'Jeenub us a tib of eeffot, yob!'

One Saturday afternoon, Dad lifted a large cardboard box from beneath his roll-top desk and pulled out a set of boxing gloves. He said they had been used by Tommy White himself, who had been a well-known professional middleweight. This seems unlikely as they were boy's gloves, but then Dad had a habit of shaking a little stardust over his gifts.

Alfie brought the gloves home and, as soon as Dad arrived to referee, we boys slipped them on, laced up and set to. My brother remembers pulling his punches in the unlikely expectation that I would reciprocate. My guess is that his dream of détente was disappointed. Stronger, heavier and older, I probably knew that he could not touch me anyway and pasted him all round the yard.

A few evenings later the Captain took us to the Coliseum, a stately pleasure-dome decayed, where Alfie sat beside me to watch half a dozen professional boxing bouts. We loved the show and were bobbing and weaving along with the contestants. Alfie was hooked and has been a boxing fan ever since.

At home Alfie and I boxed with Dad regularly. He had his own huge gloves, and forearms like legs of lamb. 'Get past that guard!' he would say, catching every blow thrown on glove, arm or elbow. Occasionally, he would pop over a left that halted an opponent in his tracks. Every young male visitor was expected to put on the gloves with Dad. Some of them did not look forward to it. Rumours went round the extended family that, in the ring, the Captain punished the merest peccadillo outside it. His sons were never aware of that. The worst blow I ever received when boxing Dad was a long, bloody cut when I leapt back too far to avoid his lethal left and hit the back of my head on a rough-cast wall.

I succumbed to the temptation to make public display of my boxing prowess at the age of thirteen. A young neighbour of similar build, Mark Henton, was cajoled into a contest to be held, not on the patio behind the house, but in the drive by the front gate. The reason for this unusual venue was that I was hoping to impress a dark-eyed adolescent beauty who lived just across the road. Alfie was to be the referee. Sure enough, on that fatal afternoon, when I shuffled down to the gate in vest and shorts with a bathrobe over my shoulders, Doe-eyes was at her front bedroom window. Alfie had to be MC, timekeeper, judge, referee and doctor, and as you might expect acted every part to perfection. He had the MC's cockney intonation exactly – 'a boxing match of three reeownds, three minutes a reeownd!' As referee, he muttered convincingly to the two battlers, though we did not catch a word of it.

When Alfie called 'Seconds out!' and made a clanging noise with his mouth, I raced across and showered blows upon my opponent – jabbing, sticking and hooking, straight-lefting, bolo punching, short-arming, upper-cutting, swinging – over the top, underneath, to the head then the ribs, windmilling, roundhousing and haymaking. I gave it every kind of punch in the book and some that were not in any book. Not a

single blow went home. Mark covered up. He just
skipped away, held his gloves in front of his face and
tucked in his elbows. I chased after him, unloading
bombs that missed their target and never exploded.
The shots landed on gloves, forearms, elbows, upper
arms, shoulders, the crown of the head and the top
of the gate post. At the end of the first round, I was
tired. The second was a repeat of the first, except that
I finally staggered back to my orange-box, exhausted.
After a minute of the third round, I could not lift my
arms. I had punched myself out. Then Mark socked
me with a shot that came in over the Isle of Wight like
the flight from Paris. I could not get out of the way fast
enough. It caught me smack on the bridge of the nose.
A hit, a very palpable hit! A second blow exploded like
a sky rocket in my left eye. The next thing I knew Alfie
was holding up my hand as the winner. It seems that I
went down and was hit while scrabbling about on the
ground. I won on a foul. That's what Alfie said anyway
– and he was referee. But it was not the performance I
had dreamt of. It was more like a performance of 'Don't
it make your blue eyes black!' And I never did get a date
with Doe-eyes.

Undoubtedly, one of the causes of the poor school
reports that so upset the Captain was Alfie's preoccupation with his business deals. On the one hand his
father was proud of the boy's enterprise, but he felt it
was no excuse for neglect of school work. Alfie had
extended his commercial empire into a very lucrative
area, gold bullion. Beginning with fourteen-carat gold
nibs from discarded pens, my brother was soon into
gold coins, medals and small jewellery. This led him
on quite naturally to silver trinkets and semi-precious
stones. He became well-known to local goldsmiths
and second-hand dealers, but still found it wise to

obtain certificates of origin from his father and others
to reassure the timid or suspicious traders.

He began to amass his own capital, which made him
independent of his meagre pocket-money allowance.
This weekly dole was small as Dad preferred to garner
the credit from occasional novelties brought home, a
policy that had the added advantage for him that he got
to play with the item first. Alfie's own efforts provided
the seven shillings and sixpence for a second-hand
bicycle. This was invaluable as a means of transport.
He was able to race round the town on it, from home,
to school, to shop, to office – all in a few minutes. His
business flourished as a result – 'Deals on Wheels', with
a vengeance.

His true delight in the bike, however, was as a plaything. He loved to pedal up to Lords Wood, where
the paths were particularly dusty and great ant-hills
abounded. There he would risk broken bone or chain
to drive his bike to the limit, swerving, with one foot
trailing, like the speedway riders, to send up a satisfying
cloud of dust that hung in the air like smoke.

At that time, like Alfie, I was floundering, too. Imagine my relief when, at thirteen, I was welcomed without
question into a local Fellowship of the Woodcraft Folk,
a co-educational organization engaged largely in outdoor pursuits. At a classmate's birthday party, a door
opened and there were twelve youngsters all in jerkins
of Lincoln green. They were so friendly and so much
fun that I was overwhelmed – and fell in love with them
all immediately. I felt I had come home. Soon after,
I joined them, writing my name on a piece of birch
bark, burning it and adopting a Red-Indian name of
my own choice. I lived up to that name when with the
boys and girls in green, and for seven years enjoyed
a separate life that had more meaning for me than

school, office or home. With my Woodcraft friends I knew who I was.

Of course, there were ructions at home. Why did I want to join a cranky, nonconformist group run by the children themselves? Why could I not enrol in a sensible organization like the Boy Scouts? Well, the Boy Scouts had no girls, for a start. And what splendid people those Woodcraft girls were – lovely, outgoing and independent. Alfie was deeply envious of my friendship with them. He ached to join my Fellowship too. But I would not let him in, swearing to leave the Folk if he joined. I liked my Woodcraft self and was fighting for survival as a personality. There was no place in my separate life for the doubts and problems that beset me at home. Alfie would bring with him all the assumptions that so paralysed me most of the time. His entry into it would threaten my world. So I fought every inch of the way, first, to stay in, despite the Captain's obstructions, and second, to keep Alfie out. The necessity for the latter course pained me then and has ever since, but I had to keep my separate world inviolate.

Alfie was disturbed and disappointed for years at my adamant refusal to take him into the green company. I hoped he did not think I was motivated by spite or sibling rivalry. For me, it was simply a matter of self-preservation. Of that period, Benny says, 'I just wanted to join a club that had girls in it. When I told Dad he said [and here Benny imitates his father's gruff voice], "What do you mean? You want to join a boy's club? That'll be all right." You just couldn't tell Dad that you wanted to go to a club that had girls in it. And there was no one that I could confide in that I wanted to be with girls.' He snaps like his father again, 'Oh eh, what the bloody hell are you talking

about?' Alfie never found a club that had girls in it.
And he was as bored at home as he was at school.
He recalls, 'Mum used to say, "Go and ask your Dad
to go for a walk." And I would say, "Mum, Mum, do I
have to?" Mum would say, "Go and ask him to go out
for a walk. He wants to go for a walk." "But, Mum,
Dad didn't say he wanted to go for a walk." "But he
does, go and ask him to go for a walk." So I would ask
him. And he would say [here Benny huffs and puffs],
"Well, huh, I don't know, my son. That depends on
whether you want to go for a walk. Do you want to go
for a walk? Well, all right, if you want to." (To Mum)
"He wants to go for a walk. Come then, we'll go for
a walk!" Oh, ho ho – ' laughs Benny wryly. 'What a
strange world!'

Then, at twelve years of age, Alfie fell in love at first
sight with a rather older girl whom he glimpsed across
a crowded Eastleigh fairground. He mooned about,
followed her and discovered that every day she took
lunch to her father in a shop in Market Street. After
that he saw her regularly. Not to talk to, just to look
at. Telling his parents he was going for a hike, he
would set off tramping the six miles to Eastleigh to
stand on the corner of Market Street. Alfie waited
for his beloved there and watched her walk up the
road and into the shop. He hung about patiently for
half an hour until she reappeared and walked away.
Then he tramped the six miles home again. He kept
this vigil every week for months. But he never spoke
to the girl.

A few years later, when he was sixteen, he saw his
old flame outside an Eastleigh cinema and invited her
inside. They sat together in the romantic darkness. At
last. But the magic had gone.

'Result? Total boredom,' says Benny. 'No sparks.

Nothing. What was all that about? I asked myself afterwards. Pillock!' Benny sighs. 'Ah, well, puberty's a hair-raising time for everybody!' he adds, with a look to make sure you do not miss the joke.

Although I became increasingly preoccupied with Woodcraft activities, there were still many interests that I shared with Alfie. Short stories, for example. Alfie liked me to read him one in our double bed before sleep every night. Damon Runyon was his favourite author and, when the books ran out, I made up similar stories and recited them to my younger brother in a Brooklyn accent. Whenever the Woodcrafters discovered an interesting walk, I would bully Alfie and Chris into retracing it with me. The Hill trio undertook some enjoyable hikes that way – to Farley Mount, through the New Forest and along the River Itchen to Winchester.

When Auntie Louie's sons, Donald and then Francis, each bicycled down from Bexleyheath, over the Hog's Back, for a short holiday at Westrow Gardens, Alfie felt that he would like to try the journey in reverse. It took the pioneers about eleven hours and Alfie knew that his 'stand-up-and-beg' bicycle was not up to it. So he dipped into his scranbag and came up with £13 for a Raleigh all-steel Continental with drop handlebars.

'Dad, bless his heart, offered to pay for it,' Benny recalls. 'But I wouldn't let him. No, I said. It's mine. I don't want anybody else to buy it. I want it to be mine.'

He set off for Bexleyheath on his splendid new bicycle very early on a summer's day in 1938. 'Alfie was due at teatime,' says Auntie Louie, 'but he didn't arrive. I was so worried I telegraphed his mother. She telegraphed back to say he was on his way. He turned up in a rush, five hours late! When I asked him where he had been, he said, "It poured with rain. I've been hung up under some woman's umbrella!" Under some woman's umbrella indeed!'

One of Alfie's difficulties was that his saddle was so high and his handles so low that he was craning his neck, straining his eyes upward to see ahead. If you see him in close-up, you will notice that the journey left him with a permanent crease in his forehead. Benny reckons he has only to raise his eyebrows to hold a pencil in that crease.

A few weeks later, Billy, Louie's youngest son, spent one of his rare holidays with the Hill boys in Southampton. 'I didn't enjoy it as I should,' he reports. 'Your dad was so strict.' The Captain took him to task for not wearing pyjamas at night. Poor Billy had no pyjamas. On that trip, he noticed that Alfie was constantly drumming with spoons and forks. 'He was restless and growing wilder, always in trouble with your father. I got the impression that he was unhappy and looking for something extra.'

When I was fifteen, I finally got through the Captain's boxing guard. Slipping his straight left, I stepped inside and belted him a solid right hand to the solar plexus. It was not a malicious blow. There had been times when I could have quite cheerfully killed him, but this was not one of them. We were boxing, and he should have known better. He had a duodenal ulcer. Although he must have been hurt, he boxed on to finish the bout. But that was the last time any of us put on the gloves. He never suggested it again. As with so many activities, Alfie and I went along with his wishes. We boys had little interest in boxing each other. Without Dad's enthusiasm, we just did not bother. When I was sixteen, Alfie and I found that we had no wish to

fight each other in any way. We became such close
friends that a girlfriend of mine later forecast that I
would never marry. 'You're already married to Alfie,'
she said.

6

Now Will You Practise?

G. P. and Nana, my father's parents, had been settled
for some years in the docklands district of Southampton, over which rang the original bells of St Mary's,
celebrated in song. They lived in a large rambling
flat above a dairy similar to Nana's first home on the
corner of Fleet Street in London. A huge, comfortably
furnished room in the front of the building served as
living room, dining room, lounge and waiting room. It
led into a small dental surgery. G. P. had developed his
tooth-pulling talents, discovered as a humble chemist,
into professional status. He was now a fully fledged
dentist (no qualifications were required in those days)
and a well-known local character.

Prosperity had mellowed G. P. into an elegant W. C.
Fields look-alike – fine grey suit with homburg to match,
waistcoat exposed to display heavy gold watch-chain,
cravat at throat, spats on feet, rings on fingers, cigar
in mouth and silver-topped cane in hand. He had the
pompous Fields manner, too, though he had never seen
the film star. He cut so extravagant a figure in the street
that his grandchildren were embarrassed to greet him.
In the district, *hoi polloi* called him 'The Lord Mayor of
St Mary's', but not to his face.

As a dentist, G. P. was certainly gentle with the
children of the family. Benny remembers waiting for
treatment, at an early age, with Nana showing him the
canary in its cage and playing the gramophone record
'Ain't It Grand to be Blooming Well Dead!' to cheer him
up. The caption on the wall, 'Don't Worry. It May Not

Happen!' did not reassure him, either. It Happened, but
G. P. ensured that the extraction was not an ordeal.

'Open moufie, dooky,' he murmured, adopting his
native Yorkshire accent. It was soon all over.

A wide range of clients sought G. P.'s ministrations.
When in town, boxers, jockeys, music-hall and circus
folk all came to visit him socially and professionally. G. P.
was grateful to dentistry for making that possible, and
for enabling him to travel first class. His only complaint
about his profession was that, breathing over patients all
day, he had to ration himself to one cigar every evening.

Nana, too, was always gentle and, despite internal troubles never explained to us boys, cheerful and
uncomplaining. With eyes like moist raisins in the pale
pudding of a face, she moved in a cloud of powder
that wafted the scent of cachous all over the art deco
furniture. This style was preferred because the contents
of the flat were recently acquired. In the past, Nana
had travelled light. Now she could afford to live in the
manner to which she was originally accustomed.

Prosperity also enabled Nana to offer members of the
extended family the richest and most succulent of high
teas. Food was important to the Hills. In Nana's huge
lounge, Alfie and I were first seduced by chocolate
eclairs. And in Nana's larder we first saw tins of
goodies stacked high enough to withstand a siege, a
sight remarkable in those days.

G. P., who for years cultivated a theatrical air with his
long hair and cloak, now had a show-business reputation. His advice on legal, social and professional matters was eagerly sought by performers in all branches
of the entertainment world. He was much respected,
particularly by circus folk. To accompany him round
Bertram Mills' or Fossett's tober, with acrobats, jugglers
and clowns tumbling out of their vardos to speak to

him, was to realize the affection in which he was held.
Years later, after his death during World War II, Nana
was visited regularly by passing circus friends.

When Alfie was twelve, G. P. took us both to the
local Hippodrome for the first time. He was able to
do this without undue expense because he was the
regular recipient of free tickets as columnist and critic
for the *The World's Fair*, a journal for travelling show
people. The Hippodrome entertainment that week in
1936 starred Horace Goldin, the great illusionist. Alfie
was thrilled by his baffling legerdemain. After that
evening, he went to the Hippodrome as often as he
could manage.

'That is where I began to take a committed interest
in show business,' he says. 'I was privileged to see the
variety shows in the company of G. P. Everyone in the
theatre smiled to greet him and was keen to have a
deferential word with him. We always sat in the best
seats – third row, on the central aisle, reserved for us.
After the overture, the conductor, made up for the
evening ritual, would look up into the spotlight and
bow to all parts of the house with a conspiratorial nod
towards G. P.

'The performers, too, would tend to work in our
direction. I felt sure that the whisper had gone round
that Harry Hawthorn Hill, the *World's Fair* critic, was
in the audience.

'Many of those turns had remained unchanged for
years. Some performers made a good living out of touring the same act round the country for forty years. I
met an old pro once, who told me that he had inherited
his act from his father, had added one joke, and still
got a lifetime's mileage out of it. Of course, the good
comedy turns were building all the time, improving,
adding and dropping gags and business. Each act was

quite independent of the others, rarely co-operated with them and was usually booked separately.

'Performers were very jealous of their position on the posters. The placing of my name on the bill reflected my climb up the ladder of success. When I began, it first appeared among "the wines and spirits", the small advertisements. As I progressed, it moved to Top Right, Top Left (because one reads from the left), Full Bottom and Full Top of the bill. Of course, my career started just as the variety theatre was fading. There might be some who say that I finished it off!

'We saw some great personalities at the Hippodrome in the late thirties – Sam Mayo, Scott Sanders, Noni and Nita. I watched them closely and learnt a great deal from them. G. P. warmed particularly to the performance of a fellow-Yorkshireman, Sandy Powell, and would give a lifelike representation of the young comedian, if pressed. He sometimes took notes for his column and would ask me what I thought of a particular act. I loved them all and was afraid to be too critical.'

G. P. was not afraid to be too critical. He gave Louis Armstrong a roasting in his column on the great man's first appearance in Southampton. The doyen of the circus folk found Louis's mock-shy stage presence nauseating and thought he played too loud. When Alfie learnt this, he was horrified. Louis Armstrong was one of his favourite stars. He loved to impersonate him. At one time, Alfie was mopping his brow with a handkerchief, croaking, 'Aw yeah!' and shaking his head at everyone in sight. And it was Louis's classic records, 'West End Blues', 'Knocking a Jug' and 'Tight Like This' that later inspired Alfie to take up the trumpet.

'Sometimes we would go to the Palace Theatre,' continues Benny, 'to see a revue – a confection entitled *Naughty Girls of 1937, Ooh La La, L'Amour!* or some other illiterate encouragement. The posters were interesting, as the principal comedian's name was billed at the top and almost always described as "The New Star Comedian". He never was a star. No one in the town had ever heard of him! It could be a heavy sentence for him, clattering round the country, working his heart out to seduce audience after audience into laughter. Some comics gave up and just walked through it, but the best were marvellous, honing their craft to a sharp edge. The greatest of them all, Sid Field, toured the provinces for years. It wasn't until he arrived at the Prince of Wales Theatre in 1943 that he became a star. I saw dozens of revue comedians. Most of them had something. One faker I saw was totally without talent. He had nothing but a smile and tremendous energy. He would work himself into a lather throughout the show, succeeding by effort alone. Another ambled through, knowing, every performance, that his last five-minute sketch would tear the ears off 'em – so that the audience left the theatre happy. One saucy beggar even left it to a sure-fire curtain speech to win the customers over.

'Every comic knew that the first half could be desperately hard labour; you didn't get much of a return in the first half-hour. After the interval, when everybody had sunk a bevvy or two, things began to pick up. Laughs were bigger and more frequent. Of course, I didn't know all that when I first went to see the revues. As far as I was concerned, at the age of twelve, the principal comedian was the creator of a warm atmosphere of hilarity and good humour. People began to smile as soon as he appeared. The women, in particular, loved his sauciness.

' "Ooh, isn't he awful? Did you hear what he said?" they would screech, enjoying every minute of it. And always the principal comedian was surrounded by glamorous, naughty girls to do his every bidding;

French maids who bent over to waggle a feather duster, sticking their bottoms up to show their frilly knickers and black stocking-tops. Just about the most ineffectual cleaning job you ever saw! I would look up enviously at the comic and, like all the other fellers in the audience, think, "You lucky devil! You've got the money and you've got the girls!" On top of that, everybody loved him, laughed at him, cheered and applauded him. That's where I caught the bug.'

G. P. could not provide Alfie with a seat on the aisle every week. Very often the stage-struck youngster had to find another way into the theatre. His schoolboy friend, Tex Southgate, a shy young trumpeter, was a source of tickets. Tex's father worked for the local newspaper and could occasionally pass on a couple to the boys. When all else failed, Alfie would press a few small coins into the palm of Horace, the lugubrious usher who guarded the stairs to the gallery of the Palace Theatre. One evening, Tex remembers, when he told Alfie that his father had no tickets, Alfie replied, 'Leave it to me. I'll drop.' Our young hero apparently provided a sop for Cerberus, as they successfully passed the guardian of the door. The pair were about to mount the stairway to paradise, when Horace cried after them, in a voice that echoed up the well, 'What? Two of you for thruppence?'

The personalities and individual styles of the variety and revue comedians, who were now teaching Alfie by example, were stored in his head. He could reproduce Ted Ray, Len Young or the young Jimmy Jewel at will, just as accurately as Will Rogers or Gordon Harker, well known from their films. However, as I was the only member of our family who regularly saw most of the touring comedians, there was little point in striving for accuracy of portrayal. Instead, Alfie's living-room performances were enlivened by a pastiche of his favourites. He used a hotch-potch of their material as well. Some of it was over his head. He would quite cheerfully rap out a witticism that he did not understand, such as 'There Was an Old Woman Who Lived in a Shoe. She had so many children she didn't know what to do. Obviously!' At the age of twelve, Alfie had no idea of the point of that one, despite his father's expertise in the subject.

These entertainments were well prepared. Alfie would employ the full range of his make-up box so that the audience was never quite sure what sort of personality would appear. He would usually wear the black George Robey bowler that Mum had bought him from a joke-shop. Underneath it might be the face of a cheerful Cockney, a mournful undertaker, an earthy farmer, a naïve parson or some other ridiculous stereotype.

Alfie's performances spilled over into everyday life. He would pepper his conversation with catch-phrases and lighten every task with quips, and cranks, and wanton wiles. The foolery in the musical and variety shows was equally exciting to me. I loved to drop feed-lines for Alfie to tag:

> 'My time is liniment.'
> 'Well, don't rub it in!'

Or:

> 'He's right! Give the gentleman a cigar!' at which Alfie would growl, 'Wattsamatta? Got a grudge against him?'

In the summer of 1938, the Captain took his two sons for a short trip to London to see the sights. We stayed at

Oxford and Cambridge Mansions in the Edgware Road with a blowsy blonde landlady who regaled us with accounts of her triumphs in musical comedy. The high spot of the holiday for the Hill boys was a visit to the Palladium to see Alberta Hunter and the Jitterbugging Maniacs in *The Cotton Club Revue*.

Friends in the Woodcraft Folk had been amused by my own antics round the campfire for some time. This led to my staging concerts to raise funds for local Fellowships, whose Supporters' Council organized an American Supper for the same cause. I invited Alfie to join me in providing a short cabaret for the occasion. He jumped at the chance and together we improvised a sketch satirizing the three styles of radio fare then popular – BBC programmes, Radio Luxembourg, and American commercial broadcasts. Among those imitated were Gillie Potter, Rob Wilton, Jack Buchanan, 'Schnozzle' Durante, Bing Crosby and the Ritz Brothers. The sketch ended with my hitting Alfie over the head with a large Chinese gong. Unfortunately this final antic was performed with such gusto that Alfie was knocked almost unconscious. He swayed and staggered. The audience laughed uproariously. They thought it all part of the fun and clapped enthusiastically. Slowly Alfie came round, his senses reeling, to the music of applause. He loved the acclamation and knew then that this kind of fooling was what he wanted to do for the rest of his life.

Also on that bill was Dr King. He entertained at the piano, singing his witty, original songs with such panache that he could have held his own in any company. Some of his admirers likened him to Noël Coward but, with his clear, strong voice, he was truly more of a British Tom Lehrer. Subsequently, the talented schoolmaster saw Alfie's solo act at several charity functions and encouraged him to persevere. Years later, after Dr King had carved out a distinguished parliamentary career, Alfie compèred a celebration in honour of his old mentor.

The double-act had been so warmly appreciated that the Hill brothers received invitations from several local organizations to perform together again. Alfie, delighted with this success, was eager to accept every offer; I had found the applause less satisfying and preferred to appear only for causes close to my heart. We agreed that Alfie should try his luck on his own and I helped the fledgling comedian devise a solo routine. It was not difficult as we both had learnt such a deal of likely material that an effective script was quickly put together. Committing this monologue to memory, my brother set off to learn his trade.

The Captain was unhappy about Alfie's theatrical ambitions.

'You'll find out, my son,' he warned. 'Show business is not like a Betty Grable picture, you know – all glamour and applause, with first-night audiences in evening dress and huge dressing-rooms full of flowers.'

Alfie was to find out soon enough, when G. P. took his son and grandson backstage to meet an old juggler friend.

'You see what I mean?' asked the Captain as he pointed out the stained mirrors, cracked basins, battered chairs and general air of bleak squalor. 'What sort of life is this for a young man?' Having just caught a glimpse of thigh and a whiff of powder as he passed the chorus girls' dressing-room, Alfie thought it promising, but did not say so.

Unfortunately, the rumble of approaching war drowned out the siren songs of show business. Alfie was prevented from taking up most of the welcoming offers. He was evacuated to Bournemouth with many of the pupils and staff of Taunton's School in the summer of 1939. This was a precautionary measure, part of a general exodus of children from cities in the firing-line from German bombs. Alfie's six-year-old sister, Diana, accompanied him to the relatively safe seaside resort.

'You will look after her, won't you?' directed his parents anxiously. Alfie, who had been looking forward to riotous times away from home, was depressed at the thought of lugging a young sister around with him.

The two Hill children were billeted with an elderly working-class couple in a semi-detached house similar to Grandma Cave's home. The fostering pair were like grandparents, kindly yet strict and narrow in outlook. Alfie chafed at the necessity to stay in during the evenings, when he suspected that his friends were out on the town. Nevertheless, he took his few chances to entertain.

By this time, Alfie owned a guitar which Tex Southgate had taught him to play. He now joined with a few schoolmates to form the Hills Brothers. The act leaned heavily on the talents of Eric Vincent, an older boy, who was the only experienced guitarist among them. They performed to their fellow-Tauntonians, in a couple of concerts organized by Dr King, dressed up in huge hats as hillbillies, with dialogue and music to match.

'What have you got in that thar bag – a turkey?'

'It ain't a turkey [taking out the guitar] – It's a guea-tar!'

The words 'performed to' have been used advisedly, as the general opinion of Alfie's schoolfriends with him in Bournemouth seems to have been that he was a poor comedian. I have been told that he 'died the death', showed no sign of talent or indication that he would ever make it in the profession. This assessment is reinforced by members of the extended family, who were more impressed by my concert performances than by Alfie's and have been surprised by his later success. The revelation of these opinions has astounded me, as they are diametrically opposed to what I felt at that time. I was always aware of Alfie's remarkable gifts, which obviously outclassed my own five tricks, for I had seen him sparkle progressively over the years. His humorous wheezes overwhelmed me so many times that I assumed he would continue to evoke laughter among ever-wider audiences.

After hearing Neville Chamberlain's declaration of war on the radio in September 1939, Alfie went into the streets to see how the conflict was going. He was disappointed to find that Bournemouth was unchanged. As he searched for clues that this was, indeed, a day of historic significance, he slipped and fell on a slope. Rubbing his sore parts, Alfie wondered if his tumble was an omen of a more fateful fall to come. It was. His slip presaged a night of shame that occurred when he was touring with the revue *Send Him Victorious* two years later. He fell off the stage and into the big drum.

When the Captain and I heard Chamberlain's fateful announcement, we were stripped to the waist resting on our shovels, deep in a trench at the bottom of our back garden. Dad reassured my mother, 'We shall be quite safe in a trench.' To me he muttered, 'Get cracking, my son. The bastards'll be over in a minute.' Everybody expected a blitzkrieg attack that very day. It did not occur. In fact, nothing much occurred for quite a long time. It was the period of the 'phoney war'. The insane optimists who forecast that the war 'will be all over by Christmas' were bewildered when Christmas crept upon us without much sign of hostile intent from either side.

In Bournemouth, Alfie was disappointed and bored. He felt cribbed, cabined and confined, both at school and in his billet. The lad wanted a man's job, with money in his pocket for gaspers and birds. Above all, he wanted the chance to entertain. These stirrings could only be resolved if he went back to Southampton, and that meant leaving school without taking his School Certificate examination. Alfie did not believe that his academic work was up to standard, anyway, but not to sit for the Certificate was unusual. That course would leave him with no evidence that he had been to grammar school and no qualifications. All that work for the scholarship would have been in vain. Alfie thought about it and made up his mind. In the new year of 1940 he began to make angry noises.

By this time, there was a feeling among many that things were not quite as critical as everyone had previously supposed. There were no signs of blitzkrieg. Perhaps hostilities might never break out. Mothers all over the country, deprived of their children for months, were lowing for their little ones. Mum was no exception. And so it was that, early in 1940, we saw the return to Southampton of 'the gruesome twosome', as I dubbed them in my brotherly fashion. Their mother was delighted, of course, to have all her children around her again. I was still living at home, working as a local government clerk. Alfie was not to stay long, however. Mum once said ruefully, 'Sons are a joy until they are sixteen. After that they're a disappointment.'

The Captain was not taken in by the phoney war. 'I think Southampton's going to cop it shortly,' he said. 'It's time to move.' He immediately set about buying a wooden bungalow on the other side of the Test, at the edge of the New Forest. Across the river and into the trees, you might say.

Upon his return to Southampton, having abandoned his school career, Alfie sought chances to exhibit his talent. He answered an advertisement in a local paper and was called to audition for the semi-professional Bobbie's Concert Party. They found him a likeable, fresh-faced performer, too young for the material he was using, with a cheekiness that did not entirely conceal his vulnerability. He was given two short spots, performing in half a dozen shows at suburban halls. For his first act, Alfie spoke in an approximate north-country accent, neither Lancashire, nor Yorkshire – a Pennine voice, you might call it. Because he had a routine of bad weather jokes, he appeared in an overcoat with a woolly scarf over his head and tied under his chin. The ensemble was topped off by a flat cap. Shuffling from the wings, Alfie would dip a hand in his overcoat pocket, throw up a cloud of small pieces of white paper, and, as they snowed down over him, cry, 'Oh, God, what a night!'

In his second spot, Alfie, wearing a dog-collar as the Minister of Mirth, addressed the congregation on Church matters:

'Would those responsible for leaving betting tips in the prayer books please desist, as the Bishop and I are already out of pocket. Ladies providing for the Easter celebration are asked to lay their eggs in the vestry. I am sorry to have to report that this year very few ladies have become young mothers, despite the strenuous efforts of the Bishop and myself. You will be pleased to learn that we shall soon be installing another font at the front of the church so that in the future babies can be baptized at both ends. Saturday's bride has requested a quiet wedding. I shall, therefore, be wearing carpet slippers for the occasion.'

At the end of each show, Alfie was offered the choice

of half a crown or a taxi-ride home. He always took the half-crown and walked home. On one occasion he was able to use his 'Minister of Mirth' act elsewhere. He entered a talent competition held at the immense Plaza Cinema, Northam, now the TVS Studios. 'I came second,' he says, wincing at the memory, 'to a bloke who ate broken glass and razor blades – and sewed buttons on his face!'

Alfie was persuaded to take a job so that he could keep himself solvent, perform in the evenings while learning his craft and apply to the theatrical companies that visited the town. The job he took was that of a weighbridge clerk with the Phoenix Coal and Coke Company.

'It'll suit me,' quipped Alfie. 'I always wanted to be another Cole Porter!'

His office was on the wharf in the shadow of a colossal coke-tower that looked like a rusty Dracula's Castle. The Castle held a princess, whom Alfie longed to rescue. She was a pretty young typist who would take dictation, but not from Alfie. He tried to impress her with his music-hall patter, but girls do not find much romance in comedy lines like, 'I could walk about if I wanted to – ' After three weeks, he decided to leave the 'tweeniks at the Phoenix' and try something else.

On our trip to London in 1938, the Captain had pumped an old acquaintance, the manager of the Oxford Street Woolworths store, for information about his employers. What Dad learned then convinced him that the 'nothing over sixpence' company offered a ladder to the top that rewarded merit. He was determined to assist his younger son on to the first rung of that ladder. When Alfie slipped away from the 'Quai des Brumes', Dad used his connections to start him in the Eastleigh Woolworths store, and set him up in comfortable lodgings nearby with a Mr and Mrs Brown at their house called The Nook.

'They were a charming couple,' says Benny, 'and did me proud – full board, my own radio and clean sheets for a pound a week!'

Alfie found himself among forty girls at Woolworths. There he discovered that, when lovely woman stoops to folly, the stockroom is a busy place. Alfie was busy humping elsewhere – usually rolls of lino, sacks of peanuts and wooden crates so rough they still retained their bark. The crates held massive loads of crockery, each piece of which had to be cleaned and checked. There were also thousands of sheets, wrapping, packages, and containers of paper, card and cardboard to be collected and stuffed into the baler to make heavy, solid blocks, which had to be carried and stacked for removal. The shop floor needed to be swept every day, and oiled every week. Alfie would stay behind at night to lubricate every square inch. It took hours.

Alfie's sworn enemies, the vandals that ruined his clean, well-oiled floor, were the dogs. Although nothing in Woolworths cost more than sixpence, every day at least one canine visitor insisted on putting down a small deposit.

'It was usually left by the cosmetics,' says Benny. 'Probably a comment on the cheap perfume we sold. Unfortunately, I was in love with the beautiful blonde in charge of the counter. I would kneel, red-faced at her feet, to clean up the mess with dustpan and brush – not a pretty sight! Perhaps it was a lesson to me. They say that "Humility is good for the soul!" '

Only once did Alfie come up smelling of violets – or rather California Poppy. Pints of the perfume had spilled from broken bottles into the bottom of their container. When Alfie was not looking, a gang of saucy girls scooped up the stuff and threw it all over him. He smelt like a seraglio for months.

'I was busy all right. I even had to make the tea for everybody,' reminisces Benny. 'Talk about "Figaro here, Figaro there, Hey Figaro!" and that was only the girls! Except that they called, "Hey, Sonny Boy!" Did they give me the runaround? The manager, Mr Dean, was a lovely feller. But he certainly kept me at it, too. "Tote that box! Lift that bale! You get a little rest when you check that mail!" '

It was the paperwork that finally did for Alfie. He hated all that checking, noting, ticking, signing and ordering. Stuck at his little table, he felt trapped again.

A week or two after Alfie had joined Woolworths, one of the girls who knew of his ambitions told him of a vacancy in a local band, Ivy Lillywhite and Her Friends. It seemed that a trumpeter had been called up into the army. Perhaps a guitarist would fill the gap. That evening Alfie knocked on Ivy Lillywhite's door at Bishopstoke, near Eastleigh.

'I play the guitar,' he said. 'I wondered if you could use me in your band. I can sing, too.'

'Before I realized it,' recalls Mrs Lillywhite, 'Alfie was in my living room, playing his guitar. He wasn't good, but he had a strong sense of rhythm and a feeling for chords.' Mrs Lillywhite was able to assess Alfie's solo at once. She was a music teacher as well as a band leader, actress and producer. When the young applicant sang for her Mrs Lillywhite was not impressed. However, bearing in mind that he was only sixteen, knowing that his voice could only improve, she looked at his cheerful, pleasant face and agreed to give him a chance. At least he would help with the rhythm.

Alfie did not help much at first. A guitar without amplification does not add a great deal to the overall

effect of a dance band. Nevertheless, Ivy Lillywhite's
Friends were grateful for the reinforcement of even a
novice guitarist. Except for the drummer.

'He was a funny old chap,' says Benny, 'the proud
possessor of a smartass set of drums', who had been
trained to play at Kneller Hall, the army school of
music. He was good, and he did not welcome the
tow-haired lad who talked too much and did not play
the guitar the army way.

'If you could play that guitar as well as you can
talk, you'd get somewhere, my lad,' he grumbled.
Ivy Lillywhite smiles today at the irony that Alfie got
somewhere without the guitar.

Whenever the drummer left the stand for physical
relief of some kind, Alfie was at the drums, beating out
the rhythm with all the showmanship of the legendary
jazz-drummer Gene Krupa, whom he had recently seen
in a Bob Hope film. He would pick up the trumpet too,
if given a chance, and eventually learnt to play it, but
not with the band. In fact, all the instruments were
tried out in turn – except the violins.

The new boy took over the vocals. 'I became the
singer in the band,' explains Benny. 'In the throat,
like this – ' He makes scarcely human, strangulated
noises as if his tender parts are being squeezed. He
surely cannot have been quite so poor a vocalist. Reference to Mrs Lillywhite brings a sense of proportion.
However, she will not be deflected from her original
appraisal.

'He wasn't brilliant, but he had charm. He sang
numbers like "Who's Taking You Home Tonight" and
"Careless Love".'

Disaster struck on the evening of the prestigious Spit-
fire Concert in Eastleigh Town Hall. Everyone was there
to see it – the Mayor and all the local bigwigs, G. P. as

informal assessor and critic, with his extended family,
the local press plus as many of the Eastleigh folk as
could pack into the hall. Dr King brought his accordion
so that he could sing, play and walk about if he wanted
to. Tex Southgate played his trumpet in another band.
Then it was the turn of Ivy Lillywhite and Her Friends.
Alfie was on guitar, as usual. All was going splendidly
until they moved into double tempo at the climax of
'Begin the Beguine'. Alfie was well into the vinegar
strokes when suddenly a string broke. Ivy Lillywhite
saw the entire catastrophe from the piano. 'I shall never
forget his face,' she says. 'Alfie was heart-broken. As
if it were the end of the world for him. I felt so sorry
for him.'

At the summing up after the show, G. P. to his credit
did not mention Alfie's shame, the matter of the broken
string. However, he found his grandson far too grim
a performer. 'Smile, boy, smile!' he counselled. 'Don't
look so pained. Honey catches more flies than vinegar.
You've got good teeth. Flash them!'

Although she was little more than ten years older
than Alfie, Ivy Lillywhite had already had experience
of teaching boys of his age. She found many of them
difficult and uncouth. Alfie was different – kind, polite,
cheerful and interesting. 'I liked him,' she says. 'He had
a brain. We would talk together sensibly. He confided
in me, telling me all about his young ladies. I suppose I
was a kind of mother confessor. There was one girl he
fell in love with at Woolworths. When she would have
nothing to do with him, he was so broken-hearted, he
had a good weep. Well, he was That Age, wasn't he?'

Ivy Lillywhite is a remarkable woman, who has dominated local show-business for half a century. 'She has
always been kind, gentle, soft-spoken and straight as a
die,' says Benny. One senses that her sharp judgement

of character has probably been honed while producing scores of local pantomimes, a fertile source of vanity and vexation of spirit, as she will testify. Ivy herself is totally without pretension. 'Alfie was very lucky to meet someone like Mrs Lillywhite,' was the Captain's considered opinion. He appeared to be suspicious of her at first, probably feeling that such a young woman must have some ulterior motive for showing an interest in his son.

The Captain met Mrs Lillywhite just after Alfie threw up his job at Woolworths and became a milkman with Hann and Son's dairy in Eastleigh. Dad was furious to discover his son so foolhardy and ungrateful. Alfie, in consequence, did not visit his parents. When Mrs Lillywhite heard of this impasse, she reminded him of his filial duty and offered to accompany him to the family wartime home, the wooden bungalow at Hounsdown on the edge of the New Forest. She took her own young son with her as escort to the prodigal and helped to smooth feathers all round.

Benny reckons he had no trouble getting another job as men were short and he was already five feet ten. He was taken on as an assistant milkman to learn the ropes. When a boy assistant was big enough and sensible enough, he graduated to a horse and cart of his very own. Alfie rode shotgun for Old Bill, an ancient milkman who knew every housewife in the district and always got his feet under the table when totting up on a Saturday.

At that time in 1940, food rationing began to bite. The system had taken a while to get under way. For Alfie's customers, meat, fish, fruit, sugar and butter were now in very short supply. One week he was delivering a single egg per person on the sunny side of the street. Those in the shade had their blues on parade. They had to wait till next week for their egg. On this particular day, Alfie was delivering milk as usual to the sunny side, Old Bill to those in the shade. Both of them were selling root vegetables and greens from a huge pile on the cart. Suddenly there was a terrifying crash from the nearby shunting yard. The borrowed Co-op horse, obviously nervous about working for Hann and Son, bolted. 'He was off,' says Benny, 'going like the clappers down the road. I ran after him and came level with the cart, which was swaying from side to side, rattling the bottles and strewing the road with turnips and carrots. Ahead of us, kids and mums and dogs flew out of our path, but the horse wouldn't slow down. I came alongside the horse's head and grabbed the reins and let him carry me. Then I remembered Dad had stopped a runaway horse in his circus days by sawing the reins. So I began to pull his head one way, then the other. It wasn't easy for me and not much fun for the horse, either. It must have hurt his mouth. Anyway, I brought him to a halt without knocking anybody down. Old Bill was more concerned that I'd saved the vegetables.'

It was not long before our young hero was awarded his own horse and cart. Or, more precisely, his own mare and cart. As Old Bill had already taught him to drive, there followed halcyon days for Alfie. He discovered the joy of a morning when the hillside's dew-pearled, the lark's on the wing, the snail's on the thorn. 'It was lovely getting up on fresh mornings and galloping for miles out into the country,' Benny recalls. 'The Hampshire landscape glistening with early morning dew is one of the prettiest sights you can see. I'd be up on the top of the cart, lord of all I surveyed. Over the Station Bridge we'd rumble, cart creaking, bottles rattling. Daisy the mare would pick up speed on the other side and we'd bowl along to Bishopstoke.

Sometimes I'd imagine that I was a stage-coach driver or a cowboy. Then I'd sing to Daisy –

  It's your misfortune and none of my own,
  Yip-a-hi! Yip-a-ho! Get along, little dogies!
  You know that Wyoming will be your new home!

At other times, I would pull up at a tiny bridge and look down into the stream. Childhood memories of that very spot would flood my mind – recollections of catching tiddlers in jars and trying to tickle trout.'

Most of his customers enjoyed the happy-go-lucky lad's songs and patter. Occasionally they would invite him indoors for a cup of tea and sometimes even a slice of home-made cake, which was a luxury in wartime Britain. Others would hold him personally responsible for the food shortages. Some customers accused him of favouritism, although Alfie worked under a very strict rationing system. Because he was so scrupulous in giving every housewife her fair share, he always ran out of eggs at the same place each Tuesday. When he assured the woman of the house that he would deliver her eggs on Thursday, she would explode:

'You've got eggs. Why can't I have my eggs now?'
'No, madam. I have no eggs.'
'I know you've got them. I've seen them.'
'I've no more eggs on my cart, madam.'
'I saw you give some to the lady across the way.'
'Yes, madam. It is because you saw me give them to the lady across the way that I have no more eggs. If I hadn't given them to the lady across the way, I'd have them to give to you now.'

The woman would begin to breathe heavily and her dangling ear-rings to tinkle as her head shook with suppressed rage. Alfie knew this was a danger signal.

'Why can't you give me my eggs on Tuesday and make her wait till Thursday?'

'Because I am instructed to call on her first. That is the way my book is made up. You will be the first of the rest of my customers to get eggs on Thursday. The ladies who had eggs today will not get them on Thursday.'

'I'm not satisfied. I'm going to report you to Mr Hann. Mr Hann is a very good friend of mine.'

'I'm so pleased to hear that, madam. He's a very good friend of mine too. And because you're a very good friend of Mr Hann, I'll make doubly sure that you get your eggs first thing on Thursday.'

Then Alfie would start to whistle until his customer huffed and puffed and slammed her front door.

'I feel so sorry for her now, but I was a saucy boy in those days,' says Benny.

One of Alfie's customers was an old woman who would appear at the front door holding a tea towel over her mouth because she did not want him to see her without her false teeth. 'She would mumble at me through the towel,' recalls the erstwhile milkman. 'Don't ask me why. I was delivering milk – not kisses! Many a time, when she was making no sense, I felt like walking away, leaving her nothing.' Sans teeth, sans everything.

'Sometimes we milkmen were a bit naughty and played Robin Hood to the poorer customers,' Benny remembers. 'If they couldn't pay all of their bill, we would stick it on a rich customer's account. There was one woman on my round with six children and another on the way. She kept saying, "I can't pay this week, I'll settle up next week." No great efforts were made to collect her debt. I think she got away with it one way or another.'

Daisy was always late when she finally trotted into the
dairy yard at the end of a round. Every day. Sometimes
over an hour late. By the time Alfie was saying, 'Whoa,
mare, you've earned your little bit of corn!' he had
earned yet another telling-off from the dairy inspector.
The bane of this poor man's life was the saucy boy who
never mended his ways.

A few years ago, Benny was running for a train at
Waterloo Station when he was grabbed by a woman
as he hurried across the concourse. 'Excuse me,' he
said, 'I have a train to catch.'

'No,' she said. 'You can't go. Hold on a minute.'

'Excuse me, I can't wait. Please let me go.'

The woman grasped his arm with two hands. 'No,
no, you can't go,' she repeated. 'Don't you recognize
me? I'm Mrs Camberlane.' Benny pulled his arm away
and looked hard at her. 'I don't think we've met,
have we?'

'Of course,' she replied. 'You used to deliver my
milk.'

'Good God,' exclaimed Benny. 'Give us a chance. I
was sixteen then. I'm sixty now. Well, it's nice to meet
you again. How are you?'

They chatted for a while. 'Mrs Camberlane had no
difficulty recognizing me,' explains Benny. 'She had
followed my career on the box. She assumed I was
equally close to her. In fact, I didn't know her from
a tin of blacking. Of course, I missed my train.' But
he kept a fan.

Alfie was rarely away from the dairy by 1.30 P.M.,
as he should have been on most days. Twice a week
all the milkmen were obliged to stay behind. On Horse
and Harness Day, they groomed the horses with the
curry comb, dubbinned the leather harness and polished the brasses. Alfie, as you might expect, cursed

the Whoreson Harness for all to hear on Whoreson Harness Day, but secretly enjoyed fussing over Daisy. In celebration of Cart Day, when the waggons were washed, dried and oiled, Alfie gave an airing to his 'in the cart', 'à la carte', 'carte blanche', and 'cart before horse' jokes.

If he finished his round before two o'clock, Alfie would walk the mile and a half to Ivy Lillywhite's house to sit in the kitchen drinking coffee and chatting to her. Alfie once told her that he wished he had learned music properly and envied people who could play the piano. 'When a dance band was on the wireless,' she recalls, 'Alfie would get cross with me because I couldn't identify it. He could recognize instantly the style of every band – and name the vocalists as soon as they started singing.'

Mrs Lillywhite reports that Alfie did not look after himself properly when working as a milkman. His clothes were poor and shabby. 'Well, he wasn't very old, you see,' she says in explanation. 'And he wasn't getting much money.' One day, in bad weather, he turned up at her house with the sole flapping from his shoe. Mr Lillywhite, who was a fireman, gave him a big pair of boots that kept the boy's feet dry for a couple of winters. 'I'm afraid Alfie was hard up and hungry most of the time,' Mrs Lillywhite continues. 'One afternoon I put the remains of a cold chicken carcass in front of him. I thought he would leave enough for me to make soup for my husband. But he was so famished that he ate every scrap. Nothing was left but bones. Bang went my husband's soup!' Only those who experienced the wartime shortages will appreciate how generous Mrs Lillywhite was on that occasion.

Ivy Lillywhite had been persuaded to allow her protégé to introduce short humorous acts to the band's

entertainment. The drummer would have said that their
audiences were suffering from funny turns. Alfie's
funny turns. The young comic practised them in the
living room at Ivy's house and rushed into the kitchen
to perform his latest bit. 'Will this get laughs?' he asked
her. 'What do you think?'

'Sometimes I would bless him under my breath,' says
Ivy, 'especially when he interrupted my cooking.'

To the vicar and the north countryman Alfie had now
added a farmer and a Cockney. This latter, a Max Miller
look-alike, was the strongest of the characterizations –
noisy, cheeky and cheerful. Alfie looked the part. He
had bought the loudest check jacket he could find anywhere from the local Co-op store at a giveaway price.
If he had pressed a little harder they would probably
have paid him to take it away. 'Are you sure?' asked
the assistant, incredulous, when Alfie asked to try it
on. 'He kept looking round for my seeing-eye dog,'
says Benny. Poverty dictated that the young would-be
comic wore the coat in the street. Benny says that,
whenever he gave it an airing, it made waves – old
ladies gasped, dogs howled and mothers hauled their
toddlers indoors.

Wearing the psychedelic check jacket, a hat with
the brim sewn up in front (the symbol of the funny
man) and a red tie ('I thought for a minute I'd cut
me throat!'), Alfie won enough applause to fire his
ambition.

'He didn't always go down well,' says Mrs Lillywhite,
in her usual honest way. 'And he took it to heart.
You could see that it hurt him.' It is not surprising
that audiences were not universally enthusiastic. The
band often played to small groups in bare huts and
halls in the afternoon because people were afraid to
go out on winter nights, at tea dances where women

predominated and danced the valeta and St Bernard's waltz with each other.

Alfie began to look for more responsive audiences. Working solo, as a semi-pro comedian, he found them. His act evoked such enthusiasm as the cabaret at one Town Hall dance that the manager apologized for the meagreness of the fee. 'I'm sorry it's only five bob, lad,' he said. 'You was worth every penny of seven and six!' Smiling at the recollection, Benny says, 'It may seem ludicrous today, but the man was absolutely sincere and I accepted his tribute seriously. Don't forget that, for me at that time, five bob was a day's pay!'

When the summer came, the Luftwaffe mounted fewer bombing raids. Ivy Lillywhite and Her Friends felt safe to perform all over the Southampton area. At nine o'clock one evening, they played the Last Waltz and the dancers made their way out of the Eastleigh Town Hall. It was still quite light when Alfie escorted Ivy on foot through the streets, on the way back to Bishopstoke. Suddenly, a huge German bomber appeared out of nowhere. 'It was flying low,' says Mrs Lillywhite, 'and didn't seem far away. I could see the black swastika and the pilot's face. It was horrible.' As shrapnel pieces sang and danced all round them, Ivy put her leather music case over her head for protection and ran with Alfie to an air-raid shelter under a local club. When they sat down, panting, they felt the ground shake from nearby bomb explosions. This led to spirited conversation among the company. Alfie was well to the fore and held forth on matters of interest with such animation that nobody heard the all-clear siren. When Mr Lillywhite, searching for his wife, arrived an hour later, he told them that the bomber had killed a little girl paddling in the river. The appalling news silenced them all. Everyone left the shelter in sombre mood.

Some afternoons Alfie spent in one or other of the Market Street cinemas, lunching frugally off a bun or a few ounces of Murray's chocolate, as shortages were slowly emptying the store shelves. Now that he was seventeen, our young milkman-about-town felt that a pipe rather than cigarettes would enhance his masculine image. He set off one day on his bicycle with a brand new briar clenched between his teeth. As he puffed away, he trailed behind him encouraging clouds of smoke, worthy of the Flying Scot. However, approaching a hill, Alfie began to breathe deeply. The steeper the slope became, the more our hero sucked down the fumes of the fragrant weed. When he reached the top, Alfie was violently sick. It was consummate timing.

Occasionally Alfie rode his bicycle into Southampton to meet Tex Southgate coming out of his workplace, Pickford's removal company, at the bottom of Regent's Park Road. At other times he took the train to Basingstoke, to pick the brains of professional comics at the Grand Theatre for the price of a drink. It was when the Smeddle Brothers, a well-known comedy mime act, auditioned him in their dressing-room that the die was cast. They were very encouraging and hoped to contact Alfie later when a vacancy turned up. It was their appreciation of his potential that persuaded him to set foot on the show-business ladder before he was called up. It was surely wise to establish himself, as far as he could, in his chosen profession, rather than wait for his draft papers. In any case, he could not continue the punishing double life of milkman and entertainer. 'It was all too much for me,' says Benny, with a twinkle in his eye. 'Up with the lark and to bed with a Wren. Ho hum.' Who does he think he is kidding?

The position was clear. All that was needed was the

courage to make the break. 'I decided to have a go,' says Benny. In the autumn of 1941 he gave in his notice to Hann and Son, patted Daisy goodbye, shook hands all round at the dairy and said au revoir to Ivy Lillywhite, who made him promise to write. During his brief farewell visit to Hounsdown, his mother packed clean clothes in a small cardboard suitcase and his father added a few oncers to Alfie's life savings of £20. The next day, wearing his check jacket, pork pie hat and a confident grin, Alfie set off with his suitcase for London and the stairway to stardom.

7

Happy, Inglorious

On that uncertain morning in September 1941, Alfie
skipped down the steps of Waterloo Station and made
his way across Waterloo Bridge. He had not visited the
capital for three years, noticing at once, under a low-
ering sky, how grim and deserted the city had become.
Most of the standing buildings were shored up with neat
buttresses of sandbags. Alfie was hardly aware of the
others – the shattered walls and rough mountains of
bricks. He was familiar with the devastated centre of
Southampton and the ruins of war about him did not
warrant a second glance. His head was full of dreams.
Clutching his little suitcase, Alfie turned left into the
Strand. He had no idea where he was. Except that
he was in the right place. For there across the street
stood a theatre. And another! And another! Theatres
advertising plays and musical comedies. Alfie's heart
leaped to see them. Somehow they had survived the
Luftwaffe's onslaughts, had sustained a precarious kind
of life, like the flowers sprouting among the rubble of
the bomb sites.

Alfie was tempted to try his luck at the stage-doors.
Perhaps one of the shows needed an extra pair of willing
hands. Older, able-bodied men were being called up all
the time. But Alfie knew little of musical comedy, and
even less of the legitimate stage. No, upon reflection, he
decided he would be more comfortable with a variety
act or a touring revue. He would look for a variety
theatre. That was more his cup of tea. He bought a
copy of *The Stage* at a nearby newsagents and eagerly

scanned the small ads. They were not much help. London variety theatres were listed together but there was little indication of their whereabouts. Where was the Clapham Grand and how could he get to the Metropolitan, Edgware Road? He strolled down the Strand with *The Stage* in his hand until he reached Trafalgar Square. Surveying the buildings around the open space, Alfie could see only one theatre, the Garrick, to the north. As he made his way towards it, the threatened rain arrived. The young hopeful hurried to join a group of people sheltering under the marquee. They were silently watching the vain struggle of a cart-horse that had fallen into a deep ditch in the road before them. Eyeballs rolling, steaming body plastered in mud, the huge beast thrashed its powerful legs in pain and fear. Workmen cursed and strained to tie ropes around the stricken animal. It was a depressing sight. Alfie thought of Daisy and found the incident a dispiriting omen.

When the rain eased off, Alfie left the confines of the Garrick. Moving towards a small park, later recognized as Leicester Square, he looked back. The cart-horse was the right way up at last, trussed, and slowly emerging from the abyss. Alfie began to cheer up. He approached a policeman patrolling the square and asked for directions to a couple of variety theatres that were close together. After checking the *Stage* list, the copper suggested that the Brixton Empress and the Streatham Hill Theatre in south London offered the best chances. Alfie was keen to try the Empress as one of his favourite acts, Sid Seymour and His Mad Hatters, was playing there. The would-be comedian had previously rocked with laughter at their exuberant musical travesty, of the kind that Spike Jones and His City Slickers were to make world-famous. Alfie could see that his own prowess in comedy and music would make him

a dead cert for a place in such a riotous band of zany
musicians. He was off to the bus-stop like a shot and
fuming impatiently all the way as the double-decker
trundled slowly south.

Alfie did not recognize Sid Seymour when he met him
at the stage-door. The great variety star did not look a bit
like a Mad Hatter. He was clearly not the anarchist who
presided over all that musical mayhem on stage. Sid
Seymour was a quiet, elderly gentleman with a facial tic
who listened politely while Alfie proved conclusively
that the Mad Hatters could not survive another week
without his own brand of Hampshire humour. Then the
band leader told Alfie pleasantly that he had nothing for
him personally, but wrote out his brother's address and
one or two others who might help. Gratefully tucking
the list into his wallet, the eager youngster then tramped
the two miles to the Streatham Hill Theatre, which was
presenting *Goodbye, Mr Chips* that week. For Alfie, it was
'Goodbye, You've Missed Yer Chips' as the company
manager shook his head in reply to the lad's enquiry.
It was too late to search further. Alfie determined to
start early next day with Sid Seymour's list to guide
him. In the meantime, he had to find cheap lodgings
for the night.

As he walked across the common, he noticed some
half-finished concrete air-raid shelters. Taking a look
inside, he found them dusty but clean and dry. Great
– a free doss where he might lay a weary head on his
little scranbox. It was not long before he was fast asleep
on the concrete floor. He slept well and woke only once
to find himself staring into the bright button eyes of a
questing rat.

Alfie's early-morning ablutions were carried out under
a notice forbidding them in a nearby Lyons Corner
House. He squared his account by breakfasting in

the café on a bun and a cup of tea. An hour later, his double-decker to the West End took him across Battersea Bridge. Guessing that he must be near the Chelsea Palace, Alfie dropped off the bus and was soon knocking at the stage-door. He was not to know then that, years later, he would break that theatre's box-office record and hold it for ever. Harry Flockton Foster, the touring show's manager, was not to know it, either. But he saw possibilities.

'You're a fine big feller for your age,' he commented, after asking a few questions. 'I think I may have something for you. We're looking for a bright, willing lad. Now, next Monday morning, report to Beak Street in Soho – you know where Soho is?' Alfie did not, but he nodded in the affirmative. 'Well, it's 11 Beak Street,' explained the amiable showman. 'At the bottom of Carnaby Street. Ask for Mr Harry Benet, he puts on all the shows – and tell him I sent you.'

So far, so good. The problem of how best to impress the impresario preoccupied Alfie for the next three days. In case he failed, the ambitious young comic decided to spend his nights in the Streatham shelter, as before, to save money. His days, however, were spent rehearsing his entrance and opening lines while staring into restaurants and food shops. This might be the most important interview of Alfie's life. He had to get it right. Who always got it right? Why, of course, James Cagney. People found the little tough guy irresistible. Right. Alfie would play James Cagney to the impresario's Sidney Greenstreet.

The Hampshire mimic began to get his act together. On the Saturday, many in the market crowds must have noticed a fair-haired young man behaving strangely, muttering through clenched teeth, poking his head forward, teetering on the balls of his feet, biting his bottom lip and grinning sideways at himself in shop windows all over south London. It was only Alfie getting into character. There was method acting in his madness.

Thus it was that, on the decisive Monday morning, James Cagney bounced into Harry Benet's office, sat on the corner of his desk, tipped his pork pie to the back of his head and snapped, 'Now, Harry, what's it all about?' The startled Mr Benet, however, was no Sidney Greenstreet. He did not rumble in reply, 'You're a man after my own heart, sir. I like your style.' Instead he swallowed hard and ushered his crazy visitor to a chair.

'Look, son,' said Harry. 'Don't think you can walk straight in anywhere as principal comedian. It doesn't work that way. You have to learn your trade first and that takes a long time. But you get there in the end. My top comedian nowadays is George Lacey, who's doing very well indeed. He started with me as property boy at two pounds a week. Now, you can do much the same. We need an ASM and Small Parts. Very small parts. No trouble for a smart lad like you. You start tonight in *Follow the Fun*, East Ham Palace, at three pounds a week. What do you say?'

'Done!' replied Alfie, though he did not know what an ASM did. But he knew that three pounds a week was twice what he had been getting as a milkman.

Alfie soon found out what an ASM did. As an assistant stage manager, he was general dogsbody, toting skips, setting scenes, preparing props, making sure that the show ran smoothly. As it included an animal act, 'Pino's Circus', with ponies, monkeys and dogs, he could scarcely have picked a show with more crises for an ASM. Alfie needed to know everybody else's job as well. To hear Benny tell of it (with songs and characterizations) today, is an entertainment in itself:

'*Follow the Fun* opened with a big scene of the entire show singing "Make it a Party!" and arriving by boat. "Here we are again in wonderful East Ham! And here are all the lovely ladies and gentlemen of the East End. Hullo folks, hullo, hullo! How splendid to be back again in Venice on Thames!" Finish song. Exit cast, close tabs. The principal comedian, Hal Bryan, and his straight man would enter from opposite sides of the stage for front-cloth patter. At that time, posters were exhorting the nation to "Go to It!", so the straight man's first words were, "Hello, Hal, 'Going to it?' " at which Hal would snap back, "No, 'Coming from it!' " On my third evening, the Wednesday, after the opening I was setting the next scene behind the tabs, laying a kitchen table, when I heard Hal Bryan out front, ad libbing for his life. "Oh, I'm dying for a drink and there's NOT A SOUL IN SIGHT to tell me where I can get one. There's NOBODY ABOUT. Do you know where I can get a drink, lady?" The straight man was obviously absent, probably enhancing his social life in the chorus girls' dressing-room about eight flights of stairs above us. So, made up for a later scene, with a boiler suit over a policeman's uniform, I strode on the stage, knees knocking, and cried, in a high-pitched voice, "Hello, Hal, 'Going to it?' " "No, 'Coming from it!' " shouted Hal. We staggered through the routine with Hal Bryan feeding me in whispers and me echoing the feed-lines as loud as I could. The audience actually applauded at the end and I walked off into a hail of congratulations from the rest of the cast. The ladies were particularly complimentary, but Hal Bryan carried on with the show as usual. Never said a word. He was a totally different man off stage. A well-spoken, public-school English gentleman, immaculate in a Prince of Wales check suit. As he didn't speak to me, I thought, perhaps I had upset him. Had I done the right thing? I worried about it all through the evening. Later, when the others had gone and I was packing up my bits and pieces, he came to me, put a ten-bob note in my hand, and said, "Well done, son. You're going to be a trouper." Oh-ho. My chest puffed up with pwide, din it? Hal Bwyan told me personally, man to man, so it must be wight!' When he comes to the climax of his story, Benny fools to the top of his bent. Even after fifty years, he can't tell it straight. It means too much to him.

Alfie loved every minute of the tour. Even his chores were exciting. One of them was to make quarts of weak tea every day to represent beer for the funny business. He had to sample it, too, when he played a small part in a three-handed sketch. Alfie showed Hal Bryan and the straight man how to get a drink after hours. 'I left the stage,' says Benny, 'to return in a moment with a half-pint bottle of beer.

' "How did you get that?"

' "I just gave her a kiss."

' "I'm going to have some of that!" says the straight man, leaving the stage the same way, to return shortly with a quart flagon of ale.

' "How did you get that?"

' "I just gave her a kiss and a cuddle!"

' "Oy-oy, stand well back! Out of my way!" sez Hal Bryan, dashing towards the same side. He halts, looks back and sez, "I'm going to do all right hereoooh!"

'Before he can say another word a female hand grabs him from the wings and yanks him off. Shouts, screams, thuds and moans, the drummer going mad in the pit! Hal reappears at last, tattered and torn, carrying a huge red barrel on his shoulder! Blackout!'

Alfie had a spit and a cough in the court scene, too. He was dressed in uniform as the policeman who echoed the usher's call for witnesses. But the Hampshire lad came into his own in the patriotic finale. 'I'd go on looking splendid as John Bull (with a pillow stuffed up me weskit!) and shake hands with an equally unlikely Uncle Sam. The whole cast was in service uniform. The girls got up as ATS, Waafs, Wrens and Land girls, everybody singing their hearts out about our boys in blue, up in the air, do or dare – "I see a valley full of corn; this is worth fighting for". Of course, they weren't fighting: they were singing about it. That's what show-business is – sincere insincerity. Most of the scrimshankers were pleading unfit or gay to avoid call-up. And all being madly patriotic on stage. You had to laugh at the hypocrisy. When we faced the audience with "Land of Hope and Glory", I had hysterics.'

Weekends were hectic times for Alfie. They began at the end of the second house, Saturday night. As the audience filed to the exits, stagehands would offer to stay behind and help the company stage manager 'get out'. For seven shillings and sixpence each, they would strike the scenery, backcloths and props and load them all on trucks for the local station. It was a responsible job for the ASM, making sure that everything was taken down, that it was all there and nothing left behind. The forty cloths, rolled up together, made a very long, heavy and unwieldy load. Occasionally, a horse and an extensive flat cart were used to transport them to the railway wagons. As it was a Saturday night, the stagehands would want to smoke and drink at their tasks. The SM and ASM had to keep sober to see that the evacuation was completed. That meant stacking every item on to the railway trucks. The backcloths needed a long wagon at the rear of the train, to be loaded from the back. The roll had to be slid in, a foot at a time.

'I had plenty of practice at loading,' says Benny. 'I learned how to fit a lot into a small space. Now, in the supermarket, they all look at me. No one can pack a carrier bag like me.'

The show train was on its way by mid-morning on Sunday, and usually arrived at its destination – which could be the other end of the country – by Sunday evening. Then for the stage staff there was the ritual of 'getting in'. If everything went well, the theatre would be open, the dock doors unlocked and the stagehands waiting, willing and wanting, for seven shillings and sixpence each, to reassemble the giant toy. The stage manager supervised and the stagehands handled the scenery. That left hours of hard physical labour for the ASM. He had to carry heavy baskets of props and put each item in place. As he lugged the skips of costumes up the endless metal stairs to the chorus girls' dressing-room, Alfie consoled himself with the thought that every step was another one nearer his life's ambition.

The young baggage master was philosophical too about the ups and downs of his off-stage life. On tour around the country, the performers were in different lodgings every week. They had to write, booking them well in advance. The tour manager, Harry Flockton Foster, kept a list of recommended digs on the itinerary of dates, theatres and towns pinned to the notice board. If Alfie had any difficulty getting fixed up for a week, there were those in the cast who would advise him. He learnt that he could hire a bedsit and facilities for twelve shillings a week and pay extra for provision of bread, butter and milk.

The landladies of these establishments were well known among the profession, the most eccentric of them celebrated in legend. Inevitably, Alfie made early mistakes. When his first landlady asked him his favourite food, the lad was nonplussed. 'Oh – er, celery,' he replied. The good woman served him celery for every meal during the week. In his first month on tour he stayed with a landlord, a strange pious young man who, singlehanded, 'did' for people in his large lodging-house. He charged for bread by the slice, and expected his guests to pay for 'use of cruet'.

Alfie soon learned that the landladies had one obsession in common. They expended a great deal of energy making sure that there was NONE OF THAT. 'There's NONE OF THAT in my house!' they would declare, with a self-righteous shrug of the shoulders. 'You think I don't know what goes on in some places? You can't tell me. There's that Mrs Hoskins at number twenty-three. No better than she should be. More like a disorderly house, that is. I've reported her to the council, but they won't do nothing. She needs the Sanitation Department, that's what she needs. But I'm having NONE OF THAT here. I had to turn one out last week – a musician he was, name of Cadenza. Threw him out, I did. Banging doors at all hours. An honest woman's not safe, I said. You'll have to go, I said. I'll give you Cadenza – you can go. I don't want you. And that goes for your tubular bells, an' all!'

'I'm afraid there was usually NONE OF THAT,' says Benny wistfully. 'And very little of THE OTHER. However, there were ways round the eternal vigilance. One could leave one's room, walk to the communal loo, pull the chain and, instead of returning, go to the lucky lady's room. Once there, time was of the essence. For it was usually not long before there was a knock on the door and the landlady's clear enquiry. "Mr Johnson, are you there? Are you in there, Mr Johnson?" Mr Johnson was in there, all right, but did not want to admit it.

He certainly did not wish to specify how far he was in there. The landlady would try again. "You know you're not supposed to be in there, Mr Johnson. You must come out at once!" Mr Johnson would be forced to tell the truth. "I'm – ugh – hugh – just – hugh – hugh – coming, Mrs Dobbs!" '

There were still old-fashioned digs without lavatories, where chamber pots were provided. It was the morning ritual for guests to slop out downstairs. They would descend, carrying their vessels, like bedpans, under square towels. In one such house, the landlady kept a much treasured vase, a present from Blackpool, on the landing table. Bright sparks from *Follow the Fun* told her that an unpopular member of the cast was going to steal her beloved vase at the last moment under cover of slopping out. On the Sunday morning, as the unsuspecting villain reached the ground floor with his hidden receptacle, the dragon leapt out on him, 'Ah-ha! Gotcha!' and whipped off the towel with such vigour that she spilled the contents of the chamber pot over the hall carpet.

Alfie's first tour was not unduly affected by air-raids. He can recall that the show was halted only rarely by the warning sirens. 'Usually, I felt that the interruption of life was just a nuisance,' he says. 'I sheltered from bombs as I sheltered from rain.' However, one midday attack is vividly remembered. The young ASM was in a Woolworths store when the deep crump of heavy bomb explosions and the wail of warning sirens sounded together. The customers and the staff, mostly women, scurried for the cellar that served as a shelter. Alfie, who was always aware of the dangers of panic, did not move at first, then, as the store cleared, he saw a woman racing down the central aisle towards him, pushing a pram before her. She was screaming with terror, wild hair bristling, eyes staring. As the gorgon approached, Alfie put out a foot and stopped the pram dead. The mother blundered on alone, still screeching, out into the main street. The baby was quiet and made no fuss when Alfie lifted her up and carried her in his arms down into the shelter. The master's hand had been trained by long hours of attending to his baby sister. Down below there was a great deal of oohing and aahing from the Woolworths girls, but Alfie would not share the baby with anyone else. He felt responsible for her. When the all-clear signal went an hour later, the baby was returned to her pram until an abject mother, now much calmer, claimed her child and embarrassed the lad with protracted thanks.

All too soon, after a couple of months, the tour of *Follow the Fun* ended. Most of its cast found themselves 'resting', or unemployed, for the six weeks until the pantomime season began. However, Harry Benet had received good reports of young Hill and wanted to keep the lad in his organization. 'Look, son,' he said to Alfie, 'if you like, you can work in my scenic workshop down the Walworth Road until I need to use you in one of my pantomimes. Stay overnight and make yourself comfortable in the top room. If you do the firewatching, it will cost you nothing.' At that time, every building in the land required a permanent guard to raise the alarm and put out fires caused by the thousands of small incendiary bombs dropped by the Luftwaffe.

Alfie was grateful for the chance to stay in work and particularly to be able to save a few pounds on accommodation costs. His only outlay was the cost of a new boiler-suit that he wore morning and night. He enjoyed his time at the huge warehouse under the railway arch in south London, and remembers with affection the camaraderie of the scene-painters, the smell of the hessian, the wood and the boiling size. As usual, he was the gofer and, regularly, he had to go for the huge backcloths. These were sewn together by a platoon of the monstrous regiment in a sweatshop near the Elephant and Castle. Alfie relished the badinage his arrival always evoked and loved trundling his barrow of hessian back through the streets of Charlie Chaplin's childhood.

In the workshop one edge of the cloth was attached to the long bar lying on the floor. Slowly the bar was cranked up horizontally, so that the top of the back-cloth appeared ready for painting. Alfie would help with that too. He is proud of the work that he did there. 'The painters let me fill in the sky, trees and clouds,' Benny explains. 'Stuff like that. But they had high standards. "Put it on like I showed you," they would growl. I can honestly say that some of my scenery was hung in the Palladium and the Prince of Wales Theatre. Of course, I had to knock up flats as well, frames of four by two, nailed or screwed together. Nothing fancy. No dove-tailing. And, of course, I had to make tea and pop out for sandwiches.'

Alfie's domestic arrangements were primitive. He slept on a pile of hessian and lived on bread and tea. When the scene-painters went home at six, he had the place to himself, but he could not leave it. Taking pity on him, his workmates worked overtime to give their apprentice an evening out. 'Git orf aht of it!' they said. 'Don't 'ang abaht!' Taken by surprise, Alfie put his raincoat over his boiler-suit and left. An hour later he was in the second row of the circle at the Hippodrome off Leicester Square to see the stand-up comedian Vic Oliver and the lovely Frances Day in the revue _Black Vanities_. As he entered the theatre, Alfie noticed the large number of uniforms in the foyer. Looking round the circle, he was impressed by the preponderance of evening dress. In their endearing English middle-class way, the wearers made it clear that they were not impressed by Alfie's boiler-suit.

For his first pantomime, Alfie was designated ASM and Small Parts; not, I think, an altogether accurate description of my brother. He was happy to accept it at the time, as the show, *Robinson Crusoe*, was staged at the splendid Bournemouth Pavilion. He enjoyed the seaside resort's relative luxury in wartime – the coffee mornings, the fashion parades and the theatre organ's nostalgic repertoire, including his favourite, Edward German's 'English Dances'. Alfie even found time to send Tex Southgate a pile of complimentary sheet music copies cadged from the orchestra leader.

The pantomime, too, was surprisingly lavish. It was well worth my bicycle ride from Hounsdown through the New Forest to see it. Although the principal comedian, Walter Niblo, was a very funny little York-shireman, I laughed most when Alfie joined four chorus boys in 'The Cannibal Dance'. Each cannibal, includ-ing my brother, was made up in blackface with a bone through the nose and wearing a black wig, brown body stocking and grass skirt. When the tom-toms began to beat and the jungle music wailed, the well-drilled line of brown chorus boys came dancing on to the stage delicately waving their spears like long cigarette holders. Imagine my hoot of recognition when Alfie followed at the end of the line, shaking his weapon in realistic rage. Compared to the line of willowy dancers, he was a creature from another planet. With his stocky figure and muscular gestures, he looked like a different species altogether. Tears of laughter ran down my face as I saw him desperately trying to keep time with the others. They danced. He stamped. He acted. They flirted. For them, the exercise was easy. They could not care less. For Alfie, the essay was deadly serious. He was giving a performance. It was his sincerity that for me made the situation so funny. His efforts were all in vain. No matter how hard he tried, he would never begin to achieve the effortless grace of the chorus boys. This was the pathos underlying the humour of his predicament. The producer missed a point there. If he had advised Alfie to play his part with rather broader strokes, he would have got roars not only from me but from the audience, too.

Alfie had already picked up hints that he was also of a different culture from that of the chorus boys. On the first night, he noticed one of the lads looking at the audience through the spyhole in the curtain. The boy turned to him and said, 'There's a lot of trade out there tonight.' Alfie felt that it showed a splendid spirit to be so concerned for the success of the show. Later, he realized the true import of the remark. On the same day, another of the chorus boys asked him if he was queer. 'No,' said Alfie, innocently, 'I'm feeling quite all right.'

'No,' said the boy. 'I mean – are you, you know, queer?'

'Well,' replied the Hampshire yokel, amiably, 'I've got me funny little ways, same as everyone else.'

Another member of the cast who made me laugh that evening was Gary Hickson, who tapdanced on a xylophone. The curtains opened to reveal him made up as Man Friday, examining a long thin table. 'Oh, Massa's left his reading eyes here!' he cried, picking up a pair of spectacles from the tablecloth. He put on the spectacles and threw off the tablecloth to reveal his xylophone. 'Ooh, look! Here am a funny table.' All this excruciating banality was necessary, so Alfie assured me, because Gary was short-sighted as well as elderly. 'The poor old boy's as blind as a bat without his glasses,' he explained. 'The stagehands, the rotten sods, keep hiding his spectacles – so he has to blunder about the stage in full view of the audience while I find out where they are.'

In one scene, Gary had to fetch the poisoned chalice from off-stage to give to the Cannibal King, who quaffed the contents and pegged out forthwith, thus facilitating the escape of . . . etc. Alfie, as ASM, had made sure the chalice was in its appointed place. However, when Gary tottered off to find it, the chalice had disappeared. He and Alfie sought high and low, while on-stage the whole entourage stood about ad libbing. Chalice-less, Gary was forced to return to the stage, where he proceeded to strangle the Cannibal King. With Man Friday whispering instructions into his ear, the King put up a struggle and made a good dramatic end. He was no sooner laid out than a stagehand motioned Gary to the wings and offered him the miraculously restored chalice. The old man fell for it and then went through the pantomime of reviving the Cannibal King in order to poison him, while the stagehands fell about with laughter at the success of their ruse. The point was not lost on Alfie, who reproduced that situation in 1961 for the American 'Jo Stafford Show'.

The sketch, as shown on American television, featured Benny as a medieval spy, who falls wounded to the floor. Lying on his back and clutching his body he croaked, 'And so shall oi doi. With yonder sword will oi truly kill moiself.' The spy reaches out his right hand to pick up the sword, but it is not there. Perhaps it is on his other side. He puts out his left hand. 'With yonder sword will oi truly ki . . . ' No sword there, either! Where is the sword? Benny feels inside his doublet, 'With yonder poisoned tablet, will oi truly kill moiself.' He has just swallowed the poison when the sword appears and he has to declaim, 'With yonder sword' ('You daft beggar!' – *sotto voce* to the stagehand) 'will oi truly kill moiself!'

At that early stage of his career, my brother was billed in the programme and on the posters as Alf Hill. Neither of us was impressed by the name and considered Al Hawthorn (referring to G. P.'s guardian) more effective. However, while I was with him in Bournemouth, I suggested a stage name with a kosher ring to it. Reminding him of the Jewish influence in his chosen profession and the long line of great comedians it had produced, I pressed the claims of 'Benny' Hill upon him. My brother demurred at first, and waited until he was serving in the army, before wholeheartedly adopting my suggestion. John Fishwick, his staunch REME friend, told me that my brother introduced himself as Benny when they met in 1943.

Robinson Crusoe was remarkable for the number of lovely women in the cast. When I went backstage after the show, my naïve enthusiasm irritated Alfie. 'If you liked the girls so much,' he said, 'why don't you try your luck?' I think he was learning about the world and had been saddened by what he discovered. I was learning too, and received a lesson that very evening.

Harry Flockton Foster had arranged for Alfie and all the chorus boys to put up at a comfortable guest-house close to the theatre. Alfie invited me to share his room for the night, and when I entered the lounge late in the evening it was occupied by four slim, handsome youths draped over the furniture in the most languorous attitudes, making bitchy remarks to each other in high-pitched drawls. Their conversation was entirely about acquaintances in their exclusive circle, expressed in a jargon of their own. They fascinated me. I had never come across a group of people so obsessively narcissistic. Every word was enunciated with stylish precision, every gesture choreographed for maximum effect. I made the mistake of sitting down and trying to make conversation with a young fellow of about my own age. I soon gained the distinct impression that not only was communication between us difficult, but that it was important that it should be impossible. After my halting attempts to find common ground had foundered, the indolent interchange of venomous repartee continued.

From time to time, one of the boys would bestir himself, move gracefully to his feet, dance a few steps, pirouette, bend over and, holding his pose, break wind on a loud and sustained note. Such panache was a revelation to me. I was later to hear a great deal of public farting in the army, but I never encountered so elegant an introduction to a physical necessity or such resolute attempts to raise it to the level of performance art. Despite my interest, not to say curiosity, I felt it wise to make my excuses, which were of supreme indifference to the company, and left for bed.

Alfie learned a little more a few weeks later. After the pantomime season he went straight into *Send Him Victorious*, another Harry Benet revue. When the show arrived at the Hackney Empire to begin the second week of its tour, Alfie discovered that an ironing board was missing. It had been left behind at the Bedford, Camden Town. It was the duty of the ASM to bring it back. By bus, if he was lucky. Alfie arrived at the Bedford and had just found his ironing board when he was buttonholed by Toni, the senior partner of Toni and Tim, a novelty dance act on the bill at the Bedford that week. Alfie knew that the senior partner owned the act

and occasionally replaced the performer playing Tim.
Toni, a slim friendly character, confessed that he was
looking for a new partner and liked the look of the young
Hampshire comedian. 'You're a fine-built good-looking
feller,' he said. 'You'd look great in white tie and tails.
What do you do?' When Alfie told him, he said, 'You're
made to measure for the act. We must talk business. I'll
phone you.' A few hours later Toni rang and proposed
a meeting after the show. That did not seem quite right
to Alfie, as it meant travelling across London after
midnight. He suggested, instead, a chat the following
afternoon when they would both be free.

'Toni had a luxurious flat in Maida Vale,' says Benny.
'Thick carpets and modern art everywhere. When I
arrived, he gave me some delicious shortcake he had
cooked himself and cold lemonade. Of course Idiot
Boy knocked it back – glug-glug-glug. "Ooh! Dat Nice!"
Only about five parts gin, it was, that's all. Then I did
all me impersonations. Toni was very complimentary.
"You're a knockout," he said. "That Eddie Cantor was
marvellous!"

'"It was Al Jolson, actually."

'"Whoever it was, you were great. Take your jacket
off and relax. Here, sit next to me. And have some more
lemonade," he said. "Now, in the act, you will do your
comedy and impersonations while I'm off changing for
the final dance. We can't miss. I really think we can
charge fifteen pounds for the double – seven pounds a
week clear for you alone. And that's just the start. Yes,
I can see stardom ahead." Arm round the shoulder. All
of a sudden, he's got his hand inside my shirt, touching
my chest, as 'twere. "Give us a kiss," he sez. "What are
you talking about?" I said, all hot and bothered. "Well,
we've got to be friends," sez he. "That's silly," I said.
"I don't kiss men. That'd be silly."

' "If we're going to be partners, we must trust each other," he sez.

' "I'm not having that," I said, pulling away from his clutches. I got up, walked very dignified to the door, drew myself up to my full height, and said, "If you want me in this act, you'll have to take me for my talent alone!" and swep' out, tripping over the mat on the way! Pillock! I never saw him again after that.'

There was a corollary to that lesson. 'Now I realized how some ladies feel,' says Benny, 'when I come on strong with, "My God, you're beautiful! I find you terribly attractive." If they really don't want to know, they always say, "Is that the time? I must go. It's time I was in bed." "Yes, I know," I reply. "No, seriously, I must get back. Is that the time?" One day I'm going to write the song, "Is That the Time?" '

As usual, Benny put the experience to good use. To point up the humour of a man in the ridiculous situation of rebuffing sexual advances, he turned the predator into a man-eating vamp in a sketch with Patricia Hayes for the BBC and later, in another version, with Stella Moray, for Thames Television. Benny wrote the skit years later, as he has written so many, on a restaurant table in the sunny Champs-Elysées with the passing show and a bottle of wine for inspiration. He had just seen the film *The Collector*, starring Terence Stamp, and it reminded him of his earlier predicament.

In the burlesque, Benny, as the naïve young man, has been plied with drink by the aggressive vamp. He wakes to find himself on a strange settee.

BENNY: Where am I? Where's my teddy? (he accidentally touches a pair of silk knickers and draws his hand back as if scalded)

STELLA (as the vamp enters): Hello tiger. How's
my tiger?

BENNY (looking at his watch): Is that the time?
Eight o'clock? I must go. I have to see Mother
before I go to bed.

STELLA: It's eight o'clock in the morning.

BENNY: Eight o'clock in the morning! Have I been
here all night?

STELLA: Yes. My God, but you're irresistible when
you're angry!

BENNY: All night? Did I . . . ? Did you . . . ?

STELLA: Did I what?

BENNY: Did you have carnival knowledge of me?

The variety theatres countrywide were graded according to size and seat capacity. Number One houses took
the more expensive and important shows. Harry Benet
revues usually played the Number Twos. However,
such a distinction was only approximate and sometimes a revue would not have enough drawing power
to fill a large Number Two house. In such a case, Harry
Benet would for one week only add an extra attraction,
usually a headliner, to the bill.

At the Hackney Empire, for example, Joe Davis, the
champion snooker player, joined *Send Him Victorious*.
His act, with its mirror tilted at forty-five degrees to
show the stalls his skill on the green baize, was a
novelty. The interest generated by his performances
left a deep impression on Alfie.

The experienced comedy double-act of Connor and
Drake was also scrutinized by the shrewd young ASM
when it was brought in to boost takings at the Brixton
Empress. Alfie admired Eddie Connor's professional
expertise and called upon it years later to assist him
with the Benny Hill Show on television. 'It took ages

for me to fully appreciate how good Eddie was,' says Benny. 'He had seen it all. You never had to explain anything to him. He would do it perfectly first time, modestly – without fuss.'

Despite the disapproving wartime railway poster, 'Is Your Journey Really Necessary?', the show continued to rattle on round the country – This Week – The Victoria, Burnley: Next Week – Salford Hippodrome. In the first week of November 1942, *Send Him Victorious* was doing well at the New Theatre, Cardiff. On the Friday night, Alfie was made up and in the wings, about to go on stage, when a voice enquired in his ear, 'Are you Alfred Hill, Alfred Hawthorn Hill?' He turned and saw that the questioner was a policeman. There were two of them. 'Yes,' replied Alfie, 'why?' 'We'll tell you that at the station. Come along, Sunshine,' said the copper, grasping his arm.

8

Snafu – Situation Normal,
All Fouled Up

When he stood before the sergeant in charge of the Cardiff police station, Benny still had make-up on his face.

'Now, son!' said the sergeant. 'The question is – have you been arrested or did you give yourself up?'

'Do I have a choice?'

'You do.'

'I certainly haven't given myself up as I've done nothing wrong.'

'You have been accused of failing to report to your army unit in accordance – '

'But that's easily explained – I'm on the move all the time. I didn't receive – '

'You didn't try to avoid call-up?'

'Of course not! How could I? My name is on theatre posters all over Cardiff.'

'You'd better give yourself up.'

'Why?'

'Because that way you will only spend a few days in the cells here. Then you will be handed over to the army to sort you out. If, on the other hand, you were arrested, then you will stay in the cells a very long time, until your trial comes up.'

So Benny was persuaded to give himself up and signed a form to that effect. He handed over all his possessions, including his shoelaces, to the sergeant and finally heard the heavy cell door crash to behind him. The tiny space contained two bunks, both in use as the evening trawl usually provided Benny with a drunken companion. Sleep, uneasy because of the permanent electric light, sometimes became difficult.

The belated army recruit did not go hungry. He was given three sandwiches and three mugs of tea a day. The food was shoved through a square hole in the door, just tall enough to allow the passage of a full mug. Thick, doorstep sandwiches scraped through also. Inside them paste or jam was spread so thinly that it was impossible to tell what it was. By the third day, Benny was longing for a tastier mouthful. Luckily he had been worldly wise enough to stuff two pounds down his sock while handing over his personal property. With the help of a co-operative constable, enough chocolate bars were purchased to enliven the diet.

On his fourth day in Cardiff police station, Benny was visited by two regimental policemen in khaki greatcoats, who persuaded the desk sergeant to return Benny's belongings. They took him by truck to an army camp outside the city, where he was locked in the guard room and ordered to scrub it – 'I want it spotless!' Although a straw palliasse made his army bed more comfortable than the police station bunk, the food provided was positively unappetizing.

Benny ate little for three days until he was rescued by a different pair of regimental policemen, who explained their mission with admirable clarity: 'We have been ordered to take you across country, through London to a training wing at Lincoln. We shall obey that order in a friendly and civilized way. No handcuffs will be used. But if you so much as even think about betraying our confidence, you will arrive in Lincoln handcuffed, having sustained a number of painful injuries while trying to escape. Understood?' Per

The two policemen kept their word. Friendly and civilized they were, but zealous, too. They stuck close to the unfortunate recruit, marching shoulder to shoulder with Benny between them and sitting on either side of him for the entire, interminable train journey. Up and down the London escalators, they squeezed him front and rear, hand on shoulder. It was quite clear that the lad was under military escort. He was mortified, and afraid that a show-business associate would spot him and spread the news to the whole profession.

Yet another cell awaited Benny at his training camp. He groaned when he saw it. 'I'd rather join Littlewood's Happy Circle,' he muttered as he was banged up once more. The next morning he was taken to the company office and chased in to see the commanding officer by the huge company sergeant-major.

'I thought the sergeant-major was off his rocker,' says Benny. 'He pushed me along and bellowed at me all the time – Leff, Roight, Leff, Roight. 'Alt. Stand still! He never spoke – always shouted, opening his mouth so wide you could see his uvula quivering.'

Benny, still in civilian clothes, stood before the commanding officer and explained why he had not reported to the unit on time. Clearly, his call-up papers had not been forwarded from one theatre to another.

'It is just possible, I suppose,' commented the CO doubtfully, 'in view of your profession, but the fact is that you have had to be brought here late. And that's a black mark against you. You will have to wipe that stain off your record. You're in the army now and you've got to catch up. You've got to work extra hard. Learn to obey double quick. Develop self-discipline. Maximize your efforts. Because the sarn't-major will be keeping an eye on you, won't you, Sarn't-Major?'

'Yessah!' roared the big man.

'And, Hill, you will do your best, won't you?'

'Yessir, yessir,' said Hill, with a sinking heart. ('Three bags full, sir,' *sotto voce*.)

The reluctant hero was marched away, put into ill-fitting khaki and taught to salute. For two days he saluted nearly everything that moved. He saluted the sergeant-major. 'You don't salute me, you dozy little man!'

'Sorry, sir.'

'You don't call me sir. Call me Sarn't-Major!'

'Certainly, Sarn't-Major, sir.'

'Not sir, you bloody Arab, you!'

'Sorry, sir. I mean, sorry, Sarn't-Major,' said Benny saluting. He has been saluting ever since.

The new recruits, Benny among them, spent hours every day marching up and down the barrack square. They practised stamping their metal-heeled boots in unison. Benny made such efforts that he injured his Achilles tendon, a complaint known as 'Guardsman's Heel', common among drilling soldiers. He limped about the camp for ten days, until at last the tendon mended. By this time, the recruits were well into fitness training – route marching, running, climbing, lifting, carrying and performing gymnastics of all kinds. Most of every morning was spent on physical exercise. The priority was fitness. Soldiers had to be strong and healthy. The army must be fit. So what berk decided to issue fifty cigarettes weekly to every squaddie, plus two hundred at a vastly reduced price? They didn't know what damage cigarettes can do to the heart and lungs? I did. Every stand-up comic did. We used to crack the one-liner – "I hear the tobacco companies have a new slogan: 'Cancer is good for you!' " '

Benny learned to loathe the asinine stupidity of the army. 'Most winter mornings we'd report shivering in the freezing cold for physical training of some sort. We'd march and race and wrestle and box (what a perFORMance! everybody tacitly agreeing to pull their punches). As the morning went on, we got warmer and sweatier. When we were exhausted and on our last legs, we'd go inside for scalding mugs of tea and a hot meal, followed by a steaming pudding. Immediately after the meal, we'd go into the fug of the lecture room for an Army Bureau of Current Affairs talk by one of the officers. He was always a tedious old chump who was bored by the subject and clearly didn't want to be there. Can you imagine it? Forty tired men, fighting sleep to the drone of a dunce from Dullsville. We could feel our eyelids drooping and knew we'd be in trouble if we were caught napping. Fingers were licked and wiped over eyelids in a vain attempt to keep sleep at bay. What were we all doing in there? It was a complete farce.'

The saucy boy kept his mates chuckling at the insanity abounding. When the Weapon Training Sergeant asked him what 'a fine sight' was, he replied, quick as a flash – 'Two dinners on one plate!' On another occasion, his platoon sergeant was demonstrating the Thompson sub-machine gun. The effect of the 'Tommy gun' on enemy morale he explained thus – 'it has a devastatin' effect on the enemy's morals'.

'You mean, it turns them into angels,' asked Benny, innocently.

Installing a new notice board in the barrack-room, the platoon sergeant varnished a piece of oak, inscribed it carefully, 'Duty Roster' and screwed it to the top of the board. Except that he spelt it 'Rooster'. He was livid when he found that someone (guess who) had written in chalk underneath it – 'cock-a-doodle-doo!' The men in Benny's barrack-room laughed when he told them that a gypsy at a local fair had just told his fortune. 'You are a leader of men,' she said. They were right to laugh; in five years' service Benny never even made lance-corporal.

One day, an invitation to a Christmas party appeared on the barrack-room notice board. 'It's for a dozen only – so you'll have to sort that out,' explained the sergeant. 'It's from the general up at the Big House – and I'll be comin' too to see that you behave yourselves.' The same thought went through every head. 'A party! There'll be girls! Classy girls! Upper-class girls who charver!' Everybody was mad keen to go. The Dirty Dozen was chosen by playing cards (aces high). Lucky beggars! Lucky Benny. He was one of them. The evening before the party, they were all busy with spit and polish, cloths and Duraglit, brushes and ebony sticks.

When the happy band, well-shaven and Brylcreemed, arrived at the Big House, they were greeted in the hall by the general's wife, who apologized for her husband's absence. 'At the War Office, you know.' She instructed her guests to make themselves at home. 'Gilbert will look after you.' She indicated the wrinkled retainer who was busy taking their greatcoats. At which she betook herself off upstairs, never to be seen by them again.

Gilbert led the puzzled party-goers into a deserted sitting room, in which a huge log fire blazed under a magnificent marble mantelpiece. He poured every man the drink of his choice and announced, 'Dinner will be served in half an hour,' then he left. The Dirty Dozen looked at each other. They were now more like the Twelve Angry Men.

'Is this it then, sarge?' asked Benny.

'Looks like it, son.'

'Well, I'm off. This is not what I call a party.' Benny stood up and several others moved into the middle of the room. 'I'm not hanging about in this morgue,'

said one. 'She can keep her soddin' chips!' cried
another.

'Hang on, lads,' said the sergeant. 'I know you're
disappointed, but it wouldn't be right to leave before
the meal. It's not fair to the cook for a start, and
another thing, we'd all be for the high jump, if it got
out that we'd pissed off before the big dinner.' So they
waited, ate the meal amid quiet, desultory conversation
and left.

At Lincoln, Benny took a battery of intelligence and
aptitude tests. They were very thorough examinations,
designed to match the right man to the right job, square
peg into square hole. What a sensible idea. Except that it
did not work. In Benny's case, it firmly pressed a square
peg into a round hole. The considered assessment of
the experts involved was that Benny was better suited
to be driver mechanic than any other kind of army spe-
cialist. When he heard the conclusion, Benny felt like
weeping. 'If there's one thing I was not cut out to be, it
was a driver mechanic,' says Benny. 'I couldn't drive.
I couldn't put a bicycle pump together. I couldn't
put anything together. During my years in the Royal
Electrical and Mechanical Engineers, I spent days and
whole nights on jobs that others could do in an hour
– because of my lack of aptitude. I was anything
but a natural mechanic. What really depressed me
was that I had already proved to Harry Benet that
I was strong, intelligent and hard-working. I wasn't
ambitious. I didn't want to be a general, I just wanted
to do something valuable, anything to make a useful
contribution. And there I was, little more than a bloody
nuisance. And not my fault. None of it my fault. From
the very first, the army had treated me like a criminal,
when it wasn't my fault. When they decided to make
me a driver mechanic it was the latest in a series of

cock-ups that had made up my short army career
so far!'

Philosophical as ever, Benny decided to keep his
head down and make the best of it. He was sent
to a civilian barracks in Staines to learn to drive.
There he was carried round the streets in the back
of a stripped-down London taxicab. Sat on a wooden
seat with two other learner-drivers, he listened as his
sergeant-instructor taught him to drive the army way.
'Handbrake off, foot-clutch, clutch; release clutch
slowly . . . ' The soldier-students were given one job
to carry out each day on the car, so that every fortnight
the daily attention added up to a complete overhaul.
They were learning to maintain the vehicle as they
were taught to drive it. After the first few days, the
sergeant-instructor decided, 'I think we'll get out of the
way. Go for a drive in the country. Only because you've
done so well, lads.' Every morning they would be off
in their camouflaged taxicab, sampling the delights of
the local cafés. Their pleasures were simple – tea and
sandwiches, reading the newspapers, listening to the
jukebox or radio and conversation about such things.
'Do you know, there's a NAAFI canteen in Mill Hill
where you can get a bloomin' great mug of cocoa and
a macaroon for a penny!' Benny laughs at his silly young
self. 'Whoa-hoa,' he cries. 'That's living!'

When his basic instruction was completed, Benny
was sent on a fitter's course for six weeks at Brighton,
as near to heaven-by-sea as a town could be. He was
in civilian billets, with ladies and other human beings.
What more could he ask? He made the most of the
holiday, very little of the course. His results made him
forty-first out of forty-two trainee fitters. 'The feller who
came last, forty-second, was the oldest squaddie in the
world,' says Benny. 'He was a regular soldier, who had

wangled himself a trip. It was only another course to him and he paid no attention at all. I paid attention. I just couldn't do the stuff.'

Some weeks later, Benny developed a large, painful ulcer on his shin and was sent to hospital, where the wound responded to treatment. He was so impressed by the gentle skill and dedication of the nurses, particularly those on night duty, that he wrote a verse in praise of them. Benny remembers that it began:

> When shutters board the twilight ward
> To bar the evening's beauty,
> When curtains close and traffic slows,
> The Night Nurse comes on duty.

The offering was initialled and pinned to the ward notice board. In the early hours of the morning, Benny was awakened by the placing of screens around his bed. A moment later the night nurse slipped in beside him. She seemed to have taken his innocent verse as a declaration of love. He did not disabuse her of the notion. Imagine his astonishment a few nights later when the new relief nurse showed her own appreciation of the verse in exactly the same way.

Benny recently told this story to his zany friend Phyllis Diller. 'It taught me one thing,' he concluded, 'to be careful about making a general statement to a woman. She always applies it to herself.'

'I don't,' said Phyllis firmly.

In July 1943, Benny was posted to the newly formed Third Light Anti-Aircraft Searchlight Battery Workshop at Arnold, near Nottingham. His REME unit of thirty men transported and maintained the battery's dozen or so Bofors guns, searchlights and radio equipment. In addition, the maintenance group was responsible for servicing and supporting the Royal Artillery Gunnery personnel. Every day brought its electrical, mechanical and practical problems. 'Benny was not much help with them,' says John Fishwick, his REME buddy. 'He was a terrible driver, an even worse mechanic and the scruffiest soldier ever. But he was worth his weight in gold as a companion. He used to keep us in fits of laughter. I never saw him miserable. Benny was always singing. I liked to sing along with him. So did Dickie Senior, who accompanied us on his ukulele. When we harmonized in the pub at West Malling, a group of Canadian pilots would join in with us. Benny had his own version of his favourite, which was, "If You Knew Suzy Like I Know Suzy, Her Father Would be After You As Well!" He was not only witty off the cuff, but he would often have the table in a roar reading a few pages of funny comments on our army life that he had written. He would stand up and deliver it as if he was broadcasting over the radio. I called him the Picasso of the pen and thought I understood him, but the other lads could not make him out. He was a most unusual soldier. I saw him really upset only once. That was when a driver doused a grass snake in petrol and set light to it. Benny couldn't forgive such cruelty.'

John Fishwick continues: 'Because he was a misfit in the REME, Benny took a lot of stick from the staff sergeants, but he always came up smiling. I felt so sorry for him when the battery moved to Anglesey in November '43. We only had a couple of miles to go to the gunsite at South Stack Lighthouse on the island. It was a black, stormy night and I was driving the last truck along a narrow road, bringing up the rear of the convoy. My partner, a staff sergeant, said, "Look, that idiot Hill's taken over the wheel now." We could always tell when Benny was driving. His staff sergeant partner was not a driver, but he could control a vehicle better than Benny, who had been trained. On this occasion I could see the tail of Benny's lorry immediately in front swinging about. Sure enough, it skidded – and down it went into the ditch. The lorry stuck there, tilted over to one side. The wheels hadn't stopped spinning before the air was blue. Benny's staff sergeant cursed him up hill and down dale. Then mine got started. They really took the skin off the poor lad. Of course, a guard had to be mounted and the lorry pulled out next morning.'

It was not long before the battery, with its attendant workshop, was sent to 'Buzz-Bomb Alley' in the south-east, to take out some of the pilotless winged missiles that streamed across the Channel on their way to London. The buzz-bombs were driven by engines that cut out and allowed the missile to circle while the gods decided whom they would destroy. Except that many people felt that the bomb was making the decision, a concept more plausible than you might imagine to a shivering wretch at three o'clock in the morning. At least the battery could throw something back. Usually in vain, as the buzz-bombs came in low and fast – sometimes to devastating effect, as in the case of two Third Battery gunners who were killed in a cinema. The loss of their two comrades concentrated the minds of the lucky survivors.

At last the battery received the call for which they had all been waiting. On 1 September 1944, a few weeks after D-Day, fair stood the wind for France. They set sail from Southampton in a landing ship transport, over a Channel so calm that the lorries were left unlashed on the decks. Surveying the scene from a sitting position on the roof canvas of a truck, John Fishwick and Benny were conscious that a sturdy wash from another vessel would be enough to send the vehicles sliding overboard. When John mentioned German submarines, Benny replied: 'I don't wish to know that. Kindly leave the stage!' After a night at sea, they arrived at the Mulberry Harbour, the prefabricated landing complex towed across the Channel from Southampton. Leaving Arromanches, the thirty drivers of the REME workshop hauled the Third Battery across northern France until they found themselves in a village near Dunkirk.

A pocket of 7,000 Germans had been trapped nearby and could not get out. Both sides knew that the encircled troops had nowhere to go. It was wiser to continue the formality of exchanging a few high explosive shells each day. The Germans were still sending out patrols and, from time to time, unwary British sentries and careless soldiers paid the ultimate price for a lapse in concentration; the Luftwaffe were regularly bombing British installations at night; land-mines and booby-traps killed several of the Third Battery gunners; bitterly cold weather closed in for months. All these factors created a grim, edgy winter for the men of the battery workshop.

Benny's presence did a great deal to keep his mates cheerful. When he learned that one of the drivers, Little Bobby, had returned *virgo intacta* from his honeymoon, the barrack-room clown took charge. He arranged an educational exercise, a trip to a house in Lille with a party of the lads. Upon arrival, they packed Little Bobby off upstairs with his instructress, while they sat at a table in the bar. Benny, as is his wont, made a joke about the barmaid's bosom. At which she hauled out a huge breast and squirted milk in his face. The lads roared at his discomfiture. When, at last, Little Bobby came downstairs, he was a changed man. After his one lesson, they could not keep him away from the girls.

'Benny joked so easily with the French girls that I thought he had a dark secret,' says John Fishwick. 'I felt sure he was partly French or had stayed with French relatives before. It was only when he learned German just as quickly at Melle that I realized he was picking it up like everyone else, but with exceptional speed. He has a remarkable gift for languages. Why the army didn't find that out when they gave him aptitude tests, I can't imagine.'

In a village café, Benny met Simone, a pale, pretty local girl. She was unwell, slowly recovering from an operation that was taking too long to mend. He felt sorry for her and did what he could to help. One night, the village was *en fête*, but Simone was alone, resting in her bed. Benny brought her a few gifts to cheer her up. He was astonished when she removed her wig, which was an unusual accessory in those days. Sweet little golden curls covered her head. It had been shaved in public a few weeks earlier when her liaison with a German soldier had been discovered. Simone told Benny that, despite the sentries on both sides, many French girls still met their German sweethearts at night in the fields and cemeteries around Dunkirk.

One night Benny was on guard at the end of a tunnel which funnelled pedestrians and cyclists from one district to another. All was quiet when Benny heard footsteps echoing from the darkness. At once a strange presentiment swept over him – something wicked this way comes. Benny listened, alert for danger. 'Halt, who goes there?' he shouted. There was a muffled reply. '*Halt! Qui est là?*' cried Benny. Ready for trouble, he clipped a round into the breech. '*Qui est là?*' Out of the shadows stepped a large dark man with an eye-patch. 'Halt,' ordered Benny. The swarthy stranger did not halt, but began explanations in a French rumble. At no time did he stop moving forward, but clattered up close and breathed a Pernod anaesthetic into Benny's face.

One-eye introduced himself as Louis Bouchier, the bistro owner. He lived a few streets away and invited his new acquaintance to visit. That is how Benny met Louis' wife, Yvette. She was beautiful and modest. Bouchier was a monster, a black marketeer who bought chocolate and soap locally and sold them in Paris.

On Benny's first visit, One-eye grabbed the cat by the tail and threw it out of the window. His second visit, when Bouchier was away on business, was hardly more propitious. Madame Bouchier was chaperoned by a much older woman, who clucked and looked most disapproving when Benny tried to compliment Yvette on her beautiful face. Unfortunately, he said, '*Vous avez une jolie fesse*,' which means, 'You have a pretty arse'! He did no better when a moment later Yvette poured two glasses of her husband's bathtub brandy. Benny tried to be affable, saying, 'After this, you will be drunk (*zig-zag*).' It came out, '*Après ça, vous zig-zig*', 'After this, you fuck!' The chaperone was so shocked that she insisted on Benny's leaving at once. Benny reluctantly bade *au revoir* to the lovely Madame Bouchier. A little learning is a dangerous thing.

In fact, Benny's gaffe was not far from the truth, for on his third visit to Yvette both Bouchier and chaperone were absent. However, One-eye returned unexpectedly. He called out as he passed the bedroom on his way to the kitchen. Benny dressed quickly, kissed Yvette goodbye, and slipped out of the house. For once, he blessed an army ordinance. Regulations insisted that he carried his Sten gun everywhere.

John Fishwick says that some of the men in the unit got wind of what was going on and feared for Benny's life. It did not stop Benny going to the Bouchier bistro a few evenings later. He was having a quiet drink at a corner table when he heard One-eye making approving comments about the British army. 'Mind you,' said the monster, in a loud voice, 'if I found a British soldier with my wife, I'd kill the pair of them with my bare hands!' Benny finished his absinthe and left. When he arrived back at the company office, he was told that the battery was leaving the next day. He never saw Yvette again.

Recently, on holiday in Provence, Benny came across a Frenchman who knew Monsieur Bouchier of the one eye.

'He survives, you understand, but he is unwell.'

'Is Madame Bouchier still alive?' asked Benny.

'Oh, yes. She is a lot younger than him, of course.'

'Of course. I first met her in 1945.'

'In 1945, oh no, that was the second Madame Bouchier, she was killed in 1945.'

'She was killed?'

'Yes.'

'Yvette was killed? Did Bouchier kill her?'

'No, he was in Paris when it happened. She was killed when a German shell hit the house.'

'Oh, my God. How awful.'

'Yes, it was very sad. Her lover died with her.'

When Benny was granted leave for England, he usually stayed with his parents at Hounsdown and, later, when the bomb damage was repaired, at Westrow Gardens. He also used to spend a few days with Auntie Louie in Bexleyheath and catch a couple of shows in London. His cousin Chris recalls a vignette of Benny with his mother, who was peeling potatoes in the sink of the kitchen at Westrow Gardens. Mum was singing 'Me and My Girl'; Benny, with his hand on his Mum's shoulder, was harmonizing. On that leave, says Chris, his cousin spent many hours upstairs in the bedroom practising his new trumpet. It drew fire, of course, from the Captain. 'How much did you pay for it?' asked the Old Man. 'Two pounds,' replied Benny. 'Two pounds? For a bit of junk like that? You've been had. You must need treatment to pay good money for that thing. It'll be a five-minute wonder, as usual, I suppose. Wasting your money again.'

'Look,' remonstrated Benny, 'I paid for it. I take it I can do what I like with my own money.'

'All right, my son. No need to get aereated. I'm only interested in my son's future, that's all. I suppose, if you practise here, you might go semi-pro one day. Bring in a bob or two. That'd be useful.' As he left the room, the Captain paused at the door, turned and asked, 'You know why Harry James is the greatest trumpeter in the world, don't you?'

'Well,' replied Benny. 'He's got a great technique.'

'That's not it,' replied the Captain.

'And he's given it years of dedication,' suggested Benny.

The Captain shook his head. Then, with an expression of infinite wisdom he placed a forefinger on his closed mouth. 'The lips!' he said firmly, and left the room.

Mrs Lillywhite remembers those leaves. 'Benny used to bring me my favourite flowers, carnations,' she recalls. 'He knew how I loved carnations. One time he brought me a bottle of carnation perfume as a gift from France. I put it in my chest of drawers and upset it by accident one day. It went over all my clothes. They were well and truly perfumed. I needed only to take a clean hankie for the room to be full of the scent of carnations. I went round in a cloud of perfume for years. People remarked on it. Benny certainly made sure I didn't forget him.'

Although the war had ended, the battery and REME

workshop moved on. Many nights the driver/mechanics had to sleep on the ground under their trucks as they had done, off and on, since their arrival in France. Thus the guns and lorries were guarded and the men relatively dry, sheltered and protected. Benny finds it ironic that he slept so soundly in such rough and dangerous conditions but now has to take tablets to induce a fitful doze on soft mattresses and pillows.

Driving through the French countryside Benny became enchanted by a landscape where every prospect pleases. From time to time, he disappeared into it. 'He was his own man,' explains John Fishwick; 'sometimes he went a bit clandestine.' Whenever possible, Benny walked away from army routine into another world – a land of splendour in the grass, of glory in the flower. He tramped along dusty roads, through lush meadows, by winding rivers, from village to village, stopping only to sample the *vin du pays* and chat, in halting French, with the locals. Though he has always taken pleasure in the parcelled park of southern England, Benny, like others before him, found France the best garden of the world. His love of it has deepened over the years, and he returns there for refreshment again and again.

When the REME workshop first drove the Third Battery across the German border, all British troops were strictly forbidden to fraternize with the enemy. Drivers were also warned of severe penalties for picking up strangers while en route. Local parents, for their part, were adamant that there should be no intercourse, social or otherwise, between their girls and the soldiery. That meant no contact at all with the local fräuleins. Benny hesitated therefore when, hammering his lorry along a quiet road, he saw ahead of him an attractive figure in a blue and white dress, waving him down. He decided that an initial misdemeanour was unlikely to be found out. He would take his chance on others that might flow from it, if he were lucky. When he pulled up, the lovely hitchhiker, to his surprise, asked for a lift in French. She came from Picardy, he learned after she had joined him, and was attached to the Allied hospital administration. Chatting away happily and driving too fast, Benny shot over a rim, bumped, and raced down a steep valley. At the bottom, a tree trunk blocked the opposite side of the road. Suddenly, what Benny calls 'a clapped-out old banger', a German wagon, rattled over the opposite brow of the hill ahead. It took the slope too fast, could not avoid the tree trunk, and pulled out in front of the REME truck.

'My way was blocked,' says Benny. 'I couldn't brake in time, so I went up the steep grass bank to my left almost to the hedgerow at the top, passed the German banger, flew down behind him and right up the opposite bank, swung down again, swerved back on to the road and drove on at twenty-five miles per hour.'

'*Vous êtes malade?*' enquired his companion.

'*Non, pourquoi?*'

'*Vous êtes devenu pâle.*'

'Gone white, have I? I can't think why.'

White faces bothered Benny later when he noticed so many pale, skinny children in the streets of Melle, where his unit was stationed. All of them were half-starved, some of them homeless. The midwinter snow that made the little German town look like a Christmas card, spelled hardship and suffering for the young-sters. Benny suggested to his mates that they should give the kids a Christmas party. The idea was greeted with enthusiasm.

'Everybody in the unit was caught up in the spirit

of the thing. The lads got cracking. They decorated the rambling old house where we were billeted and made or scrounged everything needed for a children's party – balloons, paper hats, novelties, gifts. Some of the fellers gave up smoking and sold their fag ration to buy goodies. We all pooled our chocolate ration and put the bite on everyone in sight for more – the Red Cross, the NAAFI. The Yanks chipped in with Hershey bars. Then it was all handed over to our unit cook, Corporal Bozzini. He was a master pastrycook and the last I saw of him he was working at the Savoy Hotel and showing his skills on television. He made us pastry galore and a monster cake with all the trimmings. He iced the confection and wrote "Auf Wiedersehen" in chocolate on it.

'We invited all the children we could find to the party. I even went round the streets announcing the news like a town crier – dressed up as Santa Claus with a red ping-pong ball on my nose. The kids had never seen anything like it and a crowd of them followed me round shouting, "*Zirkus Clown! Zirkus Clown!*"

'Then, out of the blue, the non-fraternization law was withdrawn. We were allowed to talk to the fräuleins at last. Not a moment too soon. There was no question of scrubbing the children's party. That was Number One priority. But we wanted to celebrate, too. Simple. We would entertain the young ladies in the evening, after the youngsters had gone. We asked the children to tell their big sisters. We advertised. More planning. Decisions, decisions. We scraped together a makeshift trio – a pianist, an accordionist and me on the wash-tub and saucepans. Everything for the evening party had been carefully arranged by the time the children's afternoon party began. And what a party that was! We had invited all the kids in Melle – and it seemed that they had all accepted. We organized games, we sang, we led the dances, we played the fool, we fed them, we grafted. They played, sang, danced, laughed and ate. They ate everything – the whole cake, the pastries, the sweets, the chocolate. At last, the children were, for a brief spell, full and happy. Eyes shining, they left our Christmas castle clutching their little gifts. As for us, we felt we had spread a little of the Christmas spirit. Now for the fräuleins' party.

'We cleaned up the debris left by the children, repaired and put up fresh decorations, grabbed a few minutes' kip, shaved and spruced up. I urged the pianist and the accordionist to start the dance music before the guests arrived so that we could have a little rehearsal. Keeping the right tempo for the dancing bothered me, as I hadn't any brushes. So we started with a slow waltz. At the end of it we still had no guests. Then a foxtrot. No one appeared. A valeta. Not a soul. The lads stood about waiting and waiting all evening. The girls had decided not to come. They had turned us down. We were all really upset. Nobody came to our party.' As he comes to the end of the story, Benny comments wryly, 'Life, you see. Aah.' Once more he suggests what his comedy so often illustrates, that in relations between the sexes the male is doomed to disappointment.

No one was disappointed by the workshop Christmas dinner. 'Louis Bozzini did us proud,' says John Fishwick. 'It was a marvellous meal. We had always been a happy, friendly crowd, despite some difficult times. And that dinner crowned it all. Benny made an after-dinner speech, from notes, that was a work of genius. I've never heard anything like it. He had everyone in stitches.'

In the New Year, it became clear that barriers of

suspicion take time to come down. Only slowly did exchanges between the native population and the occupying troops become easier. By the time Benny's REME unit was posted, German girls were attending British army dances. Soon after arrival at his new station, Osnabrück, Benny met a lovely little fräulein called Greta. When he took her to a NAAFI dance, her pale face lit up to see the piles of sandwiches, biscuits and cakes in the bar. He was glad to be able to please her so easily. 'The first time I took her out she wore a brown dress,' says Benny. 'The next time, she was wearing a black dress; on the third occasion she wore a brown dress with white piping and rosettes; then, a black dress with fringes; after that, a brown dress with fringes. I thought she had a wardrobe of different dresses. It was when she turned up in black with white piping and rosettes that the penny dropped. She had two dresses and was sitting up nights altering them with needle and thread, to look nice for me. I was touched.'

When Geraldo and his dance band came to entertain the troops, Benny was absent. To his chagrin, he discovered he had been detailed for stick-guard elsewhere while the show was going on. He read a book to take his mind off his disappointment, the life story of Coco the Clown. Already predisposed by his background to take an interest in the subject, Benny was fascinated by the biography, which he read in his off-guard periods. 'I loved it,' admits Benny. 'When I finished it and closed the book, I thought to myself, I really enjoyed that. It was made to measure for me. Then I looked at the back cover and it said, "suitable for children under fourteen"!'

One of the performers Benny did manage to see was Frankie Howerd. He was then a sergeant touring the camps with an Army Entertainment Unit and undecided about his future.

'I don't suppose I made the slightest difference to his career,' says Benny, 'but I saw his potential and urged him to realize it. After the show, I sought him out in the little canteen and asked him if he was a professional. "Well, no not really. I've done a little bit," he said modestly. "You've got a jolly good way with you. You ought to take it up," I said. "I don't know, really, you know." He was young then and diffident. "Well, that's just my opinion," I said. "But I was in the business, only ASM and Small Parts, I've been in a few professional shows and I think you would do very well." '

Benny pauses. 'Whatever happened to him?' he asks thoughtfully.

A few days later, opportunity knocked for Benny. There appeared on the unit notice board a poster from the Central Pool of Artists ('Stars in Battledress') to the effect that new regulations allowed the entertainment group to accept all fitness grades into their ranks. The change in the rules meant that, the war having ended, Benny, who was physically A1, could now apply for a post in army show-business. He could make the leap from greaseboy to greasepaint. If he was lucky, it would be the end of the 'ammer, 'ammer, 'ammer along the 'ard, 'igh road.

This chance was important to the reluctant driver/ mechanic. The war was over. He had done his bit. Now it was time to think about the future. He thought hard and decided that he might be too inexperienced to compete with established performers who would be flocking from all branches of the services into Stars in Battledress.

Benny needed an edge – and all he had was his ability to write comedy material. Some of the wheezes he had devised for himself in Eastleigh had garnered more laughs than the jokes he had appropriated from professional comedians. He set to and began to write more. While his mates spent their spare time in canteens, bars and dance-halls, Benny stayed alone in the barrack-room sitting on his bunk with pen and pad – an occupation that was to engage him for the bulk of his time ever after.

On his next leave, Benny took his precious scripts with him. After visiting his parents, he continued scribbling for a few days at Auntie Louie's home in Bexleyheath. She made sure he was not disturbed. Then, with a respectably thick parcel of comedy sketches under his arm, Benny knocked in trepidation on the door of the Stars in Battledress headquarters in Hill Street, near Grosvenor Square in Mayfair. Here they told him bluntly they had nothing for scriptwriters. They did not need them. There was no call for comedy material at all. Performers had their own material and Sergeant Charlie Chester was in charge of that department. Sorry, mate. Benny was devastated. No place for scriptwriters? What kind of Fred Karno's outfit was this? Benny was about to leave when the sergeant said, 'We're holding auditions for performers tomorrow morning – you could try out for us, if you like.' Details were spelled out for the reprieved supplicant, who took them gratefully and tottered out into the morning sunshine.

What a turn-up for the book! Now he was back to competing with polished performers. Somehow the stand-up triumphs of his milkman days seemed passé, the rag-bag routines too provincial. What was gunpowder in Eastleigh would be talcum powder in London. He needed new material. And fast. Most of the scripts he was carrying were not suitable for an audition. They were two-handed and three-handed sketches. The monologues had been written for nobody in particular. They did not make the most of his talents. One of those talents was his ability to reproduce every kind of accent in English. That verbal dexterity must be showcased in his audition piece.

Thinking hard, Benny was ambling south towards Piccadilly when he realized that the first show of the day was about to commence at the Windmill. This theatre had gained great notoriety for its revue featuring posing nudes and can-can dances. It had continued non-stop, six shows a day, throughout the London Blitz and proudly announced 'We Never Closed!', which some unkind commentators suggested should have been 'We Never Clothed!' Like thousands of servicemen from all over the world, Benny regularly visited the Windmill when on leave in London. However, it was not the girls but the comedians who were the main attraction for him. He would sit cramped, scribbling notes on performances in the programme while his immediate neighbours boggled at such perverse behaviour.

On this crucial morning, Benny felt that a visit to the Forum of Flesh and Fantasy might provide inspiration. Sitting at the back of an all-male audience, the aspirant comedian smiled to see one of his favourites of the music-hall, the stylish Peter Waring, on stage in black tie and tails at midday. In a veddy, veddy cut-glass accent, the man-about-town drawled a long throwaway monologue about his debutante girlfriend – 'comes from a good family. Her mother has shares in the Co-op.' Nonchalantly waving his long cigarette holder, the distinguished Mr Waring was teasing chuckles from an inattentive crowd which was waiting for the return of the girls. The voyeurs would not catch fire until they saw the whites of their thighs. Benny knew that, in the circumstances, the Mayfair dude was doing very

well indeed. Could he, the kid from Southampton, do
something similar? Perhaps. An hour after Peter Waring
had taken his bow, Benny was back with Auntie Louie,
requesting an early call. The rest of the day he spent in
his quiet bedroom.

With studied insouciance Benny strolled next morning in front of a tribunal of note-taking officers to tell
them a rambling shaggy-dog story about a man who
used the railway without a ticket. The traveller's adventures included exchanges with a Mummerset farmer
and a Cockney, both familiar to Benny's Eastleigh
friends, plus a Scotsman and an Irish ticket-collector.
As the quips rolled out, the tiny basement theatre
echoed with the officers' roars of laughter. The auditioning panel was enthusiastic. After his piece, Benny
could hear something of the whispered discussion
– 'authentic accents', 'spot-on characterization' and
'sharp observation' were phrases used. 'He's ebsolutely
bwilliant!' declared a lieutenant. 'What a find we've got
here, what a find this fellow is,' repeated another. When,
as chairman, the senior officer called Benny back he
said, 'Good effort, Hill. You're just the sort of chep
we're looking for. You'll definitely be hearing from us.
And soon.'

Benny was overjoyed. So far, so good. But would he
ever hear any more of it? Would this be just another
disappointment, yet another army cock-up? He could
do nothing more than return to his unit in Germany
and wait. Three weeks later he was awakened by the
company clerk, who was on duty late at night. 'Your
posting has come through, Benny. I thought you'd like
to know. Go back to sleep.'

'I shan't sleep any more tonight – I'm too excited,'
replied Starry-eyed in Battledress. In the morning, he
discovered that he had not only been transferred to

the Central Pool of Artists but was to be stationed in Grosvenor Square, near the headquarters.

In the spring of 1946, The Artist lived in Mayfair as a Young Dog for a few weeks while he rehearsed his first venture for Stars in Battledress. It was the juvenile lead, an 'Anyone for tennis?' type, in *Happy Weekend*, a musical comedy of the mid-thirties. The role had been played in the West End originally by Steve Geray, a dapper little light comedian, who became a popular character actor in Hollywood. It has to be said that Benny was not a natural for the part of Ricki, a happy-go-lucky bachelor with all the social graces. He could not dance, for a start.

Major McGregor, an experienced performer in the Jack Buchanan mould, tried to make good that deficiency. The early practices must have been fascinating to watch. Before the show was costumed, the cast rehearsed in uniform. The major was instructing in dance-pumps; Benny was following in army boots. Imagine the scene. Ricki stands alongside Deirdre, arm round waist, holding one hand. They are to sing, 'We Go Together Like Sausage and Mash, Bacon and Eggs – That's Us!' and dance across the stage. So simple. Major McGregor shows them how. He sways gracefully and skips across. 'We go together like sausage and mash, bacon and eggs – that's us!' he sings. 'Now, just take the girl and move over there like that.' Benny takes a deep breath, grabs Deirdre, bumps into her and clomp, clomp di clomp, clomp, clomp di clomp, clomp, clomp, clomp, pushes her sideways. The boots scythe a path across the stage like Russian tanks. Only nifty footwork saves Deirdre from serious injury. She looks daggers at Ricki. 'Now up on to the coffee table,' suggests the major, cheerfully. It must have been the funniest dance routine until Mel Brooks persuaded the Frankenstein monster to try 'Puttin' on the Ritz'.

Happy Weekend, an after-dinner confection for the pre-war middle class, was, of course, totally unsuitable for post-war troops. Lines like 'Lend me a pony, old chap. My tailor's dunning me again,' were meaningless to uniformed audiences. Benny was irritated by such archaisms and could not resist re-jigging the script. He set about making the dialogue intelligible and spiking up the jokes. It was all too easy to please grateful servicemen starved of entertainment. Any reference to a well-known radio character, catch-phrase or slogan would evoke a storm of delighted recognition.

'Who was that on the phone?'

'Whippit Kwik!' (a radio comedy character).

'Excuse me a moment.'

'Is Your Journey Really Necessary?'

'Would you open the wine?'

'Give us the tools and we'll finish the job.'

The part of the barman in the comedy was little more than a spit and a cough in the original script. When Benny discovered that the actor playing the character was an excellent yodeller, he wrote a special number, 'They Call Me the Yodelling Barman', for inclusion in the play. It was a great success. 'After that, the beggar got more applause than I did,' says Benny wryly.

Happy Weekend, thoroughly modernized, was well received on its countrywide tour of service camps and bases. 'The show was carried by what we all brought to it,' says Benny. 'Its major difficulty was technical. The set had to be very simple and small enough to fit into a Nissen hut. When we finally opened at the Calais Opera House, our little fit-up was lost on that vast stage. We had to pull in the side tabs to mask most of it. By that time, the scenery was looking very grubby. Jack Payne, the dance-band leader and impresario, is said to have seen it and asked why the entire play was taking place in a public lavatory.' Reports of Benny's solid contributions as a writer and performer had been sent back to headquarters. At the end of *Happy Weekend*'s tour, he was sent to the Army Entertainment Headquarters near Lüneberg in Germany to rehearse as compère of a variety band show.

I had been called up in 1942 and served first in the Infantry and then in the Royal Army Ordnance Corps. When I first heard that Benny had been posted to Stars in Battledress from the REME I sent him a gramophone record of my congratulations and advice – 'Keep at it – like the girl who worked her way through college, student by student!' This was despatched from my army station in Hong Kong, together with copies of *Variety*, *One Thousand Jokes*, and the *New Yorker*, which were difficult to obtain in Europe. The choice of magazines is significant. They all nourished our shared fantasy life which had begun in the late thirties. Benny and I both loved American humour and believed that all the interesting developments in modern comedy were taking place in the United States. We were familiar with the names of dozens of transatlantic comedians we had never seen or heard. The details of their careers were followed avidly. Occasionally, a joke or a description of a comic's act in a show-business article would whet our appetite for more. From such clues we would build up a surprisingly accurate picture of each favourite performer. For example, Benny and I were discussing the work of Henny Youngman, Danny Thomas, Zero Mostel and Martin and Lewis many years before we saw them on stage, film or television. We felt that we were discovering them, as they were completely unknown in Britain and relatively little known in the States.

On the other hand, the established American film and radio comedians were part of our life, immutable stars in the show-business firmament. We never missed a chance to see or hear them. News and reviews of recent entertainment invariably played a part in my desultory correspondence with Benny over the years of military service. In addition, we vied with each other to write the pithiest comments about our own situations. Persiflage prevailed. Early on, I included a few pages of jokes under the title, 'Gagbag', which in later correspondence became 'Son of Gagbag', 'Gagbag Rides Again', 'Gone with the Gagbag', etc. Benny, who has an elephantine memory for funnies, reminds me occasionally of the origin in the 'Gagbag' series of an item in a current show.

The first performance of the variety band show in the Army Theatre near Lüneberg was to take place in the evening. Its dress rehearsal, under the major responsible for entertainment in the area, began at two o'clock in the afternoon. The major and his sergeant sat alone in the deserted auditorium to vet the show. As compère, Benny welcomed the imaginary audience and introduced the acts. He was linking the items, making a smooth transition from one to another by performing short comedy routines that referred to the previous offering and anticipated the next. His task required not only a high level of performance but a considerable writing talent. For instance, Benny wrote special material for exchanges with the band about the music.

'Although we had an audience of only two, I did my best to twinkle,' says Benny. 'We got through the rehearsal without a hitch and I thought things had gone well. The major came back-stage afterwards and had a word with each act. He spoke to everyone but me, telling them things like – "We won't have time for the encore, leave that out," and "Shorten the introduction. Get into the song straight away." As the major was ignoring me, I felt sure that he had been pleased with my work. There was nothing he could tell me. I thought to myself, "He knows a pro when he sees one." When everybody else had gone, he took me to one side and said, "I'm sorry, Hill, you can't go on tonight. You're just not good enough. Your material is poor; your performance is weak. Some people are comedians; some people are not. You're not, and the audience won't stand for you. They'll give you the bird. Don't worry about this evening. I'll take over as compère personally. But I'm afraid there is clearly no place for you with us." '

Benny was stunned by this rejection. To be shot down just as he was taking off! It was heartbreaking. He felt ill. Not only were his dreams in tatters, but he was being sent back to the REME – to the driving and engineering he hated so much. And he could not do a thing about it. Benny was so upset that he could not eat and simply mooched about the headquarters. He was hanging about, an outcast, when the major opened the evening show. 'There was a crumb of comfort when I realized that he was using material I had considered and thrown out as inferior,' says Benny. He received another crumb of comfort when Harry Segal tiptoed alongside and invited him to the canteen for a cup of tea.

Harry Segal was the young sergeant in charge of *It's All in Fun*, an army touring revue of which he was the principal comedian. Harry, a kindly, soft-spoken man off-stage, had been in the business since he was a child star in the music-hall. He had also been in the wings during the afternoon's dress rehearsal. 'The major was wrong,' says Harry Segal, bluntly. 'I could see at once

that Benny was a good performer. He looked good,
he worked well and he had tremendous potential.
His trouble was that he was ahead of his time. His
material was too far advanced for that era. I knew he
would go places, so I had a long talk with him. He
was terribly upset, really distressed. His confidence
had fallen through the floor. I tried to cheer him up.
I said, "Don't worry. We'll take it a step at a time.
Come out with my show as stage manager. I think I
can swing it. That will keep you from being sent back
to REME. No way will the major allow you on the stage
at present. But once we get out on the road, we'll be in
charge of our own destiny. When we get away from
headquarters, you can go back on stage." '

'Harry, bless his heart, was as good as his word,' says
Benny. 'In fact, he was better than his word. He not
only persuaded the major to keep me in the Pool and
made a job for me, because there was very little to do
as stage manager, but he also forced me on stage when
my nerve had gone. He put me first into the Cockney
finale with all the other performers, then he took me
into his comedy sketches and finally he kept at me
to do a five-minute spot on my own. I was still very
apprehensive and I kept putting it off – "Not tonight,
Harry. Another night. I can't do it tonight." '

The night came when Benny was not allowed to put
it off any longer. Two of the cast were ill and Sergeant
Harry Segal was hard-pressed for performers. 'I want
you to do a five-minute spot tonight, Benny,' he said.
'Not tonight, Harry,' replied Benny. 'I've nobody else
to call on,' explained Harry. 'I shall need you in every
sketch and every scene – and in a five-minute spot on
your own. So get on stage – and that's an order!'

'Benny was as nervous as a kitten,' remarks Harry.
'I practically had to push him on from the wings.'

For his solo act, the reluctant performer sauntered into the spotlight wearing a silk dressing-gown. He told his shaggy-dog story of the character who travelled without a ticket. At the first witticism, there was a burst of laughter that brought Benny's confidence flooding back. After that he was away. The big laughs followed one another, growing louder and louder. At the end of the five minutes there was a storm of applause. The audience would not let him go. Clapping enthusiastically from the front row was Colonel Richard Stone, the officer in charge of Service Entertainment for the entire European Theatre.

'I thought Benny was wonderful,' he says. At the time, he backed his judgement by countermanding the performance ban and insisting that the craftsman comic should be allowed full scope. The major was overruled. But the story does not end there. The colonel thought so highly of Benny that, a couple of years after they had both been demobbed, he became his agent.

'Soon after I took him on to my books, I received a call from the major,' recalls Richard Stone. 'He was then a publican and wanted Benny to entertain at his pub in the New Forest. What his motive was I don't know – possibly he was trying to make amends. When I put it to Benny, he refused, at first, to accept the booking. He would have nothing to do with the major. After I had asked him to reconsider, as he was earning only twenty pounds a week for six evenings' work at the Café Anglais in London, he said he would do fifteen minutes for thirty pounds, a prohibitive fee. To our astonishment, the major agreed. However, he forgot to advertise the show. When Benny arrived at the place, there were only a few customers present. The major was so disappointed he scrubbed the event but honoured the contract by paying thirty pounds for a non-appearance. He gave Benny his cheque for doing nothing. So a kind of rough justice was done. But that is still not the end of the story. A few days later, Benny bumped into Harry Segal in Charing Cross Road. Harry was upset because he had just been offered the comedy lead in a pantomime but would have to turn it down because he was skint and couldn't afford the costume and props required. "How much do you need, Harry?" Benny asked him. "Thirty quid," replied Harry. Benny, being Benny, still had the major's cheque in his pocket. "Come with me to the bank," ordered Benny, and in a few minutes had cashed the cheque and handed Harry the thirty pounds he needed.'

9

Civvy Street

In the early autumn of 1947, when the last of their young men had returned home from military service, the extended Hill family met for the first time in years to renew their solidarity and to assess the effects of the war. Of those who had attended pre-war celebrations in Fleming Park, Eastleigh, only G. P. was missing. He had died soon after the Southampton blitzes, a prey to senile paranoia, convinced that German pilots hovering above his roof could hear his every word.

The family reunion took place by courtesy of Auntie Lena, as usual. A lively tea party was held in the packed living room of her new home at Fawley on Southampton Water. Our sister Diana, now a fine, handsome fourteen-year-old, was busy pouring out tea when Uncle Ernie traversed the room with a huge red enamel kettle of hot water. Spotting the kettle, Diana cried, 'Oh, Uncle Ernie! What a big spout you've got!' As soon as the words were out, she realized the enormity of her gaffe. Her face flushed scarlet, then suddenly she hooted. Her spontaneous reaction broke the startled silence and soon everyone was chuckling with her.

Benny reminds me that when the crockery was cleared at last, the ladies gravitated to the kitchen as the Captain held forth. He spoke for all when he thanked Providence for the family's emergence relatively unscathed from the dangers of war, and offered unstinting praise to Churchill and Montgomery for 'boxing clever' in the way they had avoided the carnage that had decimated his own generation. 'Of course,' he went on, 'we can never repay our debt to the twenty million Russians who died beating Hitler. No amount of propaganda will ever make us forget them.' No one present disagreed with him.

The talk moved on to the subject of the atom bomb. Several views were expressed about its significance. The Captain made no contribution to the argument. Neither did Benny, who never expresses ideological opinion except to mock the more obvious insanities of the politicians. He is remarkably tolerant of human folly, but finds man's inhumanity to man totally incomprehensible. 'After all,' he says, 'we're all brothers under the skin.' On this occasion, he listened to the views of his uncles until his father rose and walked to the door. The Captain turned and addressed the assembled elders. 'Don't talk to me about the atom bomb!' he said. 'You know what the atom bomb is, don't you?' The group looked puzzled but expectant. 'You don't know what it is? It's a bloody menace, that's what it is!' With that he left the room. And the remarkable consequence of his calculated exit was that the company immediately changed the subject. Everyone tacitly accepted that the Captain had said the last word.

Benny was up early next morning and soon on the train to London. A £50 gratuity in the pocket of his chalk-striped grey suit, both donated by a grateful government, bolstered his confidence. He knew where he was going. Certainly not back to humping skips. He had earned the right to call himself a comedian, and a comedian he was going to be. Within two hours he was tramping familiar territory, and within three he had paid a deposit on a room in Queensway, fifty yards from the Bayswater Road. He was to share a flat with three girls, a dancer, a secretary and a hairdresser. They had hoped for a fourth young female partner, but were cool

enough to recognize the advantages of having a man
about the place. By now a fellow who could look after
himself, my brother welcomed the chance to use the
kitchen and bathroom facilities.

When the gossips spread the news that Benny was
shacked up with three attractive young ladies, there
was a good deal of winking and nudging from people
who did not know him very well. What the winkers did
not realize was that all his flatmates were spoken for and
not particularly interested in him. For his part, Benny
was fond of all three of them. He soon settled in and
found the arrangements so comfortable that he was not
tempted to upset them. His own love life, in that period,
was peripheral. He says today that his pleasures were
taken 'on the wing'. But not in Hyde Park. On his way
home of a night, he gently refused the tarts along the
Bayswater Road. They hissed him, signifying their belief
that it was homosexuality which induced him to forgo
the delights of barked shins under the plane trees.

Benny never understood why women made so much
fuss about what the goodnight kiss sometimes led to. It
was all so easy, so natural; it cost them so little. Why
not, as the song suggests, spread a little happiness as
you go by? His frank way with young women always
reminded me of the fellow who was buying an expensive perfume for his girlfriend. 'It is called "Perhaps",'
volunteered the assistant. 'At forty pounds an ounce,'
snapped the dude, 'I don't want "Perhaps", I want "Certainly"!' Benny was like that, so he said. Even with a
new girl he wanted a prior 'understanding'. 'You can't
treat women like that!' I would remonstrate. But he said
he did – and got away with it. My view now is that
his claim was largely youthful braggadocio – he was
trying to impress his elder brother. I have since seen
him demonstrating so many times such genuine care

and concern for women friends of all ages that I cannot believe he was ever as calculating as he suggested.

We both experienced, of course, the universal bafflement of the male before the female. We would compare notes and laugh at our predicament. I always felt that one of the most risible situations between a man and a woman is when the guy is in the doghouse and he does not know what for. Has he forgotten an anniversary or what? So he says, 'What's the matter, darling? What have I done?' And she says, 'If you don't know, I'm certainly not going to tell you!'

Benny always loved the female riposte – 'I'm sure I'm not the one who's incompatible!' He told me once that, in a moment of weakness, he revealed to a close friend that he had a recurring dream in which his ideal woman, wearing a flared blue dress, appeared to him over the brow of a hill. His friend arranged to meet him in a local park and, wearing a blue dress, she appeared to him over the brow of a hill. What can you say to a woman who does that?

My brother and I were particularly close in those days in the late 1940s and looked out for each other. I had left the army at the end of 1946 and was living at home, waiting to go to college. One evening we picked up a couple of lively young women in a dockland pub in Southampton. Before long, Benny's quips had set the table on a roar. Then he went over to say hello to his old friend, Eddie, at the piano. When he returned his face was set. 'Let's go,' he said to me. When I demurred, he snapped brutally, 'Put her down. You don't know where she's been.' Outside, he reported that Eddie had said: 'You boys are sailing too close to the wind. They're fireships!'

When he first returned to Civvy Street, Benny had neither the time nor the money to sustain romantic

attachments. His overriding priority, into which he
poured all his thought and energy, was his professional
career. It is significant that, having unpacked his few
possessions in the Queensway room, he spent his first
evening at a huge party of aspiring performers. This
was the Combined Services Entertainment Celebration,
to which all personnel who had cheered up the troops
had been invited. It was an exciting affair.

Young entertainers had recently poured out of the
services in a flood of talent. They were all trying to
make their mark after the hiatus of the war. Many of
them were at the party, gossiping, joking and making
notes. There were dozens of young comedians, fascinated by who was in and who was out, who was
appearing where, doing what and for how much.
Almost without exception, they were on the first rung
of the ladder, working the working men's clubs (you
did not even need your own agent to appear in these).
Eyes swivelling round the hall, the eager comics would
regard with awe any of their number who had performed in a radio broadcast. 'Look, there's Charlie
Farnsbarns. He's done a "Workers' Playtime"!' These
were the young lions whose household names are now
to be found on every page of the television magazines. They are today's stars. At that party in 1947,
they clapped with sincerest admiration and respect
for Terry-Thomas, a young gap-toothed comedian in
the Peter Waring tradition. Thomas, who presented a
ten-minute cabaret with his inimitable aplomb, was one
of those who had already made it. He had done his own
spot at the Prince of Wales Theatre, sharing the boards
with the great Sid Field. Every man-jack of the young
comics watching the lisping story-teller dreamed that
the Big Chance was just around the corner for him
personally.

Outside the hall on that special evening rain teemed
down from leaden skies. It was a grey time all round
for most people. Families still mourned loved ones lost
in wartime, pined over inevitable separation or ached
for homes destroyed and lives blighted. The nation was
poor, hungry and exhausted. The years of hardship,
effort and suffering had taken their toll. Bureaucratic
controls, particularly rationing of food and clothes, bit
deep. In vital areas of national life, victory had brought
no respite. Hopes born in the struggle had faded. The
bitterest winter for fifty years in 1946–7 had precipitated
a record slump in all branches of the entertainment
industry. For many it was the worst of times.

It was the best of times for others, and for most of
the ex-service entertainers, in particular. They were
infinitely thankful to have returned home in one piece
when so many of their comrades had been killed or
incapacitated, they were grateful to have learned their
craft in security, before undemanding audiences; they
rejoiced that at last they were free, without the shackles
of service discipline. They were exhilarated by the challenge of unpredictable civilian responses; they were
bonded by a camaraderie of common experience and
shared ambition. That year of 1947 was an exciting
one for all would-be stars, but to be young was very
heaven.

Working in Southampton, I was able to visit the
Smoke every other week, kipping in the ex-service
clubs or bedding down with my brother. When he
was not busy, we would go to the soccer matches
or the shows, bumping into jokesters on every corner
– Peter Sellers, making passers-by turn with his zany
fooling, Alfred Marks, kidding about his thinning hair,
Bob Monkhouse, still in his RAF uniform, knackered
after writing all hours. The city seemed to be alive with

youthful clowns in full slap, racing for tube-trains, running after trolley-buses, boasting over brunch at Lyons Corner Houses, planning pranks in Soho pubs, chatting up the birds in the Bayswater Road without the lolly to pay for it.

Of course, it was not an easy life. Scores of fine, talented lads never made it. They could not stand the pace. First of all, there was Catch-22. You could not get work without an agent – and you could not get an agent unless you were in work. 'How can I book you if I can't see you working?' So you had to make do without an agent to represent you. But you soon learned to hang out in the bars and cafés where other performers might know of a working men's club in need of a funny man that night. There were hundreds of such clubs all over London, and a chance remark could send you scurrying off on a fifteen-mile journey for a fee of five bob.

Benny had it no easier than any of the others. He was paying forty-five bob (two pounds five shillings) a week for his room. But he soon learned to spend his Monday mornings in an alley opposite Wyndham's Theatre in St Martin's Lane, where one of the small-time agents might eventually stroll up to him and order, 'Right, Ben. Get your book out. Friday 15th – Tottenham, Liberal and Radical Club – and you can double up at the Edmonton Trades Hall. Saturday 16th – you've got a lunchtime one down at Tilbury. If you like to hang on, I can probably get you Saturday night also in Tilbury. Sunday, you're at the Mildmay. Eight o'clock. Don't be late!'

The usual fee was one pound – thirty bob for two acts. If 'The Insect' (as the entertainments secretary was known) nodded in the affirmative, you could earn an extra half-crown for an encore. The weekend's work might earn Benny as much as £8, but there were many weeks when he had no work at all.

Bob Monkhouse remembers those days. 'We were both bloody hungry,' he recalls, 'and looking for the next meal. But Benny would always share his information. He was generous with tips. He knew more than anyone else where the work was. Benny kept his ears open and knew every date there was. What it was worth, what time to be there, whether it was two spots or three. He was better than an agent from that point of view. But he didn't keep it to himself. He was very kind like that. I was in the Nuffield Centre once moaning to the comedian Robert Moreton that I couldn't find any cabaret work in London. I'd played the Ninety-Six, Piccadilly, and then run out of bookings. Benny was listening. "Try the Ridgeway," he said, and wrote down a few more addresses. "What sort of act should I do?" I asked.

' "A bit bluer than you do round the variety halls," he replied. "Here, this guy will pay you half a crown a joke." Benny handed me a slip of paper with a name and a telephone number. The name was Max Bygraves.'

When he could not get work, Benny spent most of his time writing comedy. Queensway was so noisy at weekends that, unable to sleep, he would often scribble all Saturday night and Sunday morning. On weekdays he would beat the coverts of the city for ideas. He still does, although it is more difficult for him now that he is recognized everywhere. He hopes to catch the manners living as they fly. The significance of his perceptive observations was first recognized by Ivor Brown, the theatre critic. 'Like Charles Dickens,' he said, 'Benny Hill has the key of the street.'

Another who has understood the sources of Benny's humour is Michael Bentine, who remarks how my brother is constantly watching, picking up signals and recording. 'It doesn't matter where he is – in a park, a pub or a plane, in London, Spain or in the South of France, all human life is grist to his mill. Benny reminds me of the artist Constable, strolling around with his sketchbook.'

Conversely, Bentine was an early inspiration to my brother, who admired his unique brand of comedy at first sight in the Nuffield Centre, a forces canteen near Trafalgar Square, where they both gave their services. Within weeks of their meeting, Bentine's career took off like a rocket when he devised a stunning act that put him straight into a big new Hippodrome show, *Starlight Roof*, with Vic Oliver and the youthful Julie Andrews. In the revue, Bentine made an impassioned political speech, emphasizing his points with one prop only – a broken chairback that, in his hands, became in turn a tommy-gun, a plough, a flag, a comb, a woodsaw and a host of other symbols. This performance was an extraordinary pantomimic achievement and Benny recognized it as comedy creation of the highest order. None of their contemporaries had written anything that approached it in quality. And for many years my brother used the 'chairback' routine as a touchstone of excellence. When he had produced something of which he was proud, he would ask plaintively, 'How does it compare with the "Chairback"?' 'It's good,' I would answer, 'but not that good.'

A silk dressing-gown, such as he wore in his army act, was in poor taste in the working men's clubs. They had a strict sense of propriety, so Benny bought himself a second-hand dinner-jacket in Soho and wore that on-stage for years. The working men's clubs were well-ordered establishments, sometimes expensively equipped with modern stages, curtains, footlights, sidelights

and spotlights. The backcloth was the usual reassuring
oak tree, sprouting local advertisements. Many clubs
closed the bar in deference to the 'concert', but all
entertainers had to adapt to noisier conditions in some
places. Benny swears that he never had any trouble,
never witnessed any violence or even bad behaviour
while he was performing. Once he noticed a mother
breast-feeding in the audience. 'After you with that,
kid,' he called to the baby. 'You'll be lucky!' replied
the young mother. 'Ooh, I do hope so,' prayed Benny,
with one of his looks. As he says, you've got to keep
coming back at 'em!

In those days, the working men's clubs did not go in
much for stag nights and agreed on an unwritten code
of practice understood by all the entertainers. Benny,
of course, bent it as far as he could without offending.
He would introduce himself as coming from Southampton, where his family shipped cattle. 'We shipped nine
thousand bulls last year. We're the biggest bull shippers
in the business. Nine thousand young bulls! I suppose
you think that's a lot of bullocks!'

Some very strange performers shared dressing-rooms
with my brother. There was The Mad Monk, a lug-
ubrious-looking mortuary attendant, who petrified his
audiences with displays of occult magic and terrified
his fellow-professionals with tales of cadavers. It seems
that he was stocktaking one night and had stood a stiff
'un in a corner when it stepped forward and embraced
him. He nearly had a heart attack. Apparently the body
was still stone dead, but rather lonely. Another interesting performer displayed a counting cockatoo. It was a
large, splendid and intelligent bird which could tell the
time and make simple calculations. Unfortunately, it bit
its owner's finger-joints from time to time. Speculation
ran rife among the profession as to how far the owner

would allow the cockatoo to mutilate his hands and whether at the moment of truth he would have enough strength left in his fingers to strangle the brute.

Benny was ready to perform at the drop of a silver coin. He always carried in his pocket a suede scrotum containing two grubby balls of 5 and 9 greasepaint. Our cousin Billy told me that he was walking with my brother one summer's evening in Hyde Park when Benny was approached by a casual acquaintance who apprised him of a few bobs' worth of work available immediately. Checking the address, Benny made his excuses and was off like a hare across the park after the job. My brother does not remember that particular incident but does recall that when he was still able to travel by tube he would sit and look up at the horizontal map opposite. He would read off the names of the stations, muttering to himself, 'Bin there, bin there, bin there!' Of well over two hundred stations in the system, he never found the name of a single one he had not used in his days working the clubs.

The life of a lower echelon performer had its heartaches. One time, Benny was booked at an obscure club in south London. He was told that the concert was a musical evening, so would he please bring his guitar. Looking handsome in his dinner-suit, carrying his guitar and a light summer raincoat, he walked the six miles from Cricklewood, where he lived then, down the Edgware Road to the Embankment. There he spent his last few pence on a tube to Kennington and tramped further from there. When he arrived at the club, the musical evening was in full swing – an accordionist leading a sing-song and the tiny changing-room encumbered with a xylophone, a ventriloquist's dummy and their respective owners. The Insect was absent, leaving his deputy with a sheet of paper and his best wishes. The sheet of paper, on which was written the running order of the concert, made no mention of Benny Hill. When my brother made a fuss, the club's treasurer was called in and ruled that no booking had been made. However, as there was a good crowd present, he decided that Benny could go on last, sing a couple of comic songs and earn his oncer.

The young humorist, feeling distinctly unhumorous, sat waiting in the changing-room, tuning his guitar. The other acts appeared to be doing two spots each and an encore. At last, Benny heard the bar closing and the rumble of feet. He rushed to the side of the stage to see the audience going home. When he grabbed the deputy Insect, the silly beggar said, 'Well, they've got buses to catch.' 'I haven't got a tosser for bus fare,' shouted Benny. 'Where's my fee?' 'No show, no pay. I only had three envelopes,' replied the official. 'They've been given out – and the Treasurer has gone home. So has everyone else. I can't authorize payment.' 'How am I going to get home?' queried Benny. 'Sorry, mate. That's not my business.' There was nothing for it but to lump it.

So Benny began the ten-mile walk home. He was wearing his summer coat, carrying his guitar and at his most exposed, in the middle of Waterloo Bridge, when a storm broke. The rain sloshed down, soaking his head, swamping his clothes and dissolving the cardboard soles of his cheap shoes. His guitar case was awash with the bilge that gathered from the many holes in the canvas. He struggled on through the deserted Strand, feeling cold rivulets running down his back and hearing the squelch of his pathetic shoes at each step. Deep rumbles from his stomach reminded him that he had not eaten since breakfast. The sky grew even blacker as he entered Piccadilly Circus. The strain was getting

to him. His body ached all over. He was sure he had
caught influenza, if not something worse. He had no
money – and no prospects. He was soaking wet and
shivering. Could things be worse? At that moment, a
young tart leapt out of a dark doorway and, playfully
chucking him under the chin, cried 'Hello, cheeky!'

It had been clear from the first that the working
men's clubs were no stairway to stardom. With luck,
they would pay the bills until better chances presented
themselves. At that time, however, the short cut to
national stardom was the radio. Benny had been worrying away at the problem since that first CSE celebration
party. He now saw just the opening he needed in the
weekly Thursday-night broadcast on the Light Programme from the Camberwell Palace. The radio show,
'Variety Roundabout', was an edited version of the variety bill offered twice nightly on the stage. If he could
win a booking for a week at the Camberwell Palace he
stood a good chance of a spot in the radio show. 'The
comedian with a personality like sunshine,' as he now
described himself, urged two agents, Phil Brown and
Joe Collins, to try for him. They were both successful.
Phil Brown persuaded the Canadian impresario Carroll
Levis, who was responsible for putting on the show, to
give Benny a favourable audition, and Joe Collins (Joan
Collins's father) received a letter from Levis accepting
the young comic. From his weekly salary of ten pounds,
Benny was happy to give each agent ten per cent.

But Brown was not happy that Benny was employing
another agent. He called Benny into his office and gave
him a vitriolic dressing-down. Benny was horrified by
such a reaction. After all, he had no contract with
Brown and was quite willing to pay the man his fee.
But Brown was not to be mollified and continued to
browbeat his client with threats of destroying his career

before it had begun. 'I felt like a dog that was being held down and beaten,' said Benny at the time. Brown's loss of control was most unwise. Though Brown tried many times later to establish a business relationship between them, Benny never forgave him.

When I saw my brother's show from the stalls of the Camberwell Palace, he looked good and registered well. In his first radio broadcast, on 3 September 1947, he made his mark in four minutes. After a hilarious first three minutes, Benny announced – 'On a serious note, ladies and gentlemen, I shall now give you Abraham Lincoln's Gettysburg address. Lincoln's Gettysburg address – "345a, Main Street, Gettysburg!" ' It brought the house down. Eric Spear, the producer, was delighted with him. Benny immediately pressed home his advantage. He made an appointment to see Spear the next day at his office. 'You're very keen, aren't you?' said the producer dryly. 'Yes, I am,' confessed Benny. At which, Spear immediately arranged an audition with Joy Russell-Smith, who presented the prestigious Sunday-lunchtime 'Variety Bandbox'. The lady liked Benny's style, and a month later, on 3 October, the Hampshire comic broadcast to a huge radio audience on the same bill as the popular ventriloquist act Peter Brough and Archie Andrews. Benny's spot was well received, and, as he hoped for more broadcasts, he felt he should polish his image. Consequently, he disassociated his name, Benny Hill, from the scrabbling world of club entertainment. But he still needed the erratic income from such jaunts, so he called himself Bob Job when entertaining at working men's clubs.

In another endeavour to make a name for himself, Benny began to contribute a humorous column with his own byline to *Show World*, a cheap weekly entertainment magazine. He was never paid for the articles in which he had fun with a fresh topic each week. Nowadays he modestly dismisses them as 'throwaway material'. I think they were a lot better than that. So does Bob Monkhouse, who is himself a maestro in such matters. I once met a well-known comedian, who confessed that he had collected the columns and used them for the basis of an act in the US. He told me he was so pleased with the scripts that he wanted more, but could not find writers in the States to produce that quality of work. Of all the persiflage Benny concocted for *Show World*, I remember only his insistence that 'A healthy musical diet should include plenty of Paul Vitamin and Cab Calorie.'

Another of Benny's ploys to get noticed was to hustle his way into *Spotlight*, an intimate revue at the Twentieth Century Theatre, Notting Hill Gate. If he was paid anything at all for the two performances, he was lucky. Few members of the cast actually received a salary. The point was that appearance in the show meant that the deadly Catch-22 could be sprung. 'Come and see me working in *Spotlight*!' the young hopeful could say triumphantly.

Intimate revue was so called to distinguish it from shows that celebrated 'the frails from the Follies', as Eugene O'Neill called showgirls. Since it was a middle-class entertainment, Benny knew that he could not use his club act as it stood: the audience would not accept it raw. But it was sound material and would be unfamiliar to the punters. So he sent it up, giving his privileged audience a glimpse of the abysmal service concert party sometimes inflicted on the troops.

Benny opened his spot as the Dreadful Dancing Sisters, suffering from foot and mouth disease – 'Hello, hello! How do you do you do?' Then an alcoholic baritone in a strangulated 'Pale Hands I Love', introducing the impressionist with a genuinely popular bit – Peter Lorre seeking the help of psychiatrist Sidney Greenstreet.

LORRE: Help me, doctor. Help me. All the time I
see these green lizards. They are everywhere.
They are all over me. I tear them off my coat.
They come back. I tear them off my sleeve.
They come back. I keep tearing them off!
GREENSTREET: Well, stop throwin' them all over me!

Benny then went into an exaggerated Cockney version of his club act as the concert party's principal comedian. The public-school punters loved it.

It was all there, even then – the essential Benny Hill. He has developed, of course, since that first blossoming, refined his techniques, added some facial expressions. But Benny's early offering was so remarkable because it takes most comedians a lifetime of perfecting their craft to achieve the quality of performance he was giving then. For example, he made a reference to a contortionist in the concert party routine.

'She gets into some terrible tangles. What you call a pontoon performer. You never know whether she's going to stick, twist or bust! She puts one foot under one armpit and one foot under the other armpit and under the circumstances – ' Here he clasped his hands together, like Hitler, in front of his genitals. There was a sudden great burst of laughter that went on and on, but Benny was continuing his sentence. ' – she deserves every scrap of applause she gets.' This was an extension of Max Miller's technique. The Cheeky Chappie would come to the punch line of a story and, as the house roared, he would cry, 'Now, then – ' as if he were going to continue the tale. Benny has employed the *sotto voce* extension ever since. It is valuable because it suggests that the comedian has been so funny he has been interrupted, it is playful, linking the audience and performer in a conspiracy of humour and, furthermore, something is still going on. It is significant that Jack Benny and Henny Youngman had great success using a few bars of violin music in a rather similar way.

Another young comedian whose witty patter registered strongly in the *Spotlight* revue was Bob Monkhouse. He met Benny for the first time at rehearsal and was much impressed by his extrovert personality. 'He was tremendously upbeat and outgoing,' says Bob. 'And, on stage, he knew exactly how to please the audience. He came over very well. It was much later, when I learned of his many kindnesses, that I realized he was really a quiet, shy person. I believe my judgement as a young man was at fault. When I first met Benny, he was inventing himself, assuming a role that he has played throughout his life.'

His triumph at the Twentieth Century Theatre led Benny to feel that he was ready for the Windmill. After all, if Peter Waring's shaggy-dog story could raise a few chuckles, perhaps the concert party routine would do the same. So he wrote a new finish to the spot. It featured a spoof on two popular tenors of the time. One was so Jewish you could not believe it; the other so Irish he was practically green all over. Benny combined the Yiddisher schmaltz and the Irish blarney to hilarious effect. The resulting song was very funny. But not to Mr Van Damm, the proprietor, who sat on his own in the dark at the back of the Windmill stalls. 'Thank you. Next, please.' He had a reputation for picking stars-to-be, but turned down as many of today's topliners as he chose. Benny was probably lucky to have been passed over. When he was dating the Windmill beauty Doris Deal, she told him she had seen resident comedians burst into tears when leaving the stage after five minutes of hostility from the girl-crazy audience.

Still without a full-time agent, Benny wangled a week at Collins' Music Hall, Islington (where, I am sure, the ghost of G. P. was watching from the third row stalls, on the aisle). A fortnight later he was at the massive Kilburn Empire, where his previous commanding officer, Colonel Richard Stone, came with an associate to watch him. Stone, now a theatrical agent, was there on business. He was helping the impresario Hedley Claxton cast his 1948 summer season revue at the Lido Theatre, Cliftonville, Margate. They had pencilled in the principal comedian, Reg Varney, an extremely funny performer, and were looking for a straight man (to feed Reg in the double-act) and comedy support. Stone, who knew that Benny was short on variety experience as a comedian, thought that the ex-driver would do nicely. Claxton thought so too. But they had another name on their shortlist – Peter Sellers, a young impressionist they wanted to see working before they came to a decision. Benny Hill or Peter Sellers, what a choice! After he had seen Peter working, Claxton could still not make up his mind. When I caught Peter's act, his Red Indian reporter had me in stitches. He was, he said, the London correspondent of *The Pawnee Graphic*.

Finally, it came down to a High Noon audition between the two young comics. Benny knew that Peter would probably bring his ukulele and lead with his knock-out George Formby. My brother decided to counterpunch by singing a humorous calypso to his guitar. The calypso was then becoming fashionable but neither Benny nor I had heard a truly English version of that exotic lyrical structure. He proceeded to write funny verses for it, but felt that the song needed a political reference, as with many authentic calypsos. My contribution seemed to satisfy him:

We have two Bev'ns in our Cabinet.
Aneurin's the one with the gift of the gab in it.
The other Bev'n is the taciturnist;
He knows the Importance of Being Ernest!

The calypso did it. Claxton chose Benny. A few signatures in a few minutes settled matters for years. Stone became Benny's lifetime agent. And Claxton signed the Saucy Boy at £14 a week for three summer seasons at the seaside. Claxton never made a better deal in his life.

As had been arranged beforehand, the winner bought the coffee and cake. Benny met Peter in Velotti's café immediately afterwards, where they exchanged addresses and promised to pass on job opportunities and other useful information.

Now that Benny's future was more settled, there was nothing for it but to go to Paris immediately. He simply had to see the Little Sparrow, the incomparable Edith Piaf, in person. I was elected organist – I organized the trip, and booked the pair of us into a small hotel on the Quai de la Mégisserie amid a welter of flower stalls and caged birds. The hotel, in the songwriter and producer Eric Maschwitz's memorable phrase, 'smelled of the three g's – Garlic, Gauloises and the Gents'. Its plumbing arrangements had us in hysterics. Half-way up the curved well of the stairway, a tiny secret handle opened a wall-papered door to reveal a small priest-hole – the lavabo. Neither of us had much money, so we ate from the markets and enjoyed the cheaper delights of Paris – the Eiffel Tower, the bâteaux

mouches, Montmartre and Le Concert Mayol. At the
latter, Benny fell in love with Magda, one of the stars
of the show, and I experienced a rare *frisson* when an
ample, naked lady tripped on the catwalk and all but
descended on me in a shower of gold.

One day, Benny heard a snatch of French accordion
music that he liked. He thought he would write some
verses to it, if he could buy a copy. So we found a
music shop and Benny sang a snatch of the tune to
the proprietor, who shook his head. *'Non,'* I said, *'ça
va – la, La, la – O'ah, o'ah, oh – ah – ah!'* 'That's it,' cried
Benny and repeated it. *'Non,'* said the proprietor. 'You
must know it,' insisted Benny, *'ça va – la, La – la – O'ah,
o'ah, oh – ah – '*

'Maman!' called the proprietor, looking upstairs,
'connais-tu "La, La – la – O'ah, o'ah, oh – ah?" '

'Qu'est-ce que c'est?' asked Maman. The proprietor
repeated the song. Then came Maman's voice from
above. *'La, La – la, Oh – ah! Mais oui! C'est "Ma Pomme"
par Maurice Chevalier!'* And so it was. Benny bought a
copy then and there. 'What a great number!' I said.
'What a great sketch!' he said. And so it proved.

My brother and I decided to spend one evening apart.
As we left the hotel, Benny said, 'Funny if we should
both wind up with the same bird.' Not that night, but
we did the next evening. She was a tiny figure in a severe
black dress, and she looked like one of our aunts. But
she was Piaf – and on that occasion she had not been
singing long before she owned the stage of the ABC,
she owned the theatre and she owned Paris. We two
innocents had never heard anything like it. The raw
feelings that evoked such shattering responses in us
were totally alien to the tradition of pleasant ballads we
were used to. We were stunned by a series of profound
experiences, not so much songs as revelations, that left

us limp until, at last, we stumbled out to the boulevard, trying to disguise from each other the extent of our emotional disarray.

On the final day we sang Charles Trenet's 'Au Revoir, Paris' (Benny harmonizing) most of the way back to Le Havre. Aboard the ferry, we discovered that tourist class meant double bunks in a dormitory for men. Struck by its likeness to a barrack-room, Benny went straight into the foul-mouthed macho monologue of the solitary squaddie posted to a new unit. The purpose of the verbal exercise is to establish that the newcomer is not one to be treated with disrespect. ' "Sod you!" I said,' roared Benny. ' "I'm not carrying that!" I said. "My name's Simpson – not Samson. I need nourishment not punishment." He said "Pick that bleedin' lot up or you're on a charge!" So I went round the back of the hut and took me boot off and put it on me fist. When he came rahnd for me, I smashed him in the mush wiv it. Then I put me boot back on and joined me mates. Hospital case. Nobody let on. It was a mystery, see? So that's why I've been sent to this shower here in the arse'ole of the world!'

The old soldiers among the passengers recognized the situation and laughed at Benny's improvisation. But the others smiled wanly and did not know how to react to his pithy comments when he inspected their bunks. The pantomime ended abruptly when the ferry began to rock and the Hill brothers made a dash for the loos, there to sit in nauseated stupor until we arrived back at Southampton.

It was on the trip to Paris that Benny told me of his feelings about our family. He hardly needed to as we had both suffered from the Captain's contemptuous attitude, but we had suffered in silence. This time my brother complained in such explicit language that I was

taken aback. I felt that it was improper of him to speak
so bitterly of his father. It was my duty as the elder
brother to reprove him. Which I did, although he knew
I shared his sentiments. Much later, he reminded me of
this act of hypocrisy when I made similar comments
about the Captain in the same terms.

Following his successful spot in 'Variety Bandbox',
Benny was signed up for eight weekly broadcasts playing character parts in a satirical radio series, 'Listen,
My Children'. He was the youngest member of 'an
experiment, being a comedy programme which plays
to no studio audience and is based on fairly subtle
humour'. This worthy endeavour was accompanied by
big-band avant-garde jazz. Despite a lack of audience
response, the BBC produced a second series of similar
format. With a virtual monopoly of the airwaves and
no ratings competition, the Corporation could afford
to try again.

This time the cast included not only my brother
but the team who later became the Goons – Michael
Bentine, Harry Secombe, Spike Milligan and Peter
Sellers. The series was called 'Third Division', the
first comedy show to be broadcast on the new Third
Programme wavelength that served those who enjoyed
good music and were interested in culture generally.
Audience research indicated that they resided mainly
in Wales. The BBC establishment was shocked by that
discovery, which would surprise no one today. We have
long since grown used to the typical Englishman's
response – 'Whenever I hear the word "culture", I
reach for my Pistols Album.'

Written by Frank Muir and Denis Norden, 'Third Division' had an astringent quality which intrigued the few
who gave it their attention. However, it was so deter-
minedly an ensemble effort that it denied any attempt

by the listener to identify individual comedians. For Benny, holding his own in such lively company could only mean a sharpening of his wits.

He was given another lesson in performance technique at about the same time when the American comedian Danny Thomas made his long-awaited visit to the London Palladium. It was a lesson Benny never forgot. He can still reproduce perfectly Thomas's slightly sibilant delivery of his opening – 'Ladies and gentlemen, there's a rumour going around that I'm a big Hollywood star, over here on a goodwill tour. Nothing could be further from the truth. I'm here for the money and I want you to like me. On the posters they have billed me as America's foremost comic – so it's understandable that when I come out here, you are saying to yourself – "Go ahead, foremost me!" I'm not that big. I have a comfortable little home. Well, to tell you the truth, Louis B. Mayer owns the place next to mine. His fence runs alongside my place. His house is four miles up the road but his fence is next to mine.'

What Benny found so refreshing was Thomas's modesty and sincerity. He was self-deprecating in a most endearing way. My brother had never before heard such comments. Stories that were clearly true or, at least, plausible. For instance, Thomas confessed that in the US he appeared on the Procter and Gamble radio show, advertising soap. 'Mr Procter and Mr Gamble, two nicer men you could not wish to meet, but their company sells three kinds of lotion that grows hair. So why are Mr Procter and Mr Gamble both as bald as a billiard ball?' asked Thomas reasonably.

Benny spent several evenings in a front centre stalls seat and was rewarded by a personal acknowledgement from the great raconteur. He was also reassured that his own method of using actual behaviour and real situations as a basis for comedy was in line with the American sage's philosophy. There was nothing of the outlandish premise of 'The Englishman, the Irishman and the Scotsman' about the down-to-earth tales told by Danny Thomas.

I was delighted when I learned that Benny, who had never set eyes on him, was teamed for the summer season with Reg Varney, whom I had met in Hong Kong and had seen a few times in Britain. Reg was, and remains, one of my favourite comics. I knew he had a couple of sure-fire comedy acts and was a talented musician as well. When he came on stage, a tiny figure in a green Wolf Cub's cap, with his spindly legs dangling below a great green jersey, he made a hilarious entrance. He could just stand there, little eyes blinking over his pink, turned-up nose and Joe E. Brown grin, and the audience would rock. In his other act, he played a ventriloquist's dummy better than anyone. He was more like a dummy than most dummies. And he would screw his head right round. 'I was doin' this the other night, and me bloomin' head fell off!' he'd say and giggle. It was the most infectious giggle I have ever heard. The audience would respond to it and Reg would laugh with them. After that they ate out of his hand. It was that giggle. Reg insists that it was genuine, that every night he laughed at the same place. He swears he has never done a cod dry-up in his life. I am inclined to think that the giggle owed more to art than to spontaneity, but contrived or not it certainly broke up the audience.

Reg reminds me that when Benny brought him home to meet the Captain for the first time, I was pleased to see him again and picked up the whisky bottle to give him a welcoming drink. My father pulled the bottle out of my hand, crying, 'Give him some. Don't mess about! The man wants a drink!' and with an expansive gesture poured Reg the smallest whisky that he had ever seen.

At that time Hedley Claxton's *Gaytime* was being run in on the south coast, before settling in for the summer season at Cliftonville, Kent. Of course, the title had not the connotation it has nowadays and the whole cast could happily sing the opening chorus without giving it a second thought:

> Gaytime, let's have a gaytime;
> Gaytime, let's have some fun!
> Say so long to trouble and care,
> Let your troubles fly like bubbles
> Way up in the air!

As the producer, Claxton took overall responsibility for the show. However, it was the scenery and particularly the costumes that were his delight. Benny would give us a wicked imitation of Hedley's lisping excitement – 'Oh, Reg, you've never sheen anything sho lovely, the shequinsh on the dreshesh in the ballroom schene!' On the other hand, the sketches provided for the comedians were, shall we say, traditional:

'Tell her, with feeling. No, not with the hands, you fool! She's a titled lady. Address her correctly.'
'Pardon?'
'Say, "Your Grace".'
'For what we are about to receive – '

Luckily, Benny was able to refurbish the ancient scripts and create new sketches of his own for the comedy duo. He was also a superb straight man. Reg recognized Benny's importance to the show by insisting on

sharing the star dressing-room with him. There they
confessed to each other that they had trouble sleeping
at night. Reg sought the help of a therapist, who taught
him a relaxation technique. It worked like a charm.
After a good night's sleep, Reg was keen to teach his
fellow-sufferer. Next bedtime Reg ordered Benny, in
his pyjamas, to lie flat on his back. 'Feel as though
you are falling through the bed. Now relax a little at
a time. Say after me – "Toes, toes, go to sleep!" '

'Toes, toes, go to sleep!'

'Fingers, fingers, go to sleep.'

'Fingers, fingers, go to sleep!'

'Legs, legs, go to sleep.'

'Legs, legs, go to sleep.'

'Arms, arms, go to sleep.'

'Arms, arms, go to sleep. Reg.'

'Yes?'

'Sod off. I'm knackered.'

When *Gaytime* reached the Royal Theatre, Bournemouth, the Captain brought Mum to see their younger
son performing. Benny had an early comedy spot of his
own and acted as Reg Varney's straight man as well.
Top of the bill were The Radio Revellers, a name act
brought in by the management to boost takings. After
the show the folks went back-stage to see Benny and
Reg in the dressing-room they shared. As they entered,
Mum was introduced to Hedley Claxton. He positively
glowed as she congratulated him on the beautiful costumes and scenery in his show.

The Captain, however, would have none of that.
Ignoring the contributions of the producer, the principal comedian and his own son, he opened up: 'They're
marvellous aren't they – The Radio Revellers? Real talent. You can spot it a mile off. No wonder they're the
top of the bill. You can play them anywhere. In any

language. To young and old. A class act. You've got to
hand it to them . . . ' And he went on and on, while the
rest of them stood about like the proverbial. As soon as
she could decently take her leave, Mum dragged away
the Captain, who from first to last offered no word of
appreciation to any member of the *Gaytime* company.

10

Saturday Night and Sunday Morning

Richard Stone is not at all the stereotype of the noisy, cigar-chomping theatrical agent. Erect and silver-haired, he is the very model of a modern major-general, a rank well within his capabilities, one feels, had he chosen to stay in the army. A much-decorated fighting soldier, he founded Combined Services Entertainment at the end of the war, an organization that entertains service personnel and civilians alike all over the world.

He is disarmingly frank about Benny's early days as a performer. 'I have to admit that I was more concerned about Reg Varney,' he confesses. 'It is an admission from an old man, after forty years of looking after Benny, who's been wonderfully loyal to me, but honestly in those days it was Reg Varney who was my star and Benny was only his feed. I was young and inexperienced and I don't think I knew that Benny Hill was going to be a big star. I think it is wonderful that Benny is still with me to this day, when he must know that, in those days, I was pushing Reg Varney. I was going down to the Lido at Cliftonville in my little Morris Eight with all the big impresarios from London to see Reg Varney.'

One of those impresarios was Bernard Delfont, now Lord Delfont. 'I well remember going to see Reg Varney, who was very popular,' he says. 'It was the first time I had seen his stooge, Benny Hill. I couldn't take my eyes off Benny. He had a kind of personal magnetism. For no reason I could understand, my eyes always focused on him. He had charisma. I felt it immediately. I thought to myself – this fellow shows great promise, I must watch him. So I took an interest in his career from the moment I saw him – and as soon as he was free, he starred for me in *Paris by Night* at the Prince of Wales Theatre. But I never expected that he would become so successful so quickly.'

As soon as *Gaytime* opened in 1948 at its summer home in Cliftonville, a pleasant residential adjunct to Margate, it became a smash hit. There were obvious reasons for its success. It was a well-run show, ideal for its venue. Reg, a cheeky young Cockney, was the perfect choice for Margate, traditionally the London day-trippers' favourite watering-place. Fresh and funny in his solo act, he made a devastating double with Benny as support. Then there were the sketches. Between them the young comedians put together five sketches a show, for five shows, twenty-five sketches in all. *Gaytime* was produced as a repertory of five entirely different revues, so that a family spending a fortnight in Cliftonville could see five shows. But it was the phenomenal rapport between Reg and Benny upon which the success was built. My brother, as a straight man, not only sustained, encouraged and provoked Reg, but he understood the principal comic's talents so much that he was able to write material that developed Reg as a comedian. The new sketches gave the Cockney lad something extra to work with and he made the most of them.

The best-loved of the routines was probably 'What the Deuce', in which Reg appeared dressed like the popular French tennis star Suzanne Lenglen, bandeau about the head, two long kiss-curls on his cheeks and frilly drawers well below his skirt. This pathetic little creature bounded on stage, swinging her racket in an agony of shyness for her first lesson with the handsome tennis instructor. The audience would howl for ages, without any need for dialogue. Benny, as the instructor, would stand quite still regarding the nervous newcomer, who bounced her ball, coughed and flirted timidly in a paroxysm of displaced activity. 'Benny was fantastic,' says Reg. 'He let me have it all. He gave me time and space. And I used it. I improvised – and added bits every night. People don't understand. They say, "Benny just stood there and did nothing." But he did nothing superbly. He registered. It would not have been half as funny without him. I needed to bounce everything off him. He was a good-looking boy – and he made a smashing tennis instructor. But above all, he was a great professional – and he waited and waited – and gave me every chance to get laughs.'

Together, they milked the whole male/female bit. The instructor becomes exasperated and says too much. The little girl is upset. She cries. She sobs. When he apologizes and lays his hand on her shoulder she shrugs it off. He soft-soaps her. She relents. And when it came to the game, Benny's dialogue did not miss a trick.

'Your service, Daphne.'

'Beg pardon?'

'Balls to you!'

By the time the tennis balls were flying about the auditorium, the routine was a riot. They talk about the Tennis Sketch in Margate to this day.

Within a few weeks of his debut, Reg was King of Cliftonville, opening bazaars, judging beauty competitions, awarding prizes, patronizing parties. The fact that he lived with his pretty wife and baby daughter in a new bungalow a few miles away did him no harm at all. Everybody in town wanted to shake his hand. News of the local acclaim brought Reg offers of West End stardom. But he was already under contract to Claxton. When

it became known that *Gaytime* was to be at the Lido
for another two summers, holidaymakers began to book
up ahead. Cliftonville took the young performers to its
heart. However, Claxton had plans for Benny to join his
Gaytime company at Newquay in Cornwall the following
summer.

The Lido was an open, spacious, informal theatre, with
long bars ever ready to serve. It was so conducive to
an easy-going, friendly atmosphere that sometimes the
cast would persuade the audience to join them in a
huge conga round the auditorium. Another custom that
I never saw in any other theatre or with any other show
was the presentation of drinks, after the interval, along the
front of the stage. Members of the audience would bring
a libation from the bar to join the line of glasses offered
for Reg's refreshment. He would appear to knock them
all back – whiskies, sherries, beers – during the second
half and kid the audience that he was fully lubricated by
the finale. In fact, he would sip from each glass, often to
loud cheers, which he would then place to the rear of a
box stool he would occasionally sit upon. 'Whenever the
tabs closed,' he chuckles, 'the stagehands would be at
my drinks like lunatics.' Occasionally, during a scene, a
child would walk to the front and offer him an ice-cream
cornet, which he might well use as a custard pie.

Most nights, after the show, there was a great crowd
round the stage door, sometimes chanting for Reg. He
often had to be escorted to his waiting car. Sometimes
he would be forced to sneak out of the front entrance.
It was no press agent's set-up: the crowd was made up
of genuine fans. They tore three suits off his back during
the years he was at the Lido.

After the hectic summer season of 1948, Benny returned
to London and moved in with two friends, Bill and June,
in Cricklewood. He enjoyed his stay at their house, but

June was in show-business too, and travelled a good deal.
This led to domestic difficulties with which Benny felt
he could not become involved. He moved to a room
with another couple nearby, where the situation was
considerably worse. He was the single lodger and a war
between the husband and wife raged around him as if
he was not present. Once they were adequately stoked
up, the quarrelsome pair paid not the slightest attention
to him. Missiles flew past him from both sides. However
uncomfortable it was at the time, his predicament inspired
a hilarious sketch in which he played the innocent lodger
for one of his BBC shows.

He moved on to a lodging-house in Finsbury Park,
north London, where the boarders were offered very
plain fare. However, the landlady, who ate in her kitchen,
enjoyed a richer diet. She was frequently at table and
whenever a boarder passed to use the bathroom, she
would put her arm round her plate and cry, 'You're not
'avin' any. Get away! You're not 'avin' any!'

It must be borne in mind that from time to time Benny
lived in Dickensian conditions because he was earning
a salary that allowed him no leeway. His next stop was
Mrs Birkitt's Victorian house in Kilburn, where half a
dozen lodgers occupied as many rooms. The Widow
Birkitt made her philosophy clear the first evening when
she pointed out a rape case reported in the newspaper.
'I don't know why men bother these poor girls,' she said
to Benny, 'when there's scores of older women ready to
accommodate them.'

Mrs Birkitt was accommodating a young Irish
labourer who was, of course, her favourite. Benny
had not been there long when someone broke the
lavatory cistern. Mrs Birkitt was so angry that, when
her lodgers came in from work, she threatened to turn
them all out without a bite to eat. Remembering her

young Irish lover, Benny much later wrote a monologue about it, which he performed on television. It ended:

> The others all turned white,
> But I said, 'I'll be all right.
> Landladies up the street I know
> Could use some extra lovin'.
> I'll not be homeless long
> Cos I'm virile and I'm strong!'
> She said, 'I'm not talking to you,
> Your dinner's in the oven!'

Hidden in the heart of residential Chelsea was a tiny theatre, the Boltons, which every year produced a prestigious revue introducing new talent. Considerable distinction but very little financial reward was conferred on those artists chosen for the show. They were paid £7 a week. Benny's confident audition won him a place one winter in the company. But his particular spot would need careful thought. Fashionable London patronized the little revue; important people would be seeing him for the first time.

Fascinated, as ever, by relationships between the sexes, Benny began to think along the lines of 'Marriage à la Mode'. He was intrigued by the contrast between courtship behaviour and the indifference that could set in after marriage. What about a young man visiting the cinema with his lady (imagined of course) before and after marriage – buying a box of chocolates before and reluctantly sharing peanuts after? There would be plenty of opportunities for making fun. The pantomime would include a little dialogue of course. And to give some piquancy for the educated audience, it could be in French. Benny worked on the skit, polished it and performed it with verve at the dress rehearsal.

Unfortunately, he then discovered that a talented comedienne called Marcella Saltzer planned to present her entire monologue, 'Walking the Dog', in French. Obviously, the two spots clashed. They could not both be included in the one programme. Benny immediately offered to withdraw his skit and returned home to write another.

The next day, the German eccentric Toto, ears splayed by his jammed bowler hat, made his first appearance on an English stage. Speaking his own brand of half-German jargon, Toto explained some of the complexities of life in the Fatherland. British visitors complained of the sound of trains all night. It was not the sound of trains but of speedy rebuilding. Polite German workers were passing along the bricks. 'Bitte schön, danke schön, bitte schön, danke schön, bitte schön, danke schön!'

Benny had devised his hilarious 'Deutschspeak' while with the REME in Germany. He used it constantly to amuse his comrades. Despite his low rank, he had been put in charge of prisoners of war because of his fluency in the language. He made friends with many of them and their long chats together paid off at the Boltons. His audiences there were enthusiastic and the critics appreciative. Godfrey Winn, an important journalist of the time, gave him a glowing review.

One day, for the Saturday matinée, the three front rows of seats were removed and replaced by a throne and armchairs. A 'No Admittance' sign appeared on the loo door. Queen Mary, the grandmother of the present Queen, and her ladies-in-waiting came to see the revue. Beforehand, it had been delicately suggested to Benny that he should omit his description of a lady's figure as 'kleine Sitzen und grossen Titzen'. He substituted, 'kleine Kürzen und grossem Burzem'.

After the show, the cast nervously lined up to shake hands with the *grande dame*. She offered her gloved hand to each performer in turn but spoke to no one until she came to Benny at the end of the line. In Edith Evans tones she said, 'Young man, I thought you were most amusing.' 'Thank you, ma'am.' Eyes down for a full house, he says. You can tell how pleased he was.

At another matinée performance, a less welcome visitor came to see the show. Phil Brown was the agent who had threatened to destroy Benny. When my brother caught sight of his hostile presence in the stalls, his performance went to pieces. He began to gabble and forgot his lines. He gasped and could not catch his breath. He stumbled off the stage with the best grace he could muster and drank a double whisky at the bar to get him back in trim for the finale. This unpleasant experience began a long and painful struggle with stage fright that Benny has never entirely overcome.

In the autumn of 1948, Benny teamed up with a rising young comedian, Alfred Marks, to provide the comedy interludes in Geraldo's 'Starlight Hour', a series of musical shows on prime-time radio. He played Scrubber, a simple-minded foil to Marks's 'wide boy'. This new comedy duo created some attention, not least among the girls, who raved about Marks's sexy, dark-brown voice. One of his female admirers invited Alfred to a party, but he was unable to attend. Not knowing my brother very well, he did not pass on the invitation to Benny. A few weeks later, after being signed to star in *Montmartre* at the Grand Theatre, Brighton, Alfred was asked to consider a bright new talent, Paddie O'Neil, as his leading lady. When he arrived at New Cross Empire where she was working, he discovered that it was she who had invited him to the party. They fell in love at

first sight and have been happily married ever since.
'But,' says Alfred, 'if I had passed on the invitation,
Paddie might now be Mrs Benny Hill.'

Alfred and Paddie made *Montmartre* the outstanding
success of the summer season, and in the autumn
of 1949, Reg Varney and Benny took it out on tour.
Charles Reading, the producer, had created a beautiful
show and the boys added their own brand of humour. I
recall that Reg gave one musical scene a touch of class
by playing bluesy jazz on the harmonium.

Benny had spent the summer of 1949 at Newquay,
where Hedley Claxton hoped that a partnership with
comedian Ron Clark would boost the chances of the
Cornish version of *Gaytime*. According to our cousin
Maurice, who saw the show, the pair were very popular.
'I picked Benny up from the theatre in my two-seater
Lagonda,' says Maurice, 'to take him to lunch. As a
friend was sitting alongside me, Benny had to make
do with the dickey-seat at the back. He insisted that I
drive slowly around town. Before I knew what was happening, he was standing up and waving to the crowds.
"Whatever are you doing?" I shouted. "Acknowledging
my fans," Benny replied, gesturing like royalty!'

Weekends were particularly hectic that season. Benny
was broadcasting with Elsie and Doris Waters and Max
Wall in 'Petticoat Lane', a radio variety show based on
the famous London street market. When the curtain
came down on the Saturday-night performance of
Gaytime at Newquay, Benny raced by taxi from the
Atlantic coast across the hills of Cornwall to catch
the sleeper train at Exeter. Arriving on Sunday morning
at Paddington he took a taxi to the People's Palace,
Mile End Road, in the East End. There the show
was rehearsed and broadcast. As soon as his stint
was finished, Benny made the return journey, arriving

back in Newquay just in time for the Monday morning run-through.

Each variety act booked for 'Petticoat Lane' featured a stallholder. Benny thought he had made a shrewd choice when he chose to sell 'Books and Sheet Music' from his pitch. An infinite number of titles were available to use in his patter. However, he discovered that the music-hall performers Elsie and Doris Waters had been even shrewder; as 'Gert and Daisy', they chatted to each other inconsequentially as if they were still in their kitchen. No structure or even reference to the market was necessary: 'Did I tell you that Bert had bought a second-hand bicycle?'

As a writer Benny felt that such random chatter saved a great deal of time and thought. While he remained with Reg, Benny whipped up half a dozen such routines, which, as 'Bill and 'Arry', they broadcast on 'Henry Hall's Guest Night' and other radio variety shows. Later, he was reminded of those routines by the Pete and Dud exchanges between Peter Cook and Dudley Moore and, later still, the Smith and Jones talking heads. *Plus ça change, plus c'est la même chose.*

Television broadcasting got under way in Britain in 1949, and Benny and Reg soon made their television début together at Alexandra Palace (known as Ally Pally) in a revue called, 'Here's Mud in Your Eye!' The title was justified by the finale when the cast threw cocoa goo at a sheet of glass in front of the camera lens. The show, however, was far from muddy, coming across as bright and crisp, with the boys very droll as a couple of hillbillies. The radio and television broadcasts brought Benny better-paid Masonic functions, club dinners and cine-variety (ten minutes of patter to break up a double-feature cinema programme). His most exciting venue in this period was the Albert

Hall, where he compèred a show associated with a cycling exhibition at Olympia. Making an entrance on a bicycle endeared him to the boisterous audience, who threw coins at him and floated fleets of paper darts, made out of exhibition brochures, from the galleries and boxes. Flushed with success, Benny entered into the spirit of the occasion. Meandering home later along Park Lane, he attracted the attention of a London bobby, who insisted on calling him a cab. 'I'm not a trouble-maker, officer,' Benny assured him. 'Of course not,' replied the bobby, as he helped my brother into the taxi; 'I'm well aware of that, Mr Hill.' Benny realized at last that he was beginning to make a name for himself.

He wondered if that name was to be the Hill of Varney and Hill when he joined forces with Reg once more in the 1950 edition of *Gaytime* at Cliftonville. Speculation and interest mounted as the Lido entertained a stream of show-business visitors from London. The professional trippers did not fail to notice that the two comedians had matured. The double was stronger than ever. For Varney and Hill the West End beckoned.

'In that last season,' Reg recalls, 'Benny was magnificent. It was a joy to work with him. I can see him now, so debonair, shooting his cuffs in feigned irritation. He used his eyes, his face, every muscle of his body – did all the voices! Benny was a marvellous feed – and such a brilliant writer. He came up with a boxing sketch for us that really was a knockout.' Every performance, Reg would swing a wild right that flung his boxing glove off his hand and out into the auditorium. One night the flying glove knocked out a young lady in the seventh row.

Another evening, when I was in the audience, Benny was knocked out, but not in the boxing sketch. He had just begun his seven-minute single spot when he started a joke told him by his Jewish friend, Harry Segal: 'There were these two Jewish fellers on a luxury cruise . . . ' A stentorian voice suddenly bellowed, 'We haven't paid to hear that kind of rubbish!' It was an interruption from the body of the hall so loud and clear that it could not be ignored. I knew that Benny had collected a dozen put-downs and wondered which one he would use in response. At the same time I was out of my seat, hurrying in a crouched position to find the heckler. 'It's only a gag,' I heard Benny say. 'Have I offended anyone else?' 'No!' shouted a hundred voices. 'Shall I continue?' 'Yes!' roared the audience. 'The liner began to sink,' went on Benny, 'and the two Jewish fellers found themselves swimming around in the ocean. "Can you float alone?" shouted one to the other. "Please, Maurice," replied his friend. "Don't talk business at a time like this!" ' There was a resounding burst of laughter and sustained sympathetic applause. My brother finished his act as I checked the aisles with two ushers, but there were no more interruptions. Benny received a tremendous ovation. 'Your support is most gratifying,' he said to the audience, and walked off the stage to faint right away, falling into Reg's arms.

Benny fell even harder a few weeks later when he fell desperately in love with a beautiful soubrette from another Margate show. She was special (good family; did not need the work; allowance from Daddy). Not like the girls he met 'on the wing'. I know because I was there, cycling over every Friday from my college in Folkestone to spend the weekend at Cliftonville. Nevertheless, he kept her well away from me. We were never introduced. Suddenly Benny appeared red-eyed after spending hours in the loo. It was clear that all was not well. He had dated the soubrette a few times and then proposed. By telephone. During the Saturday-evening interval at the Lido he had called her from a box on the front at Cliftonville and popped the question. She had promised to telephone his digs with her answer on Sunday morning. She had kept her promise and the answer was 'No'. Benny was devastated. He could not believe that she was already in love with somebody else. 'It was a terrible shock,' he says. 'I was so big-headed that I couldn't believe there could be anyone else. That affair really hit me. I had to call the doctor. I was almost suicidal.'

All I could do was to keep him fed and occupied – and remove all sharp instruments from his sight. Luckily, his stage work did not suffer. He was having problems with his single spot and that took his mind off his loss. But it has to be admitted that for a while he was, fundamentally, a pain. Benny says himself that he would stamp into the dressing-room, throw his things on the table and snap belligerently at Reg, 'Don't say a word! Don't speak to me. I don't want to talk. Let's just do the show. Not a word more!' They would put on their make-up in silence. The atmosphere became very gloomy for some weeks. It is to Reg Varney's credit that he has never said a word about it.

After a couple of months, Benny began to describe the whole episode as a narrow escape. 'Who needs to buy a book,' he would say, 'when they can use a library? Why should I make one woman miserable when I can make so many women happy?' That's what he said, anyway.

A little while later, the soubrette married a Dutch dentist – or 'a person of foreign extraction' as Benny described him. I tried to reassure my brother. 'One day,' I said, 'you'll smile at this whole affair.' 'She's smiling already,' replied Benny. 'Why should she be smiling?' I asked. 'She gets her teeth fixed for nothing,' he replied.

By the end of the 1950 season, Benny appeared to be himself once more and ready to move onward and upward. He was given an opportunity to do so when Varney and Hill were invited to take out *Sky High*, a successful revue from the London Palladium. Reg was signed for the tour to replace the youthful Jimmy Edwards, another post-war discovery, who had achieved a personal triumph with the Argyll Street audiences. Benny knew that such a lavish production would play the better houses, the Number Ones. *Sky High* was sky-high above the touring revues with which he had begun his career. Above it was stardom at the Palladium itself. This was his Big Chance. Benny would act as Varney's straight man only on condition that he was given his own seven-minute spot.

The producers of *Sky High*, George and Alfred Black, reluctantly agreed. They were doubtful about Benny's single and they were doubtful about the boxing sketch. It was clear that another comedy scene was needed to replace Jimmy Edwards's classroom chaos, but was mayhem in the ring really suitable? The Black brothers were given a chance to see for themselves when the sketch was staged as an extra item on a Saturday evening at the People's Palace in the Mile End Road.

It says much for Richard Stone's acumen as a theatrical agent that his entire stable of clients was working and paid that evening – Ian Wallace, as referee, Ian Carmichael, as second, Reg Varney as challenger and Benny Hill as the cauliflower-eared champion. It says much for Stone's judgement as a theatrical agent that his entire stable of clients became stars – Ian Wallace, of opera and the international concert hall, Ian Carmichael, of a score of films including *Lucky Jim* and *I'm All Right Jack*, Reg Varney, of television series such as *The Rag Trade* and *On the Buses*, and Benny Hill of global television comedy. With such a cast how could the boxing sketch go wrong? It was a riot. The Blacks loved it.

The tour of *Sky High* began in and around London. At the Chelsea Palace, still patronized by the fashionable crowd, Benny was surprised that his ovation was as thunderous as that accorded Reg at the finale. The Cockney comic always thoroughly deserved his enthusiastic reaction as he was a relatively unknown top-of-the-bill and could be depended upon to convulse the customers time after time, without fail. Word-of-mouth recommendation in each town ensured that *Sky High* played to packed houses later in the week.

At the Royal Theatre, Chatham, on a Saturday morning, Reg received the news of his father's death. He was desolated. 'I adored my dad,' he says, 'and I didn't know where I was or what was happening. I had to go on and be funny to a packed theatre first and second house Saturday night. I was lost; no idea of what to do. If anybody pulled me through, it was Benny. He was wonderful. He absolutely carried me through that show. Benny put his arm round me and said, "Don't worry. We'll do it." I'll never forget it. He can be very soft at times. Never showed emotion a lot, did he? But he is very loyal to people. Right there it is. I could hardly speak. Benny was as good as his word. He was marvellous – especially when we had to do the duelling scene. "What did you say?" he asked. And then he would say my line. Half the time he was talking to himself, but he got us through it somehow. We had a strange partnership, you know. We were never together during the day – not at Cliftonville, not on the road. We went our own ways. But when we were working, we had a kind of telepathy. I would look into his eyes and could tell what he was thinking. I could have cried when he left, I loved the feller.'

The further *Sky High* travelled from London, the greater difficulty Benny had with his solo of seven minutes. From his uproarious reception at the Chelsea Palace the tour could be viewed as a continuum of diminishing returns for his single spot. 'I was using smart, metropolitan comedy. It would not be recognized as such today, because that kind of humour is now part of our national cultural environment. We see it every night on our television. In 1950 very few punters north of Watford responded to it. They didn't even make sense of my pronunciation of the English language.'

The divide between the Saxons and the Danes had been accepted by travelling players for centuries. In the twentieth century, even as popular a London performer as Max Miller rarely ventured very far north of the capital. And, vice versa, when Frank Randall, a popular northern comedian, appeared at the Adelphi in the Strand, he was reduced to near apology for an act that was sensational on his own territory.

Benny's appearance and manner on that tour tended to subvert his chances of success with his solo offering. He was largely unknown, young and good-looking, not characteristics especially provocative of laughter. Throughout the show as straight man, he played the part of stern authority and he played it for all it was worth. 'I was continually pushing Reg about,' he says, 'snapping at him, "What do you think you're playing at? Get off the stage at once!" The audience knew me only in that role, so that when it came to my spot, they were puzzled at my attempts to raise laughs. They kept looking at the wings for Reg to come bouncing on.'

Reg had universal appeal. He was a funny-looking

comic. He had only to appear to evoke a roar. But the humour of initial appearance soon wears off. Reg was also a superb technician. He worked visually in broad strokes, using where necessary every foot of the stage. At this time Benny's approach was more intimate, through the spoken word. As responses became less encouraging, the approach, no doubt, grew more tentative, lacking in confidence. Plagued by stage fright, Benny probably displayed some nervousness. That is death to comedy, which is based on relaxed playfulness or, at least, a plausible semblance of that happy state.

Benny's efforts were not helped when he was struck by fibrositis in Northampton. The stiffness in his back and legs made his falls in the boxing sketch excruciatingly painful. Never an agile tumbler, he took ages to hit the floor. Every time he was knocked down, he descended in slow motion, his face working in real agony. It was probably his funniest bit in the show.

The evocation of laughter is not easy. It is unpredictable because so many imponderables are needed to create it. Benny would offer none of this to excuse his failure. He takes the view that it is the responsibility of the entertainer to entertain. If he fails, it is never the fault of the audience. Even a bar-room of hooligans will respond to a hooligan entertainer. Of the *Sky High* tour of the north, he says, 'At that time and place, I presented the wrong image, using the wrong material in the wrong language. Reg got laughs. I did not. Reg was funny. I was not.'

The end came, appropriately enough, at the Sunderland Empire, where so many comedians have died the death. That theatre was dreaded by southern funny men. They called it a comic's graveyard in the profession.

'I was alone in our dressing-room when I first heard

it,' says Reg. 'It seemed to me that Benny had only just left to go on. I had wished him good luck as I knew he was worried, and now he was getting the slow handclap. It was terrifying. There couldn't have been more than three or four people doing it to him, but it sounded dreadful. Then it stopped. A minute later Benny tottered in, ashen-faced, and sank into his chair. Then the door burst open and there was the theatre manager. "Benny Hill," he shouted. "Yes, Mr Challen?" "You're a bloody rotten act!" he yelled. It was cruel. And it wasn't necessary. It was kicking a man when he was down. We both knew the score and were as miserable as could be about it. Christ, it was already like a wake in the dressing-room. Challen said to me, "You'll have to make up his time!" and left in a fury. Then Benny rushed to the washbasin and was sick into it. He was really ill. I never felt so awful in my life. I can't tell you what it did to me.'

Challen strode back to his office, phone bells rang and in no time at all a representative from George and Alfred Black was in the dressing-room. Their orders were that the single spot was to be axed forthwith. No more seven-minute solos for Benny Hill. However, they were entirely satisfied with his work as straight man to the principal comedian. They were content for him to continue with Reg for the rest of the tour, and, as the show was a commercial success, who could tell where that would lead?

'I'm leaving. I don't want to be just a straight man, finish. I want to be more than that,' Benny said.

In hardly any more time at all, Richard Stone was in the dressing-room. He was appalled at the ruination of his plans. Benny's intransigence was risking a business campaign that had taken years of effort to put together. 'Stick with Reg,' advised Stone. 'You're getting good

money at last and you'll get more. The pair of you
work marvellously well together. Reg is going places.
He will take you to the Palladium.'

'I don't want to be just a straight man, finish. I want
to be more than that,' Benny said.

Reg was in anguish for his friend and concerned
about the future. 'I had insisted from the first that I
wanted Benny as my straight man,' he says. 'I needed
him. He was perfect for me. That's why I made sure
he always shared the star dressing-room with me. I was
desperate when he packed it in and I tried every way
I knew to get him to change his mind. "I love feeding
you, Reg," he said, "but it's not enough!" After they
had fixed me up with a new straight man, I asked
Benny what he was going to do. "I'm going home,"
Benny said.'

On his way out, my brother wandered on-stage to
take a last look at the auditorium. It did not look like
a graveyard. It was quite pleasant really – rather like
the long-lost Southampton Hippodrome. As he left, his
uncertain tread echoed throughout the theatre.

It was the second time that week he had walked off
the stage to the sound of his own footsteps.

11

'Turn Again, Wit!'

Benny got as far as London. Waiting for his coach home, he dropped into the Bijou cinema on Victoria Station for an hour. They were showing Danny Kaye's *The Kid from Brooklyn*. When the hour was up so was Benny. A glimpse of the zany American comedian had given him new hope and spirit. He had read of Danny's career setbacks, of the pygmies who said the tall red-headed clown was unsuitable for the movies – that his material was too sophisticated, his performance too calculated and his nose too long. But Danny had stuck at it and won through in the end. He had triumphed over his Hollywood critics. Benny was sure now that he could make it, too. If Danny Kaye could do it – so could he! The kid from Southampton was back on line.

Two hours later he was installed in the Kilburn home of his friends, the variety stars Billy Rhodes and Chica Lane. He had rented the smallest room in the large guest-house they used as a base, run by Connie, Billy's mother.

Strolling round the back garden, surveying the autumn shrubs with only Doolie the duck for company, Benny took stock of his situation. He knew that, as a performer on the southern stages, he could make people laugh. His career, so far, had included many more successes than failures. And when he analysed the flops, he could see clearly how to avoid them in future.

On the air, a disembodied voice, he was beginning to build a reputation for himself as a useful character comedian. Radio was then the quickest way to stardom.

At that time, *The Stage* was full of small advertisements referring to radio shows ('Catch me on "Variety Band-box" '), rarely to television or theatre.

Furthermore, Benny observed, he had contributed as a writer to most of the radio broadcasts he had made to date. With encouraging results. The scripts had all been well received. And, as for writing for the stage, he had produced a wealth of excellent material for Reg Varney – and one or two spectacular triumphs for himself. His own pieces for the script of BBC Tele-vision's 'Here's Mud in Your Eye!' had been fun to put together. Everybody had been pleased with the show, the critics kind to him. That television revue had been Benny's first in front of the camera. He had enjoyed the experience, tickling snorts of laughter from the crew without the responsibility of controlling a large audience. Was that his way forward? Did television offer him the Big Chance? Benny thought about it.

In 1950 only one house in twenty contained a tele-vision set. The response of the well-to-do was in line with their view of the cinema forty years earlier. They saw it as an entertainment for the lower orders. The lower orders affected to despise it as a toy for those with more money than sense. And a few middle-class phonies in the suburbs put up aerials without buying sets to go with them. When people said, 'Television is a seven-day wonder. I can't stand it. There's nothing in it. All those flickering lines, shadows left everywhere. You can't see a thing clearly. And it's very bad for your eyes,' Benny would say, 'I can't afford a set either.'

Families whose home boasted a television set, boasted. With good reason. Who else could say that they had seen Princess Elizabeth, Dylan Thomas and Winston Churchill in their own lounge? or, in the case of the well-to-do, sitting room? Despite the brief two-and-a-half-hour live evening telecast on one channel only, despite the plethora of worthy, not to say pious, programmes – with a goggle-box in the house, one did come face to face with some Very Important People. Appearances Were Kept Up. The mere sight of the presenter Sylvia Peters in evening dress, speaking to you, as the comedian Gillie Potter used to say, in English, would halt even today's unspeakable sofa-hogs in their tracks. For everybody on screen wore evening dress. And their obvious expectation was that the viewer would be wearing evening dress too. One could hardly disappoint such people. They craved our indulgence in a language that has almost vanished, full of clipped vowel sounds. Cant, I think, would be an apt definition of it. It was a way of speaking that Americans found incredible or hilarious or both, and it makes *Brief Encounter* a likely contender for the Funniest Film of 1946.

Cockney, of course, should have been the language of the early days of British television. Most of the viewers lived in and around the capital. The BBC producers, children of the metropolis themselves, maintained an incestuous relationship with their audience. Thus the programmes were based largely on the Johnsonian premise that a man who is tired of London is tired of life. Without a set of his own, Benny was reduced to watching these scenes of London life on smoky little screens in shop windows. They convinced him that television was going to overwhelm all previous forms of entertainment and that the BBC's output in the new medium was very short on visual comedy.

It was quite obvious why visual comedy, in particular, was scarcely to be seen on the tiny grey screen. Effective examples of it on stage or film were relatively rare, and the BBC could not afford them. Moreover, in 1950 a single humorous music-hall sketch could earn its performers a comfortable living. One television broadcast, however, and the playlet would become familiar to millions, who would no longer pay to see it at the theatre. Agents saw the danger and discouraged their venturesome clients. Even stand-up comedians realized that they would need a very long spoon to sup with this devil of a medium. Their cherished routines would disappear into the voracious maw in a couple of snaps. They tended to feed it stale and cheaper comic cuts. Benny knew he could provide comic cuts of better quality. He had been writing steadily for five years and collecting magazine cuttings for even longer. These clippings, mainly jokes, cartoons and newspaper reports of unusual occurrences ('All it needs is a pay-off,' he would say), were thrown higgledy-piggledy into cardboard boxes, to be perused at leisure. But most valuable of all were his notes, scribbled on scraps of paper or card, which also found their way into the ubiquitous boxes. These notes were brief accounts of observed behaviour (usually human, occasionally animal or mechanical) that could be extended into a joke or sketch. Benny has been a lifelong voyeur, a fascinated and amused spectator of the passing show. However, he observes not only the passing show but also the family enjoying the passing show and the photographer snapping the family and the policeman watching the photographer. The behaviour of all or any of these players may well provide him with a humorous insight into the nature of our unpredictable species.

In 1950, Benny already had access to masses of comedy material, in his notes and in his head. 'I had scores of humorous ideas,' he says, 'based on people I had met in my job as a milkman, experiences in the army and real-life incidents in London bus queues, pubs, cafés and markets. I decided to snow BBC Television with scripts until they were bound to take notice of me.' Benny began to write in his little room, with only the sound of Doolie quacking in the garden to interrupt his train of thought. After nine weeks, he had completed forty sketches in longhand. That would do, for a start.

Ronnie Waldman, the lively, dapper BBC Head of Light Entertainment, knew Benny by reputation. He was a little surprised, however, when the young comedian walked into his office and dumped a huge pile of scripts in front of him. 'Pick one,' ordered Benny. 'Any one at all.' Waldman obeyed and handed his choice back to his visitor. It was Waldman's turn to command. 'Now, you read it to me,' he said. Benny was unprepared for this response, but took the opportunity to set the scene. The sketch was based on the havoc caused by the new conveyor belts in self-service cafés. A City type has his *sang-froid* dented when his tray of food escapes, his umbrella impales a doughnut, crockery piles up, display pyramids tumble, customers are bowled over and a good deal of cream cake is widely distributed. Acting the scene involved frantic gymnastics, juggling and mime for Benny. But Waldman thought it was funny. He was laughing throughout. As Benny sat down, Waldman wiped his eyes with his handkerchief and asked casually, 'Who do you think could do it?' Benny drew a breath and said, 'I could.'

'My sentiments exactly,' replied Waldman. 'What are you doing a fortnight on Thursday?'

'I'm free,' replied Benny, smiling.

Waldman picked up the phone, called a producer, and said, 'I've filled that forty-five minutes you have open on Thursday fortnight. Yes, Benny Hill. I'll send him to see you.' He put down the phone and explained, 'Television is not like theatre. In the theatre people laugh because everybody else is laughing. Television is totally different. The audience is one or two people in a room. Like me here. I'm one person in a room. You made me laugh and you can make people laugh in rooms all over the country.' Forty years later, Phyllis Diller told me, 'Benny makes me laugh out loud, alone, in my bedroom. That's comedy!'

The producer that Ronnie Waldman had telephoned was Bill Lyon-Shaw, who took responsibility for the revue 'Hi There!' that introduced Benny Hill to the television public. My brother needed every scrap of his experience and technical expertise for the big break, his first show as star. He felt confident that he would perform well but was worried about the newspaper critics, who might well cut him down for his presumption in challenging for the territory owned by established comedians like Arthur Askey and Terry-Thomas. He feared particularly one giant columnist, who ground bones to make his bread.

After the last rehearsal, Benny showed me round the small Lime Grove studio. There was to be no audience present. The set stood in a circle, the camera in the centre, ready to pan from one scene to the next. I was introduced to the producer and to David Jacobs, Benny's straight man for the evening, before going downstairs to watch the telecast on the monitor screen. What I saw exhilarated me. Benny was clean-cut, charming and funny. Very funny. The show was bright and fresh with a style of its own.

My brother played safe by including the self-service café scene that had creased Ronnie Waldman. It exploded on the screen. Then there was a nod towards his Chelsea chums when Benny impersonated the French waiter in a Paris bistro sketch (considered a trifle exotic in the days before universal travel). A few minutes later, the Hampshire Proteus was a Cockney barrow-boy selling apples. 'Are they sweet?' asks his mate Charlie. 'How do I know?' answers Benny. 'They're for sellin' – not for eatin'!' Charlie is accosted by a gabbling Frenchman. 'What's 'e want?' asks Benny the barrow-boy. 'I don't know,' replies Charlie, 'I can't understand 'im.' 'Well, then,' says Benny, ' 'it 'im rahnd the ear'ole!' In the pub afterwards, everyone seemed pleased, but then they always do. We awaited the critics' verdicts nervously. Next morning, the newspapers exhibited a general lack of interest. The most appreciative review observed that Benny 'has more than a mere idea of visual fun . . . he could be one of the brightest comics on TV', the most unimpressed felt that 'the show ached for an experienced comedian like Arthur Askey to take it by the scruff of the neck'. We had expected comment along these lines. It was a relief – less painful than the sound of grinding bones.

What we did not know till later was that the viewers had loved it. They immediately took Benny to their hearts. He was immensely popular long before the press cottoned on. In fact, the press have never really cottoned on. I told him he was like Franklin D. Roosevelt – 'No one was for him but the people.'

As he was no longer touring, Benny was immediately available when offered his own radio series by the BBC's West Region. He was to star on the air for the first time. This chance ushered in a very busy period for him, during which he not only wrote and performed in his own show every Saturday, but broadcast other entertainment from service camps all over the west of England. Benny's series, called 'Anything Goes', included the much-loved character, Johnny

Morris, who later gained international fame as 'The Animal Magic Man'. The first broadcast from Bristol was greeted with enthusiasm by the local audience.

After the show, the cast celebrated in a local hostelry. When the landlord called 'Time!' Benny was talking to a group of young BBC executives, one of them a very attractive woman. 'What about a midnight swim?' suggests one of the bright young men. 'I know a private pool near here.'

'What about costumes?' counters the bright young woman.

'Who cares about that?' responds the b.y.m.

'All right, let's go!' says the b.y.w., who is not an executive for nothing. So, tempted by the prospect of seeing the b.y.w. in the buff, Benny finds himself at midnight climbing over the wall of a large garden with a group of noisy bureaucrats.

At the sight of the pool, the fellows tear off their clothes and dive in, whereas the b.y.w. changes in the summerhouse and emerges five minutes later to general consternation in a swimming costume. Quite chapfallen, their appetite for fun shrunken by the cold water, the naked civil servants rapidly sober up. It is not long before they are out of the pool, drying themselves on the tails of their shirts. Not wishing to put on damp clothes, Benny runs round the lawns to dry off. After exercises in the vegetable garden, he returns to find the pool and environs deserted. When he starts to dress, he discovers that his shirt and pants are soaking wet. The rotten beggars have dried themselves on his clothes. *La trahison des clercs!*

The next day, the *Sunday Chronicle* editor wrote, 'I swear Mr Hill and his show have between them something, which in the long run may cause Messrs Ted Ray, Dickie Murdoch, Kenneth Horne and Frankie Howerd some anxiety,' whereas another reviewer observed, 'Yesterday evening there crawled out from under a stone a radio revue, "Anything Goes". The young man largely responsible for it would be better employed at almost any other activity, light factory work for example.'

'Anything Goes' was a young man's effort, derivative in every way and lacking in conviction. I knew why and realized that it would be some time before Benny's self-confidence would be fully restored. However, the show made a cheerful half-hour and held promise of better things to come.

In the summer of 1951, Benny was back at the seaside as a featured comedian in a revue at Ramsgate. Top of the bill was bandleader Billy Merrin with his lively protégée, the singer Penny Nichols. Benny shared the comedy with an experienced double-act, Low and Webster, who needed no help with their sketches. The middle-aged pair were highly professional, and the comic partner soldiered on despite an ulcerated leg that by the end of the scene regularly reduced him to tears. When the poor fellow entered hospital at last, Benny took over his part in the double-act for a while. The experience was an educative one. The straight man was a fat, aggressive performer, who had the loudest voice I have heard in my life. Every word he said rang clear as a trumpet note round the theatre. Benny had to work hard to keep up with him, but enjoyed the challenge and emerged a stronger comedian for it.

When our sister Diana decided to continue her career as a nurse in Australia Benny was at Euston Station with his parents to see her off to Liverpool where she would board ship. That day, Benny had taken them all to lunch at a Lyons Corner House and to the Palladium matinée. He knew that 'the Last of the Red Hot Mommas', Sophie Tucker, would cheer up his parents as much as the sight of a rival, Dickie Henderson Junior, on the same bill would provoke him. 'Huh, who needs it?' he muttered at the time. The Tucker-induced good cheer prevailed until the train began to move, when, simultaneously, Mum and Diana burst into tears.

A recent letter to the *Southampton Evening Echo* suggests that Australia gained a prize in Diana. 'I was a patient at the Southampton Eye Hospital in 1949 and would confirm that the morale among the patients and staff was exceptionally high,' writes T. A. Fish. 'One of the young probationers at that time was Benny Hill's sister. Benny still had his feet on the bottom rung, and as a comedienne she probably surpassed her brother.'

Like many other entertainers, Benny continued to give his services freely at the Nuffield Centre, which still welcomed the troops on leave. He appeared there often, not only out of a sense of duty, but because the rapport he established with the uniformed crowd made each occasion a triumph for him. His irreverent attitude to authority, his cheeky distrust of pretension, the worm's-eye view he takes of society, all endeared him to an audience that, every day, was bound silently to suffer the insolence of office. The ex-driver's salty, down-to-earth humour was much appreciated. He became a great favourite at the club.

Bob Monkhouse recalls arriving with Benny at the centre one evening when it was packed. 'All who couldn't gain admittance had dispersed except for one little white-haired old lady in pince-nez and, so help me, a shawl!

' "Waiting for someone, ma?" asked Benny.

' "It's just that my grandson is singing in one of the turns. But all the seats are taken."

' "Perhaps not," said Benny as I left him to go inside

the centre. Sure enough, when I walked on stage, Benny and the little old lady were sitting together in the third row.

' "Boys and girls," I announced, "I am your compère for tonight and topping the bill we have, sitting right here among you, the Nuffield Centre's very own TV comedian, Benny Hill!"

'The audience erupted. Almost apologetically Benny stood up in the stalls to acknowledge the applause. After the show, he told me that the little old lady had tugged him back into his seat saying, "Sit down, young man. What would it be like if everybody stood up to look at the man?" Benny added, "When I did my act, she must have thought, 'What a helpful young man. He's standing in for the star!' " '

Benny was a natural, therefore, to compère the new 'Centre Show', an entertainment of forty-five minutes, televised monthly live from the Nuffield in 1953. Kenneth Carter, the distinguished producer responsible for the project, had only one reservation about his main man. Benny's jokes were often ribald and critical of the *status quo*, comments which could be explosive in a services setting. The master of ceremonies would need the touch of a master's hand to guide him. Carter resolved to apply it.

All his vigilance came to naught, however, when, on one show, Benny read a police message: 'A football pools coupon was lost last night in Chelsea. Will anyone who finds it, please contact Scotland Yard, telephone, Whitehall Home, Away, Home, Away.' The announcement got a big roar from the service audience and laughs in lounges all over the country.

The joke was a neat one, based on the fact that Scotland Yard's telephone number was Whitehall 1212 and that on a football pools coupon 1 meant a home win and 2 an away win. Everybody knew that – except one high ranking yo-yo, who protested that Benny had said, 'Homo Way, Homo Way', thus suggesting that the detectives of Scotland Yard were lifting shirts when they should have been lifting villains. The poor deluded fellow was probably already unhinged by Benny's drag act, 'Primrose Hill', that had appeared earlier in the show. All this doubtful hilarity must have convinced him that authority was not only being mocked, but slandered. The result was that Department AG3, the Services Entertainment Unit, sent a complaint about the joke – signed by a War Office colonel – to the Nuffield Centre Management Committee. The Nuffield managers included representatives of all three services, so they in turn could express simulated outrage in triplicate. The Committee also insisted on the right to censor all future 'Centre Show' scripts before they were broadcast.

The story was meat and drink to Fleet Street. It had all the ingredients of a great goulash – show-business, a government gaffe, a mad mandarin, blustering White-hall warriors, suggestions of sodomy, cultural illiteracy in high places, a threat to broadcasting freedom – and, presiding over the bubbling stew, the puckish grin of Benny Hill.

'I'm flabbergasted,' he said, at a press conference. 'All I know is what the BBC have told me – that some brass hat objected to the joke. They must have misheard me because they said that home-away had something to do with sex. I'm quite sure there was nothing suggestive or improper.'

The front pages played Mutt and Jeff with it – first, for laughs and then, grave concern. Ronnie Waldman was so confused by the nonsense written that he felt the need to talk it over with his protégé.

'What is this all about, Benny? And what do you think we should do about it?'

Benny explained the cause of the confusion and offered to review every script with Kenneth Carter (which he was doing already), but refused to allow his material to be vetted by outsiders, and certainly not by military officers. 'I'll agree all my stuff with Kenneth. I don't want to make life difficult for you but I can't go further. As for what we should do about it, I leave that to you. You're the guv'nor and you've got to take the can back.'

'Right,' replied Waldman. 'Here's what we do. We tell 'em – "Bollocks!" We pull out of the Nuffield and leave 'em high and dry. We don't deprive the troops! We invite them all to an even bigger monthly show at Shepherd's Bush Empire. How would you like to be backed by Eric Robinson and the BBC Light Orchestra?'

'Would I ever?' replied Benny with a smile from ear to ear. And that was how 'The Services Show' was born.

Waldman's steadiness under fire was widely applauded; Benny received matfuls of congratulatory mail and the *Daily Mirror* cried, 'Thank goodness the BBC haven't sacked Benny Hill!' Transmitted from the transformed Shepherd's Bush Empire studio and bolstered by a bigger budget, 'The Services Show' was more expansive than its forerunner. It allowed Benny to expand his repertoire too. He was encouraged to fit in more of his tailor-made bits. These were often comedy songs, gags with the band or specially devised wheezes for particular acts or guests. And each month he would play the part of yet another rum cove he had observed in his travels, another oddball to add to his gallery. They impressed the *Sunday Pictorial*'s TV critic. He named Benny as 'the surest for the big time. He looks good. He invents very funny characters. He has enough of them to ring the changes on his act. And he THINKS TELEVISION!' Benny confirmed this to another TV critic, Fred Cooke, when he told him of the crucial decision: 'The future of entertainment lies with television. That's the star to which I've hitched my wagon!'

In the meantime, however, he was still the compère of 'The Services Show' and responsible for making it fizz along. The confidence invested in him by Waldman gave Benny more confidence in himself. He remained debonair and unruffled by any unforeseen hitch. The show was broadcast live, of course, and, when the stage curtains stuck, he freed them with a flow of light-hearted banter that amused the audience and left no trace of embarrassment. If something clattered to the floor within camera view, Benny would retrieve it in such a way as to make it part of the entertainment. He would draw attention to the object and improvise a *jeu d'esprit* around it. In this way, he made a plus of a minus. He was so adept at this that, had it been a stage show, the producer would have cried, 'Leave it in. We'll do that every night!'

At this time Bob Monkhouse set up a running gag with Benny. They had a mock feud in public, the kind of rivalry that Jack Benny and Fred Allen made famous in the States. 'He did it with me for about a year,' says Bob. 'He poked fun at me in his show and I would refer to him as Belly Hill or Benny Hell. It worked awfully well, then he just stopped it. I recognized the signs. Benny was happening. In a very positive way. He was coming through that screen and he knew that stardom was beckoning. Kenneth Carter was telling him, "You're going to be a big, big star", so he was already separating himself from the rest of show-business. I'm sure he was saying to himself, "Every time I plug Bob, I am putting myself at his level. But I'm going up to another level." And I think that's the reason he dropped it. And I dropped it too. Because I sensed the same thing – that Benny was destined for something quite extraordinary.'

Benny's decision in that matter was a career move. He was clearing the way for the next step up the professional ladder. It had nothing to do with self-aggrandizement. Off-stage, Benny was always a modest person. If he had any tendency towards conceit (which he did not), Sunderland was a salutary lesson. There were others.

Top of the bill on one 'Services Show' was Charlie Chester, then a well-established star comedian. After the rehearsal, Benny took Charlie and Charlie's rather less distinguished friend, Dusty Kringle, for a cup of coffee at an Italian place across the street. Dusty was partner in a double-act that had just finished a week at Chiswick Empire. As soon as the trio sat down at a table, waitresses gathered in the corner, whispered, giggled and peeped across at them. Eventually, one came to take their order. The giggling continued. Then another young waitress approached with pad and pencil. 'Oh, Lord,' thought Benny, 'autograph time! Please God she asks Charlie first. He's Top Banana here. Senior comic. He should take precedence. That's only right and proper. She'll know me. I've had so much publicity lately. Please God, she recognizes Charlie. If she asks me, I'll pass it over to Charlie to sign first.'

'May I have your autograph, please?' asked the young lady sweetly.

Dusty took the pad, signed it and handed it back.

'Oh, Mr Kringle, I did enjoy your act at the Chiswick

Empire last week. I laughed and laughed. I shall treasure this always.' With that the nymph skipped happily away.

In addition to his other accomplishments, Benny was making a name for himself as a quick-change artist. Casting around for fresh wheezes he could use in his stage act, he conceived the idea of making the struggle, anxiety and frustration of quick change itself a target of his foolery. As the prime essential of the art is speed, he needed a situation between two people where delay was inevitable. He hit upon the classic balcony scene between Romeo and Juliet. One person playing both parts would be hard put to it to speak from the orchard and answer a few seconds later in a change of costume from the balcony.

Benny designed and supervised the building of a folding structure that resembled the decorated balcony and outside wall, with a half-hidden wooden stairway that wound up to it. Dressed as Romeo, Benny would speak his lines sonorously from the stage, then nip around, whip off his accoutrements and, throwing on the top of his Juliet costume, stumble up the stairs to arrive puffing on the balcony. After a sentence or two, he was on his way down again, doffing his Juliet cap for the Montague mantle.

As the scene is so well known, Benny felt constrained to alter as little of the original text as possible. This created difficulties for the verbal comedy, but Benny made up for that by the ingenuity of his comic business. Hats, roses, wigs, cloaks, weapons, gloves, belts and ruffs were all put to use as props to keep the laughter flowing. The confusion built to a madcap climax which made the act very successful in the variety theatres and gave some hints of

what was to come when Benny tackled the Bard in
earnest.

The balcony scene burlesque had been devised to
help cash in on Benny's growing reputation. Richard
Stone was busy booking his young comedian into variety theatres wherever and whenever possible. Benny
met two performers who induced him to question his
motivation, to ask himself whether that was a policy
he wanted to continue indefinitely and, if not, how he
wanted to modify it.

When touring, Benny travelled light. Apart from his
new balcony piece, he had only a small suitcase.
He was used to changing and waiting long hours in
dressing-rooms which contained only a cheap table,
two rickety chairs and a cracked mirror – with one
naked bulb to light them all. One Monday morning after
band call he knocked on the door of Renée Strange's
dressing-room, hoping to say hello to the attractive
puppeteer. The door opened and, to the music of
Vivaldi, Renée invited him into a well-lit, comfortable,
living room. Benny was astonished. There were pictures and prints on the wall, rugs on the floor, flowers
in vases everywhere, a beautiful mirror, lampstands,
family photographs in frames on the dressing-table,
bright cushions on basket chairs. The dressing-room
was furnished! Renée was putting up curtains. 'Why
are you going to all this trouble?' asked Benny. 'You're
only here for a week.'

'No,' replied Renée. 'I'm here for a year, many years,
even. If not this actual room, a room very similar. My
life is passing. Shall I spend it in a squalid room or a
pleasant, familiar room? It is worth a little effort every
Monday morning to remain civilized.' Such a viewpoint
was new to Benny. He had never considered his way of
life like that. He was used to putting up with things.

He did not expect too much. Five years in the army as a private soldier had taught him to rough it. The years after the war had not been easy. At times he had been desperately poor. Benny had pulled in his belt and gone without. It is a habit that dies hard. But he was impressed with the validity of Renée's argument.

Then he met Vic Oliver, the violin-playing star of stand-up comedy. Off-stage, Oliver was a prosperous, kindly *bon vivant* of Austrian origin, who travelled with a manager to smooth the way for him.

'Mr Oliver,' says Benny (he still calls him 'Mr Oliver'), 'had so many cases and baskets that he carried a permanent baggage man with him. He had golf clubs, suits, shoes, food hampers, crates of wine and the Lord knows what else. But he had a marvellous time. I never saw a man so at ease with life. He certainly knew how to look after himself.' Rubbing shoulders with a boulevardier of the old school suggested to Benny that life offered pleasures not to be found in the headlong chase after success.

When he was not performing, Benny would be writing. It was cogitate and scribble all day long. In the summer months, he sat working in a deckchair on the lawn of the large Kilburn garden. I caught him once dozing there after a night on the tiles. 'Not composing?' I asked. 'No,' he replied, ' – decomposing!'

Doolie was not always around to keep him company. When Billy and Chica were touring they took their duck with them. She was part of the act. At the climax of the pair's performance when the musical excitement was at its height, the piano would collapse, it would fall to pieces, and out of the wreckage would waddle Doolie, quacking away to the delight and amusement of an appreciative audience.

One afternoon, Connie called Benny in from the garden to take a phone call from Richard Stone. 'Get down to the Met at once,' ordered the agent. 'Joe Loss has been taken ill and wants you to front the band.' When Benny arrived at the Metropolitan, Edgware Road, Joe Loss was sat in a chair backstage, shivering despite being wrapped in blankets. Influenza was suspected. The band leader whispered encouragements to his replacement – 'You can do it, Ben. You'll be all right. Fake your way through it.' Ever the pro, Joe would not leave until he had brought Benny on-stage and croaked an introduction to the audience.

'All I was really in that show was an announcer,' says Benny. 'I threw in a few gags, of course, but I was useless to the band. I gave it all the razzmatazz I could. "And now, ladies and gentlemen, the Joe Loss band bring you 'Mule Train'! Hey, hey, hey here we go with 'Mule Train'! Take it away boys! Huh one, huh one-two-three!" Fingers clicking – all in the wrong tempo, of course. Sensibly the boys in the band paid no attention to me and took their cue from the first lead sax. Joe Loss couldn't keep away and returned a few days later. He was pleased with my work and asked me to stay on with the band as long as I could.

'We played a few weeks around London and one or two Sunday concerts. Unfortunately, Joe passed on the 'flu to Larry Gretton, a fine vocalist and father of Elvis Costello. While Larry was off ill, all his numbers were dropped. But Joe was reluctant to jettison the Jolson Medley, which was very popular. He asked me to sing it. Well, I can do a Jolson impression, but I can't sing. Not like Larry Gretton. And I certainly haven't got Jolson's leather lungs. I had nervous asthma – short of breath. Remember? I didn't want to let Joe down so I agreed – and began to practise right away. But, as it was half-past five in the afternoon and first house started at quarter-past six, there was little time to prepare. Singing in front of a band is not at all like singing in your bath. Nervousness overwhelmed me completely – my heart thumped and my ears throbbed so badly that I could hardly hear. Then, when we arrived at the Jolson Medley, I realized that the vocalist carries the melody alone for most of the time. There was nothing to sing along with. The band were playing descants and short figures that were no help at all to me. I had to decide when to come in, sing the song on pitch and hope to finish in time with the band. I was on my own. Did I learn fast to respect professional singers?

'What bothered me most was the big finish to "Mammy". My last note soon petered out. Larry Gretton could keep it going for ages but I was soon struggling. It was so humiliating that I spent all next day in my top room practising – hyperventilating, pressing down my diaphragm, inhaling to the maximum and holding a note as long as I could. The practice helped and, by the end of the afternoon, I felt sure that I could achieve a passable last note.

'That evening, I tackled the Jolson Medley with more confidence and when we came to the end of "Mammy" I filled every cranny of my lungs with air and let rip. It was a peach of a note. It went on and on. I was sweating and straining to keep it going. My chest ached. There was ringing in my ears and a red mist before my eyes but I still hung on to the note. At last, there was no more breath left in me and the song ended. The applause was as refreshing as the air that I sucked in so eagerly. I felt pleased with myself and hoped Joe would be pleased, too.

'After the show, I caught him on the move and asked him about the Jolson Medley.

' "It was all right," he said, as he passed.

' "What about 'Mammy', Mr Loss?" I called after him. Joe walked on without turning his head. "You can hang on to that last note a bit longer, if you like," he said.'

Benny was never able to hold the last note as long as Larry Gretton, but he began to enjoy his time with the Joe Loss Show. 'It was a great band,' he recalls, 'and made a splendid sound. All that brass, the rim-shots from the drums and the hiss of the hi-hat cymbals – it's a pity we don't hear so much of that ensemble playing nowadays. I loved it. Joe made life easy for me, too. He would put me on early if I had to get away for a broadcast. And he was always ready to help. I missed him when I had to leave.'

Joe Loss remembered Benny's efforts with gratitude. 'In our business,' he asserted, 'where it's always a struggle to survive, to keep afloat, it's a strange irony that there's so much temperament, so many people making difficulties. We had none of that with Benny. He was always a real trouper and a perfect gentleman – a joy to work with, always a smile. And we did marvellous business when he was with us as MC. He did his own act as well, a wonderful performer. We filled the Gaumont, Lewisham, and the Elephant and Castle, the Brixton Empire, three-thousand-seater sell-outs. Great shows!'

The call came at last in 1954 from Ronnie Waldman.

'I've got a promotion for you. No more compèring the "Services Show". You're to be resident comedian on a brand-new programme, "Show Case". It's a step up. I want you to develop your character comedy in it.'

'Why not call it "The Benny Hill Show"?' asked my brother.

'It's not your show. You're not ready yet. I'm still grooming you for stardom.'

'I'm groomed, I'm groomed already,' exclaimed Benny.

'I can't call it "The Benny Hill Show". Not yet. It's not your show,' said Waldman.

'Wanna bet?' challenged Benny.

12

Show Case

When inviting the actor and director Jeremy Hawk to lunch in town, I suggested that he should choose a quiet restaurant where he felt comfortable. 'My dear boy,' he replied in those familiar urbane tones, 'I feel comfortable everywhere.' It is quite true, of course. Whether hosting 'Criss-Cross Quiz', directing Sid Caesar's comedy show or playing golf with Danny Kaye, Jeremy has always been supremely self-assured. As a life-long neurotic myself, uneasy in my easy chair, I marvel at such insouciance.

I first saw Jeremy on stage at the Prince of Wales Theatre in Mary Chase's play *Harvey*, as the doctor treating an alcoholic Sid Field, who died a few months later from a hair of the dog that bit him in that endearing comedy. Later I reported Hawk's outstanding performances in the Globe and Lyric Revues to my brother and was delighted to learn that they were teaming up for 'Show Case'. The suave man-about-town with the aquiline good looks was to play Benny's straight man.

'It is typical of Benny that he had seen less of my work than you had,' Jeremy Hawk told me. 'He did not allow himself the time to go to the theatre – or for leisure pursuits at all. When I met him, he was a workaholic – a glutton for punishment, full of ideas that he was bursting to put into practice. I think we were good for each other. He taught me the value of dedication, showed me what hard work could achieve. And I showed him a good time, and helped him to relax. At that time, he was shy and rather tentative with girls

– but not for long. "Show Case" led to variety tours,
when we stayed at the same digs. I would drive him
round the town. We'd ogle the local talent, and pick
up some female diversion, though his taste was not at
all the same as mine. We had such fun in those days.
He was great company.'

There was, however, a side of Benny that had doubts
about Jeremy's laid-back attitude. He tut-tutted, in
particular, about the hours that his partner spent on
the golf-course. There should be time for leisure, fun
and dalliance, Benny conceded, but not too much.
He was ambitious and looked askance at people who
worked less hard than he did. He considered that
Jeremy's lifestyle was a little too hedonistic, and he
probably rather envied, as I do, that effortless charm
and social poise.

It is easy to understand why. As Bob Monkhouse
explains, 'You could always sense Benny's discomfort
at formal social occasions. His unsureness of etiquette
embarrassed him. He came only once to my home at
St John's Wood – to a dinner party. He was not relaxed.
Normally he drank very little as he was uncertain of
its effect on him. But, possibly in order not to appear
naïve, he had a couple of drinks. Immediately, he got
the giggles.'

Bob's wife Jackie takes up the story. 'I was Bob's
secretary then and Benny began to chat me up. In no
time at all he had proposed to me and, at the end of
the first course, gone out into the garden for a breath of
fresh air. He vanished into the darkness. We didn't see
him again that evening. Next day he sent me an enormous bouquet of flowers with a contrite note. I phoned
Elizabeth, Bob's wife, and she said that Benny had asked
her advice as to how he could make amends for his bad
behaviour. Later he invited me out one evening. We had

a marvellous time together. He was charming, attentive and very proper.'

'Benny had to learn to relax,' says Jeremy Hawk, 'and it took time, but anyone who says he could not enjoy himself should have seen him at the parties that I threw at my home in Eaton Square and, for those who claimed that he was gay, my goodness, you could not find a man more resolutely heterosexual. The people who thought he was homosexual should have talked to some of the young women he met on tour or at Eaton Square. But he didn't go for just any girl. He was quite fussy about the partners he picked, and loyal to them as long as the affair lasted. However, nothing, but nothing, was more important to him than the show.

'I well remember the first sketch we ever performed together for "Show Case". I was the shopkeeper selling a small electrical gadget to a very simple punter (Benny) and demonstrated that it could be adapted at the touch of a button to do a dozen jobs around the home. Benny was delighted and bought it immediately. As he walked away with it, I called out, "Don't forget the battery, sir!" and heaved on to the counter a huge, old-fashioned acid battery! Blackout! That was the first of scores of marvellous sketches Benny wrote for the show. I enjoyed appearing in them. It was so rewarding. Everybody was on your side. Audiences everywhere loved Benny, the home audience loved him and the camera loved him. We had a first-rate director in Kenneth Carter, for whom Benny had immense respect and from whom he learnt a great deal. Of course, it was a live one-take-only job in those days. No recording. You had to get it right first time. If you made a mistake, you just had to plod on. But Benny was so quick that he'd usually make a joke of it. And he was so professional – never late; never lazy; never difficult; never forgetful; always hard-working. I

admired him tremendously, and was grateful that he
kept me in television's top comedy show for so many
years.'

For his part, Benny was indebted to Jeremy for the
excellence of his work as a straight man, for his versatility as an actor in dozens of different roles, and for
adding a dash of elegance to the show. On a personal
level, he liked his stage and screen partner, enjoyed his
company and, despite some reservations, was much
impressed by Jeremy's example of gracious living.

Hawk was one of three men who met Benny at about
this time and were all influential in his life. Another was
Peter Charlesworth, an engaging, articulate theatrical
agent, who invited me to his office for a conversation
that was interrupted by phone calls concerning the
interests of his client Joan Collins. However, I soon
learned that he had not always been so well connected.
In the middle 1950s he was a song-plugger, who tried to
persuade Benny to sing a Guy Mitchell number on the
radio. Peter had bearded the up-and-coming star in his
dressing-room at the Alma Theatre, Luton, and amused
him when trying to sell this frothy inanity. There was
instant rapport between them and they became, and
still are, firm friends. When they met, they both had
regular girlfriends, and often went out as a foursome.

Benny's escort at that time was the dancer Doris
Deal, whom I found a charming and serious-minded
girl. My impression was that she wanted a stable relationship and an early marriage whereas Benny felt
that he was too busy with his career to contemplate
so permanent an undertaking. It seems probable that
Doris sensibly brought matters to a head and broke
off the affair. Benny was very fond of her and was
upset for some months. However, he is, I think, a
loner and Doris was proved to be right when she

later fell in love and made a happy marriage with someone else.

Peter's own tandem affair slowed down and finally conked out. At last the natural bachelors (neither of them has ever married) turned to each other for consolation. Or rather, together they turned to other young women for consolation. Peter could spin a line that had Benny speechless with admiration. In the early days, when they had one battered banger between them, the silver-tongued song-plugger once impressed a couple of wide-eyed beauties with, 'I've sold the other Jag, Ben.' 'About time too,' replied my brother, choking with laughter at his friend's audacity.

'The stories about Benny that were going around at that time,' says Bob Monkhouse, 'were as thick and furious as they ever became. Somehow he caught people's imagination. It was something to do with his desire for privacy, which most of us showbiz people did not share. So, of course, everyone speculated about him. It was said that Benny's technique for picking up female companions was to go and wave his face in the downstairs bar at the Empire or Hammersmith Palais or any one of the dance-halls until the girls noticed – "Look, there's Benny Hill!" When a crowd of them gathered, he would sort one out and whisk her away. The girls said that if you owned three pairs of different coloured knickers, three different coloured see-through nighties and one bottle of Primitif perfume, you had been out with Benny Hill seven times! And the fellers said that he'd got it all wholesale!'

Benny certainly disappointed at least one young lady. She was the delectable Ann Ling, nineteen years old and secretary to John Browell, the BBC Light Entertainment radio producer. My brother was, at this time, a keen keep-fit enthusiast. One afternoon, he walked

six miles to the Aeolian Hall in Bond Street to dic-
tate a script to Ann. When they had finished, it was
five o'clock. 'Which way do you go home?' asked
Benny. 'Oh, I catch a train from Victoria,' replied
Ann. 'Would you like to come that far with me?'
invited my brother. 'Oh, thank you. That would be
nice,' said Ann, with visions of being whisked along
in a taxi by this handsome young star. How romantic!
Alone in a cab with Benny Hill! This was Life with
a capital L. The next morning John Browell asked
her, 'Well, how did you get on?' 'We bloody well
walked,' Ann answered in disgust ' – every bloody
step of the way!'

Such incidents gave Benny a reputation for meanness
that he did not deserve. His own needs are modest, his tastes simple; he is content with very little
and cannot understand why others are not as easily
satisfied. His early training disposes him towards moderation.

Our parents came from families that had known
poverty; both had suffered hardships; my father had
endured hunger as a child and starvation as a prisoner
of war. Benny and I were never stinted as children,
but we were always made to clear our plates. Benny
still does so today. So do I. Our home achieved an
unostentatious comfort but was a frugal one. From our
parents' actions and attitudes we learnt:

If you cannot get it wholesale, buy it second-hand.
Do not even think of hire-purchase.
Taxis are for weddings and funerals.
Never buy processed food unless it is tinned.
Arcades are for looking, not spending money.
Hotels, restaurants and cafés are not for you.
Take home-made sandwiches.

Walking is pleasanter, healthier, cheaper and more
educational than public transport.

With so implacable a background of thrift, Benny took
a little time to adapt to new expectations. He became
used eventually to staying in hotels, eating in restaurants, taking taxis and giving expensive presents, but
he has never been able to conquer a certain unease
about such a way of life, which smacks too much,
for him, of vanity and vexation of spirit. He sees it as
folly, a view entirely proper to a clown.

'How anyone can say Benny is mean beats me completely,' says Peter Charlesworth. 'He is the kindest,
most generous person I have ever known. And the
girls we used to date would all agree. It was chocolates, flowers and a taxi at the door for all of them.
We met some damn nice girls. And had wonderful
times. There wasn't a desperate rush to bed the ladies.
Some of them remained just friends. We all relaxed
and had a ball. Of course, we avoided starlets and
showbiz types. They always wanted favours. But the
dancers were good fun. I hope I am making it clear
that Benny is far from being gay, because there is a
school of thought – no, I can't call them that as
they are so pig-ignorant – there is a view that insists
that Benny is homosexual. That is the joke of the
century!'

Although I never joined the evenings out, I can
confirm Peter's point about the caring nature of
the relationships. It seemed to me that Benny was
always off with a bunch of flowers to some hospital
or other to visit an ailing girlfriend. I thought then,
that, in such a situation, most men would not have
bothered.

Benny met the third man to influence his life at this

time, while changing in a bathroom the size of Salisbury Plain and washing in water from huge golden taps. He was Dave Freeman, a huge former Special Branch detective, then club officer of the American Officers' Club that occupied the Woolworth heiress Barbara Hutton's home in Regent's Park. He had booked Benny at the suggestion of his wife for the club's Saturday Night Dance Cabaret. While Benny made up in the luxurious bathroom, Dave confessed that he had himself written a few comedy scripts for radio. 'I'm always in the market for fresh ideas,' said Benny. 'Why don't you put something on paper and send it to me?' Dave did. It was 'The Wheelbarrow Tester', a sketch that Benny adapted to introduce Fred Scuttle to the television audience for the first time. Their co-operative effort was a great success, they became friends and began a long, easy association.

Dave's assistance meant that the pair did a great deal of walking, talking and lying about in parks. They described themselves as layabouts and tried to write a new style of comedy dialogue in the desultory manner of their own conversation. As he had always done, Benny kept his eye open for the absurd. Now he had a companion with whom to discuss it. Regent's Park, Hyde Park and Hampstead Heath were the scenes of their rambling discourses. When they got hungry, they usually made for the nearer of their two homes. One morning they arrived at the Kilburn guest-house just in time for lunch. 'I'm glad you two have turned up,' said Billy Rhodes, as they all sat down to table. 'I want your advice.'

'What's the trouble, Billy?' asked Benny, tucking into the chicken curry and rice.

'Well, the fact of the matter is that we need a new finish to the act,' explained Billy.

'What's wrong with the present one?' asked Benny. 'It's a knockout, Billy. Down falls the piano and out steps Doolie. Pandemonium! What could be better? That reminds me, I haven't seen Doolie today. Where is she?'

'You're not listening, Benny,' said Chica Lane, softly. 'We need a new finish to the act.'

'Oh, I see. You need a new finish to the act,' said Benny sadly, realizing that the curry he had been eating was not chicken.

As ever, Benny made a virtue of necessity. Walking and talking to Dave later, he realized that there was humour to be mined out of the hypocrisy and ambiguity with which people treat animals. Even a dead bird could be funny. So the ambling pair wrote a sketch on the subject that Benny promptly performed on television. It was well received but Dave still had the feeling that it was ahead of its time.

The scene depicts a customer entering a taxidermist's shop to pick up the duck he had left to be stuffed. Unfortunately, the assistant has cooked and eaten the duck, so the taxidermist is reduced to passing off a dead parrot as the stuffed duck. With the dead parrot on the counter before them, the dialogue becomes a long argument and includes a good deal of straight-faced idiocy.

Customer: It's gone a funny colour hasn't it?
Benny (as the taxidermist): Yes, I'm afraid that
    happens sometimes. It's the steaming, you
    see sir. We have to steam them before we
    stuff 'em.
Customer: But its beak's a different shape.
Benny: Ah, well, sir. That's the shrinkage, sir. It

shrinks, you see, sir, with the application of
the embalming fluids. Upon occasion.
Customer: But it looks like a parrot.
Benny:. Yes, it does a bit, doesn't it? Now that
you mention it.

Dave felt that such laconic, realistic dialogue in playlet
form was breaking new ground. It was based not on
traditional question-and-answer music-hall jokes, but
on the observation and reproduction of genuine contemporary exchanges. Later Dave was to join Benny
on screen in a series of sketches depicting Lofty and
Albert, a couple of street-corner yobs of the time.
Benny played a would-be Jack-the-Lad or Teddy Boy,
Dave the tall simpleton in an ill-fitting suit. They were
usually to be found languidly chatting up a couple of
working-class dolly-birds.

Benny: Well, of course, since the war, I mean,
I haven't – well, I mean, what happened to
me during the war, that was it, wasn't it, you
know what I mean?
Dolly-bird: Well, what happened to you during
the war?
Benny: No, no, don't ask me! I can't. My gawd,
it was terrible. You wouldn't – I mean, I don't
want to talk about it.
Dave: I fought you was a cook at Catterick.
Benny: I was. But it was terrible. I don't want to
talk about it.
Dave: You wanna go down the Regal to see
Apache Vengeance?
Dolly-bird: No, I don't like nuffing brutal.

Dave Freeman reminded me of how easily upset

viewers were in the fifties. The following exchange, which Dave describes as 'the mildest comedy in contemporary terms', drew fire from two national dailies when it was first shown. It was considered 'gross and offensive'.

> Farmhand (Benny): 'E dropped the sledgehammer on moi foot. Didn't 'e do no 'arm though. I'll show you (taking off boot and sock). There. I got very strong feet.
> Clergyman (recoiling): Oh, yes, you have indeed. You certainly have.

Not only were the television critics waiting to pounce on unwary scriptwriters and careless performers, there was always the strident group from Surrey with a lunatic fringe on top. In addition to the amateurs, the BBC laid down its own rules. Benny recalls that certain words were *verboten*. There was a long list, including the obvious obscenities and blasphemies, that were not to be used in any circumstances. The list also banned the employment of quite reasonable words like vicar, knickers, ruddy and damn. A honeymoon was not considered a proper subject for humorous observation. The diktat even covered the way words were to be pronounced. The BBC forbade the imitation of any kind of speech impediment.

John Browell, who produced the Benny Hill Show on radio (beginning in January 1955), struggled constantly to save the laughs. He succeeded in the scene where the terrible Edie Grimthorpe grabbed Benny by the hand and dragged her reluctant companion into a deserted field.

> Edie: Ooh, look at that tree!
> Benny (morosely): I know, I can see it.
> Edie: Ooh, look at that flower!

Benny: I know, I can see it.
Edie: Ooh, look at that —
Benny: I know, I can see it.
Edie: Why did you step in it, then? (laughter)

'The BBC, in those days, would not allow me to imply that Benny had stepped into a cowpat,' says John, 'so I asked him how we could save the sketch. He came up with an extra line after the laugh:

Benny: I shall have ants running up and down
    me legs all day! (Suggesting that he had stood
    in an ants' nest.)

'We got another big laugh with that, which was a typical Benny Hill ploy. He teases you into a naughty thought but then punishes you because there is a perfectly respectable explanation. I must say that Benny responded amenably to direction. He would get away with everything he could, but he knew to the comma how far to go. He never gave me anything like the trouble that Max Miller did.'

Benny and Bob Monkhouse performed bits they had written themselves in the BBC radio's 'Showband Show', between musical numbers conducted by Cyril Stapleton. Benny presented a piece in which he played a German animal psychologist. A farmer brings him a reluctant donkey.

'He won't do a thing I tell him,' complains the farmer. 'He doesn't listen to a thing I say.'

'I'll tell you vot you do,' says Benny, in a stygian Black Forest accent. 'You get a railway sleeper and schmack der donkey on der kopf mit it.'

'What do I do that for?' asks the farmer.

'To get its attention!' replies der Professor.

'No, no, Benny, you can't do that!' interrupted the

director. 'We'll have the animal lovers down on us like a ton of bricks. We can't suggest cruelty to animals. We'll get shoals of complaints.'

'Can I be a German psychiatrist and suggest hitting Cyril Stapleton on the head with a railway sleeper?' asked Benny.

'Oh, that'll be all right. No problem,' replied the director. With Cyril Stapleton, the band leader, as the butt of the joke, it got a big laugh and not a single letter of complaint.

Bob Monkhouse, unknowingly, did Benny a good turn on that show. They were continuing their public rivalry at that time, and Bob quipped, 'B. H. stands for Broadcasting House, Benny Hill and Big Head!' A lovely lady in the audience later told my brother: 'I thought Bob was awful to you. You looked so sad. So I decided to cheer you up.' She sought him out and did just that. Several times.

Benny was up to every kind of dodge to get his comic capers past the BBC watchdogs. Knowing his reputation for naughtiness, Ronnie Waldman and other top echelon television executives made a point of attending final rehearsals for 'Show Case'. The script usually contained a cheeky line or two that they would wish to excise. It might look harmless enough on paper, but when Benny gave it the full weight of his arch delivery they would consider it too dangerous to leave in the show. So when he arrived in rehearsal at a piece like:

> Her dress was green as clover;
> I jumped with glee
> 'Coz I could see
> Her dumplings boiling over!

he would begin to giggle.

It was a cod corpsing, feigned laughter, when a performer pretends he cannot continue. Benny would chuckle and mumble his way through the doubtful line so that the would-be censors never actually heard it properly. 'Sorry, Ken,' he would call to his director and move on swiftly.

Concurrently with writing and performing in 'Show Case' on television, Benny was playing Archie Andrews's tutor in 'Educating Archie', a highly popular, long-running radio series. The star of the show was a ventriloquist's doll, a naughty boy whose falsetto treble voice was unmistakable. The ventriloquist, Peter Brough, like his transatlantic equivalent, Edgar Bergen, made no effort on radio to conceal his lip movements. One of the reasons for the show's continuing freshness was that Brough made efforts to change Archie's tutor regularly, each time employing yet another post-war discovery who was reaching stardom. Benny followed Tony Hancock, Robert Moreton and Max Bygraves, among others.

Peter Brough had worked with his doll for so long that he treated him as a real person. When Benny first arrived at the studio, Peter said, 'Come and meet Archie.' He ushered my brother along to his dressing-room, where he picked up the doll. 'It's so nice to meet you at last, Benny,' said Archie, in his high-pitched voice. 'I want to welcome you to the show. We love all your work on television and hope you'll be very happy with us.' As they shook hands, Benny replied, 'Thank you, Archie, very much. I hope things will go well for all of us. I'm looking forward to a successful series.'

'Now, Benny,' said Peter, 'I'll introduce you to the rest of the cast.' Nobody smiled, not even Archie.

Since Benny's first television appearance in 1949, there had been a receiver explosion. Due largely to the broadcasting of the Queen's coronation in 1953, a quarter of the country's homes now contained a set that was switched on most of the evening. When there was a BBC monopoly, broadcasting live on one channel only, the previous evening's television programme was the prime subject of conversation everywhere, every day. Except in the tallest of ivory towers. When, at the end of a panel game, the Australian film star Ron Randell blew a goodnight kiss straight out of the screen to the ladies watching him, there was a furore. The next morning, the tabloid front pages were agog with illustrated excitement at the extravagant gesture. The fuss went on for days, and the loss of the actress Barbara Kelly's ear-ring on camera was the subject of exhaustive conjecture among millions.

The nation was hypnotized by the small screen. Those who possessed sets had frequent uninvited visitors who crowded round the box to see their favourites. I was such a visitor to neighbours and friends and am deeply grateful to those who sacrificed a certain domestic sovereignty to allow me to see my brother's early shows. As I had no television set for years, I often depended on the kindness of strangers.

The inexorable growth of the television-watching population led to a transformation in the cultural life of the nation. People of all ages, classes and tastes found that they shared one common experience – television. As in the early days of the cinema, some commentators were slow to see the implications of such a unifying preoccupation. Benny appreciated the significance of the development at once and exploited it. He was the first to satirize television shows on television. This was something entirely new. It was a genuine breakthrough in comedy entertainment. Benny began to guy, on the small screen, figures familiar to his national audience only through the small screen. He had always, of course, impersonated extraordinary people – film stars as a child, stage performers as an adolescent, radio voices as a young man, eccentric characters in 'The Services Show'. Now he turned his attention to the personalities whose faces flickered in millions of lounges. He was plugging in to the common experience.

At first he reviewed the experts whose demonstrations had made them household names in household roles. There was the bald, bearded, roly-poly Philip Harben, with floured hands and butcher's apron, who was an earnest cook and a serious trencherman. When Benny appeared as the tubby television chef, the likeness was remarkable. And when he began to explain how the viewer could make his own gorgonzola cheese, he was a hoot. 'First shred the gorgon into a basin. Make sure the gorgon goes in first. If you put in the zola first, you will get zolagorgon cheese. And there is no such cheese.' Philip Harben was a good sport and, on a later show, allowed Benny, as a phrenologist, to examine his bald head for laughs. However, he withdrew from a scheduled further appearance, because, as he told the press, 'It indicated that I could not cook.'

'Do and say whatever you like about me. Let's have some fun with it!' was the response of 'Mr Teasy Weasy', the flamboyant Raymond, more showman than hairdresser, who teased tired housewives out of the kitchen and into the lounge to watch his antics. He invited Benny to his hair-styling salon, showed him the tricks of the trade, then wafted him and other guests to a hotel in Bray where he introduced my brother to oysters and other seafood delights.

Benny liked and admired the cheerful, hardworking Mr Teasy Weasy, who had created an exciting personality from unpromising beginnings. The stylist made an

impressive picture on screen, with his huge head of
wavy hair, satin-lapelled smoking jacket and voluminous cravat. Extravagantly posturing and gesturing, he
was deliberately larger than life. Raymond conjured up
his creations with great panache, but he added to the
gaiety of the nation – and Benny, along with millions,
loved him for it. The impersonation was, therefore,
something of a tribute to a fellow-performer who was
already guying himself. Benny had Mr Teasy Weasy off
to a tee, including the working-class accent that could
scarcely be disguised.

'We're combing the 'air over this ear. This 'ere ear.
Then over that ear, over 'ere.'

As Mr Twirly Whirly, with a wig that waves like
Medusa's snakes, Benny flounces along the line of
seated models, his attentions causing a wince here,
a black look there. He stops and adjusts a customer's
curl, only to find he cannot remove the roller from his
finger. He moves on, at last, to a silver-blond head
and talks knowingly about the highlights on its ringlets
when he is interrupted by the charlady, who grabs the
head, which we now see is a floor mop – 'Do you
mind? I've got work to do!' she chides, as she stalks
away with it.

Everybody enjoyed the take-off, including Mr Teasy
Weasy himself. It helped to persuade readers of the
London *Evening News* to choose Benny as their TV Personality of the Year. In subsequent shows, Benny turned
his mordant attention to rather staider personalities
like Raymond Glendenning, the sports commentator,
Peter Haigh, the interviewer, and Cliff Michelmore,
anchorman of the 'Tonight' news programme. The
viewing people enjoyed the affectionate mockery of
these near-Establishment figures no less than the 'characters' of television.

It must be remembered that the BBC then had a reputation for being the most reliable broadcasting service in the world. People had faith in it. It appeared as unshakeable as the Church of England, the Houses of Parliament or the monarchy itself. The influence of the austere, autocratic Sir John Reith was paramount. He had ruled the Corporation like a strict Scots nanny, giving the audience what he knew was good for it: nourishing but very plain fare. According to public perception, in the natural hierarchy of things, Sir John had come to occupy a very high place indeed. The British public, by and large, accepted his firm control without complaint. Nanny knew best. The BBC therefore acquired an aura of authority which clothed even the regular stalwarts of evening television. Thus, there was a particular *frisson* for the viewers when Benny began to take the mickey out of the pillars of a revered institution. His targets were arrogance, pomposity and pretension. As Leslie Ayr of the London *Evening News* noted: 'His art is not so much that of the impersonator as the caricaturist, unerringly picking out this and that and playing it up with a fine sense of the ridiculous.' Benny's wicked mimicry could be disturbing, possibly even anarchic. The authorities, of course, kept a wary eye on it.

In 1954 Benny's position as British television's top comedian was confirmed by the acclaim that greeted his most ambitious project – the impersonation of all four members of the panel of 'What's My Line?' In this well-known television game, a group of celebrities took turns to elicit clues from unknown guests to establish their trade or profession. The contrasting personalities that made up the panel tested my brother's skills as an impressionist to the limit. Barbara Kelly was a wise-cracking Canadian actress, Lady Isobel Barnett a qualified doctor and famous hostess. Barbara was fair-haired, attractive and laid-back; Isobel brunette, elegant and more formal. Gilbert Harding was a thick-set, hairy, gruff ex-policeman, David Nixon a thin, balding, amiable professional magician. Impersonating them one after another, broadcasting live, with the cameras on the question-master Jeremy Hawk and the guest, as Benny changed in front of the studio audience, presented the most exciting challenge ever accepted by an entertainer on British television.

Benny met it calmly with his usual skill, application and sureness of touch. The performance was a *tour-de-force*. Next day, everybody was talking about it – of how he had Barbara's voice and accent just right, the way he sucked in his cheeks to show Isobel's fine bone structure, sank his head into his neck for Gilbert, so that, with the military moustache and horn-rimmed glasses, he was a dead ringer for the old grouch, his mockery of David's habit of fluttering his eyelashes in simulated surprise. People felt that television history had been made that night. So did the press – 'the most original and refreshing comedian that British TV has discovered', wrote Moore Raymond in the *Sunday Dispatch*; 'so entertaining that all the other acts . . . faded into nothingness', claimed Clifford Davis in the *Daily Mirror*, and another critic insisted, 'he could play the condemned man, the firing squad and the officer giving the order to fire with the lift of one eyebrow'. There was general agreement that Benny had, with that particular effort, won the right to wear the laurel and hardy crown of triumph.

After that, things began to happen fast. Ronnie Waldman announced that Benny would star in his own series in the New Year to be called, at my brother's insistence, 'The Benny Hill Show'. Bowing to public demand did not save Waldman from criticism. Benny should have been elevated years before, grumbled some scribes. James Thomas, TV critic of the *News Chronicle*, celebrated: 'The Battle of Benny Hill (Lime Grove 1953–4) has been won. It seems by sheer dogged persistence in their loyalty to the 28-year-old comedian of "Show Case" the customers have forced TV to give him his own series.' Thomas went on to claim that Benny had made previous 'pottering programmes worthwhile by the sheer weight of his own personality and the original fizz of his wit. Furthermore Mr Hill writes all his own scripts.

'In at least a show a month since January 1953, he has not had a flop. This week he towered over his mediocre supporters ... TV, scraping for comedy talent, persisted in the ridiculous statement: "we are grooming him for stardom". They have been grooming with a rather worn brush a man the public have long considered a star.'

Other changes followed. In his stage appearances, Benny dropped the 'Romeo and Juliet' sketch and substituted the take-off of 'What's My Line?' This was also a quick-change act. Theatre audiences were fascinated to see how it was done, something that had been kept from them on television. And as for laughs! Benny was able to make it a lot broader. For instance, as Lady Barnett, the rascal would flex his chest and back muscles to make the evening dress slide down, revealing his nipples. The dignified dame would suddenly appear to be topless. An explosive roar of laughter invariably greeted this unlikely treat.

Benny had been booked for some time to appear as second top at Finsbury Park Empire. Top of the bill was the popular singing pair Teddy Johnson and Pearl Carr, who had a record of success which included winning

Above: The Hill family during World War I. Standing from left to right: William, Benny's uncle; Uncle Leonard (who already looks very dark from jaundice, from which he died shortly after this photograph was taken); our father, Alfred Hawthorne Hill; Uncle Ernest; Auntie Violet. Seated from left to right: Aunt Cecilia, our grandmother (Nana) and grandfather (G.P.) Hill.

Below: Grandpa Cave at Newcombe Road in 1910.

Above: Grandma Cave in 1918; on the right is our mother, Helen Florence Cave, and on the left Auntie Louise (Louie).

Above: The perfect baby: Benny at six months.

Left: Benny's father and mother at their wedding in 1920.

Above: The circus tradition: Uncle Leonard as a clown in 1912.

Left: The author, dressed as a clown in 1924, aged two.

Above: The Hill brothers in Southampton, Christmas 1927, when I was nearly six and Benny nearly four.

Above right: Seven-year-old Benny, then called Alfie, in Ryde, Isle of Wight; our father captioned the picture in the album 'Every little helps'.

Above: Benny at fifteen; sitting next to him is our mother, then further along is Uncle Alan, across the table Grandmother Hill (Nana) and our sister Diana.

Left: Benny, aged eight, boxing with me in the back garden of our house in Westrow Gardens.

Above: Portrait of Benny as a driver/mechanic in France, 1944.

Below: Benny (on the right) with his mates in the REME in France, 1944.

Below: Benny as cockney comedian, when he first began to entertain professionally in Eastleigh. This photograph was taken by Norman Page, a neighbour in Westrow Gardens.

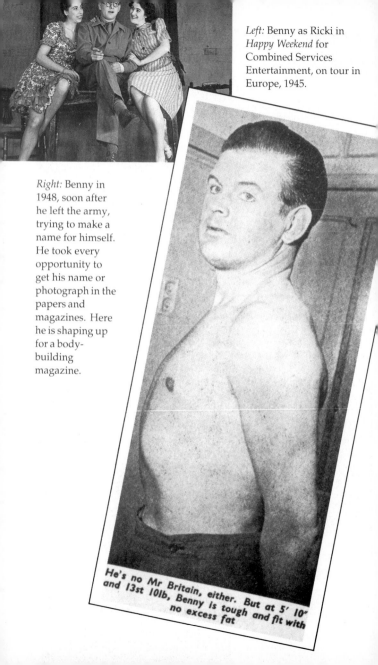

Left: Benny as Ricki in *Happy Weekend* for Combined Services Entertainment, on tour in Europe, 1945.

Right: Benny in 1948, soon after he left the army, trying to make a name for himself. He took every opportunity to get his name or photograph in the papers and magazines. Here he is shaping up for a body-building magazine.

He's no Mr Britain, either. But at 5′ 10″ and 13st 10lb, Benny is tough and fit with no excess fat

Above: Ferrier's Showbusiness Cartoon, a weekly cartoon in a popular magazine, 1949. It celebrates the debut of Benny Hill as Toto, the German comic.

Below: Reg Varney reminds us today that he was Top Banana when Benny was Bottom of the Bill in *Montmartre,* a saucy revue that toured the country in the early fifties.

Left: Benny in 1950, in his room at Cliftonville, Margate. During the summer season, he was feeding Reg Varney in *Gaytime*, the show at the Lido Theatre, Cliftonville.

Below: Benny with his father and mother in the Pigalle Restaurant, London, 1953.

Left: Benny starring in the *Folies Bergère* Show, *Paris by Night,* at the Prince of Wales Theatre in 1955.

Right: Benny congratulates the winner of the *Blighty* Magazine Beauty Competition, Albert Hall, in the early fifties. He met a lot of pretty girls this way, and got a lot of kisses.

Left: In his second film, *Light Up the Sky*, Benny does a wartime song-and-dance act with his brother (played by Tommy Steele). Dancing in army boots again!

Below: Benny and Michael Caine together in *The Italian Job*: not the first time Benny had played a milkman.

Right: In a tense scene from the film *Chitty Chitty Bang Bang*, Benny and Dick Van Dyke look worried. But it turned out all right in the end . . .

Below: 'Bog-dweller Benny' tells the Lord of the Manor, writer/actor Dave Freeman, of the magic drink. Schweppes advertisement, early 1960s.

Right: Stuntman Ken Sedd shows souvenirs of twenty-five years' association with Benny Hill.

Opposite page: Benny with his long-time stooge Jackie Wright in 1982.

Left: Phyllis Diller is delighted to receive a picture of her pen-pal, Benny Hill, at her home in Brenton Park, Hollywood.

Above: Dennis Kirkland, trapped between Benny as Fred Scuttle and his Madame Tussaud's lookalike, 1987.

Left: Benny is playing with fire again in this backstage pose with his friend Sue Upton.

Opposite page: Benny performs a trick as one of a troupe of similarly-clad males forced to perform by a female man-tamer with a whip. This circus-style sketch resonated in a way rare in television comedy.

Above right: Prince Philip shaking hands with Benny at the Eric Morecambe London Palladium 'Bring Me Sunshine' Tribute Show. Petula Clark and Cannon and Ball look on.

Below right: Cannes 1989: Benny with business associate and friend Don Taffner and distinguished newscaster Walter Cronkite at a Thames Television publicity junket.

Below: Benny Hill's team as the Crook Report, featuring, from the left, Henry McGee, Benny (as Roger Crook), Jon Jon Keefe, Bob Todd, and Duggie Small.

the Eurovision Song Contest. The bill had been arranged and printed before Benny's remarkable broadcast. Suddenly, there were queues for tickets around the block and packed houses every night. Nobody appeared to know why. Lew Grade knew why. Now Lord Grade, he was one of a formidable theatrical partnership with his twin brother Leslie. Lew suddenly appeared in Benny's dressing-room as the comedian was preparing for his performance. 'Why don't you come and join us, Benny?' invited the impresario. 'You could do a show with us. We would look after you.' He looked round him. 'We've got dressing-rooms too, you know. Bigger and better than this one. You can have a nice time. You'll do well with us.'

'Don't stand there talking,' answered Benny, 'make yourself useful. I'm on in a minute. Do me up at the back.'

Lew started to help my brother into his stage clothes. 'See what I mean about joining us, Benny?' said Lew. 'We've only been working together for three minutes – and you got the highest paid dresser in the business, already!'

Benny saw what he meant and joined the Grades in a happy and easy-going association. He was immediately promoted to top of the bill and signed for a tour of the stage version of the Benny Hill Show. It did sensational business. The record for box-office takings at the Chelsea Palace had been broken the week before Benny was due to open there when the heart-throb singer Dickie Valentine had packed the place out during the week of his much publicized wedding. But Benny topped the takings a few days later to hold the record of the Chelsea Palace for ever.

I was in the audience on one evening and have never seen such remarkable scenes of acclaim. One could not move about the theatre for the crush. Groups of screaming teenage girls added to the confusion. I was amazed to see them, as I had always considered my brother a laughter-maker, not a figure of female adulation. Of course, with his fans, some from his club days, packing the theatre to the rafters, it was a time for tear-stained faces and aching ribs. Everyone went home happy and exhausted. It was the same everywhere. Even in Sunderland.

In the four years since the audience had slow-handclapped Benny from the stage of the Sunderland Empire, there had been a revolutionary change in the entertainment industry. The ailing variety circuits were now in their death throes, the Benny Hill Show being almost the only large touring show making large profits. Television had exploded from being the plaything of the metropolitan *nouveau riche* to a countrywide service with millions of avid viewers in all the great cities and towns. The regions had suddenly become much less provincial.

The shared experiences, evening after evening, meant that although London still dominated television production, half the population were being sensitized to national concerns. Television's visual impact reinforced the awareness of an English, if not a British, culture, sustained by the radio network. Watching their favourites on the small screen speaking largely in Standard English or Cockney, the viewers were willy-nilly imbibing lessons in the understanding of southern speech. The changes in leisure-time habits led to a growing sophistication, newly acquired tastes, familiarity with a wider range of subjects and style, including humour.

Thus, when Benny returned to Sunderland as a star, he arrived in triumph. He was no longer an incomprehensible alien, muttering strange comments on esoteric subjects. He was the cheeky young fellow who regularly appeared in the lounge to keep the family in stitches – and, as such, he was trebly welcome. The Empire Theatre was sold out. From his first entrance on the Monday evening, Benny was given a tumultuous reception. The response was so warm that he wondered how many in these enthusiastic audiences had seen his original débâcle.

On the Saturday evening, my brother sent a note to the manager requesting him to watch the second-house show from the back of the auditorium. At the climax of his performance, Benny repeated, word-for-word, the seven-minute solo spot that had, years earlier, sent him home in disgrace. This time he really socked it to them. This time they understood it – and loved it. Roars of laughter and cheers greeted every sally. Standing among the crowd who could not get seats, the manager smiled wanly. The rapturous applause rolled on and on. At last, with a farewell volley, Benny was through. He took bow after bow and finally walked off-stage as the old theatre shook with the thunder of stamping, cheering approbation.

13

Britain's Brightest Boy

The Captain rarely revealed publicly the disappointment with his sons that he vouchsafed so freely to them in private; such an admission would have reflected adversely upon him. Among his cronies, he described unlikely virtues that my brother and I had obviously inherited from their father. So that, when, in the New Year of 1955, Benny was selected as TV Personality of 1954–5, the Captain felt able to boast about it to a group of elders at a Jewish wedding reception we were all attending. However, they told me later that he was stumped for a moment when the cantor drew attention to my presence across the hall. As I was an assistant schoolmaster at the time, the Captain was at a loss to find something to say in my favour. He looked at me, paused, and, touching his temple with a forefinger, solemnly intoned – 'Deep Thinker'.

Benny had taken a few days from rehearsals to see his parents off at Southampton Docks. They were cruising by liner to Australia to visit Diana for the first time. Mum was overjoyed at the prospect of seeing her daughter, who was now married and working as a nurse in Sydney; so was the Captain, but he was also looking forward to employing his skills as a bowls champion and active Freemason. He was likely to be making a host of new contacts in the year before Mum and he were due to return.

While on the south coast, Benny took the opportunity to try out a fairground organ stored in an aircraft hangar near Chichester. This exploratory jaunt came about because he loves the sound of a steam organ: he had considered calling his own show 'Benny Hill's Merry-Go-Round' and was much taken with the idea of a fairground scene to open it. Accordingly, Cyril Ornadel, the composer, was commissioned to write a jolly piece for fairground organ, only to discover that such an instrument was difficult to find. They traced one to the Kursaal fairground, Southend, where they were told it had been moved to West Sussex for safety. Even more difficult to find was the only man in the country who could transcribe music from the manuscript to the card with punched holes that would activate the organ. It took months of letters and telephone calls for Benny's idea to reach the stage where the splendid music was actually peppered on the card that would depress the keys of the mammoth instrument.

On a bitter winter's morning, Benny and Cyril stood shivering in the aircraft hangar as the organist fed the card into the machine. There was a sudden blast that made them jump as the giant pipes began to pump out the music. Except that it was not splendid – or even music. An ear-splitting stridulation made the hangar sound like an iron-foundry. The cacophony was soon stopped. 'The organ is frozen,' said the expert, 'we must allow it a couple of hours to warm up.'

After a couple of hours, Benny, Cyril and the organ had all warmed up. The card was inserted again. This time music emerged. But it was not splendid music – not at all the glorious racket that Benny was hoping for. It clearly would not do.

'Never mind,' said Cyril. 'I'll arrange the piece for the orchestra. It'll be okay. You'll see. We'll make a gorgeous noise. Just like a fairground organ. No one will know the difference.'

'I shall,' said Benny, sadly.

'You will,' said Cyril. 'But the audience won't.'

There was insufficient time to find another organ. On this occasion Benny had to accept second best. But the story illustrates the efforts he has always made to achieve the highest values for his shows. A week later, the first Benny Hill Show opened to the music of a carousel, on which sat a bevy of beauties, their long hair blowing in the breeze from a hidden wind-machine. Benny had ensured the support of two of his favourite performers, Alma Cogan and Beryl Reid. Alma was a bright soubrette of immense talent and charm; Beryl could play every kind of female character from the 'jolly hockey-sticks schoolgirl' to 'Sister George' in the play by Frank Marcus in which she made an international reputation. The presence of two such stalwarts gave Benny the confidence to attempt the higher slopes of comedy. He was hilarious with Dave Freeman as Bill and Ben the Flowerpot Men, two string puppets from a children's programme whose splendid language, 'Oh, clop-a-loppa-lop', took a terrible beating.

The *pièce de résistance*, however, was yet another quick-change travesty, concerning a medieval king besieged in his castle 'by the French'. The king summons several advisers (all played by Benny) to him, one after the other. The first is a French prisoner already shackled by ball and chain. After questioning, the prisoner is dismissed, but it soon becomes apparent that off-stage the shackles cannot be removed. Benny has therefore to play all the other parts encumbered with a huge iron ball. He enters with it hidden on his back, as a hunchback: in front as a pregnant serving wench: on his leg, under his tights, like an obscene carbuncle, and between his thighs like some monstrous codpiece. It was a brilliant piece of visual comedy.

Next day, the show was given a mixed reception by the press. Several of the newspaper critics affected to be disappointed. I was mystified by this response. My brother suggested that possibly the ball-and-chain sketch was more suited to the stage than television. As none of the critics had made this point, I felt that their sourness was due more to a perception that dissatisfaction made better copy than the excellent reviews Benny had been receiving. However, the critics found that, having paid attention to their strictures, his next show in February was very much better. 'The show perked up with a bang,' wrote one. 'Here was Mr Hill in sparkling form.' In fact, he was in his usual sparkling form, with a hilarious send-up of the panellists on a game show called 'Find the Link'. 'If there is one word which describes the essential of good TV,' wrote another columnist, 'it is intimacy . . . there is only one light entertainment show to have both grasped this principle and be trying to act upon it – The Benny Hill Show.'

In the first few series, the hour-long presentations always ended with a cod musical comedy finale. Starting with a mock 'Student Prince/Chocolate Soldier' that boasted an authentic drinking song, 'It's Ruby-red Sherry-style Imported Algerian Wine, Drink Deep and Your Eyes and Nose Will Shine', Benny and Dave went through the well-known types of musical. Eventually they were reduced to writing a 'Dracula' operetta ('Just Remember, My Daughter, Blood's Thicker than Water!'), a 'Frankenstein' and finally a melodious 'Highway Patrol', with Benny as a baritone Broderick Crawford.

After the success of the 'What's My Line' spoof, Benny set about satirizing most of the popular television shows. When Benny turned a sardonic eye on 'Six-Five Special', TV critic Ronald Stott called the burlesque of

the rock 'n' roll show 'a miniature masterpiece. It was
a stroke of genius to prefilm Benny in the guises of
half-a-dozen or more types of . . . idolaters, so that the
varying shots could be inserted at brief intervals. It is
a long, long time since I had such a hearty Saturday-
night laugh.' What Stott failed to report was that the
device had made Benny the first TV recipient of an ovation by telephone. The BBC switchboard was jammed
with a record number of congratulatory calls – more
than ten times the previous record. The *Daily Herald*
reported that in his 'Six-Five Special' impression he
imitated Freddie Mills so well that the ex-boxer's own
father-in-law thought it really was Freddie.

The excellence of this show led the Deputy Director
of Television Broadcasting to write an internal memo to
Ronnie Waldman.

Subject: The Benny Hill Show: Saturday, 1 February, 1958: Produced by John Street
   This, I thought, was in places brilliant. At the
same time, I am always worried that Hill will say
or do something unacceptable!
                    (signed) Cecil McGivern

That comment is the kind of accolade to which all
young comedians should aspire. They cannot hope
for continual brilliance; even Chaplin produced some
duds. Occasional brilliance is the most even the greatest comedian can achieve. But it is the traditional duty
of the fool to reveal folly even at the risk of a whipping,
not only from his master, but from others, too, who
would deny the truth. McGivern's note makes it clear
that Benny was already dangerously close to giving
offence to some – and giving offence to some is a risk
that a true comedian should be prepared to take.

In his impression of the popular 'Juke Box Jury', Benny wanted to appear as the four members of the panel, all of them on-screen *at the same time*. He was pushing television techniques to the limit. Luckily, his producer, John Street, had movie experience and knew that he could photograph and record four times on a section of 35 millimetre, winding back the film each time. It would take very careful timing both in length of take and dialogue. Benny wrote the piece according to specified time limits and it was performed, shot and recorded and broadcast successfully. On the screen before their very eyes, the viewers could see and hear the four celebrities (all played by Benny) in one long scene. They were astonished by the comedian's versatility. But this remarkable accomplishment was a tribute to his producer's versatility too.

For the many who have seen Nicholas Parsons only as an impeccable master of ceremonies, it may come as a surprise to learn that he was once a professional impressionist. His impersonation of the film star Barry Fitzgerald is a knockout. So that when Benny asked Nicholas to impersonate another Irishman, Eamonn Andrews, in a take-off of 'This Is Your Life', he picked the right man. Nicholas played the part to the hilt as he introduced the sketch. Benny, off-stage, protested in mock astonishment – 'He's getting bigger laughs than I do!' He kidded Nicholas for years about his success, but must have appreciated the contribution since the one-time impersonator later became a regular on the show.

'A minute before The Benny Hill Show was due to open on BBC television last night,' wrote Kenneth Bailey in *The People* on 31 March 1957, 'electricians threw the switches and plunged the studio into darkness.' It was a lightning strike.

'I'll never forget it,' says John Street, the producer. 'I was in the television gallery at the studio in the huge Palace Theatre, Hammersmith. We were just about to go on air when all the studio lights went out. Only the theatre house lights stayed on, but we could hardly see by those. I rushed down from the gallery with Duncan Wood, a senior producer, and we found that the camera dollies were still. They could not be moved. We left Hettie Tack, my secretary, alone upstairs to direct the show and we manhandled the cameras. When he wasn't quick-changing or performing, Benny worked like a dog too. He was an unforgettable sight, dolled up in drag, pushing the cameras around and encouraging everyone to keep the show on the air. The electricians, who you might think would be murderous, were all on Benny's side. His determination won them over. Although they obeyed their union's instructions, it didn't stop them cheering Benny on and shouting advice – "Come on, Ben. It's not a close-up. You want a two-shot here!" I couldn't believe what was happening. It was surreal. We finally got enough power to put the show on air seven minutes late, but had to keep it on by our own efforts.'

Kenneth Bailey went on, 'As though spurred on by the electricians' walkout, Benny Hill surpassed himself in his BBC show. Benny's mimicry alone is rich enough for an hour's programme, and he does not need to risk himself on sketches. But this time the mimic reached new heights – as Shirley Have-a-care with zither, as Havasneezia Bergman in "Anastasia" and as Baby Doll in a mock TV film excerpt.'

After polishing off 'Guess My Secret' and 'Tonight', Benny turned his attention to the popular pairs that graced the small screen for several years. There were the naturalists Armand and Michaela Denis, who roamed

the Bert Lahr country, 'Gnora, Gnora'; Hans and Lotte
Hass, who were indirectly responsible for Benny being
half-drowned; the Danish pastries Nina and Frederick;
the Israeli singers Esther and Abbe Ofarin ('Cinderella
Rockefeller') and Sonny and Cher. In most cases, Benny
played both partners.

Michael Bentine's favourite skit was one redolent
of cooking sherry – the Craddocks. Benny played
Fanny, who insisted on cooking her marvellous dinners caparisoned in the most gorgeous gowns while
husband Johnny, in evening dress, pottered amiably.
'This endearing image was the supreme target,' says
Bentine. 'What Benny did in that kitchen made one of
the funniest scenes I have ever viewed on television. He
could not stop himself from laughing. When a small,
round potato rolled away from the turkey, Benny ad
libbed, "Oh, look. It's laid an egg!" He was so quick I
nearly bust a gut! As I did at his Square Dancing sketch.
This was a scintillating set piece, a classic construct
of visual comedy. It was a perfectly enjoyable, proper
square dance, with no miming or mugging at all. It goes
on in a very pleasant manner – except that, no matter
which way he turns, or to whom he advances, Benny
always ends up with the ugly, fat girl while the other
men find themselves the pretty partners. This is one
of those remarkable inventions that Benny produces
every now and again. Put together they represent a
considerable body of work at the highest level. Nobody
else has created such excellence for the small screen,
which is why I believe that when this post-war period
is assessed, Benny Hill's will be the only name to join
the pantheon of great comedians.'

The presentation of popular pairs was climaxed years
later by one of Benny's 'remarkable inventions'. In one
show, he offered three skits, each including a pair of

stars. Impersonating all six on film, he conjured up Mae West and W. C. Fields in *My Little Chickadee*; Richard Burton and Elizabeth Taylor from *Who's Afraid of Virginia Woolf?*; Marlon Brando and Rod Steiger in the cab scene from *On the Waterfront*. In addition, he played all three Marx brothers and Oliver Hardy. My brother was then at the height of his powers and still slim enough to accomplish each of the look-alikes with ease. I do not believe that a *tour-de-force* of that kind has been equalled on television before or since.

After his successful launch, Benny presented regular, packed, elaborate shows for the BBC for well over ten years. He became their most durable and popular personality, whose supremacy at the top of the ratings table beat off all attacks from ITV. With frequent help from Dave Freeman, he wrote the entire show, words and music, as he still does.

Into the many entertainments he created for the BBC over the years, he poured the comedy cornucopia of his mind – an immense wealth of material, not all of it original, but most of it new to television. He was the great innovator. Until he burst upon the scene, small-screen comedy had been locked into insular music-hall stereotypes. Benny opened it all up. He introduced a vast new world of humour: not just funny Frenchmen, but jolly Japanese, ludicrous Lapps, and preposterous Peruvian Indians. No race or country was safe from his hilarious caricatures, no incident or period in history, no book, play, film, newspaper story, radio broadcast, television programme or item of interest. His shows brought numerous novelties to the small screen – comic choirs, funny folk dances, muddled marching bands, calypsos, talking statues, dream sequences, silent films, graffiti, amplified sound sketches, black theatre illusions and dozens more. He pressed his producer and crew for techniques never before used in comedy – a narrowed picture, for example, to make him look thinner.

Benny's innovations, technical or otherwise, were soon taken up by others. 'Much of my original material has been used, without acknowledgement, many times,' he told me. 'Some of it has been repeated so often that even people in show-business do not believe I invented it.'

'Give me a "fer instance",' I said.

'Well, take the first sketch I ever wrote for "Show Case" – the lightweight device powered by a heavy battery. That came straight out of my head. I have since seen it performed three times by comedians in other shows.'

Dennis Kirkland, Benny's director, has to deal with a more serious aspect of his comedian's fecundity. 'I have responsibility for security. Quite frequently Benny will come up with a totally new concept, an idea or a sketch that has never been done before. This is like a nugget of gold, money in the bank. Some comedians would give their right arms to get a crack at it first. I have to watch over that comedy bit from conception until it is safely on the air. Which is why I abhor a delay between shooting and broadcast.' The danger has always been there; from his earliest BBC days Benny Hill taught everyone how to use television for comedy. Scores of comedians and shows in Britain and the USA have, for forty years, fed on the crumbs from his table.

Benny would be the first to bid them *'bon appétit'*. He has himself partaken freely from traditional and classic sources. He knows you cannot copyright a humorous concept. Every now and again, if it fits the context, my brother will quite openly include an undisguised gag from Chaplin or Keaton as a kind of tribute. He will adapt old jokes from seaside postcards or refurbish music-hall sketches. 'When I was with the BBC,' he explains, 'I took the view, accepted by most comedians then, that anything we heard on shortwave radio from the States was fair game, because using it here was unlikely to damage anybody's career.'

'Occasionally, when he was younger,' says Peter Charlesworth, 'he would buy the germ of a sketch. Whenever he did, he invariably paid over the odds for it.'

Benny is always careful in his selection of sources. He likes to be sure that they are in the public domain or his own creation. And it is his own observation that provides him with the most characteristic and trenchant comedy. John Street, the maestro who has edited scores of Benny Hill shows for the US, France and other countries, probably knows my brother's work better than Benny himself. 'One of his great strengths,' says John, 'is his ability to recycle his own material. Not only can he polish up one of his forgotten stories from forty years ago to astonish a modern audience, but he can adapt a skit that was seen a year ago so that it is unrecognizable today – and still get delighted laughter with it.' Unfortunately, Benny is disorderly in his habits and throws away valuable scripts and papers. As he has totally forgotten many of his performances there is no access to much of his early work, for it appears to have been destroyed.

Many years ago, a couple of misguided accusations of plagiarism were levelled at my brother. One well-known comedian wrote to complain that Benny had used a joke that the complainant had bought for £150. He was soon apprised of the fact that the joke he thought he owned had earlier been broadcast in an obscure American radio show and had appeared in the Judy Canova film *Broadway Gondolier* in 1935. Another funny man once wrote to allege appropriation of material. My brother relished the irony of the situation as his critic, unknowingly, had broadcast two days earlier original material written by Benny and stolen by the writer's producer. Not wishing to embarrass the complainant, he did not reply.

'Benny Hill does not steal material,' says Michael Bentine. 'He has no need to. His own ideas are usually better, anyway. He is completely honest. He can afford to be. In the early days, Benny once said to me, "Sometimes you worry me, talking so openly about comedy. You are so full of ideas that you may think I shall nick them from you." I never thought that for a moment. He has never nicked a thing from me. But he's the only man to have thanked me for an idea in public. I have helped quite a few comedians and played a large part in the success of a couple, but the only one publicly to acknowledge my help was Benny. I gave him the idea of a male fashion parade – with all the crazy jargon, he did it beautifully on television. It was very funny. And, at the end, he said on air, "I'd like to thank my friend, Michael Bentine, for giving me the idea of the fashion parade." That's a very rare gesture for a comedian. They usually take over an idea and, before long, have convinced themselves that they thought of it first.'

Benny can testify to the paranoia that possesses some performers about their stock-in-trade. Many years ago, Richard Stone asked my brother to help out one of his clients, a comic of some reputation, who was going into a summer show as principal comedian. 'Please give him a hand,' requested Richard. 'He's short of material.' When they met in a quiet pub, the comedian paid serious attention as Benny explained the scripts he had brought along. The papers were strewn all over the table before them, when, suddenly, another famous comedian entered the snug. Immediately, my brother's companion leapt to his feet and cried to the newcomer: 'The cheek of this feller – he thinks I need his help! Me – that's topped bills from Brighton to Glasgow! Me, that's had thirty years in the business! And look at the stuff.' He picked up a page and read a line in a manner calculated to kill it stone dead. 'I don't need crap like that!' he shouted, throwing down the paper and storming out.

By the time the first Benny Hill Show was completed in April 1955 my brother was already committed to two other major projects. He had signed to star in the Folies Bergère show, *Paris by Night*, at the Prince of Wales Theatre, and in his first film, an Ealing comedy called *Who Done It?* Benny had set himself a punishing programme in attempting the two ventures in tandem. However, it all began well.

'This was the third Folies-type show starring a British comedian that I had put on,' explains Lord Delfont. 'When it was announced that we were featuring Benny, we had the biggest advance bookings ever. He was a tremendous draw. The theatre was packed for eighteen months. I invited Maurice Chevalier over from Paris for the opening. He sat with my wife and me in the stalls, beaming with delight at Benny on-stage. "Thees boy ees wondairful," he said, in his famous French accent. I believe that when I introduced them backstage, Maurice and Benny took to each other at once.' Benny confirms this view of his feelings. 'Maurice was a lovely, gentle man – so sensitive,' he says. 'He wanted no embarrassment or awkwardness at the press conference, just like me, and as I do, made suggestions to avoid any difficulties. We were on exactly the same wavelength – except that he reassured me by being even more nervous than I was.'

In *Paris by Night* the 'smilingly impudent scamp', as *The Times* called him, presented 'The Fashion Parade' (after thorough rehearsals round the halls). Benny used two ravishing fashion models who showed off the latest creations and then he, as Digby, would echo their presentations with a crazy male model equivalent. Jeremy Hawk intoned the commentary – 'And now Digby models beachwear for the gentleman.' Enter Benny, intent on covering his nipples with inadequate braces while carrying a beachball that has a life of its own. The beachball escapes, is pursued and bursts upon capture. 'This year the Riviera Superdark sunglasses protect the traveller from midday glare.' They don't protect Digby. He can't see a thing and crashes into the scenery. Second scene: 'Casual wear for the smoker'. Digby reveals the inside of his jacket to show serried ranks of pipes, cigars, cigarette packets, matches and lighters.

'For the non-smoker – ' the other side – rows of lollipops all different colours.

'May be worn with or without the belt' – without – down fall the trousers.

Such basic visual comedy provoked roars of laughter from the packed houses. Lord Delfont would drop in from time to time to watch Benny from the wings. 'I just enjoyed hearing those marvellous waves of laughter,' he said, 'then I'd walk out feeling very happy.'

Benny could scarcely believe that he was occupying the dressing-room where five years earlier Sid Field had sat and made up. He could almost hear Sid's husky voice protesting – 'What a perFORMance!' My brother has never had the slightest doubt that Sid Field was the funniest stage comedian ever. To be following such a

peerless performer into that room meant a great deal
to him.

To Benny they were hallowed boards. But not to
Jeremy Hawk. He incited the most notorious of the
young ladies of the chorus – well known for her
vicious tongue and voracious appetite – to attack
Benny in his dressing-room. Jeremy and his fellow-
conspirators eavesdropped at the door while Benny
tried to keep his cool. His protestations and attempts
to escape the attentions of this man-eater had them in
hysterics. After he had been chased round the room a
couple of times, Jeremy burst in to rescue him. It was
typical of the japes engineered by Jeremy.

Benny had only just begun the twice-nightly stints at
the Prince of Wales Theatre when Sir Michael Balcon
put him to work every day at Ealing Studios. By this
time, *Who Done It?* had been written. T. E. B. Clarke,
who had earned an international reputation for the
screenplays of half a dozen successful Ealing comedies, had accompanied Benny on his music-hall tour
of the country to try to capture the funny man's particular charisma and write a film to showcase it.

Tibby came up with a story about an ice-rink attendant turned detective, who with luck on his side every
time outwits and captures a nest of Soviet spies. It
was a knockabout comedy with a great deal of racing
about, suitable for any one of several slapstick comics
of that time.

While making the film, Benny's day began at six,
with a car calling for him in the Edgware Road to get
him to Ealing in time for make-up at seven-thirty to
be ready for shooting at nine. Most mornings he slept
through make-up, although some of his disguises were
elaborate. He also slept on the set. In one scene, when
the villains shot him, he sank to the floor and promptly

fell asleep where he lay. In another scene, where he was sitting comfortably, the director, Basil Dearden, gave him instructions on how to turn his head. Before Basil could say 'action!' Benny was fast asleep. After a tiring day, a car rushed him to the Prince of Wales Theatre for a busy evening.

Even there, he dozed. Sometimes, Harold Collins, the conductor, had to tap his baton to alert Benny, when in his exhaustion he repeated the verse of a song. He was learning fast that being a film star was not all moonlight on the terrace at Riviera parties. For one gag, they sat him on a tray and shot him across the ice rink. Unfortunately, the safety surround was not effective and he hit the bottom of his back on a solid wooden corner. He was badly bruised, but it could have been worse. He might have broken his spine.

The rising luminary did, however, enjoy a taste of *la dolce vita*, one of the compensations of stardom, on a Good Friday evening when, flanked by a couple of delicious Windmill girls, he awarded the *Who Done It?* trophy to the winner of a stock-car race at the West Ham track. This was a publicity stunt, paid for by Ealing Studios to advertise the film, which climaxed at a stock-car race meeting.

After a dinner of smoked salmon, washed down by champagne and shared with his two decorative escorts in the restaurant overlooking the track, Benny drove a jeep twice round the circuit to start the race. At its end he presented a metal trophy to the winner, who ignored the blood running down his face from a head injury, to wave his prize in triumph as Benny drove him on a lap of honour round the track. It was, apparently, a night to remember.

'With the wind blowing through my hair, the champagne tingling in my veins and the roar of the crowd in my ears,' he confesses, 'it was an experience I shall never forget.'

Ealing Studios decided not to show the film in London's West End. The critics tended to agree with them. The doyenne of the film columnists, Dilys Powell, wrote in the *Sunday Times*, 'an amateur detective (Benny Hill) entangled in espionage, ice-skating, weather-control, stock-car racing, the Radio Show – I found it a sad bundle.' Fred Majdalany in the *Daily Mail* thought that 'Mr Hill – a green Hill who's always far away, bungles through it like a huge and charming innocent born to be a victim.'

Several critics noted the poverty-stricken nature of the script. 'Situations and stock ingredients are corny,' said *Variety*, to the point as ever. *Kine Weekly* remarked that 'Benny Hill works tirelessly.' I thought that he so underplayed his part that he was practically invisible. However, an unlikely viewer was very much impressed. 'I first saw Benny in *Who Done It?*,' Burt Reynolds told me. 'He made me laugh. I didn't like the picture, but I thought he was marvellous. You can learn from a bad picture, you know. At that rate, I must be brilliant. Anyway, I saw something there the first time I set eyes on him. Somebody had thrown a net over him, but he was struggling to work his way out of it. They had a stranglehold on him but he was coming through. I saw something there that was wonderful.'

In November 1955, Benny was invited to appear before the royal family. The *Daily Telegraph* described the occasion thus: 'In a gay, brilliant setting, the Queen, accompanied by the Duke of Edinburgh, Princess Margaret, Queen Elizabeth the Queen Mother, and Princess Alexandra, last night attended the twenty-sixth Royal Variety Performance at the Victoria Palace.

'Thousands of people gathered around the theatre to

welcome the royal party. Many had been waiting for hours and extra police, mounted and on foot, were called in to control the crowd.'

'I was President of the Fund and producer of the show,' explains Lord Delfont. 'I picked the list of performers and submitted it to the Palace. Obviously, Benny had to be considered. He was a big, popular star, carrying a successful show in the West End, who had never been honoured before – an eminently suitable candidate. We did not want to lose the evening at the Prince of Wales Theatre, so special arrangements had to be made. We were worried that Benny would not be able to manage it at all. He had to play some of the first house in *Paris by Night*, race by taxi to perform before Her Majesty, return for the rest of the first house and the second house at the Prince of Wales Theatre and, after the finale, rush over to the Victoria Palace Theatre to join the line-up to shake hands with the Queen and other members of the royal family. Benny made it by the skin of his teeth. He appeared early on in the royal show and did very well in spite of the tough audience that could be difficult. They responded marvellously to him and he certainly enhanced his reputation that night.'

Several newspapers reported that Prince Philip was particularly amused by Benny's performance. Lena Horne, Johnnie Ray and George Jessell were favourites of my brother who also made an impact in the Royal Variety Performance. Benny took the opportunity to spend some time with George Jessell, the legendary American entertainer, for whom he had great affection and respect.

Starring in *Paris by Night* had, from the first, presented problems for Benny. His pre-eminence had always been

challenged from two quarters – the beautiful girls and
the supporting comedian Tommy Cooper. In the early
months of the show's run, Benny had more than held
his own. He was the darling of, first, the London
crowd and, then, the coachloads of admirers from
all over Britain. They knew, from television, every
idiosyncrasy of his face and voice. They understood
every nuance of his speech. However, his audiences
of fellow-countrymen and -women were gradually
replaced by foreign tourists and businessmen unfamiliar with his brand of humour. Strangers may have
enjoyed the visual comedy of his sketches, but they
failed to appreciate the patter in his opening spot and
final seven minutes.

Not only was the audience balance being tipped
against English-speakers; it was clearly showing an
increasing predominance of men over women. Bus-
loads of Japanese businessmen were filling the front
rows of the stalls. They had come to see the delectable models, and to them Benny was merely an irri-
tating distraction. It was the Windmill dilemma all
over again. But one comic who had beaten the sul-
len antipathy of the Windmill watchers was Tommy
Cooper. He had learnt to get on with his act – and
laugh at it himself. A naturally funny man, with a
rough and ready manner, he never appeared to let
anything get him down. As his performance was largely
visual, he was usually well received at the Prince
of Wales, but did not give a damn if he was not.
Although they were both Southampton boys, Benny
was totally different. If he was not getting laughs,
he worried. Even if the laughs were coming thick
and fast, he worried that they might stop. Now the
ghost of his Sunderland failure had come back to
haunt him.

'After I finished the filming, things got really tough for me at the Prince of Wales,' says Benny. 'I knew my stuff wasn't going as well as it should, and I felt trapped. It was almost impossible to get the sketches or spots changed, because in those days every word and gesture had to be passed by the Lord Chamberlain. I was stuck with the agreed script. It was a deeply depressing time for me. When taking my bath every afternoon, a black cloud would descend upon me.'

I was aware of my brother's predicament, and actually made matters worse by sending him a long letter of suggestions that probably would not have worked even if he had been able to carry them out. It was that last seven-minute spot that had him reeling off the stage at the end of a show. Peter Charlesworth confirms my observation. 'Benny would be white with tension under his make-up,' Peter recalls. 'As he struggled to get the patter across to an uncomprehending audience, he would sway as if about to faint. I felt for him.' At the end of a show, Benny would crawl home like a wounded animal, to lie all night dozing fitfully in a foetal position.

One evening, as he left the theatre, a group of yobbos caught sight of him, gathered round and shouted, 'Lucky ole Ben – Off to a party then?' Climbing painfully into his cab, Benny muttered, 'Party? I'm in no state for parties.' The next morning, when he picked up his mail from the mat, he glanced at himself in the hall mirror. His eyes were bloodshot and his complexion grey. He stuck out his tongue and was disgusted to see that it was white and furry. No wonder he did not feel at all well. Regarding the sorry figure in the mirror, he opened the largest of his envelopes. It was from the editor of the comic, *Radio Fun*. They intended to feature Benny, the editor wrote, as the central character in a regular series of humorous cartoon stories.

'We are going to call you,' said the editor, 'Britain's Brightest Boy!'

14

What's It All About, Alfie?

When it became clear that battling impassive foreign audiences at the Prince of Wales Theatre was affecting his health, Benny went to Lord Delfont. He did not need to spell out his predicament. The impresario understood at once and immediately released him from his labours. In return, Bernard suggested that my brother might consider writing and starring in a couple of his Saturday Night Spectaculars on television. Benny agreed then and there, delighted at the prospect of returning to the familiar clutter of the television studio.

A few months later, Benny's self-esteem was nourished by an invitation to lunch from George and Alfred Black. Mindful of his painful dismissal by the Blacks from the cast of *Sky High*, he brought his agent, Richard Stone, with him. He was wise to do so. They wanted him to take over for three weeks from the comedian Dave King at the London Hippodrome, beginning on the Saturday evening in November 1956. Dave could no longer delay an appendix operation, and would be away until he had recovered from it. Knowing all about Benny's original failure in Sunderland and having heard of his difficulties at the Prince of Wales, the Blacks were understandably a trifle tentative. Their minds were concentrated on the risks they were taking. Was Benny up to the task? Richard Stone, who had no such doubts about his main man, was considering other factors.

'I understand your concern,' he said. 'So, instead of a straight salary, let's put Benny on a percentage. That way, he won't cost you a penny he doesn't earn.' That sounded like good sense to the Blacks. They agreed to a generous percentage. What Richard was banking on was the fact that the following month included the Motor Show and Smithfield Cattle Show, two weeks when the city would be full of punters up from the provinces.

The next Saturday-evening performance at the London Hippodrome was a surprise to all concerned. At such short notice, Benny played safe by using his spots and sketches from *Paris by Night* as far as he could. He was astonished when his opening lines were greeted with great gusts of laughter. 'I couldn't believe it,' he says. 'I opened with a roar and just built from there. I had to pinch myself in the sketches to convince myself that it was all happening. We just flew all evening and never came down.' A crowded auditorium that had come to see Dave King gave Benny a standing ovation. The Black brothers were relieved and delighted. The fact that they had to pay a fortune to their stand-in star did not worry them unduly. Benny played to packers for a month, so the Blacks made a fortune, too.

As my brother's agent, Richard Stone was always keen to find work for his client. However, after Benny had made his name, he became less interested in continuous employment, preferring to achieve high standards by spending months in careful preparation. He began to refuse some of the offers Richard elicited, and later evolved a way of life in which he spent most of each year writing and planning, much less time in performing. My brother was concerned to limit his television performances so that his huge audience was always glad to see him. Most years he appeared only in a series of six Benny Hill Shows for the BBC. After the mid-sixties, he rarely made commercials in Britain for fear that they would expose him too often.

Now that Benny was able to command large fees, Richard arranged for accountants to handle his financial affairs. The money was not of the slightest interest to my brother. He grudged any time spent talking about it. However, he listened to Richard when he suggested that he could afford to relax his self-discipline somewhat. Friends urged Benny to take up the income tax allowances he had never bothered to claim. They kidded him that spending so little on expenses made everybody else look irresponsible. Benny took their advice in one respect only. He started to use the telephone more often. Thus began the ritual of the weekly telephone call. Every Sunday morning he was available, I would walk to a public telephone box a few streets away in Worthing to call him collect at his home. We chatted for ages until I was interrupted by other would-be callers hammering on the glass door. When I could afford my own telephone, our conversations grew even longer, sometimes lasting two hours. They were always a source of fascination for me. I enjoyed vicariously the brouhaha of Benny's life in show-business. I loved to hear of his adventures but was never tempted to follow him into the profession. My early essays into the world of amateur entertainment had taught me that there was a heavy price to pay in wear and tear on the nerves. As comedian Eric Morecambe used to say to him, 'It's the fear, Ben. It's the fear!' I had experienced that and never felt envious of Benny's success, although I think he sometimes might have thought I was.

My brother and I must have spent months in telephone conversation with each other over the years, if all the units were added together. Most of all, we spoke of the Benny Hill Show, reviewing the last one and mulling over plans for the next. Very occasionally I could help by suggesting an angle or recommending a performer. Though his memory of events is extremely poor, Benny never forgets a gag and always acknowledges the slightest contribution. 'You gave me that,' he will say long after I have forgotten about it. The rest of our time on the telephone we talked shop – show-business shop. News of the family, boxing and soccer sometimes occupied us for a short while, but we soon returned to our muttons. I was struck by Benny's concentration on his professional studies. His resemblance to Sherlock Holmes, in this respect, has always intrigued me. Holmes, as I recall, could recognize one hundred and forty kinds of tobacco ash. Benny can write and perform one hundred and forty different jokes about tobacco. And many other subjects.

When we had dealt with the agenda of our telephone conversation, my brother and I would often play showbiz games such as 'Movie Players' or 'Songs from the Shows'. 'Donald Cook?' he would ask. 'Showboat,' I might answer. 'Forty Minutes for Lunch?' I'd say. 'One Touch of Venus,' he would reply. On a good day, of course. Despite my greatest efforts, Benny invariably won the contest.

Our calls to each other remain much the same today. Except in two respects. They are no longer confined to Sunday mornings and we rarely mention the Captain. In the fifties and sixties scarcely a conversation went by without a reference to his incorrigible ways. We were both over forty years old before we began to understand our father's own difficulties and the sources of his irascibility. At about the same time, the Captain mellowed enough to accept his younger son's success and give him the kind of respect Benny had worked so hard to gain. This led to a certain unspoken reconciliation between them, which eased our father's remaining years.

Cosy though he was in his single room at Connie Rhodes's guest-house in Kilburn, Benny felt that the time had come for him to leave for a larger place. It is significant that he made a calculated move to a base four miles nearer to the West End. He chose an unpretentious three-roomed flat in a red-brick block that looked abused rather than weathered. It presided over the seamless union of Maida Vale and Edgware Road, that northern lifeline along which Benny had tramped a score of times.

Benny was always a reluctant home-maker. He appeared unaware of what was required and tended to respond occasionally to the suggestions of friends by officially opening a store in return for a few pieces of furniture in varying styles. He would put up with the discomfort of any lack of amenity rather than make a shopping expedition to remedy it. His home was a den in which he could, with varying effort, satisfy his needs, the most vital being food, composition, girlfriends and Latin American music. These were accommodated with the minimum of personal property. Which sometimes led to difficulties.

Dave Freeman was once invited to the flat for a meal and asked to toss the salad while my brother sautéed the potatoes and grilled the steak. Benny's concentration went into the cooking. Dave therefore found himself, a little later, sitting on the edge of the sofa, contorting his enormous frame into the shape of a letter G so that he could eat from a heaped plate on the lowest of coffee tables. He struggled manfully for a while stabbing with a small fork and sawing with a blunt knife. Suddenly the steak shot one way, the plate another, and the salad all over the carpet.

'What a perFORMance!' cried Benny, as they collected the debris. 'When I said "Toss the salad", I didn't mean, "Toss it on the floor"!'

'I ate at Benny's flat fairly often in those days,' said Dave, 'and it was usually a free and easy affair. That suited me fine. But what a difference when he was entertaining a lady! I was invited when he was trying to tempt Hattie Jacques to join the cast of his show. On that day, he pulled out all the stops – cooking the lobster and decorating the table himself. It was a work of art – flowers, silver, plate. I have no idea where all the crockery came from. Never saw most of it before or since. And the meal was superb. However, Benny's efforts to win Hattie over came to nothing. She never joined his show, but teamed up instead with Eric Sykes and won global fame in the "Carry On" movies.'

The never-ending stream of letters that the postman fed through Benny's letterbox induced his downstairs neighbour Mrs Jones to offer secretarial help. This was gratefully accepted but led to five years of unremitting mutual bafflement. Benny and his new secretary established between them a perfect misunderstanding – that of the irresistible force faced with an immovable object.

Mrs Jones, the widow of an RAF officer, made the most conscientious efforts to assist Benny – to bring some order and a semblance of civilized standards to his life. My brother, on the other hand, required speedy efficiency in a few basic tasks, silent obedience and no interference with the even tenor of his ways. At bottom, he wanted to be left alone in peace to write his shows and compose his songs. He found the deepest satisfaction in the creation of comedy and would polish it for months on end, with breaks only for food, girlfriends and music. Benny watched television and listened to the radio every day but always as a source of material. Because it stole time and attention from his work, most correspondence (in fact, human contact of any kind) was something of a nuisance to him. He found it difficult, therefore, to tolerate Mrs Jones's eagerness to stay working in his flat, keeping it orderly, tidying his possessions and dusting the furniture. When he had distributed his papers all over the carpet, he could not understand why Mrs Jones could not work around them. There was rarely any pressing need, he felt, to clean anything at all.

'Benny used to drive her up the wall,' recalls Dave. ' "Leave it," he would say. "I can never find anything after you've tidied up." "I can't leave it," she would reply. "I've got to dust the place!" She was very lady-like, so the poor woman was never able to express her frustration properly.'

Another female unimpressed by Benny's immediate environment was Dobie Milchrist, who met him at a dance and had been on the town with him and Peter Charlesworth a few times before visiting the Maida Vale flat. As she remembers it, 'I was totally unprepared for what I found – "astonished" is the word. Benny was a massive star then – and he gave me star treatment. I had never tasted champagne before I went out with him. We had marvellous times, and he was always most attentive to me. But I had been brought up on films and assumed his home would reflect his position. So when he invited me to his flat, I expected a huge, sumptuous apartment. It wasn't like that at all, but very ordinary, rather untidy – absolutely nothing smart about it. My own poky place was nicer.'

It must be admitted that Benny's lifestyle in the Maida Vale flat was a modest one. 'You live like a ten-pound-a-week man,' said one journalist to him.

'In a couple of years I may *be* a ten-pound-a-week man,' rejoined Benny.

When Richard Stone called a meeting to discuss his client's financial plans, he suggested that they could realistically forecast no more than five years at the top for Benny. If carefully invested, my brother's earnings before his star waned would provide a steady income for the rest of his life.

No such rosy prospect offered itself to Benny's friend Peter Charlesworth, at that time. 'When I was made redundant,' he recalls, 'nobody wanted me. During my nine months' unemployment, I was down to my last three quid. The only person who supported me in that time was Benny Hill. He was extraordinarily kind and generous. And he managed to save my pride. He would say, "Come over to dinner and lend me a hand. I need help with the script of the next show." He always paid handsomely for my few suggestions. Before I had to sell it, I drove Benny around in my beat-up old Ford Consul. He could have had a Rolls, and chauffeur, but he used me instead. Even the way he suggested a trip allowed me to retain my dignity. If I were free, he would say, "How about this? Charlesworth will supply car and drive Hill to Oxford for Sunday concert. Hill will pay for petrol and lunch. Charlesworth will perform in double-act with Hill. Okay?" I must have been the worst straight man ever, but he paid me twenty-five pounds every performance, and that took care of my rent for five weeks. The trips were never less than great fun. They did my morale a power of good. They made me feel worthwhile, that I was still in show-business and that somebody cared. Above all, they kept my pride intact. Benny always considers people's feelings and I know that he has helped many others in similar ways.'

I was one of the many others that Benny helped. He

made me a director of his company in the late 1950s, passed on the fee for his column in the *Picturegoer*, although I furnished only a few jokes for it every week, and paid me for ghostwriting stories for him in the newspapers. Not to mention his impulsive gestures of extravagant generosity at other times.

Once Peter Charlesworth had established himself as a theatrical agent, his fortunes improved. There followed great days for the bachelor pair. Benny was much in demand as a judge in beauty competitions, a function for which he was eminently suited. Peter continued to drive him to these celebrations.

'It wasn't easy being a judge,' says Benny ruefully. 'I rarely agreed with the other judges, and with only three winners, tended to make very few friends and a host of enemies. Most of the contestants held me personally responsible for their disappointment, although, in fact, my preferences were usually among their number. I was cornered by local bigwigs, upbraided by angry mothers and attacked by jealous boyfriends.'

There were compensations however. He got to meet some very lovely girls. At one contest he introduced himself to Irma and Ellen, friends who were both beauty queens of London districts. On the drive home, Peter confessed to his friend that he was much taken with Irma and asked Benny for her telephone number. Benny changed the subject.

A week later, Benny was entertaining Irma's friend Ellen, in his flat. After one of his spectacular meals, they sat together on the sofa in front of the television set. Sleepy with food and wine, Ellen dozed off, her head on Benny's shoulder. Suddenly, she farted. 'I'm sorry, Peter,' she murmured. 'I'm sorry, *Peter*?' Benny realized with a pang that Peter, the crafty beggar, had been there before him – and had said not a word about it!

When Peter next called his famous friend, he was surprised to be offered Irma's telephone number. He lost no time in contacting her. 'I subsequently took her out. It was the most horrific night I have ever spent with a girl in my life. She started the evening in the most charming and delightful manner, looking very beautiful and calm. Then she had a few drinks. When we got back to my flat, I turned the lights low and she suddenly attacked me verbally, along the lines of "You bastard – you've brought me back here for only one thing – what you can get out of me!" I was taken aback, as I hadn't actually even gone near her. It seemed best to get her home as soon as possible. I stammered, "Oh, I'm sorry. It's all right. I'll call you a taxi." Then she started to cry, sobbing, "Nobody loves or wants me." So I thought I would comfort her. The moment I put a hand on her shoulder, she shouted, "Don't touch me, you swine! I'm not going just because you want to get rid of me! Look at all you rich people with your cars and property. You think you're so clever. Where I come from people get booed if we don't like them." Then she threatened to smash up the room. "Look at you, you swine!" she said and collapsed into tears again. "I haven't a true friend in the world. Be tender, be kind to me. Love me." "All right, sweetheart, everything will be all right," I said. "Don't come near me! Get away from me, you bastard!" It took me four hours to get her out of the flat. Exhausted, I fell into bed at about five o'clock in the morning, having been terrorized by this lunatic all night. When I called Benny the next day I didn't get much sympathy. "Did she run you ragged?" he asked. She had previously driven him crazy, blowing hot and cold all night – and he had deliberately let me in for it.'

Once again, Benny made use of the experience. The real-life farce was re-created for the small screen, with a schizoid beauty's abrupt changes of mood giving Benny hell. The re-enactment was a winner, because so many of the viewers recognized the truth of it. It was yet another opportunity for Benny to make comedy on the theme to which he has returned so many times – the ridiculous predicament of the disappointed male.

Luckily, Benny was not always so disappointed in his own love life. He had many romances, and is, I have no doubt, remembered with affection by matrons all over the country. My brother won hearts not only with the obvious attractions of his good looks, wit and fame, but by his strangely old-fashioned courtesy and thoughtfulness. He was and still is a great one for flowers. Of course, the females he approached were those most likely to be impressed. As Bob Monkhouse points out, 'Benny's relationships with girls have always been with younger women, not older, more demanding or mature women who would expect more from him perhaps than he wishes to give.'

Benny was quite frank about his predilections at the time. 'I like girls who come from working-class backgrounds like myself. Factory girls, shop girls and typists. I get a kick out of taking ordinary girls to places they would not normally visit.'

When we were both very young, I remember walking through the East End with my brother one wet winter evening. He stopped and pointed to an old tenement block standing ominously black against the sky. 'I'd like to marry a girl from a place like that,' he declared, ' – a poor girl, who'd never had anything. I'd take her out of that hole and give her all the things she'd missed. I'd do my damnedest to make her happy.' We were both, as I say, very young at the time. But Benny cherished that dream – of taking some unsuspecting working-class girl out of the slums and creating a better life for her. Always his dream made him the source of good fortune. He bestowed his gifts on her. His dream girl was never very active. Benny finds positive women something of a threat: particularly educated, positive women. He avoids them. On the other hand, no one admires more than my brother the successes of active female achievers.

'Give 'em the chance. Let 'em do it!' he urges. No one cheers louder than he when a woman wins. He is delighted to see her making things happen. But not in *his* life. Benny likes to be in charge. He insists on taking control. One of the traumas of his life occurred when a woman was in control. Benny was being interrogated by a formidable middle-class dame for a women's radio programme. She could not follow his usual chat-up banter and tried to make sense of his throwaway humour. It was clear to the listeners that there was a problem of communication between them. Benny stuttered, coughed, began again and offered explanations of his remarks. He started to bray, 'Y'know', between every other word and generally lost his nerve as the interview went slowly down the tubes. He laughs about it now, but it was one of the experiences that has made him wary.

That he was so wary with women was always a matter of regret for his mother. She appeared to hold an inborn belief in the Talmudic notion that 'a man without a woman is not a human being'. An inkling of his amorous adventures did little to console her for his bachelor status. She wanted to see him safely wed, enjoying the deep, deep peace of the double bed after the hurly-burly of the chaise-longue.

Mum was constantly on the lookout for likely

daughters-in-law. She combed the families of friends and acquaintances, and checked females on Benny's television show. She would urge the merits of every candidate in turn, trying to fan any flicker of interest into a flame. Mum described each of them as 'a lovely girl'. They had only to be female to get her seal of approval. She was a dedicated gender recommender – and always reminded me of the Jewish matchmaker who was trying to interest a prospective bridegroom – 'Have I got a girl for you? Miss Popular herself, Becky Firestone. You know her. Lives down by the canal. Walks with a limp and has a little trouble with her speech. You know! Her with the buck teeth and the cast in one eye. Lovely girl.' Mum demurred at only one suggested fiancée, a beautiful French girl whom Benny had met in Paris. When he confessed that he might like to marry her, Mum said, 'Oh, I don't think that would be a good idea, Alfie. She'd never be able to manage in the checkout at Sainsbury's!'

Benny's relationships with women have been a matter of intense interest to the national press for many years. The journalists find him both a problem and a source of good copy. His Protean nature makes him difficult to stereotype, but it allows him to present a bewildering array of personal aspects. He reveals, therefore, that side of himself most appropriate to the enquirer and the occasion. Benny will play one of several roles – the lighthearted lady-killer, flashing photographs of his conquests from all over the world; the forlorn lover, unlucky in love; the happy bachelor, busy and self-sufficient; the earnest seeker after the girl of his dreams; the hedonist, with a penchant for Eastern saunas; the tender romantic, all hearts and flowers. To blow a little air into the bladders, my brother dips into his stock of one-liners on marriage and his single state from time to time. 'I don't yell, I don't tell and I'm grateful as hell.' When asked bluntly how many of his Hill's Angels he had been to bed with, he grew serious. 'Off the record, I can put my hand on my heart and tell you honestly. I haven't made love to one of those girls,' he said with quiet sincerity. 'I think her name is Sandra.' He was less forthcoming to another reporter. 'I am not allowed to talk about my current love affair,' he stated. 'Well, it wouldn't be fair, Royalty aren't allowed to answer back. All I can say is that I sometimes hold her horse for her.'

By the autumn of 1957 there was no sign that Richard Stone's calculated forecast was coming true. The steady growth in the sale of television sets made Benny's fame wider still, and wider. He was packin' 'em in at Great Yarmouth that summer. Bernard Delfont saw him several times in his seaside show and reported that 'the audience rose to him on every occasion'.

After that successful season, my brother felt that he deserved a holiday. In Spain perhaps. The arrangements were left to the travel agents, who booked Benny into the grandest hotel in Barcelona. Upon arrival, he felt disappointed. From its ambience, he could tell that it was not a truly Spanish establishment. This was not the real Spain. The hotel might just as well have been situated in London. And Benny does not like grand hotels anyway. So, next morning, he checked out and wandered through the streets observing and taking notes. Fascinated by the sights, sounds and smells of the baroque city, the voracious voyeur examined the markets and alleys all day. Evening found him drinking cheap red wine in a bodega near the docks. With the stench of tobacco, raw fish and tar in his nostrils, he felt that at last he had arrived. Across the street stood a dilapidated hotel that could offer only the smallest of top rooms. In a mood of euphoria, Benny took it and lay next to a boiler that puffed and grumbled more than he did. Feverish and sleepless, he consoled himself with the thought that this was Adventure, Romance, Foreign Parts, the Real Spain.

The next morning the hotel was filled with the sound of chattering starlings. Descending the stairs, Benny turned the last corner and stood paralysed by the sight that greeted him. The chattering ceased abruptly as sixty young eyes regarded him. An army of children was taking breakfast.

'Luke!' cried a treble voice. 'Thur's Benny 'ill!' Pandemonium erupted. The place was full of Yorkshire schoolgirls. The innocent abroad paid up at the double, grabbed his things and fled.

Despite his initial blunder, Benny began to develop a taste for short jaunts to Spain or southern France. Occasionally a girlfriend would accompany him. That almost always ensured an active holiday and, if he was lucky, a trip to the moon on gossamer wings. But it was not invariably a success. One time, the experience was like a short course of marital strife. Another excursion was a bore for them both. Once, in the early days, it cost a deal more than Benny thought it was worth. A particularly reckless young woman, whose memory is treasured by a handful of his oldest friends, caned him for four pairs of expensive Italian shoes. 'Four pairs of shoes!' he cried upon his return. 'Who needs four pairs of shoes? Judas Priest, you can only walk on one pair at a time!' He did not get over the shock for ages. The few closest to him chortled over his discomfiture at the time and still kid him about it.

Benny once encapsulated the relationship in an original sketch he performed on television with the brilliant actress Patricia Hayes as the Dolly-bird.

Benny (as the Teddy Boy) approaches.
Benny: Wanna wine gum?
Pat: No, thanks.
Benny: Go on have a wine gum.
Pat: No thanks, I don't want to be under
obligation.
Benny (incredulous): Get away, it's only a wine
gum. You won't be under obligation for a wine
gum. (pause) It's not like a bar of chocolate!

A friendship totally unlike the one suggested above
began when Benny met a young actress by chance.
She came with friends to see the summer show in
which the cheeky comedian was starring and they
literally bumped into each other back-stage. As soon
as he heard her laughter, Benny was a goner. Luckily
for him, her home was in London, and she often
worked in the television studios. When the season
was over, they became lovers. Benny's sweetheart was
a slim, tomboyish girl, not unlike Audrey Hepburn in
appearance. Besides being a good enough actress to
be in demand in the theatre, television and films, she
was a talented sculptress. Her work with hammer
and chisel had developed corns and calluses on her
hands, slight imperfections that Benny grew to love.
The couple appeared to be very happy for some time,
until she met the man she was to marry. When she
left Benny for her new love, he was very depressed
for months. He found solace when he began seeing
another actress, who rescued him from the Slough of
Despond. Although she resembled his previous inamo-
rata in few particulars, Benny became besotted with
her. But their affair was too intense to last. When his
shapely girlfriend began touring in a play there were
fewer opportunities for them to meet. They both wrote

and telephoned at first, but she began to respond less eagerly. It soon became clear that the relationship was becoming one-sided. Despite strenuous efforts, Benny was forced to accept defeat. He grew so miserable that, if his actress flame appeared on his television screen, he would have to switch off or leave the room. It was a very long time before he was completely free of strong feelings for her. When both his actress lovers appeared years later on his screen, on different channels at the same time, he was able to flick from one to the other, regarding their sweet familiar faces at last with equanimity.

One of the last shows to be staged at the Chelsea Palace before it closed for ever in 1957 was produced by Richard Stone and starred Terry Scott and Hugh Lloyd. Richard wanted to make the opening night an occasion. To this end, he used his wide circle of acquaintances to persuade the stars of stage and screen to attend the celebration. Benny was requested to put on a dinner suit and partner Sabrina, a zoftig beauty, who was, at that time, titular queen of British blondes. As Benny observed that she always appeared to be nearer to him than he was to her, he was not indisposed to escort her. Imagine his chagrin when, safely ensconced in their box at the theatre, she revealed that she had been paid £50 to come with him. 'Oh, that makes me a very attractive fellow,' he thought gloomily, 'if they have to pay the girl fifty pounds to sit in a box with me.' Sabrina was kind enough to feign surprise that he had not been paid for his services as well.

At the party after the show, Richard approached Benny, pointing out the raft of photographers present and suggesting that his client should dance with Sabrina for publicity purposes. The paparazzi were focusing on her frontage to the exclusion of everything else. Benny was pleased to oblige Richard and the lady was polite enough to oblige him.

Next morning, at his judo lesson, my brother made a painful mistake. Instead of releasing his seventeen-stone instructor and slapping the floor, he pulled him on top of himself. The fall left him gasping. His good friend, Dr Page, diagnosed a fractured rib and strapped him thoroughly about the rib-cage. Benny had just arrived back home and was changing when Richard called in to see him. 'What's the matter with you?' asked the agent, horrified to see his client's chest so bandaged.

'I've broken a rib,' replied my brother.

'However did it happen?'

'It's your fault, Richard,' said Benny. 'You made me dance with her. This is what you get when you dance with Sabrina!'

When Benny first saw the intimate revue, *La Plume de Ma Tante*, that Robert Dhéry brought from Paris to the West End in 1955, he was enchanted. Here was a show crammed with surprises and visual fun. For example, a beautiful soprano dressed in a gorgeous hooped crinoline is singing a lyrical ballad when the audience is suddenly startled, staring in disbelief. The lovely chanteuse appears to be rather taller than she was. How can that be? The hem of her crinoline still sweeps the floor as, unperturbed, she continues her song. Sure enough, she is growing taller every minute. And amazingly, so is her crinoline! Without a break in the melody that pours from her throat she is elongated until she finishes her ballad atop a soaring dome of shimmering fabric. Stuff like that stimulated my brother to emulate it. He approached Bernard Delfont, who, with the impresario Emil Littler, set about finding backers for a similar revue, starring Benny. Dave

Freeman was co-opted to help write the show and immediately came up with a splendid title, *Layabout Laughing*; however, Emil Littler's suggestion, *Fine Fettle*, was preferred. Ronnie Hazlehurst, Leslie Bricusse and Ron Grainer contributed words and music. Benny began to practise his Paraguayan harp, for which he had paid a fortune. He was at this time under the spell of Latin American music and had introduced the rich and exciting melodies of Los Paraguayos to the British television audience. In return, the popular quartet taught him the secrets of the Paraguayan harp. Whenever he had played guitar, drums or trumpet previously on the small screen, everyone assumed, wrongly, that he was miming. Now he was determined to stun the public with his expertise on stage. 'That harp was a damn nuisance,' says Dave. 'Every time Benny was needed for a script conference or a rehearsal, he was off practising on the bloody thing. In the end, the show overran and when Kenneth Carter, the producer, cut out the Paraguayan number just before we opened,' recalls Dave with a chuckle, 'the irony of it all tickled me. I was in stitches.' Layabout laughing, so to say.

Benny went to the pre-opening party with his hair already cropped to facilitate the traffic of wigs that passed over his head in the course of a performance. He has never forgotten that night. 'It was a marvellous affair, the trees aglow with coloured lights, a lavish buffet and everybody from *Fine Fettle* there. Tommy Cooper entertained and I did my party piece. But the high spot of the evening was when the brothers Bernie and Lew, now Lords Delfont and Grade, danced up a storm. They had been Charleston dancing champions when they were young – and they hadn't forgotten a thing. Didn't they go! Everybody loved it of course. It was great to see them letting their hair down.' Lord

Delfont adds, 'When we finished our dance, Benny said, "I must put you in one of my shows." '

'Fine Fettle, a musical romp in cloth-cap and tails' opened at the prestigious Palace Theatre, Cambridge Circus, in August 1959. The assembling audience was treated to a slide display of mock local advertisements with voice-over – a parody of the ordeal by boredom that cinema-goers have endured for decades. There followed an introduction to an elephant act by a trainer looking remarkably like Benny. He was seized by a trunk which snaked through the front cloth curtains and raised him aloft. The poor fellow tried to continue his talk from high above the orchestra pit despite the difficulties that the elephant was clearly causing at the back. However, it was not long before he disappeared through the curtains, whisked away to bottomless perdition.

Another unlikely creature to be found in a London theatre was the centaur, played by Benny, with an attractive young dancer representing its rear end. She was in intimate contact with Benny's rear end and he warned her, 'I've got one up the spout ready for you. If you make a mistake, I'll fire. One false step and I'll asphyxiate you!' However, in order not to offend accidentally, he doused himself each evening in cheap scent ('Fourpence a gallon,' he says, 'from Woolworths').

Among other delights were a musical marching display by the massed bands of the Milk Marketing Board and a version of 'This Is Your Life', featuring Robertson ('Oh, calamity!') Hare, a veteran of the Aldwych Ben Travers farces, whose first revue this was. W. A. Darlington of the *Daily Telegraph* felt that the billing had misled him: 'While the cloth cap element, which is designed to suit the attractive personality of Mr Hill, is well to the fore, one is rather at a loss to find any justification for "tails" . . . the piece's expectation of life depends fairly and squarely on the likeability of Mr Hill, which is a formidable asset. He is funny and likeable as the front half of a centaur in a classical skit, pathetic and likeable as a country boy at a fair in a mimed solo, gently lewd and likeable as Lady Godiva's stable-boy and generally likeable no matter what he is.'

In the *Evening Standard*, Milton Shulman looked a little closer at the star. 'His cherubic face, with its eyes fluttering like some berserk windscreen wiper, represents on the surface the orthodox little man buffeted and baffled by fate. But he brings to this traditional comic characterization a secret, lipsmacking irreverence which gives his humour a boisterous even bawdy quality.' *The Times* made the prophetic comment that Benny 'is a great hand at marshalling comic amateur performers, showing something of Nick Bottom's anxious care that his friends shall do themselves justice and, inevitably, becoming himself the chief cause of disaster'.

After a few months, business at the Palace began to decline. The shrewd Bernard Delfont knew exactly what to do about it. A programme of excerpts from *Fine Fettle* promptly replaced the popular prime-time television show 'Sunday Night at the London Palladium'. The next morning, the Cambridge Circus box-office ratings took off again and remained buoyant until the end of the run when the musical *Flower Drum Song* was slated to open at the Palace.

At the *Fine Fettle* farewell party, Benny danced with his centaur partner. 'I have to tell you this,' she confessed. 'The scent you splashed all over yourself was terrible. I hated it. I'd much rather have smelled you.' *Fine Fettle* was such a disappointment to Benny that he has never attempted a stage show since. Dave Freeman admits, 'We lost our way on that one.' When Lord Delfont told me frankly, 'It was a mistake to put an intimate revue into a big house like the Palace,' he put his finger on the central weakness. But I believe that there was another important factor that might have made the show a smash hit. *Fine Fettle* was nearly there. It had excellent sight gags, but not as many as *La Plume de Ma Tante*. Benny did not know at the time how much Michael Bentine, who was then in Australia, had contributed to Robert Dhéry's success. Had he known, he might well have called for help from Michael, whom he has always regarded as a master of visual comedy. With another bright idea or two the show would have been a winner.

While at the Palace in 1959, Benny was tempted once more into making a film, *Light Up the Sky*, in which he co-starred with Tommy Steele and Ian Carmichael. This time the director, Lewis Gilbert (*The Spy Who Loved Me, Educating Rita*), ferried my brother to work every day. Benny took the opportunity to learn from the distinguished film-maker. On the first ride, Benny asked him about the background of the character he had to play. 'Background?' replied Lewis. 'You don't need to know that. Just speak the lines and get 'em right every time. That's all.' On the set, just before lunch one morning, Lewis was explaining the afternoon's first scene to the actors. 'It is Christmas and all you soldiers are a little drunk. I want you merry, not staggering about.'

'I've got a few bottles of wine in my locker for visitors, Lewis,' offered Benny. 'Why don't we kill 'em for lunch, and then we will really be merry. We won't need to act.'

'No,' replied Lewis. 'I don't want drunken actors playing soldiers. I want sober actors playing drunks.

You may think you will do it right, but I'm telling you that, if you're really pissed, you'll get it all wrong!' Later, Lewis took Benny aside and explained further. 'Audiences don't want the real thing. They want what they think is the real thing. In *Sink the Bismarck*, for example, we built a huge Ops room with immense maps on the wall and uniformed Wrens with long poles moving small models on a huge table. Ops rooms are not like that, but the public think they are – so we give the public what it wants.'

In the film, Benny and Tommy Steele play brothers, a music-hall song-and-dance act, who have been called up. They made an engaging pair. One critic wrote, 'they never missed a trick'. Tommy never missed a trick off-stage. He is an indefatigable practical joker, a master of the ingenuous private comment that's overheard by everybody. If you believe him, you're in trouble. Benny had to keep his wits about him.

Light Up the Sky was not generally well received. Derek Hill wrote in *Tribune*, 'Of all the lying, perverse, dangerous tributes to the merry romps of our brave lads in that difference of opinion twenty years ago, *Light Up the Sky* is the most appalling. Life on a searchlight unit in the last war, it shows us, was just a round of jolly frolics under the apparently sarcastic, but oh-so-fatherly eye of Lieutenant Ian Carmichael, who now makes a pilgrimage to the site every year, and guess what it's become? A cricket pitch. Deliberate parody could go no further, but Tommy Steele and director Lewis Gilbert take it seriously. Benny Hill loafs around the fringes of the screen wearing a grin, which suggests that he alone was prepared to treat the script with the contempt it deserved.'

Kine Weekly noted that 'Ian Carmichael is a bit stagey,' but the other actors 'make a grand team and play the old

army game with tremendous zest'. It is interesting that
the critic should single out Carmichael. He was singled
out in reality. Benny observes, 'Ian was portraying an
officer who was really quite friendly, yet most of the
cast kept away from him in the restaurant. All the
actors playing other ranks ate together. We were all
working-class. Some, like me, had served as private
soldiers in the army. Even an actor playing an officer
made us uneasy.'

In the spring of 1960, Richard Stone turned impresario to put on the summer season show at Weymouth.
Benny agreed to give the venture lift-off by starring in
it for the first month as his next commitment was for
Channel 7 in Australia, where he was due in the autumn
to appear in four television shows. That gave him eight
weeks to meander half-way round the globe. Richard
could not understand Benny's reluctance to earn them
both a hatful of gelt by working out the whole season
at Weymouth. 'You can fly direct to Australia later,'
he argued. The suggestion that he should fly over the
great cities of the Middle East and the Orient without
dropping down to explore them shocked my brother.
He was not to be deterred from the journey of a lifetime.
With a small suitcase, two plastic cards and a ticket to
Istanbul he set off.

It was an exciting and eventful experience. In Istanbul
he was bundled into a cab and dumped intact miles
out of the city at an expensive restaurant, where he
was obliged to dine before transport was provided; at
a casino near Beirut he watched the most extravagant
Follies revue he has ever seen, featuring a chariot race
with four white horses on rollers, galloping towards the
audience; in Colombo, the standards of the Raj were still
being maintained at a hotel, which chided, 'Gentlemen
have been seen wearing braces near the hotel swimming

pool'; a Chinese play in Singapore showed him how one performer could represent two people, one riding on the other's back; from his hotel window in Hong Kong he witnessed a gun battle between rival gangs that left two bodies on the street; in Tokyo, an English-speaking hostess from a Ginza nightclub taught him her repertoire of Japanese funny stories. Among other things.

Benny's reception in Australia was rather less welcoming. Those responsible for looking after him insisted on his sharing his accommodation with his associates from Britain, who had just arrived. That meant that his director, Kenneth Carter, was put up in the bathroom while the straight man, Peter Vernon, slept in the kitchen. My brother soon changed all that but was incensed by the disrespect implied. The press showed more courtesy. Despite his being 'virtually unknown' in Australia, Benny, the *Sydney Morning Herald* suggested, might become The Comedian of the People. 'Good-looking, with a freshness of complexion that marks him out in Australia as an Englishman, he is a delightfully normal fellow; there is no smell of greasepaint or histrionics about him. In a classless society such as our own, where, moreover, "you can't put anything over on us, mate", that's a good start.' In answer to a television columnist, Benny revealed that the ubiquitous Australian adjective 'bloody' could already be heard on British television. 'I predict that in a few years there will be no swear words or obscene phrases that you cannot hear on the box. But I shall never use them. My material is as balmy as a summer breeze.'

With a largely Australian cast in support, Benny's hour-long 'Curtain Call' shows were a great success. So great a success that ten minutes before the fourth and last broadcast the Musicians' Union called a lightning strike. As the show was about to open, Tommy Tico, the band leader, came to Benny and, with apologies, told him the bad news. The musicians would not play for the final 'Curtain Call'. The *fait accompli* had to be accepted. The hour included a great deal of music – funny ballads, songs and dances. There was no instant remedy for the stricken programme. 'Take it as a compliment,' suggested Tommy. 'We chose the most popular show on the air.'

The broadcasting authorities advised Benny to wait. The musicians would soon be back at work. After three weeks' stalemate, Benny decided to put on 'Curtain Call' without musicians. He would use singers instead. The orchestra was replaced by a choir humming 'Boing boing boing!' like Les Compagnons de la Chanson (or Champignons, as Benny calls them). There were still gaps in the programme that had to be filled by filmed excerpts. One of these must have been as hilarious as a Benny Hill sketch: it was Basil Rathbone's rendition of 'The Green Eye of the Yellow God'. The much-patched 'Curtain Call' went on air at last. Next day, a local television critic wrote of the presentation, 'I could not quite put my finger on it, but something was missing.' 'How very perceptive,' commented Benny at the time.

My brother fell in love with Sydney, as his sister had done before him. He knows exactly what he likes about it. 'It has everything a city should have plus a wonderful beach you can reach in five minutes, and six of them in a quarter of an hour by hydrofoil. The good news about Sydney is that it is the home of thousands of beautiful women. The bad news is that their menfolk are equally good-looking. The good news is that the menfolk don't bother with their women. Good news for me, that is.' While in New South Wales, Benny took the opportunity to visit relatives in neighbouring states. He was delighted to see Diana again and meet her husband,

Noel. They were invited to see him entertain in the Lord Mayor's Command Performance, a charity show held in Sydney Town Hall. On that memorable occasion he was supported by June Bronhill, John Larson and leading entertainers from all over Australia. With only two exceptions, this was his last performance on any stage.

A few months later, Benny was back in Europe, in Paris, in the Champs-Elysées in the rain. Whenever the Parisian sky threatens, he goes to the cinema. There are always dozens of interesting films to be enjoyed in that city. He hurried into the nearest art house. It was showing *The World By Night*, a documentary of night-life entertainment, which Benny was pleased to see was very well made. He was even more pleased to see, during its description of London after dark, a lingering shot of the Palace Theatre displaying the legend in lights – 'Benny Hill in Fine Fettle'. This was followed immediately by a picture of the Queenbee Nightclub in Tokyo. 'The hostesses in this establishment,' intoned the commentator, 'are among the most intelligent and charming in the Orient.' And there smiling, before his very eyes, was his beautiful Japanese chum.

'What a moment,' exclaims Benny. 'Images of the pair of us, together again, on the screen, in Paris!'

15

Shakespeare and Company

At home, Benny calls himself 'a *status quo* man'. He likes to leave matters as they are, changing things only when pressured. It took a barrel of hints, comments, and jokes to induce him to leave Maida Vale for a residence more in keeping with his position. This time he moved to a fashionable district in the heart of the city. Benny chose a large flat of tall rooms in a prestigious mansion terrace on the north-west side of Queens Gate near Hyde Park. His balcony looked out on to Queens Gate itself, a boulevard that leads straight into the park hard by the Albert Memorial and Albert Hall. Benny was to joke about it later: 'I live a stone's throw from the Albert Hall. The feminists meet there to throw stones at me!'

One of the regular visitors to 'that dreadful flat', as he calls it, was Jeremy Hawk. 'I used to pick Benny up to take him in my car to the studio. His home was furnished with the barest essentials – a table, a few chairs, a bed, a chest of drawers, cardboard boxes. And always a guitar well in evidence. While I was waiting for him to get ready one morning, he asked me to find him a pair of black socks in the chest of drawers. The top drawer was stuck but, as I tugged it open, I could see that it was stuffed with great wads of cheques. "What are these cheques doing here?" I asked Benny.

' "I dunno. I don't need them," he said.

'I looked at a few. They were made out to Benny for hundreds and hundreds of pounds. "They're all out of date. Half of them are way over six months old. You must do something about them!"

'But Benny wasn't bothered, he had been paid, had popped the cheques in the drawer and left them there. He wanted to forget them. They weren't cashed and spent because he didn't need to spend them. Benny has a total disregard for money – which has nothing to do with meanness. He's a very generous man. It's just that he's not interested. He's found a way of life where he doesn't seem to need money. He has no use for it. I'm sure he's the same today. People like that don't change.'

Another visitor surprised by what he found in the mansion flat was the youthful songwriter Tony Hatch, best known for the number 'Downtown', who had provoked questions in the House of Commons by making a fortune, while in the Coldstream Guards, from hits written before his army service. As an in-house producer for Pye Records, he had come to set Benny's lyrics to music. He told me of his initial bewilderment.

'Benny is one of the most likeable people I've ever met and a delight to work with in the studio. But when I first went to see him, he kept me waiting on the steps outside the Queens Gate building. Once inside, I was put at ease immediately. He welcomed me warmly, ushered me into his lounge and poured me a drink. "Excuse me, I'm busy for a moment," he said and disappeared. I sat nursing my drink for half an hour. When Benny returned, he showed me his Welsh harp, his Paraguayan diatonic harp and the trumpet he had played at the Palladium. He strummed his charango, which could be a Benny Hill joke, but is actually a South American ukulele made from an armadillo shell. At last I persuaded him to take up his guitar and sing a few of the witty ditties that were so popular with the television viewers. My previous impressions were confirmed. The melody, structure and rhythm of each song resembled the others. Benny used the limerick form continually. Therefore, we had to create variety, to differentiate each song. But first we had to make a successful single or two. If Pye were to issue an album of Benny Hill songs, which was their aim, we had to test the market. Benny and I were immersed in musical technicalities, when a woman appeared from another room. I thought for a moment that she was the housekeeper, but when I was introduced and saw how young and nubile she was, I realized, of course, that she was Benny's girlfriend. As I expected to visit again, I memorized her name. She then left the room, allowing us to concentrate for another hour.

'When I returned to the flat a week later, I was given a similar reception – a wait on the steps; the warm welcome; the drink; the excuse; the half-hour delay; Benny's reappearance and an hour's work; then the sudden appearance of his girlfriend. Except that, this time, it was a different young lady. I realized then that his television image was the reflection of an aspect of the real Benny Hill.'

Tony set to work writing music inspired by each song and its lyrics. He composed in terms of a basic rhythm section, plus instruments, to give the individual number its particular flavour. Thus, 'Andalusian Gypsies' uses four guitars and 'Gather in the Mushrooms!' is in a folksy, rural style. Where appropriate, Tony employed a female vocal group. Benny co-operated by altering the length of the lyric lines, thus affecting the rhythm of the tune as required by the composer.

The efforts of the talented pair were successful.

They produced popular songs that were very different from the American and Liverpool sounds that were dominating the charts. Three of their jolly pieces, 'Transistor Radio', 'Harvest of Love' and 'Gather in the Mushrooms!' moved smartly into the Top Twenty. Encouraged by the sales of the singles, Benny rejigged several hardy favourites and provided new songs for an album entitled 'Benny Hill Sings?' When the prolific partners finally booked the studio, Benny insisted on putting together the musical nosegay in three days, at a rate of four items per session. He wanted to keep the work spontaneous.

'Three days!' exclaims Tony. 'Today some artists will take a year on an album. We didn't waste time or use a large orchestra. Which kept down the costs. And we had a wonderful time making it, so many laughs together. He used to say to me,' and here Tony exactly reproduces Benny's Hampshire accent, ' "Tone, moi dear boy, Oi haven't a clue of what Oi'm supposed to be doin' here. Whatever you say is roight!" He was always generous in his attitude to me. I was honoured at so early an age to be associated with a great artist like Benny. It did a lot for my credibility in the business.'

The cover of the album depicts Benny looking like a well-nourished Beatle in a dark turtle-necked sweater, singing to his own guitar. However, there emerges from the record a looking-glass world very different from that of the Beatles. I learned, for example, from a song called 'I'll Never Know' that 'Great aches from little toe-corns grow', which has a pleasing touch of Lewis Carroll about it. His singing, however, echoes particular artists of the period when the album was produced – Elvis, Mick Jagger, Bob Dylan, Phil Harris and, with a partner, Nina and Frederick.

Sung in a familiar whine, the pungent 'What a World!'
exposes a hypocrisy still fashionable:

The folk singer came from America
To sing at the Albert Hall.
He sang his songs of protest and fairer shares for all,
He sang how the poor were much too poor
And the rich too rich by far,
Then he drove back to his penthouse
In his brand-new Rolls-Royce car!
What a world! What a place!
Ain't you glad you're a member of the human race?

The man who nowadays trusts the newspapers to get
only the date right has not changed his views about
them. A quarter of a century ago, he was singing,
tongue in cheek, 'It's in the papers, I know it's right,
it's in the papers in black and white.'

Benny is funniest when he allows himself to relax
into a broad Hampshire accent as in 'The Old Fiddler',
what he would call a 'recitatitive'. Here I recognize
the influence of Billy ('Almost a Gentleman') Bennett,
the famous music-hall monologist, and that of the Mrs
Malaprop of St Mary's, Mrs Scruggs.

He played cantatas and fewgoos and orio-oratoratorios,
    too,
By composers like Johann Sebastian Bach, to mention
    only a few.
He played woltsies by Strawss and Die Fleidermawss,
And Tales from the Vienna Wood,
Then Tchaikovsky's Piano Concerto,
But he din't play that quite so good!

Yes, definitely by Billy Bennett out of Mrs Scruggs.

The theme of male disappointment is, of course, to be found here, as in all Benny's works. 'My Garden of Love', a ballad of splendidly contrived puns, tells a familiar tale.

> But Gus the gardener's left now,
> And you went with him too.
> The fungus there reminds me of the fun Gus
>   is having with you.
> Now the rockery's a mockery,
> With weeds it's overgrown,
> The fuchsia's gone,
> I couldn't face the fuchsia all alone!

In 'The Egg Marketing Board Tango', Benny, as a Hampshire Hog swept along by the magic of the dance, is intense and passionate.

> But in the Tango, you gits the chance to
>   'old 'er oh so near,
> You gaze into her lovely eyes of blue,
> And while you're dancing, you whisper sweet
>   nothings in her ear,
> And she says, "sweet nothing doing!" back to you!

The wistfulness characteristic of much of Benny's comedy is to be found in the song 'Golden Days'.

> 'Why do you cry, young Jimmy?'
> I heard your grandad say.
> ' 'Coz I can't do what the big boys do,
> That's why I cry,' said Jim.
> 'Move over, then,' said your grandad,
> As he sat and cried with him.

*   *   *

If those who remain unconvinced by Benny's visual comedy would allow themselves to listen to this collection of hilarious observations neatly encapsulated in song, they might be more likely to agree with John Osborne's assessment that 'Benny is a talent unto himself. The world would be an even more miserable place without his unique gifts.'

When Benny climbed into drag for his first female impersonation on television, he knew that he was taking a risk. Some viewers might be disturbed; there would be whispers about him. He felt that such agitation was the gossips' problem, not his. He had been brought up to regard female impersonation as a legitimate part of comedy. The Captain made up his young sons as clowns and women. We boys accepted both as natural to show-business. Later, Benny worked with fine comedians like George Lacey and Arthur Askey, who played dames in the pantomime tradition. The fact that they wore dresses was not grounds for speculation.

There were those who took a different view. One cab-driver was quite sure. He told Dave Freeman, 'That Benny Hill's a poof, innee? Stands to reason. Any man who wears a dress must be a poof. 'E's a poof all right.' At which the cab-driver began to whistle, as if to say, 'I rest my case.'

I remember the exact occasion when Benny first became concerned about the myth of his homosexuality. We were on a train to West Ham to see a soccer game. As we passed an open space we saw facing us on the boundary wall a slogan painted in letters six feet high – 'Benny Hill Is My Girlfriend'. The alarm bells rang for us both. In those days, public opinion was very hard on any expression of what it considered morally unconventional, and that covered a wide range of lifestyles. Those who did not conform were vulnerable. We knew entertainers who had been ruined by unsubstantiated smears. A comedian friend of Benny's had been toppled from the pinnacle of success by a widespread belief in a travesty of the truth about his private life. No one would employ him. Showbiz whispers could have serious consequences.

There had been gossip about Benny before, but this graffito meant that the misapprehension was widespread. We immediately discussed ways of combating the rumour. Radical action was needed. It was decided to drop the mainstay of Benny's comedy – the drag sketches – at least for a while. At that period in his career his female impersonations were the talk of the town. He had leapt to stardom imitating Barbara Kelly and Lady Barnett on 'What's My Line?' He was, of course, as with all his innovations, the first to make female impersonation popular on television. Cutting it would be a drastic remedy. But it had to be done. In its place he would introduce the compulsive lecher and feature more heterosexual sketches. The gaps would be filled by a wider range of subjects. And his sentimental catch-phrase, 'Bless your hearts', would have to go. That was a pity, because it had originally been a spontaneous expression of his gratitude to enthusiastic audiences.

Surgery had the desired effect. The spate of stories slowly began to abate. However, bar-room know-it-alls have displayed their ignorance by keeping the myth alive for decades, into an era when rumours of a particular sexual orientation are much less likely to destroy a person's livelihood.

One person totally destroyed, perhaps, by the insensitivity of others was Marilyn Monroe. Benny is among her millions of admirers.

'They say everyone remembers where they were when

Kennedy died. I don't. But the memory of where I was
when Marilyn Monroe died stays with me – and how I
came to be there. It began after a jolly party that Richard
Stone threw for his clients at his house in Primrose Hill.
I walked home in the early hours to clear my head, fell
into my flat and flopped spark out on the settee. When
the morning sunlight woke me, it dawned on me that
there was nothing urgent in the book for a week. So
I called the BEA office and asked about lunch-time
flights. They offered me a choice of European cities. I
picked Hamburg, threw my toothbrush and razor into
a briefcase, and, wearing a frayed shirt (that would
serve as a pyjama jacket for the rest of my holiday),
set off.

'Upon arrival, a little later, I bought a couple of new
shirts, changed at once, fixed up accommodation in a
hotel at the end of the Reeperbahn and went to see a
football match. In the evening, I did what everybody
does when they go to the Reeperbahn, but it wasn't
as exciting as sitting outside a tiny café on an island
in the middle of the street watching the lorries hurtle
straight at me to miss by inches. The lorries never
stopped hurtling past the island and kept me awake
all night. Next day I took a plane to Paris, a train to
Lyons and a boat to Marseilles. It took three days to
get there, of course. A night in Lyons, getting up
early in the misty morning to catch the boat down
the Saône and the Rhône. The effort is worth it because
the food aboard comes from a five-star restaurant. We
glided down the river to Avignon, where we stayed
the night. I sat in shirtsleeves at an outdoor concert
in the evening to see Les Compagnons de la Chanson.
They sang splendidly, as ever, in spotlights, with the
Pope's Palace illuminated as a backdrop. On the final
stretch, the boat pulled in while we took a short coach

trip to see the black bulls and white horses of the Camargue.

'We reached Marseilles in the evening. I booked in at a modest hotel and was taking a bath in preparation for a night on the town, when the radio told me of Marilyn's death. Suddenly, I didn't feel like a night on the town any more. I walked slowly to a quiet place on the cliff, drank a little cognac and looked at the sea. I felt so stricken, not just because the most beautiful woman in the world had died, but because one of the most intelligent, funny, witty, talented actresses in the world had gone. It was as if I'd lost a show-business friend. She was one of us. A performer. The next day I came home.'

The performers Benny most admires are those who have honed their natural gifts to make a sustained contribution to the gaiety of nations. He has, therefore, always enjoyed spotting talent and encouraging it. In the early sixties when the young folk singers and pop artists began to flourish, he was delighted. 'A kid with flair can come from the back of beyond and get somewhere quickly while he's young enough to enjoy it.' One such was Donovan, who impressed my brother well before his first hit arrived at the top of the charts in 1965. Benny sought him out at the *Weekend Mail* Ball. 'I think you're going to be big,' he told the unassuming poet, 'and I want to be the first to impersonate you. Will you sit in the front row at my next television show and then, while I'm imitating you, the camera will keep shooting your reaction? That will be a plus for the show – and it won't do you any harm, either.'

It was agreed that Benny would leave a couple of empty seats for Donovan and his friend to see the impersonation. Unfortunately, the seats remained empty. The camera remained on Benny throughout his performance. At the end of the evening, as the audience was leaving, Donovan and his friend rushed into the auditorium. 'Are we too late?'

'I'm sorry,' said Benny. 'It's all over. We couldn't delay the show for you.'

'We couldn't get a bus,' lamented Donovan.

'Why didn't you take a taxi?'

'We didn't think of that, did we?'

It had not occurred to them to hail a cab. Such naïvety endeared the young singer to Benny. It had been a long time before he himself had become used to taxis. 'Lovely feller,' he says of Donovan fondly. 'Him in his little hat.'

In 1962, Benny had been persuaded to change the entire format of his comedy. There appeared to be a widely held view in the business that the future of television light entertainment belonged to the situation comedy series. This was easier and cheaper to produce in terms of air-time than the more traditional revue structure. A successful sit-com formula could be extended into a run that would provide regular viewing material for years. The BBC had promoted and developed several such series that commanded audiences large enough to offer a tentative challenge to Benny's supremacy. He was invited to follow the band.

My brother was doubtful, and his co-writer Dave Freeman very doubtful. Neither of them wanted to surrender to the deadening routine of the weekly sit-com, trundling out the same characters in the same kinds of scenes for twenty-six episodes. They had always tried to make the Benny Hill Show a special event, a celebration that the British people would hurry home to see.

Benny agreed to attempt the genre but refused to do it the easy way. He would undertake a trial series of twelve half-hours. However, unlike every sit-com before or since, each episode would be a totally independent playlet starring the moon-faced comic in a number of parts. This, of course, was yet another Benny Hill innovation. As the *Sunday Telegraph* pointed out, 'the idea of a comic imitating a whole range of new characters every week has not been tried before'.

The opening show, 'Portrait of a Bridegroom', depicted differing views of a young man, as seen through the eyes of guests at his wedding. The bride's mother saw him as a common idler engaged in a shady second-hand business. His ex-girlfriend, on the other hand, knew him as a fastidious connoisseur of antiques, who had rescued his bride from the gutter. To his own mother he was, of course, simply a naughty schoolboy. Other perceptive characterizations revealed irreconcilable opinions.

This first episode was applauded by critics and public alike, who looked forward to a ground-breaking series. There followed a show that owed something to a couple of Hollywood films that had adapted the plot of an O. Henry story – the adventures of an item of clothing. In Benny's case it was 'A Pair of Socks', which was passed from shop assistant to electrician, to waiter and finally to a character much relished by the viewers and one critic in particular – 'an oily, pencil-moustached musical comedy tenor called Mornington Cressant. Hill hit off to exactitude the plummy accent and uneasy smile that only sixteen years on tour with "Maid of the Mountains" can really develop.'

'The Before Man' featured a sad wimp of an actor always cast as an unreconstructed mess in advertisement films. Being given, by accident, the role of 'The After Man' does wonders for him. He responds to

expectations. The plot gave Benny the chance to guy
macho characters, such as a racing driver, an airline
pilot and a red-coated Mountie in London. ('We don't
get many Mounties in here.' 'At these prices, I'm not
surprised.')

A Walter Mitty character, 'The Constant Viewer',
was much influenced by television programmes. He
appeared in short fantasies as a handsome doctor in
a hospital soap-opera, a game-show winner, an investigative reporter and a famous violinist. Dave Freeman
well remembers the half-hour burlesque of a classic
H. G. Wells story, 'The Time Bicycle'. 'I shall never
forget it. It was the only time I saw Benny lose concentration. He was nowhere for a second. It was a
live broadcast, and I was up in the box watching
the production. The camera was on Benny's face.
Usually he is in absolute control of every nuance
of expression, but suddenly his eyes grew wide and
his mouth dropped open. I knew at once that something was wrong and looked at the other screens.
Then I saw what Benny was staring at. His attractive
partner had stretched her arms up, and in consequence raised her natural assets above the decolle-
tage of her strapless dress. "Lift and separate" I'd
heard of – but this was a case of "Lift and flop!"
Before the unsuspecting millions could cop an eye-
ful, the enthusiastic actress had put the twins to
bed, Benny was back in character and all continued
smoothly.'

An episode that provoked some disapproval was
'Mr Apollo', the tale of a bronchial, chain-smoking
con man, who advertises body-building courses in
magazines under a picture of his face superimposed
on a muscular body. A printing error in his course
literature leads a customer to ruin himself physically.

Some critics found the half-hour too clinical altogether, as 'Mr Apollo' ends up in the hospital bed next to his victim.

The series as a whole was well-liked by the public, but it was not the resounding success that Benny had repeatedly achieved in the decade since his first starring show. He could not understand why the episodes had not been more popular. Reading the scripts recently convinced him that they were well-written. That point was generally agreed at the time. Dave Freeman says, 'Once again we were ahead of taste. The public were not ready for those stories, despite their quality and great values. Over the series, Benny played fifty totally different characters and he never repeated one. That was our weakness. We didn't play to the strength of the sit-com series, which is repetition. Benny wouldn't allow himself to do it. Each of our episodes was a one-off, with fresh characters in a different situation at a new location. It all had to register in the one half-hour. Just think of what happens today. If the average sit-com had to stand on its first episode, most of the series would never see the light of day. But the producers persevere; in time people begin to get used to the characters; after eighteen months the audience has become comfortable with television fare which is, at bottom, third-rate. But today's viewers have to be trained to accept it. They would welcome the originality and respond immediately, I think, if Benny were to refurbish his "Half-hours".'

One evening in 1964 at Brighton's Theatre Royal, I was watching my favourite play, *A Midsummer Night's Dream*, for the twelfth time when I spotted my brother and his agent sitting near me in the stalls. After the performance, I waylaid them in the foyer and was introduced to Richard for the first time. Benny explained that he was there to study Ralph Richardson's portrayal of Nick Bottom; he himself had been offered the part in Associated Rediffusion's television version of the play. I was overjoyed: there was no doubt in my mind that Benny was a natural for the role of the boastful weaver. Not everyone in the family was so pleased to hear the news. When Benny telephoned Mum, he outlined the plot of *The Dream* and described the character he was to play. 'Oh, Alfie,' she replied. 'Why do they always give you parts like that? You should be playing Lysander!'

The director of the television spectacular, Joan Kemp-Welch, was convinced that Benny was exactly the right choice to play Bottom. She was accused, at the time, of 'wooing a large audience' by offering my brother his first Shakespearian role. 'This is totally untrue,' says Joan. 'The reason that I cast Benny as Bottom was that I couldn't think of anyone who could play it better. I had seen many of his shows and I always felt that Bottom needed to be played by a marvellous comedian, who possessed a roguish sense of humour. This describes Benny Hill. He had an endearing way with him. You laughed and you were fond of him at the same time. This is exactly how I felt Bottom should be played – that he should be somebody who was wildly enthusiastic; he wanted the best part; he wanted this; he wanted that. At the same time he was enormously endearing. And this is why I took up my courage and phoned Benny to ask, "Would you like to do Shakespeare? Will you come and play Bottom?" And I thought his miraculous performance justified this. He was magnificent.'

Benny had assistance, of course, with the interpretation of his part: from his director Joan Kemp-Welch, from Professor George Rylands of Cambridge, the foremost Shakespearian scholar of the day, and me. The professor not only edited the script but sketched in the background, elucidated the play and helped construe the characters for the cast. My contribution was kindly recalled by Anna Massey, who made a delicious and strangely compelling Titania. Benny confessed to her that I had taken him through the part on the telephone. 'He was very impressed,' she told me, 'when he rang you with a question one night, and you were quoting him lines without the book in front of you. He knew the text backwards before we started and understood it as well as most of us. Incredibly professional.'

His director was also won over by my brother's dedication. Joan Kemp-Welch remembers: 'At midday, when everyone else went out to lunch, Benny would stay in with an apple and a sandwich. I would see him going through things he had done at rehearsal, perfecting movements, and I thought to myself, "Oh, that man is going to be the biggest star," because that sort of work is what makes a star great.'

Joan feels that it was at such times that Benny revealed himself. 'All the very young children who played fairies loved Benny. But one tiny, angelic boy, no more than three feet tall, who took the part of Mustard Seed, absolutely adored him. Every morning he would find his friend and announce "I've got a good story for you," and tell some absurd, childish joke. At which Benny would fall about with laughter and say in return, "And I've got a good story for you." Then he would recount a story for the little boy. I always loved to see them together.'

The fact that a fellow-comedian, Bernard Bresslaw, whose work Benny admired, was also cast as a mechanical, made my brother feel more at home. Bernard has fond memories of their association. 'We had a wonderful time on that show. One incident particularly tickled Benny. Miles Malleson, who played Quince, was a wonderful old chap who had rather a thing about his hair. He maintained the fiction, as people do, that it wasn't a wig, although it didn't fool anybody. I happened to be sitting in the chair next to him in the make-up room, when the make-up girl brought him a wig for his part. She said, "I'll take off your wig, Mr Malleson, if I may, and put on this wig." Quick as a flash, Miles put one hand on his head and cried, "Wig? What wig?" in that funny voice of his, grabbed the other wig from her hand and bolted from the room. No doubt he sorted out the wigs in the privacy of his dressing-room. When I told Benny the story, he collapsed!'

According to all accounts, everyone in the cast enjoyed creating the magical play. That the project was undertaken not solemnly but very seriously was due to the inspired leadership of the director. Joan Kemp-Welch had come to direction from a distinguished career on the stage and screen, where she played opposite stars such as Robert Young and Leslie Howard. She had to struggle against male prejudice, first to produce drama in the theatre and then to become a television director.

It might be assumed, therefore, that Joan would find Benny difficult to handle. He is said by some to be a male chauvinist. This is untrue. He is also said to make television directors weep with frustration. This is true. Why, then, is Joan able to recall, 'Benny was a joy to work with. He absorbed instruction like blotting paper'? The answer is simple. Joan is a director of wide experience and immense talent. Anyone, male or female, so well qualified has Benny's ungrudging respect. It is only Benny's insistence on the highest professional standards that reduces incompetent directors to tears.

Anna Massey was concerned to achieve the highest professional standards in her first Shakespearian role. Despite her preoccupation, she noticed how technically precise and economical Benny's acting was. 'He made our scenes together so easy and enjoyable to play. They were great fun. And his portrayal of Bottom, I thought, was truthful and touching.'

The infinitely experienced playwright, screenwriter and actor Miles Malleson was also enamoured of my brother's performance. He was particularly complimentary about a piece of theatrical business that Benny contrived when, as Bottom, he awoke from his dream of dalliance with the Queen of the Fairies, Titania. Traditionally, Miles intimated, on the line, 'Methought I was, and methought I had,' it was customary for the actor to raise his hands as if to feel the long ears that had sprouted so recently from his asinine head. Instead of the expected movement, Miles was astonished to see Benny make a gesture to imply that he had tupped the Fairy Queen. 'I wanted to suggest that I had given her one,' explains Benny. Miles was entranced by the fresh dimension imparted to the scene. He had never before seen or heard the line given that particular meaning. My opinion is that Benny's view is that of the clown. He picked up immediately what Shakespeare laid down so long ago for the clown who played Bottom. The interpretation was always there to be used. Without any knowledge that the proximity of Bottom in the ass-head and the Fairy Queen would have resonance for Elizabethan audiences still secretly in thrall to pagan fertility beliefs, Benny saw it at once.

The television production was given a rapturous
reception by the British press. Several newspapers
could not resist the headline, 'Benny Hill's Bottom was
Tops!' Among the regional encomiums the *Western Press*
averred, 'Benny Hill as Bottom scored a great triumph,
his unique comedy fitting the part perfectly.' The critic
of the *Liverpool Daily Post* was pleased to report: 'Mr Hill
turned in one of the finest performances, as Bottom,
it has been my delight to see.' The *Observer*'s Maurice
Richardson was rather more judicious. 'Benny Hill's
Bully Bottom, as you might expect from this highly intelligent clown, was a pleasingly original variation. His
idiot-boy embroidery was done on a firm background
of megalomania and his skipping gait metamorphosed
with a Dali-esque ass's head was delightful.'

'Mr Benny Hill made his innate conviction of superi-
ority, his reaching towards grandeur of manner and
diction, a lively vehicle for the ebullience of Bottom,'
wrote *The Times*, ' . . . a very happy unbullying leadership of his colleagues asserting the unlikely and
impractical with unshakeable force.'

When the play reached American small screens the
New York Times critic, James Gould, hailed 'a lusty,
hilarious, joyous production . . . such contagious rel-
ish and gusto, such immense charm and naturalness
. . . a side-splitting burlesque. Benny Hill is the Buddy
Hackett of the Thames and a funny man. Joan Kemp-
Welch, the British director who fashioned this television
lark in the enchanted grove, is the medium's leading
lady this morning. *A Midsummer Night's Dream* is the hit
of the season.' From Cambridge, Professor Rylands sent
a letter of congratulations to Joan – ' . . . your triumph
of creation and interpretation . . . would have rejoiced
Shakespeare's heart.'

The excitement was too much for Philip Purser,

the television critic of the staid *Sunday Telegraph*. The presence of Benny Hill in Shakespeare on his screen so agitated him that he completely lost all sense of propriety. In true Benny Hill style, he complained of Bottom's top billing over the Fairy King and Queen. It was, he wrote, 'a case of putting the arse before the court'!

16

Film Fun

Chuck Horner, the veteran American writer of the Jack
Parr, Gary Moore and Arthur Godfrey shows, reminded
me recently of the brilliant monologue that came out of
Benny's experience of the Bard. Chuck loves the piece
because it burlesques the reticulations of constraint
under which he and Benny and all television writers
struggle to create comedy.

'Yes, Mandy love? Who's on the line? Will who? He's
not the bloke who wrote that "Saint" series, is he?
Shakespeare? I don't remember him. Well, put him
on. Hello, Will, what can we do for you? What have
you written, then? *Romeo and Juliet* – Oh, that sounds
nice. Is it funny, Will, sort of like "Bootsie and Snudge"
is it? Sort of, you know – It's about a boy and a girl? Yes.
She's what? How old? Thirteen? Oh, dear. Well, how old
is he? Will, I really don't know. They're children, Will,
they're children. You know what I mean, don't you?
It's a bit – you've got to be very careful nowadays you
know. Well, all right. Yeah. Could we – do you think
it would run to twenty-six weeks? You know, half the
season? Oh! They both die in the first one? Oh, Will!
Well, that's that. You sure you're not the bloke who
wrote the "Saint" series? No, I didn't, no. What else
you got, Will? You've written what? About a fellow on
a moor. I don't know. Well, it's so difficult to mock up
a moor in the studio, you know. You have to go on
location and that costs a mint of money, Will. Oh, it's
not a fellow. That's his name, "Othello". Oh, yes, and
he's in love with who? Des O'Connor? Oh, Desdemona!

Yes, a nice love story. Yes, yes. She's a lovely blonde girl, is she? That's fine. And he meets her on the moor? No? He *is* the moor? Oh, I see. A Moor from Morocco. He's what? Ooh, I don't know, Will. I don't think the public is ready for that. No, they're not ready for it. No, not yet. It's asking a lot, you see. "The Merchant of Venison"? Yes, I know – Oh, *The Merchant of Venice*. Yes, of course I know – in the South of France, yes. Who is this Shylock, then? He's not, you know, is he, Will? He's not – he's what? Is he? And he wants what? Will! That's not very nice. No, it's a touchy subject. We won't get it past – we don't want trouble with the Race Relations lot, do we? They'll come down on us like a ton of bricks! How about what? *The Taming of the Shrew*. It's not about a mouse, is it? It's a kiddies' show, is it? Well, what is it about, then? He beats her down? How does he do that? He makes her what? Will, for Heaven's sake! The feminists will be picketing the studios! They'll put us out of business! Haven't you got something lighter? *A Midsummer Night's Dream*. That sounds better. Very jolly, yes? There's fairies in it? I'll bet there are! The Queen of the Fairies. Oh, that's very nice, that is. That's all we need. What's her name? Titania? Oh, Will, I mean – there's a clown in it? That's more like it, Will, a funny clown. Make 'em all laugh. And his name is? Ah! You see, Will, I mean. "Behind" they would stand for. "Bum" we might get away with. But "Bottom"! It's erotic, Will. It's erotic, you see. I don't think we dare do it. What's the little feller's name? Puck? Well, I tell you what, Will, I'll have to think about it. We'll call you. Yes. Mandy, get me Johnny Speight, will you, love.'

At the climax of the monologue, Benny once again picks up what the Bard laid down. He has drawn attention to Shakespeare's bawdy puns. The characters are by no means innocuously named. Nor are others that spring to mind – Doll Tearsheet, Mistress Overdone, Belch, Dick and Gobbo, for example. Shakespeare's bawdry is a vital part of his work and most of it is accessible to a modern audience, although a great deal of his humour, particularly the verbal by-play (as in *Twelfth Night*) is not. However, despite the flux of fashion and the changes in language, the basis of comedy remains unaltered.

Many of the figures of speech used by Shakespeare are still alive and well and living in the Benny Hill Show. Such as the Reference Direct. In *Romeo and Juliet*, Mercutio announces, 'The bawdy hand of the dial is now upon the prick of noon,' whereas Benny says, 'She is going to make a clean breast of it!' Then there is the Syllable Misleading, as in Hamlet's teasing enquiry of Ophelia, 'Do you think I meant country matters?' as against Benny's, 'I'm not interested in legs, I'm a titmouse!' The Innuendo or Reference Oblique is illustrated by the musings of Malvolio in *Twelfth Night* – 'These be her very Cs, her Us and her Ts; and thus she makes her great Ps.' A model use of Innuendo is 'The Intelligence Test' when Benny asks little Johnny Vivian, 'What may be seen on a billiards table that are found inside a man's trousers?' One word immediately reverberates round the skull of every viewer. It is inescapable. This time, Benny's gone too far. But, once again, he skates away scot-free from thin ice. The answer is 'Pockets!' Benny peers to see what Johnny has written. 'Rub that out,' he mutters, with a look of distaste that punishes us all. When we stop laughing, we realize that, from first to last, the naughty word has not been mentioned, seen or illustrated. It's all in our minds. Benny has caught us at it again.

Despite Benny's frequent usage of the verbal devices that Shakespeare employed so effectively, in the matter of bawdry he is careful not to offend large numbers of his vast viewing public. The blatant references to primary sexual organs, entirely acceptable to Elizabethan audiences, would be tolerated today only on late-night television. Benny has never exploited that area, preferring the challenge of evoking laughter by a more delicate expression of the indelicate. As Henny Youngman, the doyen of American stand-up comedians, told me, 'Benny is not doity. I never hoid him say a doity woid.'

Although they contained no hint of bawdry, Benny was equally careful in the composition of the scripts for his television commercial spots. He guarded them jealously from the attentions of the advertising copywriters. Every year in the early and middle sixties, Benny made half a dozen sketches of fifteen or thirty seconds for Schweppes, the soft drinks company. Dave Freeman shared the writing and sometimes performed in the short scenes. Occasionally, Benny would re-write or adapt the scripts to suit his own personality. The cameos were marvels of compression. One of them, selling tomato juice, won first prize at the Cannes International Festival of Commercials in 1961. This was the scene where Benny in a smock, as an expert vegetable gardener, appears in his greenhouse with a magnificent potted tomato plant on the bench beside him. He warns of the dreaded tomato blight and claims that there is only one cure for it. At which he takes a cricket bat from the shelf beneath his bench and swings it over with one hand, casually flattening the entire tomato plant with a single blow. Then he picks up a small bottle of tomato juice from the shelf and suggests that, if we want juice, we would do better to buy it rather than try to grow it. The remarkable aspect of the commercial was the precision and economy with which Benny destroyed the plant. It was obliterated in a split second, which necessitated a vertical clout exactly down to the fulcrum, the base of the central stalk – a dextrous feat of which W. C. Fields would have been proud.

John Holmes, account executive for Clifford Bloxham and Partners, responsible for producing the commercials, was present at the filming of nearly all of the thirty-six episodes. He remembers that my brother was so professional that the crew, directed first by David Poltenghi and later by Kenneth Carter, called him 'One-Take Benny'.

However, on one occasion, due to no fault of the cheeky comedian, they were beset by technical difficulties and had to take the same shot sixteen times. Benny was playing an old lady, drinking a glass of fizzy tonic water to the camera. They could not get it right and tried repeatedly, as first one thing and then another caused trouble. 'After many takes,' recalls John, 'everything seemed at last to be going smoothly. There were no technical hitches at all. They had almost completed the shot when the old lady let out the most explosive belch you've ever heard! Everyone fell about laughing in surprise, as nobody had considered what the repeated takes were doing to Benny's stomach. He had swallowed gallons of fizzy tonic water.'

Another episode took place on location at a lake in Surrey. Benny, as Hiawatha, was required to paddle his canoe across the water. No expense had been spared to ensure authenticity. Benny was bedecked in genuine Redskin garb, a wonderfully impressive costume, and the canoe had been loaned by a London museum. The mighty chief paddled his craft across the lake and promptly drove it underwater. He went down with it. Benny was immediately hauled in, dried out and

cleaned up. When they rescued the canoe, it was
floated again. Hiawatha climbed aboard and pushed
off. He hadn't made two strokes of the paddle when
under went the canoe, tipping him into the drink once
more. More like Duck Soup than Shining Water! Once
again, assumptions were misplaced. Anybody can paddle a canoe. Wrong. Not a Red Indian canoe. It requires
a skill passed on from father to son. In the end, the
television crew stood up to their how-do-you-dos in
water to photograph Benny posing, paddle in hand,
rigid as a cigar store Indian for fear of capsizing the
canoe. My brother's efforts were not unappreciated.
Videos of those commercials are now treasured in the
new TV Library, set up by Coca-Cola/Schweppes in the
US. They are widely regarded in the business as models
of their kind, seminal in effect and ushering in a new
era of wittier, more engaging television advertising.

Both Dave and Benny had reservations about the
generous rewards widely on offer in the advertising
industry at that time. Dave had struggled for many years
as a comedy scriptwriter, working long hours for relatively little pay. The Schweppes commercials earned
him enormous fees over five years that ensured security and a comfortable life ever since. He is grateful,
but has doubts about the justice of such discrepancy.
'The advertising business was self-indulgent: so many
unnecessary conferences; such long lunches.'

Benny feels much the same. 'For five years I made
more cash from the commercials than from anything
else. I got a fantastic amount of money. The contract
involved me in two weeks' work a year, from which
I received enough to live in luxury for the rest of the
year without doing a stroke. Ridiculous. People in this
business are hopelessly and idiotically overpaid.'

During his 'resting' periods, Benny began to make

plans for a film career. That would be, he felt, another
step up the ladder. As a television comedian in the
early 1960s, he considered he had inferior status to
his counterparts in the cinema. He recalls an elegant
function at which he sat down to dinner next to Richard
Todd, the British film star. The waiter was most obse-
quious to the distinguished actor. 'Yes, Mr Todd. As
you wish, Mr Todd.' To my brother he babbled, as he
filled his plate, ' 'Ere y'are, Ben. Git this lot dahn yer
an' you'll be fat as a pig!' Loved but not respected.

As the last of the Schweppes commercials were
being filmed and Benny began writing screenplays,
Dave Freeman realized that their professional association was coming to an end. He began to look further
afield for writing opportunities and has helped Benny
only rarely since. The friends have kept in touch,
however, and Benny often calls to ask Dave's advice
and exchange news.

In 1964 the first star booked and the first star filmed
in *Those Magnificent Men in Their Flying Machines* was
Benny. With Norman Rossington vainly assisting, he
played Fire Chief Perkins misdirecting operations from
the top of the airfield tower. The part was little more
than a spit and a cough. The scene took only four
days to shoot. As ever, Benny tried to bring something
fresh to it. He suggested that, when he poured himself
a cup of tea, an off-camera wind-machine should blow
the liquid from the mouth of the flask straight into the
cup two feet away. The crew experimented with the
visual gag, but could not make it work. Nevertheless,
Benny was grateful to the director, Ken (*Battle of the
Bulge*) Annakin, for attempting it. He had chafed under
directors who spurned all suggestions from others. This
time he enjoyed his work, except the time spent up
the tower. Benny suffers from vertigo, so that, when

the cameras were shooting from behind him, over his shoulder, he cried, 'Don't touch me, don't touch me!' for fear of losing his balance and falling.

When he saw the finished film, my brother was pleased with his thumbnail sketch, feeling that he had registered effectively in a short time. He began to think seriously about a career in the movies, contriving to meet directors and producers like Bud (*Inspector Clouseau*) Yorkin and Ben (*The Jokers*) Arbeid. Benny wrote a couple of treatments of his own imaginative screenplays. One was 'I Love You, I Love You, I Love You', a comedy about a beautiful, incredibly rich widow, who attracts adventurers from all over the world to compete for her hand. I thought it was a winner. So did John (*Deliverance*) Boorman, who wanted to direct it. He ferried Benny round London in a battered van to see likely backers. My brother used to act out the plot before them, performing all the parts himself. Conferences were organized, finances sought and plans made. As so often in the film industry, all the excitement led nowhere. The screenplays remained unplayed.

In line with his ambitions to star on the silver screen, Benny thought the time had come to live a little more like the film entrepreneurs with whom he was now associating. He was occasionally invited to a home so luxurious that it induced in him a dissatisfaction with his own. He felt that he needed a new, more spacious flat, one in which he could throw parties for the movie crowd. He thought at first of moving, but when the neighbouring apartment came up for sale Benny decided to buy it, knock down the dividing wall and turn the whole place into a huge luxury suite. Shrewd as ever, he offered the *TV Times* magazine exclusive coverage of the process if they would employ and pay a distinguished interior decorator to re-design and glamorize his new home. Benny gave the designer no instructions, which is why the immense L-shaped lounge (made up of three former rooms) sported a thick, sculpted oatmeal carpet on the ceiling and dark blue fabric on the walls. Buttoned oatmeal velvet sofas and easy chairs floated on an ocean of dark green carpet. Benny soon made it more like home. It was not long before a couple of cardboard boxes and a plastic shopping-bag were to be seen decorating the huge sitting room.

When it became clear that a film career was likely to be a long haul, my brother signed a contract to star in another BBC series in the mid-1960s. He had, by now, abandoned the sit-com format and was moving towards a faster, funnier, revue-style Benny Hill Show, which contained more social comment. The targets of his caustic wit were, according to the television critic of the *Daily Mail*, 'Money. Pomp. Self-importance. Greed. In short order he sent up the lot.' Viewers everywhere seemed to approve the changes. The hard-hitting, streamlined spectaculars were so successful that he was named BBC Television Personality of the Year in 1966.

The interest that Benny had shown in screenplays paid off in 1968 when Cubby (*Goldfinger*) Broccoli asked him to undertake comedy re-writes for a family film, *Chitty Chitty Bang Bang*, from a book by Ian Fleming. Dick Van Dyke, playing the starring role, felt that his part as the crazy inventor, Caractacus Potts, needed funnier lines. My brother was called in to supply them. He worked closely with the director, Ken (*Cromwell*) Hughes, for five weeks, spiking up the banquet and staircase scenes. When they discussed casting various parts, Ken suggested that Benny might like to play the

Toymaker. This was the part of an endearing old German craftsman who, clad in knickerbockers and braces, helps the children save Potts's magic car from the villains. It was not a comedy role, but my brother knew that it would be useful experience and might further his career in films. He accepted and flew immediately on location to the fairy-tale town of Rothenburg in the heartland of Germany, the quaintest little place he had ever seen.

'It was full of funny, medieval houses – not a television aerial in sight. You could walk right round it in half an hour. Nothing ever happened there. The town was so quiet that people would gather at midnight to see the ancient iron figures on the church clock come out to strike the bell. When an accordionist entertained in the café, it was an event. One cinema was showing *Mary Poppins* at the time. The fact that the film starred Dick Van Dyke made it of great professional interest to me.'

Dick Van Dyke was the first American star comedian with whom Benny ever spent any time, although he had worked on single television shows with transatlantic singers like Jo Stafford, Abbey Lane and Paul Anka, who had been pleasant and co-operative. But there had been stories in the profession about the predatory nature of American comedians. Tommy Trinder had told of his experience in the New York nightclubs. 'Trinder's the name,' he said, introducing himself. 'Why don't you change it?' growled Orson Welles, from the audience. 'Are you proposin'?' asked Trinder, quick as a flash. One night, according to Tommy, his act was interrupted by a native megastar comedian, who crept up behind and laid hands upon him in an attempt to steal his audience. An ugly, violent scene ensued.

Another cautionary tale concerned Jewel and Warris,

who had been booked for an American television show, starring a celebrated funny man. When they appeared in the New York rehearsal studio for the run-through, they saw the tyrannosaurian star destroy a famous Broadway singer before their very eyes. 'If he does that to a singer,' said Jewel to Warris, 'what will he do to a pair of comics?' They fled at once and flew straight home.

Benny had never forgotten those stories. No wonder he says, 'When we were introduced, I was a little in awe of Dick Van Dyke. I had never met him before and felt rather uneasy about my position as a supporting actor. I had been Top Banana in my own show. Now, Dick was Top Banana and I was Second Banana, as it were. I had to keep a lower profile. As Second Banana, one cannot take command or move up front to keep the press happy with joeys and funnies. I needn't have worried. Dick was very understanding. He soon reassured me. I found him an awfully nice man. And he was so professional, so highly disciplined in his work. I watched him closely and learnt a great deal, too, in our chats together. At all times, on the set and off, Dick was always impeccably courteous.

'I was most impressed by his behaviour one morning, when he was being made up in the open as he went over his lines. He was concentrating on his work when a group of American tourists, who had probably come to see the church clock, gathered round him. He greeted them warmly, joked with them and responded to their questions in a most friendly manner. I knew that he had a lot on his mind – his responsibility for the film, his appearance and his part. He was also trying to psych himself for the next scene. Most stars I've encountered would have dismissed the tourists at a time like that, but Dick heard them out and finally bade them good-bye most affably. It was a lesson to me in the attainment of grace under pressure.

'Later, when I made a television commercial in which I did a funny piece made up as a dog with floppy ears and a red nose, Dick was very complimentary about it and made sure I knew that he had seen it and liked it. He was always generous like that.'

For his part, Dick had seen Benny on British television long before he became famous in the US. When he met my brother, he was astonished to discover that the British comedian was, in the flesh, not at all what he expected. 'Benny is quiet, retiring, gentlemanly – totally different to the extrovert, gregarious persona he displays on camera. It was a pleasure to associate with such an unassuming person, so unlike the noisy, aggressive people that abound in show-business. I recognized his introversion in myself because, like him, I have no really close friends. We used to talk a great deal about comedy. I thought we had a lot in common as comedians. We were both very physical and visual (I throw myself about a lot). I told Benny that we had been born twenty years too late – we both would have been bigger successes in the twenties and thirties.'

My observations at the time led me to believe that Dick Van Dyke's example of professionalism and integrity influenced my brother to adopt a similar punctilious regard for others, both in the business and in the exchanges of everyday life. Benny has always been a very caring person, but in Dick Van Dyke he saw a model of the verray parfit gentil knight whom he has tried to emulate ever since. A matching feminine generosity of spirit was demonstrated by their leading lady, Sally Ann Howes, who, at a largely male party of cast, crew and assistants, danced non-stop to partner every man-jack of the company.

The film was a great success, particularly with children everywhere. Critical assessments were 'A charmingly inventive fairy-tale' and 'A super, smashing, spectacular pantomime'. I described it earlier as a family film. *Variety*, in an unusually schoolmarmish way, insisted that it was a children's film. 'A children's film is not synonymous with a family film. Only *Mary Poppins* was both.' As ever, *Variety* was right. *Chitty Chitty Bang Bang* is still one of the most popular children's videos in Britain and the US. The critics generally felt that Benny had turned in a creditable performance. Margaret Hinxman in the *Sunday Telegraph* found 'a rather subdued Benny Hill, cuddly and lovable'. My sentiments exactly.

Soon after the success of *Chitty*, Benny met Blake Edwards, the prolific film-maker, in his suite at the London Hilton. My brother was being considered for the part of a Frenchman in *Darling Lili*, starring Julie Andrews and Rock Hudson. After pleasantries had been exchanged, Benny asked for more details.

'Does my character speak with a special accent – Parisian, say, or Northern French? Maybe from Marseilles, or would you prefer the accent du Midi?'

Blake Edwards sighed wearily and said, 'Mr Hill, God hates a smartass!'

'But He forgives a nervous ass,' replied my brother. His honesty broke the ice. Edwards smiled, nodded tolerantly and they continued their discussion in a more relaxed atmosphere. However, Benny did not get the part, which was no disaster as *Darling Lili* was not a great success.

Two years earlier, in 1966, Benny had finished his last radio series, 'Benny Hill Time'. He had used the BBC Light Programme to make a name for himself and to

rehearse his material. It was no longer needed on either
count, as he had developed an uncanny ability to predict the general response to his comedy wheezes. Even
Ken Dodd, who must be the world's master at handling
live audiences, is at a loss to explain such a gift. He
finds he has to try out everything he does on stage.
'How can Benny just write it, perform it immediately
on camera and be sure it will get laughs?' he asks.

By 1968, therefore, Benny no longer wished to embark
on further radio series. The fees for such work were,
anyway, laughably inadequate. As Mohammed Ali told
the BBC at the time:

> Don't get me wrong,
> I like your style,
> But, if you don't pay more,
> I won't be back for a while.

But John Browell, his Light Programme producer for
years, still occasionally called upon him. 'Benny would
do practically any single broadcasts I asked him. In that
way, he repaid me for the work we had done together
previously.' John was grateful for Benny's assistance
one afternoon when a top-of-the-bill was required for
a radio variety show. Benny stepped in, presenting an
act that finished with a comedy song accompanied by
the BBC Light Orchestra. In the evening, relaxing with
a lovely companion in a candle-lit restaurant, he was
delighted when the violinist of a trio played his way
to the table to serenade his partner with a soulful
gypsy melody. The lady drew her clasped hands to
her cheek and closed her eyes in appreciation of the
romantic mood. 'She's melting,' thought Benny. 'She's
away!' Still playing, the gypsy fiddler moved round the
table to my brother. 'Aldo Tomer, BBC Light Orchestra,'

he announced, in a voice that could be heard all over
the restaurant. 'You done great this afternoon, Ben.
Loved the one about the false teeth dropping down
the loo pan!'

A few months later, Benny was sent a script by Troy
Kennedy Martin ('Z-Cars'): *The Italian Job*, a caper
film about a huge bullion snatch. He was offered
the part of Professor Peach, an eccentric computer
expert recruited by the villains to paralyse Turin by
creating the mother and father of a traffic jam through
feeding damaging instructions into the control system.
A model locomotive freak, Peach was bribed to join
the gang by the offer of a huge toy train-set. Benny
found this motivation unconvincing.

'I couldn't imagine anyone going to Italy on a bullion
raid, risking his neck for a train-set. It was bizarre. But
what would tempt me? Crumpet, of course. If the nutty
professor were like me, he'd go for the right kind of lady
– or ladies. What kind? For laughs, fat ladies. I could see
the gang leader pulling back the curtains and showing
Peach a brand new open car – and in the back, a couple
of the loveliest plump charmers ever.'

Benny's suggestions were accepted and he re-wrote
the part to suit himself. He enjoyed both the writing
and the performance because he worked hard on the
characterization and felt that he had got it right. 'It was
great fun to do. I played Peach as a deaf Yorkshireman.
Now, deaf people often talk rather loudly – and there's
a recognizable intonation to their speech. My portrayal
caught some of that, I thought. It pleased me because I
had never seen an actor represent that kind of delivery.
However, the producers thought that the American
audience would not understand my Yorkshire accent.
I was saddened by their request for me to re-dub the
whole part in clear Standard English. Which I did. Of

course, that took the edge right off the characterization; all the subtleties and most of the humour went down the plughole. But that's the film business. My disappointment led me to resolve that, in future, I would keep control of my own work.'

Nevertheless, *The Italian Job* was far from unprofitable for him. Even without the subtleties, most of the critics enjoyed his performance. 'Benny Hill in fine bumbling form', wrote Cecil Wilson of the *Daily Mail* and 'Raises some useful yocks', commented *Variety*. Among other positive outcomes, he met Noël Coward and Michael Caine. Benny played a funeral scene with Coward and others in a Dublin cemetery. They were shooting in Ireland because The Master, as director Peter (*The Earthling*) Collinson always respectfully referred to him, lived abroad for tax purposes and had used up his annual quota of residence in the UK. Benny found the great man quiet and judicious, with a dry sense of humour. Coward gave a polished performance in this, his last film. 'He played his usual urbane self,' judges Benny. 'But Michael Caine turned in a superb portrayal of a very cool, very smart Cockney villain. If I had to call either of them The Master for screen acting, it would be Michael. He's a consummate performer. There's no one I admire more. I was lucky enough to observe him closely on the set, but the whole nation was privileged to see his television Master Class on the art of screen acting. It was riveting. And Michael's such good company off-stage too. Very intelligent, honest and down-to-earth. No pretensions at all. He was once asked what qualities in a girl turned him on. "Her ability to make me laugh," he said. It had never occurred to me, but I recognized a similar response in myself.

'Michael organized a party for the company in Turin. Afterwards I walked home alone along the river bank to clear my head. When I crossed a bridge, I vomited into the water. Even that was a joke. I was being sick into the Po.'

Michael Caine remembers that party, too. 'Benny enjoyed himself once he got going. I made it impossible for him not to come. I can be very persuasive when I like. It was almost a party for him, because he had finished his part and was going home. He had this habit of disappearing after a day's work. The rest of us would have a meal in the hotel or a drink in the club, but Benny would be off on his own. He was one of the shyest, quietest men I have ever met in my life. I'm sure he wasn't insecure. That was just his way. On the set, he would talk to me about quite strange things on a far higher plane than you would expect and seemed to be an intellectual rather than a bawdy comedian. The number of languages he could speak was amazing. I enjoyed his company very, very much and have seen every show he's ever done. A lot of them ten times, in the States.'

For Benny, keeping control of his own work meant, primarily, directing his own performances on film or television. It also meant the authority to space the screening of his television shows for maximum impact. My brother has always trodden the tightrope between neglecting his British viewers so that they forget him, and appearing so often that they become sated with his presence on the box. At the time of Benny's resolution not to accept, willy-nilly, the direction of others, Leonard Buckley of *The Times* observed: 'Most television comics outstay their welcome. But not so Benny Hill. Not for him the guest appearances, the constant grinning from some plug for margarine. He rations his performances. So he comes to us fresh. And fresh he is. The fatuous face exudes good health. He is every mother's notion of a well-nourished son. A walking, talking advertisement for apple dumplings and early to bed.'

The BBC directors who had made such vital contributions to Benny's television career, Duncan Wood, John Street and Kenneth Carter, were no longer assisting him. He missed their guidance. In addition, the BBC authorities decided, without consultation, not to repeat his 1969 series. Benny had understood, when he made it, that it was to be shown again. The timing of the second showing was important in the campaign to keep his name before the public. He never left matters like that to chance if he could help it. He was unhappy, therefore, that his concerns were not being accommodated. When Philip Jones, of Thames Television, approached him with a generous offer of four one-hour spectaculars in colour, which was just being introduced, and the opportunity to direct a silent film, in colour, Benny jumped at the chance. He signed to appear exclusively for the London company, thus beginning a long and remarkably successful association.

Thames immediately put him up front, showcasing him in 1969 in a Christmas Day Special, entering one of his hilarious hours for the Montreux Festival and launching the campaign to sell the Benny Hill Show abroad. Within months of joining Thames, Benny pushed his show to the top of the ITV ratings with a viewing figure that topped every other programme for two years, including the Apollo moon landing. The ink was scarcely dry on his signature before he was made ITV Personality of the Year, and shortly afterwards his spectaculars won the Society of Film and Television Arts' Light Entertainment Award for Production and Direction, plus the Craft Award for Best Script. He deserved the acclaim, as the hours of television entertainment he created contained items that were never less than interesting and often riotously funny. One of them caused a sensation when Benny, in drag, played Katie Boyle as hostess and all six contestants in his version of the Eurovision Song Contest.

Philip Jones was as good as his word and, within a year, Benny had made two silent colour films, each about half an hour long. Paramount had beaten Thames to the punch and in 1969 financed Benny's first starring film venture, *The Waiters*, which catalogues the demolition committed by two layabouts, Benny the venial one, and David Battley, the stupid one, hired for a small dinner party in a country house. After a disastrous evening, as Benny cycles home, a glow in the sky behind him suggests that the destruction is complete. The film was shown in cinemas all over the country, but the television programme-makers cut out most of the comedy sequences in favour of the plot when it finally reached the small screen. Benny is rightly proud of the original half-hour film, which he also scripted.

In the second film, *Eddie in August*, made in 1970 under the banner of Thames, Benny returned to the theme of the unlucky male, whose dream-girl chooses someone else. He ends up marrying her fat friend. Unfortunately, my brother appears rather too worldly and well-nourished to be wholly successful in his attempts at pathos. The most successful set-piece in the picture was a parody of a hospital soap opera, in which a broken-down old car, rather than a human being, needed frantic surgery.

Fifteen years before *Eddie in August*, Benny had written his first screenplay, a short comedy about the adventures of a milkman. He composed a song to introduce it, which was never heard, as the venture was shelved for lack of finance. In January 1971, Benny introduced the song in his television show. It was called 'Ernie'. Later in the year, Wally Ridley, A & R man for EMI, asked Benny to put his latest songs on an LP, 'This Is Benny Hill'. With the help of his favourite backing group, The Ladybirds, the LP was polished off in two days at Abbey Road, where the Beatles made their records. Driving my brother home after the second session, Wally suggested casually that he might promote 'Ernie' as a single Christmas number. Benny agreed that it was a likely contender. A champion, as it happened.

'Ernie' perched at No. 1 for five weeks and stayed in the charts for weeks over the Christmas period. A deflationary echo of the whole Frankie Lane genre, it described the amorous exploits of a milkman who drove 'the fastest milk cart in the West'. The song was partly autobiographical. 'When I say, "He galloped into Market Street, his badge upon his chest", that was me,' asserts Benny. 'As I had a country round, they always gave me the most spirited horse – so when I returned, I let 'em know I was coming, over Station Hill, round into Leigh Road and swinging into Market Street, we galloped as fast as we could. I imagined I was driving the stage coach into Dodge City, hoofs drumming, bottles rattling and every living thing flying out of our way!'

As always, Benny refused to take part in radio and TV chat shows to plug his record. When 'Top of the Pops' begged him to appear, he made a short film for them, dressed once more as a milkman, showing off his Dodge City driving with a horse and milk-cart. Because 'Ernie' had come from nowhere to surprise everybody, Benny not only earned royalties for words and music, but cleared the board moneywise with a deal masterminded by Richard Stone, that astonished

the record music world. Wally Ridley chose to back
'Ernie' with a number called 'Stick Your Finger In
Your Ear', which sprang from my irritation with the
insanely jolly songs of that era. Bright soubrettes were
insisting, at the tops of their voices, that one only
had to smile, repeat some gobblydegook phrase and
'everything would be all right'. So I suggested, 'Stick
Your Finger In Your Ear, Go Ting-A-Ling-A-Ling!' as a
suitably ridiculous formula. With a little help from me,
Benny wrote and performed it, but it went nowhere.
Except that, years later, my brother called to ask me if
I had heard the 'Spitting Image' hit, 'Stick A Deckchair
In Your Ear, Wave A Chicken In The Air'.

Yes, I had to admit, it did sound a trifle familiar.

17

Family Matters

Although Benny was kind enough to take up a suggestion of mine occasionally, it was clear by this time that he needed very little help from others in creating, performing and directing his work. *The Waiters* proved that. I felt that he was rather like Fred Allen, the American radio wit, who 'liked writing on dirty paper'. Benny resembled Allen in the way he would take someone else's script and use it as the basis for a flight of fancy that would leave the originator ruefully envious. But he rarely needed to be prompted by another's ideas.

In the early days, when Benny first swam into their ken, some watchers of the screen took him to their hearts immediately. Others had to be persuaded. It was not long before he was winning over the great mass of viewers to affection and high regard. Because his reputation had not yet been established, Benny took opportunities to publicize himself, and accepted many arduous assignments. However, I was aware that he lived in a state of tension in preparation for and during public appearances. My feeling was that each of these occasions took a great deal out of him. It seemed to me important for his health to keep these periods of high stress to a minimum. I have, therefore, never asked him to attend a function for my benefit or any cause in which I was interested.

By 1970, each new edition of the Benny Hill Show went straight to the top of the ratings. My brother had been the nation's best-loved comedian for over a decade. Everywhere he went, he was mobbed. Whenever we ventured out of doors together, I waited for ages while he signed autographs. Our walks were punctuated by cries from every direction. Labourers on scaffolding, taxi-drivers in their cabs, typists from office windows, yobbos in the parks – all called out to Benny. No matter how rude they were, he always waved back. 'I must acknowledge them,' he explained. 'Even if I only put up two fingers to them. They love it.'

Benny was once walking with Tessa, his beautiful Australian niece, in Hyde Park when one of a group of hobbledehoys shouted at him, 'You're just a dirty old man.'

'You're wrong,' called back Benny. 'I'm not just a dirty old man. I'm a rich and famous dirty old man.' The lads were satisfied. The god was among them and had recognized them. Immortality by proxy.

Now that Thames were selling the Benny Hill Show aggressively abroad, my brother could no longer wander unrecognized round the villages and ancient towns of Spain and southern France. It was a delight he gave up reluctantly, resorting to disguise sometimes to safeguard his privacy and tranquillity. He ordered a specially constructed pair of dentures that fitted in front of his natural teeth and altered the shape of his face. He would wear this mess of horse's teeth when standing on the terraces of the London soccer grounds, ideal vantage points for the observation of his fellow-man and the appreciation of Cockney wit.

I was always amused on these occasions when, rubbing shoulders, our immediate neighbours thought they recognized Benny. There would be nudging and muttering. Then, looking at the face, some doubt emerging. When they clocked his scruffy cap and coat, they would shake their heads. No one in his right mind who could afford better would stand on the terraces in the rain dressed like that, would he? If Benny thought a challenge imminent, he would launch into a long diatribe against the referee in the ripest Cockney street language. That settled it.

Of course, my brother did not hide from most of his fans, to whom he is ever grateful for support and encouragement throughout his career. He always stops to chat while he signs autograph books and, if there is no book, he will treasure a name and address scribbled on a crumpled piece of paper until he can send a signed photograph to it. Benny remembers Arthur Askey's dictum, 'I begin my performance when I leave my house in the morning.' He is so conscientious in his endeavours to please his fans that a misunderstanding which occurred years ago still haunts him.

'I was leaving the Palace Theatre with some friends to get into a hired car, when the driver shouted, "Will you please hurry? There's Royalty in the offing and the police are getting very edgy about the traffic. They've warned me already." We climbed in quickly and were about to go when a young woman in a red coat, who had probably waited half an hour for me, handed her autograph book into the back of the car. I was furthest from her and the driver was anxiously calling for us to hurry up. He was afraid of being nicked by the police. So I pushed the autograph book away, saying I hadn't time to sign it. We pulled away immediately and, through the window, I saw the young woman's head go down in disappointment. I felt terrible, really sorry about that, I really did. It's the only time I've ever knowingly disappointed a genuine fan – and I hope the lady concerned reads this and contacts me so that I can make amends.'

Benny has always discouraged the setting up of an

official fan club. Once again, he had doubts about being associated with an organization over which he has no control. I have met groups of Benny Hill fans in Britain and the US but they tend to meet on an informal basis.

Large quantities of mail ceaselessly arrive from all over the world. He answers it all by hand, except the most abusive and the obviously mendicant. Nearly all the letters to him are pleasant to read and answer, as they reassure him that his efforts to make the world laugh are succeeding. But they do take up a great deal of his time, which is why he will not enter into a protracted correspondence with any one person.

Sixty per cent of Benny's mail comes from women. It is usually encouraging, grateful, even adulatory. On rare occasions, Benny receives a *cri de coeur* from a lonely girl or an unhappy wife, which casts him, Angels and ministers of grace defend us, as a fantasy lover. 'I always take particular care with my reply to one of these, keeping it light, friendly and optimistic in an endeavour to cheer up the recipient. A similar number of women complain about the show – a minuscule proportion of my mail. I reply to them in the same manner.'

One day a letter arrived which began, 'I have the hottest desire to meet you,' continued in that vein and closed, 'With my deepest love, Georgio'. He was obviously a Greek young man. Benny wrote a guarded reply and was surprised to receive dozens of letters from Greek men and women expressing the same sentiments in exactly the same words. My brother guessed that a magazine had displayed a sample letter for its readers to copy. An enraged American wrote once, claiming to be Benny's bastard and threatening to kill him. 'I had never been to the US when he was born,' says Benny, 'and I've

never known many American girls that well.' In fact it
was not until 1984 that he first went to America.

Some correspondents claim to be comedy scriptwriters. When they are asked to send a sample of their
work, most do not reply. Of those that do, only one
in a hundred provides an idea or joke that Benny can
use. If he includes a contribution in his show, which
is a rare occurrence, he pays exactly what it is worth
to him, usually a proportion of his script-writing fee,
based on airtime plus a 'quality percentage'.

'I never profiteer on items I am offered,' he claims.
'Unfortunately, most would-be contributors have no
idea of the restrictions under which I work. One
gentleman suggested a scene in which I was chased
down the Edgware Road from Lord's Cricket Ground
by the actual England and Australian teams followed by
the crowd. Even if possible, that would have cost more
than the show's entire budget. A number of writers, at
bottom, offer nothing. They describe in detail a very
elaborate scene and add, "I leave the funny actions to
you. After which, laughter will reign supreme." That's
all right, then. Occasionally, a film script will be left at
the post office for me to pick up. Sometimes it is not
even a comedy. There is no part in it for me, but the
writer wants me to spend the afternoon reading it and
the evening writing an assessment of the work. "Be as
frank as you like," he says. I wish I could be.'

Most would-be writers do not appreciate frankness.
At the Prince of Wales Theatre, a couple of nervous
young men came to Benny's dressing-room to sell him
a two-minute cabaret solo that depended on his wearing a giant rabbit outfit. 'I do a 45-minute cabaret act,'
explained Benny. 'What happens when I'm changing
into and out of the costume?' They had not thought of
that. Emboldened by my brother's whisky, the young

writers soon passed from, 'Would you be good enough, Mr Hill', through 'You have to admit, Benny' and 'I'm telling you, Ben', to 'It's better than the crap you're doing, anyway.'

In the neighbouring dressing-room, the easy-going Tommy Cooper was taken in quite ruthlessly by a complete stranger who appeared on the Monday evening, claiming to be a fellow-magician. Tommy gave him a drink and chatted civilly. The next evening the chap turned up three-handed to introduce his wife and son. On the Wednesday, it was drinks all round for the sociable magician and a couple of his mates. By the Saturday night, when Tommy returned from his stint on-stage, the room was full of strangers drinking his whisky with their feet on his dressing-table. 'Tommy was too generous for his own good,' says Benny.

The wish for fame is a common dream in the twentieth century, particularly among the young. But those who long for celebrity status may well be disappointed if they gain it. Fame presents an attractive face, but those unacquainted with it have no idea how difficult at times the Bitch-Goddess can be. Even reflected starlight can be corrosive.

Benny's conquest of so many hearts in his own country evoked a few emotions that, for me, opened a Pandora's box of troubles. It is not my recollection that I invited them. I was proud of my brother's work, always accepted plaudits on his behalf as modestly as I could, and answered questions frankly. When I confirmed my relationship with Benny, questioners invariably grew animated. They would cheer up no end for about three minutes, always complimentary and interested. After I had satisfied their curiosity, most would close the conversation in a friendly and agreeable manner. I was always glad to talk to people like these. However, I discovered, after some time, a different pattern of response in a sizeable minority. I learned to watch for the signs.

These others would begin exactly like the majority, full of praise and questions. After about three minutes, they would light up like a pinball machine. 'This is not only exciting,' said their eyes, 'it could be valuable to me.' At this realization, they would begin the spiel about their position in the local Ratcatchers' Club/Carpolishers' Lodge/Ladies' Institute/Odds and Sods Brigade. After a review of all the good work their organization was doing, they popped the question – 'Will you get your brother down to open our summer festival?' Then the shit hit the Benny Hill fan – because I would have to say, 'No!' I explained. Try as I would, they never understood. 'Why can't you just ask him?' sometimes degenerated into 'Who the hell do you think you are, you jumped-up little pipsqueak?' I had made another enemy.

At least, besides self-aggrandizement, these petitioners were usually working for a good cause. To others, I offered a short cut to the cheap commercial advertisement. To one or two, a stage-door into show-business. Suppliants, usually complete strangers, called upon me at home and often expected to be offered hospitality while they conned me. I had no telephone of my own, but was no safer from interruption in school. Producers, researchers and journalists found me via the single school telephone – in the headmaster's office. He was livid, as he was obliged to take my class while I answered a string of fatheaded questions.

Even in my classroom, I could not escape inappropriate kinds of attention. Serious exposition or discussion

would be interrupted, written exercises spoilt, by personal comments, most often from disturbed children.
On a few occasions my presence evoked displays of
misplaced envy and malice among members of staff
and parents. Unflattering graffiti about my brother and
me appeared on lavatory and school boundary walls.
Outside the school, yobbos would call after me on my
way home.

One day a local representative of my professional
union visited my home to discuss a serious complaint,
as he described it, from a fellow-teacher. The aggrieved
schoolmaster was threatening to take me to court for
slander. It seems that the poor fellow was under a
couple of delusions – one, that I was a previous hostile
pupil of his, two, that I was using my brother's radio
show to ridicule him. It all came about because, like
so many comedians, Benny used outlandish names for
his characters. In order to avoid litigation, let us say
that, with a nod to Groucho, in one radio episode
Benny called himself Rufus T. Firefly. Believe it or
not, this would-be litigant was actually named Rufus
T. Firefly. He was hopping mad at being portrayed as
a simpleton, and what was I going to do about it? What
I actually did about it was first to laugh heartily and
then offer the complainant a short, sharp imperative.
However, the local representative, enjoying the only
exciting item of union business to cross his agenda
in his entire career, prevailed upon me to raise the
matter with my brother. Benny's reaction was, in both
respects, the same as mine. Finally, after a good deal of
quite unnecessary hassle, as we were told that the old
fellow was very distressed, Benny agreed in future to
call the character Rufus T. Barfly. The whole incident
was a storm in a teacup, but it was also, for some time,
a source of considerable anxiety to me.

Benny, of course, was occasionally occupied with concerns similar to my own, but he endured them cheerfully as inevitable concomitants of his career. On the other hand, I was beginning to feel that being a kind of appendage to my brother was making my professional life difficult. My dissatisfaction peaked when I was chosen from a short-list of six for a more responsible post in a new school. After an interview with a ten-strong board, during which I was at pains to offer educational reasons why I was an eminently suitable candidate, the headmaster welcomed me with congratulations. My heart sank when he followed them with, 'Of course, you will get your brother down for our summer fête, won't you?' I knew I was about to make another enemy.

After that fiasco, depression was followed by determination to make changes in my private and social life that would obviate such difficulties. Accordingly, I decided to distance myself from my brother, in some respects. We met less often and never in my home town. There were fewer long telephone conversations as I needed all my spare time for some serious study I had undertaken. Relatives and close friends were the only ones entrusted with news of my brother. I never spoke of him to casual acquaintances and evaded questions about him.

Benny understood my difficulties and felt, I think, that we had been taking each other a little too much for granted. My adoption of a low profile in our relationship gradually succeeded. With every move of home and school, the trail became colder. Fewer acquaintances knew of my links with Benny. The even tenor of my professional life went undisturbed. Eventually, the day came when I was delighted to read in a national daily the news of my own death.

Inevitably, as we were no longer in close contact,
Benny and I tended to drift apart. That is to be expected
in brothers who have their separate lives and interests.
Our mother and sister both urged us not to lose touch
with each other. A few years ago, Diana wrote to me
from Australia of Benny's plight: 'The poor old bugger's
got nobody over there that really cares about him but
you.' I took her words to heart and made efforts to
renew our former affability together. Since giving up
teaching for a writing career, there has been more time
for fraternal exchanges. Benny and I have made good
use of it. However, there are some who have a vested
interest in making a drama of the hiatus in the relationship between two brothers. There was no drama. No
quarrel, no raised voices. I have not quarrelled with
Benny since I was sixteen. There has, of course, been
a severance. I no longer feel an appendage. I have found
my own voice.

Twenty years ago, Benny took his parents to lunch at
an excellent restaurant in Southampton. After smoked
salmon washed down by a couple of green chartreuses,
the Captain announced, 'What I would really like would
be to go to Spain with my son.'

'So I took him,' says Benny. 'And I'm awfully glad
I did, because, during our holiday there, we got to
know each other at last. My father loved the nightlife
in Barcelona. A few days later, we went to a cabaret
in Madrid and, when it finished at half-past two in the
morning, the Captain insisted on staying. We didn't
leave until the morning light, strolling back along the
Gran Via to the sound of birdsong.'

After ten days of sightseeing and shows, the Captain
was ready to return home. My brother, who intended
to travel further, saw him off at the airport one morning. Afterwards, Benny made his way to a favourite

restaurant in Madrid for a late lunch. As he was busily engaged at an outside table, he noticed an attractive auburn-haired woman passing. She hesitated and walked over to sit a few yards away. After she had ordered a drink and been served, she said, 'Hello, Mr Hill. May I join you?' 'Please do,' replied Benny.

His new-found friend proved to be a most interesting and charming person. She told him that her husband was a toy manufacturer who was in Madrid for a convention. After some time, she said, 'You don't remember me, do you?' Nonplussed, Benny answered, 'No, I'm sorry to say I don't.'

'Well, we met some years ago when you worked with my mother.'

'Your mother?'

'Yes. My mother's Marlene Dietrich. I'm her daughter, Maria.' Then, of course, Benny remembered that he had once compèred Marlene Dietrich's shows at the Café Anglais in London. As they chatted, Maria told fascinating stories of her childhood in Berlin.

'Of course,' she said, 'my mother was already a star, even then. Everyone loved her. Head waiters would fawn upon her. My father was ignored. He reacted by making a terrible fuss everywhere he went. Nothing was good enough for him. In restaurants, he would complain about the wine and send back the food.'

'How strange,' replied Benny. 'I've just put my father on a plane. He's the sort that goes through life calling for the manager.'

'I know exactly what you mean,' said Maria. They both chuckled ruefully.

Two years later, the Captain became very thin and entered hospital with a painful spinal condition. When

I visited him, he was in a characteristic bad temper.
He had bullied all the other members of the ward
into accepting a picture of Benny – and God help
the man who had not displayed the photograph on
his bedside locker. A week later he was discharged,
and a week after that he called me on the telephone.
'Just my bloody luck,' he complained. 'I gave up
smoking forty years ago and now they tell me it's
lung cancer. I've only got a few months to live.'
I was stunned. 'I don't believe it,' I said. 'You've
had a pain in your spine.' We talked about it for
a while and I promised to visit him within a week.
A few days later, my mother called to tell me the
Captain was dead. I was not only shocked, but mystified. He had sounded vigorous enough on the telephone.

An hour or so before the funeral, I managed to talk to
Mum alone about the nature of Dad's death. I told her
how staggered I was by the suddenness of his passing.
'He always reminded me of the Viking warrior who
wrestled with death. He was a survivor. As a young
man, he spent years on the Western Front without
leave; he outlived all his comrades in the Machine
Gun Corps unit; he endured the gas attacks and was
one of the first to walk out of his prison camp at
the end of the war. It's obvious that he remained
alive despite all the odds. He must have used every
ounce of muscle and every grain of intelligence to
win through. And he carried that sense of struggle
ever since.'

'If he hadn't been a most remarkable man,' replied
my mother, 'he would never have survived the war.
But this time he wrestled and was overthrown. And
he knew it. So he just turned his face to the wall
and died.' I went alone to the dining room where the

body of my father was lying in his coffin and spent a few minutes in valedictory silence with him. As I was about to leave, I noticed the snowy shroud folded back to reveal his face. 'I see you finally got your piece of clean white cloth, Dad,' I said.

I learned later that, on his dying day, when Benny was at his bedside, the Captain had said to him, 'If any man should thank another man for anything, I thank you for that holiday in Spain.' My brother was much distressed by his father's death, as they had become a great deal closer in the last few years. Benny took charge of the funeral, paid all outstanding bills and made things as easy as he could for his mother, as he had done for years.

Mum continued living in the semi-detached house in Westrow Gardens. Despite the most painful and crippling arthritis, she insisted on looking after herself. The only arguments Benny ever had with his mother were over provision of help for her. She adamantly refused to change her ways and made an almighty fuss about money spent to make life pleasanter for her. However, the greatest gift Benny gave her was himself, and she lived for the frequent visits he made to keep her cheerful.

In Benny's calendar, Thursday is *Variety* Day. The immense show-business weekly newspaper reaches London's West End in the morning and Benny is there to pick up his copy. If the weather is fine he hides behind its huge pages on a park bench. Long hours are spent poring over every item relevant to his business. One day in the mid-seventies, he read that Sid Caesar had transferred ten sketches direct from his television 'Your Show of Shows' on to 35-millimetre film to make a movie for the cinema circuits. Benny was much taken with the artful promotion. It was cheap and simple. He decided to do likewise – to splice clips of his shows together on film for public showing. He called Richard Stone, who immediately suggested that Bernard Delfont was the man to talk to. The next morning, Benny and Richard arrived in Lord Delfont's office in Soho for a preliminary discussion. Bernard told them at once that he would be pleased to back the project. My brother thought to himself that they ought to obtain a copy of Caesar's film and see it before making a decision. 'Well, Bernie,' he began, 'there's just one thing – '

'Don't worry,' said the impresario smoothly, anticipating him, 'it's downstairs ready to run. Let's take a look at it.'

'You clever beggar,' thought Benny in admiration. 'No wonder you're where you are. You're a bloody genius.'

They watched the American compilation and followed suit by employing John Robbins of Thames TV to transfer videotapes to celluloid, making what must be the cheapest ninety-minute comedy feature film in the history of cinema. *The Best of Benny Hill* cost only £30,000, and became one of the trade's most remarkable financial successes. In April 1974 it went on general release at cinemas in London and all over the country.

Later that year, Benny flew the long way round to see his sister and her family in Australia. It was the first of a number of trips he made in the middle and late seventies, combining business with pleasure, to produce a show or a number of commercials down under. This time he stopped off in Tokyo to see an international boxing match, his favourite spectator sport. He was on foot, as usual, looking for the stadium, when a couple of Japanese policemen, finding his behaviour suspicious, approached him. They did not understand his explanation. So Benny started to shadow box in an effort to show them he wanted directions to the boxing match. They leapt back alarmed, thinking that he was shaping up to attack them. Then they grabbed him and dragged him struggling to the nearest police station. The sergeant there sorted it all out and it was not long before a police car delivered my brother to the stadium in time for the big fight.

Upon arrival, Benny gave Australia the Big Hello. He told waiting reporters at the airport that he had been subjected to a body search. Far from being annoyed, he said that, if he could be searched by a beautiful female customs officer he had spotted, he was 'going back for seconds'. Benny was flying high all that trip. John Jukes reported in *The Australian*: 'Benny Hill swept through the lobby of his Melbourne hotel yesterday, charming the women, insulting the men and leaving laughter in his wake. During a 20-minute foray into the lobby, normal bar and lunch service came to a halt as businessmen, tourists and hotel staff stopped to enjoy Mr Hill's staccato delivery of throw-away lines and gags. Mr Hill could not make more than three steps at a time as autograph seekers kept thrusting pencils and pieces of paper into his hands.' When he was asked what he thought about Keith Witham, the Australian impressionist, who imitates Benny as Fred Scuttle in his cabaret act, my brother said, 'Great! Just so long as I don't get the blame for his mischief. If there's mischief, I want part of the action.'

All the publicity did not impress Diana's children, Tessa, Peter and Mick, now in their early teens. They

were determined not to fall for the tall stories of their
Pommie uncle. They were fascinated, nevertheless.

'Have you ever met Brigitte Bardot?' asked Peter.

'Gordon Bennett! If she phones me up again, I'll go
mad. She's crazy about me. What a bore!'

'Yeah?'

'Yeah!'

'How about Sophia Loren?' queried Mick.

'Oh, don't talk to me about Sophia Loren. I can't go
anywhere – what can I do? I don't want to hurt her
feelings. But it's so difficult when you're young and
attractive like I am.'

'Yeah?'

'Yeah!'

Then the children showed Benny a newspaper picture of Abigail, Australia's current sex symbol, then
stripping in a Sydney nude revue.

'I bet you've never met Abigail,' said Peter.

'She wouldn't look at you,' said Mick.

'Not a great fat pudden' like you, she wouldn't,'
added Tessa.

'Right, you little buggers,' thought Benny. 'I'll show
you!' and straight away he sent Abigail a dozen roses,
phoned and suggested a joint photo-call. Abigail was
enthusiastic. 'I'm making an LP,' she explained. 'Come
down to the studio. I'll invite the press.'

When Benny arrived, the photographers were there
– so he and Abigail cuddled and clowned for the
newshounds. Then they went to the Summit Restaurant
where they held hands over lunch for photographs.

Next day, Benny bought three local newspapers, all
with front pages full of the happy pair. He threw them
on the kitchen table. 'Read 'em and weep!' he commanded. The boys were silent. When they saw the
pictures they were stunned. The fat old Pom had

actually made it with Abigail. But Tessa refused to
be impressed. Looking at a photograph of Benny and
Abigail taken after their lunch, she saw that their table
was covered with shells and claws, the debris of a
lobster salad.

'Gee, ain't she a messy eater!' said Tessa.

When the show Benny made in Australia was televised in Britain, James Thomas of the *Daily Express*
wrote, 'He had his Australian audiences rolling with
laughter . . . The amazing thing is how much Hill can
pack into an hour. No comedian in the business can
get through so much brisk material without having to
resort to time-filling songs or unimportant guest artists.
He takes the whole thing on his shoulders, and no
comedian is more adept at using the medium . . . I
don't know why he had to go Down Under to do all
this brilliant tomfoolery.'

On his way home, Benny took Diana and Tessa for
a week's holiday to Singapore, then went on alone to
the UK, where he travelled post-haste to his mother
with news of Diana and her family. Mum was still
struggling on her own in the family house, but it was
not long before Benny finally convinced her that
she would be more comfortable with assistance elsewhere. He arranged for her to stay close at hand, in
a pleasant room of her own, at a Portswood nursing-
home.

Although she stoically accepted the move as wise,
her heart was in Westrow Gardens. She tried once to
go home for good, but it did not work out. However,
any visitor with the strength to push her in the wheelchair found himself ordered to head for her beloved
semi-detached, if only for an hour's stay. Occasionally, she would ask to be bowled round Southampton
Common, a four-mile exercise that brought the colour

back to her cheeks and tested the lungs and the thighs of her companion. But Heaven was her destination and, until she was called, Westrow Gardens would do. It was there, with Benny at her side, that she became ill. He called the ambulance and a neighbour, Doreen Anderson, a one-time nursing sister who often helped his mother. They travelled with Mum to the General Hospital, where the doctors diagnosed a serious heart condition that demanded an extensive operation. Mum would not countenance it. 'Put me out with the dirty washing,' she insisted. 'I have had enough.' Benny arranged a private room for his mother, where she lay awaiting the outcome. He called me and, when I arrived, it was obviously a great comfort for Mum to have her two sons at her bedside. She looked remarkably well to me, though I knew, of course, that she was not. However, Benny and I felt that there was no immediate danger and returned to Westrow Gardens for the night.

Next morning Benny had to return to London and I stayed with my mother for most of the day. When her main meal arrived, she tucked in like a good'un and cleared every spoonful of her rice pudding. Remembering the H. E. Bates story of the dying woman who refuses her husband's rice pudding, I took Mum's trenchervaliance to be a good omen.

Everyone who knew our family had always admired my mother and tut-tutted about the cross she had to bear. In all those years of lowered eyes and whispered comments, what everyone did not know and most never suspected, was that, despite his regular outbursts, my father adored his wife. When I sat by her bedside that winter afternoon, she told me: 'I have been loved as no other woman has ever been loved.' I believe her.

At three in the morning, I was awakened by a telephone call which informed me that my mother was dying. After waiting ages for a taxi, I arrived at her room a few moments after she had died. As I felt sure she could still hear me, I spoke privately to her for a few minutes.

Later that morning, I called Benny with the bitter news. He took it calmly, although I knew it was a painful blow to him. As usual, I left the arrangements to him and returned to my home. On the day of Mum's funeral, I was ill and fell on my back trying to dress myself. It was clear that I had not the strength to get to Southampton. I phoned Benny, who told me that his old friend Harry Segal had arrived the previous day and had been a great comfort to him. They had sat up all night together, just talking. I was pleased that Harry was there, not only because he was such a support for Benny but because he had always been most attentive to Mum and she was very fond of him. Harry took my place alongside Benny at the graveside.

A person's death may not end a relationship. As Robert Anderson's perceptive play, *I Never Sang For My Father*, suggests, bonds will sometimes strengthen after loss. Certainly, Benny is aware of the continued presence of his parents. When he puts flowers on their grave, he hears his mother say, 'You shouldn't have spent all that money on flowers, Alfie. It's a terrible waste. A tiny bunch would have sufficed. We don't really need them at all. I don't like you to throw your money about so.' And when Benny is breaking the stalks to put them in a pot, his father is beside him, saying, 'Give it here, you bloody idiot! Can't even break a few twigs properly. Taking hours over a few flowers. Talk about incompetent! I'm surprised you found the right grave. You wander about with no bloody idea of what you're up to!'

The Captain will also come to me sometimes at night, which always astonishes me. 'But Dad,' I cry, 'I thought you were dead!'

'Don't you believe it, my son,' he tells me. 'Don't you believe it!'

18

Westward Look, the Land is Bright

A few years ago, visitors to London's Bloomsbury district were surprised to find a new blue plaque in the north-east corner of Bedford Square. Blue plaques denote the former residences of famous people of the past. Around Bloomsbury, they are to be found on walls in nearly every street. But this fresh decoration celebrated the home of 'Eleanor Taffner – born 1922'. The quotation beneath her name was from Rider Haggard: 'She who must be obeyed'. It was all very puzzling to the tourists. Who was Eleanor Taffner? And, if she was still alive, why was she being honoured in this way?

The truth eventually emerged. The plaque was one of Don Taffner's little jokes, a typically lighthearted tribute to his wife. It stayed on public show until the Westminster City Council got to hear of it. So now the colourful disc is displayed in the hallway of the Georgian house that serves as the London offices of D. L. Taffner Ltd, which markets the Benny Hill Show, Rumpole of the Bailey and other Thames productions. The head of this global organization is, not surprisingly, Don Taffner himself, a tubby firecracker of a businessman who jumps from city to city, throwing off ideas and jokes like sparks.

He is much in demand. A distinguished actor preceded me into his basement office. Closing my first twenty-minute interview, Don told me that a famous television tycoon was waiting to see him next. The

important visitor had recently moved on to a supreme
position in the nation's musical establishment. As I
stood up to leave, Don winked and said, 'If I can't
get to see the opera, the opera comes to see me!' On
my way out, I looked again at the plaque. Of course.
The quotation on the plaque is a line from Rumpole of
the Bailey.

Brooklyn-born Don Taffner, who has spent his working life at the business end of show-business, was
marketing Thames Television programmes in the US
from the company's inception in 1968. When he was
given the Benny Hill Show, he realized immediately that
it could not be sold to the nationwide networks, such
as CBS or NBC. They insist on controlled programme
content and there could be no interference in the
creative process that produced the Benny Hill Show.
The British comedy hour was, also, as it stood, a little
piquant for the staid networks, who prefer blander fare
for their viewers. The show would have to be syndi-
cated directly through the local television stations. This
would have the added advantage of denying publicity
to any political lobbyists looking for an issue to give
them nationwide coverage. It is relatively easy to blow
up a storm over programmes shown all over the States
at the same time on one of the networks. If the comedy
hours were sold to the independent stations, however,
the owners would air them at different times and days
in all the cities and districts served. Only local interest
would be aroused by a particular episode.

For eight years, Don and his team tried to interest television executives in the hour-long Benny Hill
Show. They were not impressed. 'He's British. We
can't understand him,' said the programme directors.
Nobody bought the show. 'If only I could get it past the
station managers, I'm sure it would be a success with

the public,' said the battler from Brooklyn. 'Benny's a
really funny guy. All he needs is a chance.' 'Don always
had faith in me,' says Benny. On one Saturday morning
in the spring of 1978, an event occurred that was to
reward Don's faith. An old friend did Dick Signorelli
a favour.

Sig's old friend was Ron Gold, a slim, boyish figure
of a man, who was then station manager of the ailing
WTAF in Philadelphia and is now one of the most
respected top executives in the business. He was
sorting out a stack of tapes Sig had been given to
review by Don Taffner, who had signed him that very
week. Ron and Sig were looking for new shows that
might be sold to the US markets. On the Saturday
morning in Ron's office, several tapes of unknown British programmes had been fast-forwarded and labelled
'unpromising' when one entitled 'The Benny Hill
Show' was put in the player. They watched the titles
come up.

'Who is Benny Hill?' asked Ron. 'Not another British
comedian?' Sig nodded. 'That's all we need,' grumbled
the station manager. Everybody knows that very, very
few British comedians make it on US television. They
fast-forwarded the tape.

'Just a cotton-pick'n minute,' said Ron. 'This looks
interesting.' The tape was switched to normal speed.
After a couple of minutes, Ron exclaimed, 'This guy's
terrific! We've gotta put him on the air.' The pair
watched the rest of the tape enthralled.

As it was rewound, Ron said, 'This reminds me of
the old Jackie Gleason variety shows.'

'That's right,' replied Sig, 'it's even got a troupe of
girls – the equivalent of the June Taylor dancers. Will
you buy it, Ron?'

'I'll buy it, but not as it stands. Benny Hill himself is

sensational, but the show is too slow. I can't use it as
an hour show. It needs to be cut down to half an hour.
And we can't do that with each show separately. We
need to re-programme all the shows available. Canni-
balize them. Throw away the singers, the guests, the
difficult bits that our people won't understand. Extract
all the Benny Hill gems from all the tapes and put them
together to make half-hour segments of pure non-stop
comedy. They'll be fantastic.'

'Will you buy it, if it's in half-hour format?' asked
Sig.

'You can tell Don Taffner that, if he edits them the
way I propose (and you must stress to him that it's
necessary to take pieces from many shows), I'll buy
and air every half-hour he can produce. He's got my
word on that.'

Sig gave his boss the message. There followed, in
Ron's phrase, 'a lot of back and forth' between him
and Don Taffner. It is easy to understand why. Re-
programming would be a complex, expensive and risky
business. There was only one sure customer for the
product. Ron insisted. Don took advice.

Finally, Don decided to produce a half-hour demo
tape along the lines Ron suggested. He realized that the
editing could make or break the project. Richard Stone
recommended John Street, Benny's former television
director and a master editor, for the task. Now retired
and living in Cornwall, Street was uniquely qualified to
undertake it. He knew Benny and his work intimately,
understood and admired the comedy star, and had a
sound background in films, having learned his trade
at MGM. Further, he had worked in American television and travelled widely in the States, where he had
relatives.

When he was approached, John saw at once Ron

Gold's point about cannibalization and insisted that a minimum of four British one-hour tapes would be required to make one American half-hour show. He carried ten tapes to his Cornish cottage, watched and timed them. In assembling the demonstration show, it seemed appropriate to open with a forty-second teaser that introduced Benny as a ridiculous old-time Western deputy. John worked out the running order at his country home and brought the blueprint and tapes to the London studios for editing. The transfer from the British system of 625 lines to the American 525 was a costly procedure but, at last, the test edit was ready.

Re-programming would only pay for itself if other station managers and programme directors could be persuaded to follow Gold's example. The pilot American-style Benny Hill Show would have to be screened, therefore, at the next convention of the National Association of Television Program Executives (NATPE). Don booked a suite for that purpose at the Bonaventure Hotel in Los Angeles where the conference was to be held.

On the day of the launch, the bad news was that a torrential storm was raging around the hotel, halting the external glass elevators that, in the autumn of 1978, were such an elegant innovation. The good news was that Don had a captive audience for his exposition. He told the trapped delegates of Benny's phenomenal success in Britain and Europe and suggested that American audiences would respond to it even more enthusiastically than those in non-English-speaking countries. One American audience that responded to it enthusiastically was the assembly of station managers and programme directors that autumn day. They loved the show. As soon as the titles were screened, they began to chuckle. The chuckles built to roars and the roars to tears of laughter. At the pilot's close, a burst of

eager chatter gave Don hope, but he was an old hand
at the game and knew that, however complimentary
the buyers were, they would be very cautious when
ordering for their station. With one customer in the
bag, he needed only another five to make full-scale
production of the half-hour shows viable. Don was
mentally keeping his fingers crossed. When he began
to answer questions from the floor, a deep Southern
voice drawled, 'Ah cain't buy it, Don. It won't make
sense to my people. Ah cain't understand a word Benny
Hill says.'

'Well, I can't understand a word Marlon Brando
says, either,' replied Don firmly, 'but can that man
sell pictures!' Appreciative chuckles from the audience indicated that Don's shaft had struck home.

As he had expected, Don was given no definite commitments at the launch, but a great deal of interest was
expressed. It would need to be followed up. He felt sure
that, if he went ahead with production of the half-hour
tapes, by the time they were ready his salesmen would
have won over enough station managers to cover all
costs. Much would depend on Philadelphia's response
to the Benny Hill Show, which Ron Gold had booked
for the autumn of 1979. The re-editing began.

The new segments were actually 22$^{1}/_{2}$ minutes long,
allowing 7$^{1}/_{2}$ minutes for commercial breaks. In these
first entertainments for the US, John Street ruthlessly
cut to the bone. Sketches were trimmed to an introduction and a pay-off. Out went any items or references
unintelligible to American viewers. Out, too, went most
of the dialogue. The songs and girls were left in, but
everything else was pruned right back. Sometimes John
used just forty seconds of an hour's tape. This resulted
in a very fast show of riotous hilarity.

John's raw material, forty hour-long tapes, had been

produced over ten years. Therefore, as Benny has a weight problem, he looked fatter or thinner, younger or older, from one sequence to another. John did his best to overcome this by dropping in a quickie between the ill-matched sequences. The discrepancy would be bridged by the appearance of Benny in a beard, a moustache, a wig, or in drag to take the viewers' attention from his age or size. Another unlikely consideration was financial. Benny's team of supporting stars were on full pay, even when appearing in crammed scenes. John had to cut these appearances down to essentials to avoid crippling costs.

Suddenly it seemed too little and too late. There were only three of the new American-style shows ready when Ron Gold desperately needed the forty he had ordered for the autumn. A rival station was having internal troubles and its 11.00 P.M. NBC News ratings were tumbling. Normally, such programmes were unassailable, but Gold believed that he could take advantage of his competitor's weakness to win the time slot by running the Benny Hill Show opposite the news. That meant 'stripping', putting the British comedy half-hour on at eleven o'clock for five evenings every week. Ron pleaded with Don Taffner for tapes so that he could start airing them at once.

'It'll be tight,' said Don. 'We have only three of them ready.'

'Ship 'em down,' ordered Ron. 'I'll run them every evening as soon as they arrive. Get the fourth one to me as soon as you can. And the rest.'

'Right,' agreed Don. 'You shall have the first three right away. And I'll hurry them up in Britain to fly the rest to you, one at a time, as they are edited.'

Ron flew into a barrage of flak over his daring plan. 'You're mad! Nobody's ever been crazy enough to do that before. You can't strip three shows a week for weeks!' sneered the critics.

'Bullshit!' replied Ron. 'Watch me. I believe in Benny Hill. And I'm putting the joker on. Every week-night from now on!'

Gold was as good as his word. When the first three tapes arrived, all the staff of the station were waiting for them. They cheered, as they hoped the Benny Hill Show would help to rescue the foundering WTAF. The first episode was put on almost unannounced. The station was so poor there was no promotion budget, no money to publicize the series. Luckily, it was shown to Lee Winfrey, who gave it a boost in the *Philadelphia Inquirer* on Monday 8 January 1979, under the headline, 'Healthy Vulgarity'.

'The Benny Hill Show is hilarious vulgarity. Benny Hill has been a popular comedian on British TV for almost a decade. His first appearance on any American station will be tonight at 11 on WTAF (Channel 29). Don't miss Benny Hill. He'll make you laugh out loud, not once, but often . . . a master of mugging and a maestro of mime.

'Channel 29 has purchased 40 episodes of the Benny Hill Show and plans to air them five nights a week, Monday through Friday. If I were working for the 11 P.M. local newscasts on Channels 3, 6 and 10, I'd be worrying about Hill decimating my audience. Until the Benny Hill Show finishes its run, the only heartwarming homilies by Ron Hunter that I'm likely to hear will be the ones that friends tell me in my office next day.'

Ron Gold continued stripping the first three shows for a fortnight until the fourth tape arrived (once more to cheers). By this time, the Benny Hill Show was the talk of the town. If you could not discuss it knowledgeably, you were socially dead. Word of mouth spread the excitement to all corners of Philadelphia. WTAF's eleven o'clock ratings climbed slowly from zero to sixes and sevens, an unheard-of phenomenon for an independent station in such circumstances. The NBC Network News was like the bear from the fair – it was nowhere. As each new episode was added to the WTAF stock, the effect on audience figures snowballed. Winfrey was later to assess the impact on Philadelphia: 'I think people were startled by the Benny Hill Show at first, but it was novel and refreshing. People were amused and charmed by it.' The Philadelphia story was not lost on station managers and programme directors all over the country. They were persuaded rather more by Ron Gold's success than by his courage. During January, WTAF were joined by Seattle/Tacoma, Miami and Cleveland, all of them buying the half-hour. They were soon followed by similar independents in New York, Boston, Dallas, Los Angeles, San Francisco and Washington DC. Immediate success induced some station managers to think they were as good as Gold. They urged Don Taffner not to wait until autumn, but to deliver their orders at once, in mid-season spring. As for Ron Gold and his WTAF (now WTFX) team, it was months before they had a breather in the comedy cycle race.

When the show was introduced on WOR, New Yorkers went wild about it. They changed their social habits to make sure they saw it. Some stopped going to evening sports. Others threw Benny Hill parties. Scores dashed off letters to the newspapers to express their delight. 'Oh, it is so, so good,' wrote Joe Mango to Marvin Kitman, television critic of *Newsday*. 'Last night I laughed so hard, paranoia set in for fear I was making too much loud, happy noise.' And an old French lady, Jeanne Bombled, struggled with her English to tell him,

'Benny Hill is so fun, just seeing his face makes you feel better and to forget our problems.' All over the city, jokers in caps and berets were giving the splay-fingered salute. It was a common boast among the hip crowd, 'I dig The Benny Hill Show, man, bristols, too.' As Tom Sullivan, under the headline, 'The Never Predictable Mr Benny Hill', explained in the *Herald-News* to his fellow-citizens: 'If you happened to make a grotesque social gaucherie and ask "Who is Benny Hill?", you'd know you were in the presence of a true fan of the British funnyman if the answer was "Who knows?" It is a difficult business to know who he is. Or, for that matter, what he looks like, because he is quicksilver. Above all, he is almost consistently funny, and never predictable. He is also the runaway success story of television syndication. Incredibly, his following knows no age barrier. He is as much an in thing with grammar school students as he is with their teachers, and that situation applies on the college level, too. Cab-drivers love him because he is their kind of person. And lawyers, noted writers and some top company executives have been known to gear their evenings to catching his acts.

' "But he is a low-class British comedian," some station owners said when D. L. Taffner, Inc., the programme distributor, started offering the half-hour episodes around. That estimation, made without the benefit of knowledge, could hardly be further from the truth. Benny Hill, at 55, is a consummate showman, whose sense of humour can only be described as brilliant and, since it is viewed by millions in the far corners of the world, it is obviously universal, too.' Bill Carlton of the New York *Daily News* had succinct advice for the buyers of Benny's latest record: 'Keep a doctor nearby – or you'll die laughing!'

WOR, Channel 9, stripped the show from the beginning, with awesome results. 'Since the series started here last April,' reported George Maksion in the New York *Daily News*, 'the ratings have skyrocketed, making it the highest rated show on the station. It also tops all the independents in the week-night 11 P.M. period . . . "It's sexy but not offensive," said a station spokesman. "It beats Monty Python coming and going." '

When the public clamoured for more Benny Hill, WOR were forced to act. They put the show on twice every night, adding another programming in the early evening at 7.30 P.M. This meant that Benny's hilarious antics were monopolizing the Channel 9 screen for five hours a week. The extra early-evening slot was soon seen to be justified when, some nights, Benny's audience took the total equivalent viewing figures for the three network-owned stations, Channels 2, 4 and 7, altogether. This was described as 'an unbelievable rating for a non-network station at prime-time'. Obviously euphoric over the British comedian's success on his station, Pat Argue of WOR asserted, 'Benny Hill Shows are like oil, a rare resource that will run out one day. Benny Hill is a genius. It's as simple as that.'

Like a presidential landslide, city after city all over America fell to the revolutionary candidate – revolutionary because the independent stations were not supposed to be able to take on the almighty power of the networks and actually beat them.

'The fact that Benny did not appear on the networks meant no media hype, no nationwide publicity, in fact, scarcely any advertising at all. He crept into the US in sneakers,' Joan Rivers told me in one breath. 'And that runs right against the grain in this country. Nobody was told how good he was. People had to find out for themselves – and he is such a great clown, so absolutely brilliant, wicked, merciless, wonderful and audacious, that they did discover him. They looked in the newspapers; they checked the magazines; they searched the channels and phoned up their friends. Word of mouth did it. That wasn't newspaper talk. It was genuine admiration and affection.' Once more, nobody was for him but the people.

Benny's triumph was reported by David Levin in the *Daily Mail*: 'Bruce Forsyth tried to and couldn't . . . Morecambe and Wise wanted to but haven't . . . Benny Hill, without even trying, has succeeded. He is the first English comic to appear coast to coast in America in his own television show. Hill has become the cult comic hit of the season. He has done it alone, a singular achievement.'

David Bianculli added his confirmation in the *Fort Lauderdale News*. 'Benny Hill has conquered American TV audiences like Sitting Bull conquered Custer. Stations fall over themselves to schedule the Benny Hill Show, an enjoyable, addictive 30 minutes. Conversation stops in bars when his impish grin appears on the screen. People stay up to watch this fat man with the rolling eyes even when they've seen his shows enough to sing along with the rapid-fire production numbers.'

Most of the reviews of Benny's work in the US were favourable or enthusiastic. However, some newspapers trawled the continent for the few complaints and made a great fuss about them. Acres of newsprint, particularly in Britain, were used on emotional accounts of a petition organized by teachers of younger children at a school in Miami. Yolanda Olrich of the *Miami Herald* gave the details. 'Teachers at Avocado Elementary School, 16969SW19, Fourth Street, are distributing petitions asking WCIX-Channel 6 to move the popular British comedy to a time slot that's past the students' bedtime. "Please understand that we are not asking the station to remove the show, only change it to a later time-slot," said Pat Clifford, a second-grade teacher at Avocado and leader of the petition drive. "I don't know why they changed it (from 11.30 P.M.)," she added.

'WCIX Station Manager, Edward Adams, said he would not comment on the timing of the show until he receives the petitions. "Until that time, I have nothing to say on the matter," he said.

'Clifford, who does not watch the half-hour programme, said she became aware of its popularity among children after listening to them imitate suggestive jokes and laugh at sexual innuendoes they saw and heard on the show. "While the youngsters are only seven or eight years old, they fully understand what is going on," Clifford said. "Hill's humour is definitely for adults," she added.' As an international news story, a dud Avocado, I would have thought.

The numbers of American viewers disturbed by the Benny Hill Show must be very small indeed, according to the evidence provided by Caroline Chang, programme manager of KTVU, San Francisco. In a letter to me, she refers to a written complaint from a local minister who 'was outraged when he turned on KTVU at 11.00 P.M. and Benny Hill was on and he saw a brief scene featuring a woman that was naked and there was a shot of her bare breasts. The viewer was very upset and couldn't believe we could air such material. I checked our records and discovered that this particular episode had been aired twelve times before and this was the first complaint.'

Don Taffner confirms that complaints from the US are so rare that John Street has never had to edit out a single piece of tape for that reason. Nor does he ever cut to pre-empt criticism on those grounds. One or two

American party-poopers sometimes claim to speak for
the Moral Majority. Not so. The Moral Majority loves
the Benny Hill Show. The dissidents, in fact, represent
the Minute Minority.

'What we've discovered,' Benny explains, 'is that
Americans seem to love our saucy humour. Let me
give you one example. We did a filmed sketch called
Scuttle's Tunnel about a little old man trying to dig a
tunnel from England to the Continent. We threw in lots
of sight gags, like someone accidentally sitting on a
detonator and blowing people up and a cement-mixer
churning out puddings. At one point, the old man
tunnelled his way into a beach cabaña, where there
was a luscious girl wearing bikini briefs and clutching
a tiny towel to her bosom. So, I came on as the beach
attendant – and it was all split-second – offered the girl
my apologies and said, "May I shake you by the hand?"
and, as she offered her hand, the towel fell off. My
producer, John Robbins, who lives in Los Angeles, told
me that, when this was shown in the States, the phone
lines were jammed – not, as I thought, with protest, but
with people saying "Marvellous! When are we going to
see some more?" '

The much-respected James Walcott, of New York's
Village Voice, gave his considered opinion. 'Since Hill
and his male co-stars are long past the first flush
of boyhood, their lusts are without heat or menace.
They're like crusty satyrs, enjoying a brief romp before
curling up in front of the fire ... Benny Hill is free
of female-loathing malice and the women on his show
have ripping fun. He remembers that life's a nasty
treacherous comedy and sex a glorious joke.'

'When I was over there, selling the shows,' explains
Philip Jones, late of Thames, now of Taffner, 'I was
asked if I felt Benny would upset a portion of the

American viewing public. I told them, "You always upset a minority with whatever you show." What we hadn't realized was how great would be the adoration of the majority.'

Rather late in the day, the independent stations began to put a little money on their ace-in-the-hole. T-shirts, bumper stickers and posters appeared displaying my brother's face or slogans – 'I'm going home to see Benny Hill on WPBT2!' KTVU sent their San Francisco viewers a hand-held fan that proclaimed 'I'm a Benny Hill Fan', and a warning sign to hang on a doorknob – 'Do Not Disturb – We're Watching Benny Hill!' When this Californian station decided to run a two-hour Benny Hill Spectacular as a New Year celebration, Don Taffner sent them a special insert, a tape of the British comic, with Big Ben in the background, counting down to 'Happy New Year!' Don supported the campaigns of all the independents with photographs, posters and other British material from Thames. At his suggestion, Benny was always pleased to make promotional television commercials, such as, 'See me on your very own station, WOR, New York.'

After about eighty half-hour shows had been produced, John Street felt that he had come to the end of what he called 'the cream'. By that, he meant the best of the comedy material readily intelligible to American audiences. All of the first eighty episodes had been cut sharply for speed. John wondered whether viewers in the US would respond to slower, longer items. Some of the rambling cross-talk sequences, Fred Scuttle, for example – he of the skew-whiff cap and army issue spectacles. His maunderings often lasted ten minutes. The Americans would not accept so drawn-out a duologue, would they? Even a British audience had been known to grow restive. 'These are the jokes,' Benny

had said, implying, 'Eat up your porridge. You'll get
jam later.' Bob Newhart once expressed his admiration
for the 'undaunted' way, on these occasions, Benny
would step up a gear and drive the routine home to
a hilarious conclusion.

John Street began experimenting. He tried five-, six-
and seven-minute sketches. He had nothing to worry
about. US audiences acclaimed them as enthusiastically as ever. Now that the viewers had grown to love
the Saucy Boy, they welcomed everything he offered.
They were quite prepared to savour more leisurely
humour and found, as Eartha Kitt suggested, that
there are advantages when an Englishman takes his
time. They learned to lie back and enjoy it. The sounds
of satisfaction reassured John Street, who added pieces
from the latest British hours to create, in time, more
than 120 shows for the US.

'Benny's great gift to me,' says John, 'was freedom.
He trusted me. "Do as you like," he told me. "Whatever
you think is needed. You know best." ' John's great gift
to Benny was sustained editing of such a remarkably
high standard that it made a key contribution to the
success of the Benny Hill Show in the US.

There were times when individual stations decreed,
having repeated many times every episode available,
that they would show no more Benny Hill tapes for
a period. They awaited fresh material from Britain.
These decisions inflicted withdrawal symptoms of the
severest nature on the fans. Marvin Kitman described
his in *Newsday*. 'It was a sad day when they took Benny
Hill off Channel 9 week-nights at 11. His show was
really fun . . . Benny Hill was my favourite alternative
to the bad news: rape, murder, corruption, inflation,
the Pirates losing. And then they took off the 7.30 P.M.
edition of "Benny Hill", which was replaced by "Dating

Game". Talk about culture shock. I had become what Chris Mezzolesta of Selden called "a Benny Baby". I needed my two "Benny Hills" a day for the world to be right.'

Marvin urged his readers to protest at such deprivation. However, he cheered up a few months later.

'I had an incredible TV experience the other night. I was sitting there, doing my homework, as I call it, watching all the stellar attractions, most of which are dogs. And suddenly I was laughing my head off. It scared me. Anybody who had heard me would have thought I had gone crazy, finally snapped. Nobody laughs at anything on TV in the summer. Why bother to laugh at the new shows, anyway? The laugh track does it for you. What made me laugh was the new Benny Hill show on cable. Uncut Hill. And no commercials. It's like mainlining it right into the funny bone for those of us who get our thrills on Benny Hill. Well, luvs, he's funny, and I don't care if I fry in hell for thinking so. Hill does a video burlesque. He is a master of low comedy. Watching Hill work is like attending a festival of the early work of Buster, Harold or Mel. He has every old screwball sight gag since Edison. You have to see them to believe them. He is such a nut. He is not growing, as we demand of our own TV comedians. He is a full-grown comedian, that's why. He does what he does and he is very funny at it.'

The cable service Home Box Office produced a Benny Hill Special every year. In 1984, J. J. O'Connor of the *New York Times* described the latest as 'a vaudeville-burlesque roller-coaster. The pacing is frantic, as sketches, skits and sight gags spill over each other, some hilarious, others merely silly. At the centre nearly always is Mr Hill, who, in repose, could be mistaken for a rather pudgy, middle-aged shoe clerk. With impish grin and devilishly gleaming eyes, he looks suspiciously like the kind of man described by one of his own female creations: "You have to take him everywhere twice – once to apologize." '

In the same year, Benny visited the US – but not to apologize. He was going there for the first time, hoping to chat with Americans of all backgrounds and look at their television programmes. It was to be a clandestine scouting trip that was also a quiet, relaxing holiday. Benny decided to fly, with his friend and director, Dennis Kirkland, to San Francisco. No reporters would be waiting there. No publicity, no hassle, no fuss. He would slip in and slip out. He slipped up. When the two tired travellers arrived at the Bayshore Airport, a reporter and photographer from a British newspaper were waiting for them. Benny traded a few hours' peace for a promise of pictures the next day. The following morning, he found that the story of his trip had already been written. He was to 'leave his heart in San Francisco'. To that end, the newspaper had flown in a couple of delectable models from Los Angeles, four hundred miles away. 'Couldn't you find any pretty girls in San Francisco?' asked a puzzled comedian. However, he implied no further criticism when he discovered what delightful company Laurie Tollefson and Colleen Neeham were. So the funny man relaxed – and gambolled through the day, clowning to keep the girls and casual spectators in fits of laughter. As they waited for lunch at a Mexican restaurant, he threw a red blanket over his shoulder, grabbed a guitar from the resident trio and promptly serenaded Laurie with appropriate Latin fervour. Later, he stood in front of every likely landmark, including the Golden Gate Bridge, whipping on his beret and spectacles for a

picture of the Scuttle Salute. Cuddling Laurie first,
then Colleen, and finally both beauties, he gave the
photographer the shots that the long-suffering fellow
had come more than five thousand miles to take. After
which, in the early evening, the reporters and the models flew back to their respective patches.

The next day was spent at the University of California
in Berkeley, where Benny was mobbed by the students, who greeted him warmly and enquired after
little Jackie Wright and Hill's Angels, the show's resident dance troupe. He found that even the feminist
wimmin seemed to be pleased to see him. Some of
the young people he spoke to were well versed in
the art of comedy. One or two, who were already
trying out stand-up routines at local clubs, impressed
Benny by their determination, personal optimism and
wit. While on campus he took the opportunity of seeing again the Black Theatre of Prague in a magical
show of such startling illusions that it inspired him to
employ more special effects in his subsequent television
presentations.

On that trip, everywhere Benny went he was besieged.
The locals called, waved and asked for autographs and
chances to photograph him and be photographed with
him. He shook hands with shopkeepers, kissed babies
and cuddled fat ladies. Surrounded by happy crowds,
Benny was overwhelmed by the warmth of the welcome
given him. Even when he ducked into a Spanish restaurant for lunch, he was greeted by a group of fans from
his favourite stamping-ground, Barcelona. They invited
him to their table to chat of strange adventures in the
Old City.

Benny found some respite from the non-stop excitement when he arrived at the Westwood Marquee Hotel
in Los Angeles. He slept for fourteen hours and awoke

on a sunny morning to spy from his window two inviting swimming pools in the hotel grounds. As visions
of water fun with a bevy of beautiful nereids inflamed
his imagination, he hurried down to the pools. There
was nobody there. The whole glorious sunlit playground was empty! Shome mishstake shurely? Was
this not the city where, throughout the daylight hours,
longstemmed American beauties paraded in swimsuits
around blue lagoons? Perhaps playmates would arrive
a little later. He settled down to sunbathe. He ordered
lunch at the poolside. He ate lunch at the poolside.
Nobody turned up. At three o'clock in the afternoon,
a solitary figure entered and approached. It certainly
was not beautiful. It was not even female. It was Bruce
Forsyth.

News got out that Benny was in town and a reception
for him was hastily organized at Chasen's Restaurant.
Famous and important people cut appointments and
altered arrangements at short notice to be there. One
of the first to arrive was Steve Allen, who convulsed
my brother by introducing himself with a string of witty
one-liners. Not far behind him was Jack Lemmon.

'I had to meet Benny,' Jack told me later. 'There's no
way I would miss it. I first heard of him in 1957 and,
when I saw his television show, by chance, I watched
ten seconds of it and said, "Oh, my God! This feller's
wonderful. He's like a burlesque comic!" You see, when
I was young, the thing that really grabbed me was burlesque. I would do anything to get a cheap seat at the
local theatre. Not just to look at the girls. That was great,
too. It was the comics. The work that they did was very
similar to what Benny does. Some of them were absolutely brilliant. I admire them immensely. I can't tell you
how much I learnt from them. The best of them worked
at a level of excellence that's terribly hard to achieve.

'I had always wanted to be an actor – so I paid attention, watched and studied them – long before I had a
shot at anything myself. The realization came to me that
burlesque was a wonderful art form of entertainment,
and that many of the performers in it were not only
funny men, but damn good actors. My greatest respect
is for someone who can do both. I doubt that I could
stand up in one and do a comedy turn. God knows,
Benny can. He does it all the time. I've tremendous
admiration for that. But, to be as successful as he is,
you also have to be a hell of an actor. And I believe
Benny is. I can't think of a comic that I saw then – and
to my dying day, I will admire them and be grateful for
their influence on me – I don't know one of them that
was better than Benny and I'm not sure that they were
as good. In fact, I don't know anyone today who tries
to do that kind of work who is anywhere near as good.
He's the best. Benny's the cream of the crop. So, you
see why I just had to meet him at Chasen's.'

When they met, Benny discovered that they had a
great deal in common. Jack was seven years old when
he learnt from laughter at a school play that he had a
talent for comedy. Benny explained that, at the same
age, he was clowning at home. Jack confessed to
my brother that, later, he had padded his shoes and
stood on tiptoe to look old enough for a burlesque
show at the wonderful 'Old Howard' Theatre in Boston. Benny remarked that, in the same year, he had
his first taste of similar delights at the Southampton
Hippodrome. Jack spoke of comedians Peanuts Brown
and Willie Howard. Benny countered with Max Miller
and Jimmy James. The American film star extolled
the merits of Phil Silvers and Bert Lahr. The British
comedian commended the talents of Sid Field and Max
Wall. Which led to a discussion of comic performances

on the screen. Benny instanced Jack's transformation
into the English Toff for the film *Irma La Douce*. He
expressed his admiration for that particular portrayal,
in which Jack had changed his entire appearance, his
face, his voice, his age, his class, his nationality – so
that he was unrecognizable. 'For me, that characterization has always been the touchstone of performance
attainment,' he said, 'because it was achieved by acting
– and not, as some do today, with a plastic mask.' They
agreed that young actors generally would benefit from
the experience and discipline once widely afforded by
touring plays, revues and burlesque shows and went on
to compare notes on the universal problem of obtaining
finance to back any kind of entertainment project.

Dennis Kirkland interrupted Benny's conversation
with wellwishers to pass on two messages. Clint East-
wood had phoned to say that his plan to fly down by
helicopter to the reception had been stymied by bad
weather. 'Tell Benny we love him,' said Clint. 'His is
the only television show my son and I agree about.
We both think it's great.' Benny was delighted by the
compliment, which tended to confirm a story he had
heard that Clint's restaurant, the Hog's Breath, in Car-
mel, California, featured photographs of the Benny Hill
Show. The other communication, from Burt Reynolds,
apologized for his absence due to indisposition, and,
in a very English way, invited the English pair to take
tea with him at his house the following day.

Tea at Burt Reynolds's house was not as formal as the
invitation.

'I understood he wasn't well,' recalls Benny, 'but he
looked fine to me – handsome and tanned, a little slim,
maybe.' Burt was putting on a brave face. He felt tired.
His jaw ached from dental wiring that had reduced his
diet to liquids. He was down to 140 from 200 pounds.

'I was skinny as a rail,' Burt told me later. 'I looked like Frank Sinatra used to look, resting in my room, trying to get well. I wouldn't have met anybody but Benny. But I thought, "I'm not going to pass this up." And I'm so glad I didn't. Benny was everything I wanted him to be – shy and interested, a very sweet man. I wasn't a bit surprised or disappointed. I'm not a fan of Milton Berle-type humour – "I just said sumpin' funny. You'd better laff or leave the room!" I've met a lot of comedians and my favourites are always shy. Jack Benny was, so is Dick Van Dyke and Richard Pryor. Sometimes you can wait for ever for them to be funny. But not Benny. He's capable of being terribly funny when he gets to know you a little better.'

The tea party moved on to other beverages. By the time Dom De Luise came over to join them, the English pair felt thoroughly at home. As Dom fizzes with good humour, it was not long before they were all kidding and laughing. 'Burt is a very funny man,' reveals Benny. 'He had us in stitches. A great impressionist, he does a knock-out Gabby Hayes and a wicked Walter Brennan. He told me he'd like to appear in my show. If working with him is as much fun as drinking with him, it will be hilarious.'

Burt offered to take the party out to dinner but, he said, he had to make a brief appearance on television in 'Starsearch', a talent discovery show. At his invitation, they piled noisily into the chauffeur-driven limousine and sped off to the studios. When Benny repeated Arthur Askey's observation that 'comedians are playing at being children', Burt exclaimed, 'By God, that's right! Look at the four of us here – giggling and larking about like a gang of kids!' Upon arrival at the television theatre, the tall film star took Benny to Vic Damone's dressing-room. The romantic balladeer gave my brother an astonished but enthusiastic welcome, opening a bottle of champagne in celebration. As Burt was about to perform on-stage, Benny joined Dom and Dennis in the auditorium seats. They had hardly finished applauding Burt's appearance when he introduced Benny. There was a roar of audience laughter as Dom De Luise stood up to acknowledge the applause. Then, when the name of Dom De Luise was announced, there was a burst of thunderous clapping as Benny stood to receive the ovation. My brother smiled and waved to the audience, and to Burt on stage. 'The camera's to your right,' instructed Dennis, ever the director. 'Turn right and smile. Wave to the camera.' Benny was grateful for the guiding hand.

After the show, Burt took the party to a fashionable Italian restaurant, very popular with the show-business crowd. 'It was fascinating,' remembers Benny, 'full of Hollywood wheeler-dealers, rising stars, fallen stars and would-be stars, and their agents. A touch of *The Sweet Smell of Success*.' The food was interesting, too. 'I chose the place deliberately,' explained Burt. 'I thought it would amuse Benny to eat those wonderful Italian dishes surrounded by bullshit.'

The English pair had been invited to stay the night after a party next evening at Hugh Hefner's residence. They were on their way when Dennis expressed some disquiet about their visit to the Playboy Mansion. 'I hope there's no embarrassment about our staying the night,' he said. 'After all, I'm a happily married man.'

'I'm surprised at you, Dennis,' replied Benny. 'That stuff is for the punters. Hugh Hefner is a much respected businessman. His home will be the last place in the world for hanky-panky.'

It is also the last place in the world for unauthorized entrance, according to Benny. 'The Playboy Mansion is

in an immaculate district,' he told me, 'under total sur-
veillance, with discreet security guards at the Hefner
main gate, obviously well organized to keep out riff-raff
like you and me. The house itself is a beautiful English
country manor. Although it is in acres of manicured
grounds, it looks a little out of place. Hugh Hefner is a
charming man and the perfect host. At least, we found
him so, as he spent much of his time looking after us,
although he had crowds of important guests at the
party. He spared no effort or expense to give us a great
time. We enjoyed ourselves enormously. I was pleased
to be introduced to Buck Henry, who is not only a
fine actor, but a writer of great comedy. He was a little
chubbier than I remembered him. Vice versa, I guess.
He's a real kidder and pulled my leg mercilessly. It was
a warm evening and the gardens were beautifully lit by
green lights behind the trees. Hef organized a walking
tour of the estate for Dennis and me. Two delightful
ladies showed us round the aquarium, the aviary, and
what appeared to be a man-made river, driven, I think,
by electric pumps.

'Later, as I was strolling on the patio, a tall,
distinguished-looking man approached me. He had
snowy-white hair, moustache and beard, and a glowing
complexion. When he spoke, his voice was familiar. "I
love your show," he said. Then I looked at his eyes and
recognized him at once. It was Cornel Wilde. The white
hair had fooled me. I was pleased to have the chance to
tell him how much *The Naked Prey*, which he directed,
meant to me. That film almost exactly represented a
recurring dream of mine, so I had completely identified
with Cornel as the runner fleeing for his life.

'As it grew late, the crowd thinned and Hef, bless
his heart, told us he was tired and going to turn in, but
we were to stay up as late as we wished. The Mansion

staff would look after us. He went upstairs to bed, but
hurried back a minute later to tell us that Burt Reynolds
and Dom De Luise were on television. Dennis turned
on the set and we were just in time to hear Burt say,
"We thought Benny was a little disappointed that there
were no girls at my house. So Dom De Luise and I took
turns at wearing the dress!" Dennis and I fell about at
that – and the Johnnie Carson audience roared, too.'

Benny was right, of course, about the Playboy Mansion. He reported later that all was 'as chaste as a night's
lodging in a nunnery'.

When the pair arrived in New York, they stopped
at the luxurious Taffner residence, which includes an
upstairs visitors' suite. Eleanor made them very welcome and threw a party for them in her own restaurant,
close to Don's office. It was a splendid affair with a
jolly crowd of friends and business associates. 'Don
and Eleanor are charming people – a fun couple, who
look like they've just stepped out of a movie,' Benny
explained to me. 'They have a New York sense of
humour that tickles me pink, and were in fine form
that night – so we had a wonderful celebration and
met a host of interesting people.'

When most of the guests had gone, Don began
reminiscing and mentioned an elusive Mexican song
that had haunted him for years. Benny also remembered
the opening bars but, like Don, could go no further.
They asked the waiters and the cooks, but nobody
knew the tune. Don found the address of a Mexican
restaurant and telephoned. 'Have you Mexican musicians at your restaurant?'

'Yes, sir.'

'Can they play "Cuckoo Roocoo Roo Paloma"?'

A minute later, back came the answer. 'Yessir, they
can.'

'Then book me a table for eleven people right away,'
commanded Don. And off they all went in cars to
another party at another restaurant, where a band of
strolling Mexicans with guitars played Don's favourite
number 'at least fifty times', according to Benny.

Another evening, my brother had an exhilarating
evening at Madison Square Garden. He watched the
preliminaries on a television screen in the restaurant
while being interviewed by reporters. When he finally
got to his seat for the big fight, it was occupied, as
all good empty seats are, by a creeper from the cheap
seats. As usual, the interloper wanted to fight for it,
while the crowd behind shouted, 'Siddown, ya bum!'
and 'Get your ass down, feller, I paid a hundert dollars
to see dis rumble!' Benny says that such badinage is
great fun, as it is perfectly in order, in such company, to
shout back, 'Shaddup, ya bums, or I'll come back dere
and pull yer stinkin' livers out!' He finally ousted the
pretender to his throne and settled down to enjoy the
majestic battle between Marvin Hagler and Mustapha
Hamsho.

When Twiggy heard that Benny was trying to buy
tickets for her huge Broadway hit *My One and Only*,
she called to offer him a couple and invite him to her
dressing-room.

'I hope this doesn't sound awful, but I've been a fan of
Benny's since I was a little girl of four. I thought he was
the funniest man in the world then, and I think so still.
I was thrilled that he was coming to see us. Of course,
at that time we had lots of famous people coming to
see our show. Every evening it was, "You know who's
out there tonight? So and So." But I've never seen such
excitement among the cast, especially the chorus line
of ten girls, as when Benny was in the audience. It was
amazing. During the first production number, everyone

in the cast was trying to spot him in the auditorium. As the girls danced past me off the stage, they would tell me where he was sitting. By the time I made my entrance, I was able to look straight at him.'

To some effect, it seems. Benny was much taken by her performance. 'I had never seen her before and I was astonished at how talented she was. I should have realized that no one can carry a blockbuster Broadway show like that without being something really special. And Twiggy was certainly that. I loved Tommy Tune, but Twiggy was a revelation. Her singing voice knocked me out. She's only a little thing, but she's so strong. Playing the lead in a tremendous hit like that is one hell of a responsibility. All that work and weight. I was lost in admiration for her. She was marvellous.'

After the show, Benny went back-stage for their first meeting. According to Twiggy, they did not get much time to themselves. 'The girls in the cast begged me to introduce them. They crammed into my small dressing-room and I thought it was touching and enchanting because he was English and I felt so patriotic that they loved him so much. They had never shown that amount of interest in any of the other superstars. I think it's wonderful that he's become such an enormous cult figure in the States. It's amazing. But, trapped in my dressing-room, I think the poor man was quite over-whelmed by all that female adulation.'

'Yes,' I replied, 'I can see how he would just hate being mobbed by beautiful girls.'

'When we went out to dinner, we got chatting about things. It became a nice conversation. He's a really sweet man. I found him very much quieter and more low-keyed than I expected. It was a pleasant surprise, actually. Because I've met some comedians who are very manic, who feel they have to be funny all the time. Benny was different, I must say. I found him relaxed and quite shy, in fact, which I thought was very sweet and refreshing. It was a great thrill to meet him. I think he's a very special man – a huge talent. That's one great thing about America – they are open to talent and success. Benny's comedy is timeless and universal and they appreciate it. In Britain, success can be a little bit of a dirty word. I don't think that, in his own country, Benny gets the praise he deserves.'

Benny flew back to face the usual dismissive strictures of a few critics in his own country after encomiums of affection, gratitude and respect in the US. He did not return to America until March 1987, when Thames Television put on a show at the Lincoln Center in New York as a response to the honour bestowed upon the company by the National Academy of Television Art and Sciences. It was said to be the most expensive evening Broadway had ever seen, as it cost the British organizers over a million pounds to fly the cast, including six of his dancers, the director, wardrobe mistress and others all first-class to stay at deluxe hotels. Arriving at Kennedy Airport, Benny was mobbed, and remembers a man pushing his way through the crowd to grab his suitcase. 'It's all right,' said my brother, 'I'll take it. It's not heavy.'

'No,' said the stranger. 'Let me have it. I want to be able to tell my grandchildren I carried your suitcase.'

Margaret Forwood described the show in *The People* newspaper: 'Mike Yarwood was Prince Charles with Suzanne Danielle as Princess Di. Janet Brown almost convinced the audience she was Margaret Thatcher. Scruffy Cockney songsters Chas and Dave sang the sort of songs Americans think all Londoners sing. Edward "The Equalizer" Woodward was the host. But the jewel in the Thames crown is Benny Hill. The 63-year-old comedian's shows are shown five nights a week on many American stations and to them he is God ... Afterwards there was a glittering banquet at the Plaza Hotel on swanky Fifth Avenue ... Chas and Dave were actually moved to hire dinner-jackets for the first time in living memory in honour of the occasion. And in the middle of all the glitter and glamour sat the hero of the hour. You could practically warm your hands in the glow from his plump cheeks.

' "Just look at that man," crooned one of the waiters in broad Brooklynese. "He does things and says things and gets away with things on TV I never thought I'd see in all my born days. I love him." '

'It was a helluva show,' reported Dennis Kirkland, its director. 'Benny was amazing. When he came out as Fred Scuttle, he got a huge ovation. And roar after roar of laughter. He was brilliant. You know how nervous he is before a stage performance. That's why he did the Diary for his second spot. So that he's got all his words in front of him. The taglines, everything. Well, he came out as himself, in a dinner-suit, and he was so relaxed, I couldn't believe it. Afterwards, I said to him, "You walked that!" and he said, "I know. I felt so much in command that I got bored with it half-way through." He didn't let up on the audience, though. I have to give him credit. He tore the balls off 'em!'

Let us leave the summing-up to the perceptive Marvin Kitman of *Newsday* who wrote, under the headline, 'All Hail, King Leer!':

'There are only two kinds of comedy, as far as I am concerned: funny and not funny. Benny Hill is funny. For years I've been getting my thrill on TV from Benny Hill, my favourite show on Saturday nights at 11 on Channel 9 since 1979 – in the meantime, when is

Benny going to be recognized publicly for the great artist he is?

'This roly-poly cherub of a little devil makes me feel good, like having milk and cookies before turning in. I feel like I know the man already. I've seen some of his shows four or five times, or forty or fifty times. In person, Hill turned out to be quiet, soft-spoken, very intelligent, charming, relaxed.

'It was a great honour to see Benny Hill in this country, much less to meet him. He was actually scheduled to appear on stage at Alice Tully Hall, his first live performance here.

'He didn't do his famous flashing number, either, for the dignitaries. Instead, he played a stage-hand in an "I Love New York" T-shirt, who kept interrupting a fellow in a tuxedo who was telling us how great Thames TV was. Also, he read to us from his diary about his experiences in New York. Very funny stuff. And he brought along the famous Hill's Angels. Hill and Hill's Angels! It was one of those fabulous nights TV critics and TV viewers dream of.'

One of those nights dreamed of by a fair-haired teenage lad, fifty years before, in Southampton.

19

The Sane Subversive

Deceived by the art that conceals art, James Walcott, of the *Village Voice*, damned the Benny Hill Show for its unacceptable raunchiness when he first encountered it. Like other American critics, he changed his mind upon closer inspection and apologized for his earlier 'Calvinistic tantrum'. He realized that it was Benny's earthiness that made the British comedian 'so subversively sane'. Precisely. 'Subversively sane' is praise of the highest order when applied to a fool (using the noun in its Shakespearian sense) who is also very funny. The fool's function is to prick pomposity, puncture pretension and mock the mighty. It is he who reminds us that the most exalted of our species is little more than 'a pig in a silk suit', to use Katharine Hepburn's splendid phrase. Such revelations make Benny Hill 'maybe even a threat to the establishment', according to some who spoke to Kay Gardella of the New York *Daily News*. However, he is not only subversively sane in performance. He is disturbingly independent in attitude, dangerously unconventional in lifestyle.

At the moment, my brother lives in a modest, rented flat in Teddington, close to the Thames Television studios. He is comfortable there, much more at home than in the huge mausoleum at Queens Gate, which he left in the mid-1980s and where he was said by one reporter to look like a passenger waiting for his flight. Benny pretends that he is searching for a magnificent home suitable for a successful man of his status. He has been improvising this charade for three years and has found nothing that pleases him yet. Though he will not admit it, he is happy in his present, cramped, untidy pad. It is quiet, so that he can indulge himself in the practice of his solitary vice, the addictive, voluptuous pleasure of creative scribbling. The place is mined with cardboard boxes and large plastic bags, full of obscure, esoteric and useless photographs, letters, bills, programmes and cuttings. Once a week, he pushes the bags and boxes to one side, while machines shatter his peace to ingurgitate the latest layer of dust.

The Teddington flat is not his only home. He was left the semi-detached family house in Southampton, with the proviso that he was not to sell it but to use it. Possession of two homes embarrasses him. As a bachelor, he feels the Teddington flat is quite sufficient for his needs, although he loves to visit his home town. Ownership of the extra house makes him uneasy. He betrayed this disquiet recently by organizing the redecoration of the Southampton home, inside and out. The catalyst for this unlikely activity was probably newspaper interest. Two very doubtful stories appeared at about the same time – one, that the place was being shamefully neglected and, two, that he was keeping the interior untouched as a shrine to his mother.

Benny's flat contains a television set, a VCR, a radio/recorder, tapes, show-business books and a telephone. His one luxury is an ancient radiogram and a vintage record collection of Latin American singers and musicians, largely unknown in this country. Apart from a few musical instruments, everything else is junk. Benny explains that such frugality discourages burglars. The truth is, that he has no interest at all in possessions. Ownership to him means responsibility. He can do without it.

Benny does without a car, and always has. Automobiles are noisy, poisonous, unpredictable, murderous machines and Benny believes that the Victorians who walked in front of them with a red flag had the right idea. He looks back nostalgically to the days when he could use the London tube without exciting public disorder. Luckily, he is fit enough to travel a long way on foot, and still walks more miles in a week than any other man I know. When there is enough time, he will arrive by Shanks's pony. If he has to use a hired car or taxi, he feels guilty. 'I don't like riding in taxis. Somehow, it seems wrong to take up a man's time and his petrol just to make a journey. It seems slightly immoral to me.'

He is equally unworldly about clothes. Most mornings he will put on the first garments to hand. It does not matter to him what he looks like about the house or in the street, as long as he does not frighten the horses. But he is extremely particular about his professional clothes and the outfits that he quick-changes into for a performance. Everything about them has to be exactly as he demands. Benny knows that comedy success hangs on detail. He is, therefore, prepared to spend hours at fittings, stripping off and climbing into costumes, walking up and down in front of mirrors. His wardrobe mistress knows that in these matters he is a very patient client, but a stickler for precision. He will make an effort, too, to look acceptable for a special function or social occasion from which there is no escape. He is likely, then, to wear one of his three good suits.

In the mid-sixties, it was the fashion, on a Saturday afternoon, for young people to parade up and down the King's Road, Chelsea, in fancy dress and crazy hairstyles. They were doing their own thing, to the astonishment and disbelief of the tourists. One such afternoon, Benny, in brown suit, brown shoes, white shirt and plain tie, was about his business on the famous thoroughfare when he espied, among the brightly clad revellers, Peter Wyngarde, a darkly handsome brute of breathtaking panache, who had played Oberon in the television *Midsummer Night's Dream*. Peter, looking like the prince in a Russian fairy tale, was wearing a fur hat and an overcoat with fur collar and trimmings. He held on a leash, as his accessory, a large hound of exactly the same fur. Had he, wondered Benny, as Peter approached, killed the animal's mate to make his hat and trimmings? When Peter deigned at last to see Benny, he stopped in exaggerated horror and declaimed to the gods with an actor's resonance, 'Oh, Benny! Look at you! You're OUTRAGEOUS!'

It is never Benny's intention, at any time, to outrage people. He will, however, stick to his guns and if some folks are outraged by his personal preferences, he feels that is their problem, not his. The vagaries of fashion are matters of little concern to him. For example, he likes Pina Colada. At the time of writing, nobody drinks Pina Colada. It is out. It is passé. Only wallies drink Pina Colada. Benny likes Pina Colada. He orders it. He drinks it. In public.

These days Benny drinks in moderation. He keeps no alcohol in the house. When he was young he drank little. The excesses of his middle period were stopped abruptly by an experience in Paris fifteen years ago.

Aboard a lunchtime flight, Benny had been slipped half a tumbler of brandy by a steward who had worked with him on the ice-rink sequences in *Who Done It?* As my brother left, the friendly skater dropped a few miniature liqueur bottles into his pocket. Arriving in his hotel room, Benny did not want the miniatures to

clutter up the place, so he downed their contents and
threw the tiny bottles into the waste basket. Fortified,
he set off for an evening's entertainment. It was not
long before he had booked a ringside seat for boxing
at the Palais de Sport. However, with a few hours to
kill, he made his way from bar to bar until he reached
Place Blanche in Pigalle. Then he remembered nothing
until he was nudged. He opened his eyes to find that
he was actually in the boxing stadium, but in the back
row, with the big fight about to start. He staggered down
the steps to find his ringside seat occupied. The usual
altercation ensued and ended when he heard one of
the contestants hit the canvas behind him, knocked
out cold. That was the last bout of the evening.

Realizing the extent of his incapacity, Benny decided
to sober up by walking back to his hotel. Unfortunately,
he stumbled in the wrong direction and eventually discovered that he was in the countryside. He knew it was
very late and, as he was tired, he lay down, without
taking off his grey suit, in the middle of a grassy field.
He slept soundly, waking once to admire the brilliance
of a sky full of stars. In the early morning, he found himself afflicted in terrible ways and made off post-haste to
his hotel. A 'Do Not Disturb' sign was hung over his
doorknob outside, while he was hung over inside, on
a trip to a three-ring circus – shivering, muttering and
suffering.

Later in the day, he craved the dark of a cinema and
tottered out to lose himself in the velvet blackness of
a local fleapit. During the intermission, he joined the
other candidates for premature death in the murky fog
of the foyer, but was so nauseated by the smell that
he resolved then and there never to smoke or drink
foolishly again, a vow he has kept to this day.

Benny's resolution did not guarantee the end of all

his follies abroad. He remained capable of coming a cropper without the aid of alcohol. One Easter holiday, my brother spent an evening in Marseilles before his train left for Barcelona. He changed some of his French notes into Spanish ones and sauntered round the southern port. When rain began to fall, he sheltered under glass at an outside table in a beautiful restaurant. He was astonished to see that a wide choice of menu was provided for the equivalent of £20, 'Tout compris' (wine and service included). As he was hungry, he ordered, and was delighted by every aspect of the meal. Replete at last, he called for the bill ('Garkong, l'addition, silver plate!' is the way he tells it). Although £20 covered everything, Benny plonked a £30 note on to the silver tray. It was an extravagant tip, but they had done him proud. He was well satisfied. The waiter, however, could not accept it. 'It is too big a tip,' he explained.

'Easy come, easy go,' said my brother airily, thinking of the old Jack Radcliffe sketch. The waiter brought the manager, who looked worried.

'Excuse me, sir, but we cannot accept so generous a gratuity.'

'Worth every franc of it,' replied Benny. 'I'll come again.'

The next morning, at the Spanish border, my brother found that, in the confusion of changing money, he had given the waiter a note for the equivalent of £300. He chuckled at his own stupidity. It is only when rogues try to con him that he gets upset. Two years later, he kept his promise and returned, this time with a girlfriend, to the Marseilles restaurant. 'All the waiters are staring and talking about you,' she observed. 'Do they know who you are?'

'No,' replied Benny. 'They are saying, "Here is the

mad English milord again. Now we can buy the bicycle!" '

Benny is a seasoned traveller and more than a match for your average thief. While on the move, he has always hidden his money effectively, often on unlikely parts of his person. Before he was well known on the Continent, he had a week-long contest with a couple of knockabout pickpockets in Madrid that added a little spice to his visit. My brother noticed, on leaving his unpretentious hotel for the first time, that an odd couple were standing conspicuously at the corner of the street. One man was large and ugly, the other small and rodent-like. They reminded him so much of the pair in Steinbeck's *Of Mice and Men* that, as he approached them, Benny was already muttering, 'Do I get ta feed da rabbits, George?' As they moved to allow him to pass, the big fellow bumped into him, while his little partner was busy at my brother's back pocket. Benny smiled tolerantly as he knew all his notes were safely between map and guidebook in his inside pocket. Foiled at their first attempt, the knockabout pair did not give up. The next day, they trailed my brother to the crowded city centre and, in the throng, made a concerted attack upon his inside pocket. They failed again, as his serious money was in his right shoe. By this time, Benny felt he had established a relationship with them. They were Lennie and George to him – so that, when next they bustled and fumbled about him, he castigated them in Spanish. 'You are without doubt the worst pickpockets in the world,' he told them. 'You are clowns – a disgrace to your profession. Why don't you accept defeat gracefully and leave me alone?' They did not reply. At no time did he hear them speak.

But they continued to dog my brother. For a few minutes, in the heat of the day, he thought they had

caught him. He was returning to his hotel along a
deserted street when Lennie, the big guy, appeared in
front of him. George was obviously close behind. This
time, they are going to get rough, thought Benny. So he
began to laugh. As loud as he could. He roared, and
the guffaws echoed up and down the street and into
the open windows. It was siesta time and behind the
open windows folk were resting and sleeping. Benny
continued to bellow with laughter and, in no time at
all, people were at their windows and on their balco-
nies to see what the crazy hilarity was all about. My
brother pointed at the two clowns, which led some
of the watchers, also, to laugh. The pickpockets were
nonplussed. They could not attack a man in front of a
score of witnesses. Benny pushed by his pursuers and
laughed his way back to the hotel. On the last day of his
visit, my brother relented. He placed a bank note that
would buy dinner for two in his outside handkerchief
pocket and set off on a day's sightseeing. He did not
encounter his eccentric friends until he was returning
to his hotel very late at night. They were waiting for
him. Lenny approached and, without a word, pointed
to Benny's right. My brother turned his head and, at
the same moment, George dipped a small paw into the
pocket and was off, like a rabbit, with the note.

'Olé!' cried Benny, and clapped the disappearing
couple. 'Olé!' Their persistence had been rewarded
at last.

When my brother is abroad, he is always charmed by
the recognition and admiration that fans demonstrate.
However, the memories he cherishes most are the little
human touches from people to whom he is, apparently,
a complete stranger. Once, when Benny had been
visiting some show people from the Tent Theatre at
the Attractions Park in Madrid, he stumbled out of a

caravan at half-past one in the morning to walk back to his hotel. Crossing the old fairground, he smiled at the notice which said, 'The children's section closes at midnight.'

'What a shame,' he muttered. 'The kids have got nowhere to go at one o'clock in the morning!' Spying a cheap wine stall, he bought himself a tumbler full and was slowly sipping it when he became aware that he was being watched. A solitary girl of about twelve had left a caravan and was looking at him. My brother assumed at once that she recognized him and expected her to ask for his autograph. Why else would she stare? As she moved slowly towards him, he began the little game he plays with children. 'You're not going to kiss me on the cheek, are you?' he asked her in Spanish. 'Because you're not allowed to kiss me on the cheek. Only good children are allowed to kiss me on the cheek. Oh, all right then, if you must.' At which, the girl leaned forward shyly to place a chaste peck on his plump chops. Then she just stood there, saying nothing. 'Would you like my autograph?' enquired Benny. The girl said nothing. 'You do know who I am, do you?' he asked her.

'No,' she replied.

'Then why did you kiss me?'

'Because you look like a nice man,' she said.

Recently, boarding the boat to the Château d'If off the coast near Marseilles, Benny noticed a tall, elegant lady who reminded him of Queen Mary. Suddenly, *la grande dame* dropped her book on the deck. Benny picked it up. 'Madame,' he said, as he bowed and handed it to her.

'*Merci, jeune homme*,' she replied.

'Jeune homme!' Benny exclaimed. 'She'll never know

what those two little words meant to me. That lovely lady made an old man very happy.'

On his journeys abroad, Benny prefers comfortable to luxurious hotels, sound rather than fashionable restaurants. However, he is no stranger to the high life, as he is occasionally offered the grandest entertainment by corporations and large companies. If he is under contract, he stipulates first-class travel and accommodation for two, so that a girlfriend may share his good fortune. Such charming and delectable company has often given his efforts another dimension and transformed many a dull business trip into a halcyon never-to-be-forgotten experience. However, much depends on the particular companion. In recent years, Benny has taken to travelling more with his director and friend Dennis Kirkland. At first glance, Dennis does not appear a very prepossessing alternative to the lovelies that have graced my brother's arm previously. In comparison, he has, as Peter Cook might observe, 'obvious deficiencies in the chest and leg departments'. However, he has much to commend him.

Dennis is always cheerful, friendly and helpful. He understands jokes and makes good ones himself. Dennis does not fuss, create difficulties, become unaccountably dumb, expect flowers, take two hours getting ready to go out, sulk if Benny makes no mention of his hair, whinge about the noise at a boxing contest, grumble at the wind during a football match, or complain of too much Worcester sauce in his tomato juice. He anticipates, contributes, guides, supports. And, best of all, while Benny scribbles, Dennis sits reading his paper for hours WITHOUT A WORD.

Possibly, Benny has turned to Dennis for the sake of a little peace. Perhaps he is afraid that some sweet young thing could destroy him. 'I sing along with Maurice

Chevalier,' he asserts. 'I'm glad I'm not young any more. I never want to fall in love again. It's too painful. Your feelings are so strong that it's like a pain in the chest, literally choking you. You worry so about the girl. "Why hasn't she phoned? Has she met someone else? What did she mean by that? Why did she look so upset?" At the same time, you are anxious about yourself. "Am I pleasing her? Did I say the wrong thing? Perhaps I ought to tell her. Should I call her?" I don't need a syndrome like that. Nowadays, if the thought of a girlfriend gives me a pang, I take my own amorous temperature, check that I'm not sickening for love and pray that I've not caught it again. Woody Allen remarked somewhere that sex is relaxing but love is stressful. I think he's right. Love is too intense for me. Give your heart away and you give your life away. I'm opting instead for a little fun and a chuckle or two. At this stage of the game, if my heart gives a leap at a pretty face, I run. I've no intention of carrying a torch into the twilight of my years.'

Despite his protestations, Benny is no misogynist. He has great affection for women of all ages. One of the closest to him is Sue Upton, head girl of Hill's Angels. Over the thirteen years he has known her, my brother has stayed at her home many times, has become a friend to her husband, Roger, and an uncle to her young children, Richard and Louise. He regularly takes the children on trips, plays Santa to them at Christmas and has even visited their school. Roger, on the other hand, took on the job of decorating the Southampton home. 'Benny has become part of the family,' says Sue. 'The children love him. He's always kidding them. When he rings them up, he calls Louise Richard and vice versa. They still find it funny. A few days ago, Richard was writing Christmas cards to a couple of his schoolfriends. He asked me to help him with his card to Benny, the only adult he wanted to write to.

'We all enjoy Benny's visits because he's such good company and so easy to cater for. He likes all kinds of food. Benny lives and breathes nothing but show-business, of course. The only exception is boxing – and that's a branch of show-business, too, I suppose. I have had to learn about the sport so that I can join in the conversation when the two men watch it on television. I have always loved old movies, but Benny has encouraged me to study the comedies in particular. We chat for hours about them. I think Benny enjoys his stays with us. He's not a great one to express his feelings. But sometimes he says, "When I come again, I'll . . . ", then I know that sharing our everyday family life has been a nice change for him.

'Benny is a sincere, considerate and quiet person. At rehearsals, he is always giving the Angels advice about their careers and their boyfriends. They don't often take it, but I've never once heard him grumble about that, swear, raise his voice, or say a disrespectful word to any of the girls. He's not a bit like the parts he plays. People should remember that he's an actor. Benny is very much a man, of course, and he is attracted to women. But he's a very caring man. Knowing what he's like professionally and in his private life, I have the greatest fondness and respect for him.'

Perhaps the person closest to Benny in all the world is his beloved Auntie Louie, now 94, who still lives at Bexleyheath. When he spends a few days with her, as he often does, he unwinds completely. The pair of them potter about her tranquil home totally at ease in slippers and dressing-gowns. Supping tea, reading pieces from the paper to each other, singing old music-hall songs in harmony, making jokes, recalling ancient films and players, they have a whale of a time together. Anyone who knocks at the door is an interloper, breaking the thread of their rapport.

'It really is lovely when Alfie comes,' says Auntie Louie. 'As soon as he gets inside, we have a good old laugh. We laugh to kill ourselves. All the time he's here. It's wonderful. I only feel miserable when he goes. I never want him to leave. When he walks out the front door, I get a lump in my throat.'

For many years, Benny has enjoyed the company of women who have no connection with show-business. He offers his friendship, apparently, when he observes a genuine need. He lends a hand – often literally. He cleans, he cooks, he pushes wheelchairs – and he pays bills. Usually for disabled ladies. Some I know about; there are others, I suspect. He looked after a retired soldier for ages until the ancient warrior died. At one time, he would not talk about these friendships. 'I have genuine affection for my friends,' he told me. 'And I hope they like me. It's not a matter of duty or charity. I won't say anything for fear of appearing to be one of those show-business phonies, who say, "Look at me, everybody, I'm doing good!"'

Unfortunately, others talked, so that now two of his friendships are common knowledge. Phoebe, who is largely confined to a wheelchair, met him nearly forty years ago, after a Sunday concert at the seaside. When he returned to London, he called her and was invited to visit. He has spent holidays with her ever since, and now stays in a guest room at the special complex where she lives. 'Benny's television image could not be further from the quiet, homely atmosphere he enjoys best,' says Phoebe.

Benny has known another lady, Netta, for over twenty

years and, as she has a great sense of humour, he has encouraged her to write comedy. She cannot walk unaided, so Benny takes her out and never forgets to send her postcards from foreign parts. Whenever possible, he escorts each lady down to London for dinner at the Savoy and a West End show. On a recent trip, he hurt his back manoeuvring the heavy wheelchair. 'I'm lucky,' he said. 'I deal with such problems a few days at a time. These brave ladies have to live with them always.'

Benny's loyalty to his friends evokes a reciprocal affection. 'He is lovely – so kind. I think the world of him,' says Phoebe. His one-time sergeant and fellow-comedian, Harry Segal, feels the same. He became so enraged a few years ago by a spate of tabloid stories suggesting that Benny was a skinflint that he stormed down to London from his home in Leeds and bearded the newspaper lions in their den. With that morning's edition in his hand, Harry had the *Daily Mirror* office in an uproar. 'Who wrote this tripe?' he demanded. 'Where did you get this rubbish from? You've insulted my friend and I want an answer! Why don't you tell the truth?' Harry was in no mood to be fobbed off with excuses and insisted on some redress. 'After a lot of toing and froing, I was put up at a splendid hotel,' he told me, 'and Hilary Bonner, the show-business editor of the *Mirror*, interviewed me there. She's a lovely, genuine person, and she recorded hours of my story. I showed her masses of documentation – photographs, postcards, letters, to back up my claims. It was all there in black and white.'

To her eternal credit, Hilary Bonner printed it all, with photographs, in a huge spread, over pages.

' "Benny Hill is the most generous character I have ever met, and the best friend in the world," says Harry.

"How dare people say he is mean? So he walks about
with a carrier bag when he goes shopping, does he?
Don't we all walk about with bloody carrier bags when
we go shopping?" Harry knows the truth about Benny
and money better than almost anyone. Over the years
there have been countless expensive nights out – paid
for by Benny – and an extravagant West End birthday
dinner for Harry. There has been encouragement for
Harry's script-writing ambitions ... Hefty payments
for comedy ideas. "I want to hit back at the dreadful
things that have been said," he says. "Benny does good
that people don't know about." When he got that thousand pounds, Harry was at an all-time low. The heart
attack had floored him. "I was really struggling," he
says. "Nobody will ever know what that money and
that letter meant to me." Harry has never forgotten the
phone call from Benny that followed the arrival of that
desperately-needed cheque. For Hill came to stay with
him for four days, and no expense was spared. "That's
all rubbish about him travelling everywhere on cheap
buses," says Harry. "He came first class on the train.
He may walk a lot, like they keep saying, but he needs
to walk, doesn't he? The man's got a weight problem.
Mean, indeed! He picked up the tab for everything,
absolutely everything." '

The flurry of interest in Benny's lifestyle had been
generated, in the first place, by a report in an obscure
Sri Lankan magazine that he was worth ten million
pounds. There was no evidence offered for this figure,
but it was eagerly taken up by British journals because
it was just enough to put my brother at the bottom of
the list of the 200 richest people in Britain. 'In fact,'
says Benny, 'my guess is that I would barely make it
into the top thousand. I am not a money person. I
have always found the whole subject boring, but I'm

sure I'm not worth ten million pounds.' I can confirm his unworldliness concerning money. When we were young, he gave me a huge cheque that I had to refuse because I felt sure he simply could not afford it. And when he was asked more recently how much the Stock Exchange crash – Bad Day at Black Stock – had cost him, he had no idea. 'Ask my accountants,' he replied. And his instruction to them is always, 'Don't call me, I'll call you.'

'Mean? That's rubbish!' exclaims Dennis Kirkland. 'I know from personal experience that he's not. I've never known him mean. And when he does charity work, he doesn't brag about it. If there's a charity dinner, he buys a table and gives the ticket away. He pays for it, but he won't go. He doesn't show off. He doesn't like to do charity work in front of the TV cameras. He just does it. He did the links for the charity Telethon recently. No fuss. No fee.'

Benny's director from BBC days, Ernest Maxin, says Benny was always the same. 'Years ago, I organized a midnight matinée at the London Palladium, a charity show for spastic children. I asked about forty stars to give their services. Of those who agreed, most were concerned about where they would appear on the bill. Not Benny. He was first to accept and he made no fuss at all. And he stopped the show, of course. Another time, I was responsible for a similar function at the Coliseum – a charity show to raise funds for a school attached to a poor synagogue in the East End. Once again, Benny was first to agree. It didn't matter to him that he was doing it for Jewish children. Children needed his help – so he gave it. This I like so much.'

The late Alice Moore, Benny's neighbour in Westrow Gardens and lifelong friend, knew the truth about him. 'Benny's not mean,' she said a few years ago. 'He's very

generous, but careful. He's badgered by people trying
to take advantage, but, if he sees a good cause, he
will make a big donation.' Benny gives fortunes away
every year – to dozens of individuals and charities.
'It's just figures on a piece of paper to me,' he says. 'I
can't believe I'm rich.' What Benny deprecates and is
unlikely to consider is unsolicited approaches to him.
He feels assailed by such demands. 'Everybody wants
something from me,' he complains. 'Nobody ever says,
"Here, Ben, this is for you . . . " ' He resents being put
in the position of the spoiler – the one who says 'No'.
Benny has to refuse often to protect himself, but he
detests the embarrassment. He eschews confrontation
and will go to great lengths to avoid awkwardness or
scenes.

Benny's wariness is entirely the result of experience.
As a lad, he was open and trusting. He got hurt when
certain people in the business took advantage of him
in the early days. He grew more careful. My brother
has always responded to human contact. He warms
to people. He likes to help them. As he became more
successful, he attracted the attention of expert cheats.
He began to get begging letters by every post. He never
replies to them now. He has been caught too often. The
counterfeits made him look hard at every proposal.

'Benny has a pathological fear of being cheated,' confirms Peter Charlesworth. 'If anyone makes a serious
attempt to take advantage of him, they will find a very
stony Benny Hill. He expresses his icy rage with cutting
sarcasm, and departs immediately. I have seen him like
that only once. Apart from that occasion, I have found
him the most tolerant and amiable of men. Benny is one
of the few whom I would call "friend". He is a strange
friend. He doesn't communicate weekly or monthly.
But suddenly the phone will ring and you will have

an hour-and-a-half conversation. And you can rely on
what he says. He never lies. He may be evasive or make
no answer. But I have never heard him tell an untruth.
He has integrity. Benny is a very private person who
has one extraordinary quality that I have never known
in any other individual. He is totally comfortable with
his own company. Night after night. He can easily
spend weeks on his own – writing, watching TV,
making notes, reading, cooking, eating, walking. He
rarely needs the society of other human beings.'

Before any impression is created that my brother is
suffering from deep-seated misanthropy, due to some
dark untold secret, I have to register a fact that may
throw a rather different light on his solitary lifestyle. His
great-aunt Lucy Russell, who died aged 108, held the
British record for living on her own. After her husband
died, she looked after herself alone for decades, until
the age of 105. There are others in the family who have
lived long, useful lives in solitary splendour. Maybe
the Hills just happen to be a breed of independent
beggars.

Benny's self-sufficiency has led to the shedding of
buckets of crocodile tears by the press, especially
at Christmas time. Described as a recluse, a broken-
hearted clown, Mr Lonely, or a latterday Scrooge, he
is always good for a few paragraphs of tear-jerking copy
at Yuletide. He is described as shivering in solitary
misery while the rest of his fellow-countrymen eat,
drink and make merry. The truth is that, in the matter
of Christmas celebrations, he has more choice than
anybody else in Britain. He has commitments to no
one but himself. He is free and can easily afford to
spend the seasonal holiday anywhere in the world. He
has declined to visit members of his family so often
that they no longer mention it. His wide circle of

friends and professional associates would be delighted
to welcome him into their homes, thousands of families
of all classes would be proud to change the old boast
from 'We had turkey for Christmas' to 'We had Benny
Hill for Christmas'. At the drop of a plastic card, he
could be on a plane to friends in Australia, America,
Japan, France, Greece and a dozen other countries –
friends who would fall over themselves to give him a
good time. Or he could be winging his way to any
one of a dozen sunny beaches in exotic corners of the
globe. He will not go.

Let us face it, he is perfectly happy spending Christmas
on his own. It is a busy season for him, the season when
all the TV comedy stars come out to shine. Benny is
watching and taping non-stop over the holiday. He is
making notes that will give him some structure for his
next show. Occasionally an item will spark off his own
ideas, but mainly he is concerned to avoid including
anything that will induce the viewers to say, 'We saw
something like that last Christmas!' He is watching the
trends, too, so that his parodies will not be old-hat, but
catch the current topics and fashions by the time his
show hits the airwaves.

So the man is not suffering. He is enjoying himself, doing what he likes doing, sitting in front of the
goggle-box with pen and pad, sipping an unpretentious
little wine culled from the southern slopes of Marks &
Spencer's. The only tears appropriate will be tears of
laughter at the results of his efforts six months later.

Benny is not so independent that he does not enjoy,
from time to time, taking a lady to lunch and a matinée
performance of a musical show. His escorts on these
occasions are usually old friends who choose the entertainment. On all other visits to the theatre, Benny's
professional needs are paramount.

'I go to a show to learn,' he explains. 'If I see a serious play like *A Streetcar Named Desire*, it is because I hope to burlesque it on television; if it is a comedy, I hope it will inspire me.'

Being so familiar with the work of British performers, writers and directors in the realm of comedy, Benny finds the London theatre less interesting than that of Paris and Madrid, where he quite often catches two revues and a cabaret in one long evening. However, on the Continent he is more likely than in Britain to be mobbed by adoring fans at places of entertainment.

Benny has always been a film buff – with a preference for funny pictures and an abhorrence of pretentious symbolism, which he has occasionally sent up on television. In recent years, he has made full use of the smaller auditoriums in the modern cinema complexes. However, he appreciates the ambience of certain older picture palaces and never misses a chance to visit his favourite, an ancient Arab cinema in Marseilles.

Benny occasionally craves company for physical reasons. He has had more hot dinners than sex – and it is to hot dinners that I refer here. Occasionally, he will cook for others, and he is very good at it. Over decades, he has entertained some of the greatest clown heads of Europe. He is quite capable of producing delicious, authentic Malaysian or Paraguayan dishes. But he prefers the challenge of whipping up a tasty, nourishing meal in half an hour, out of ingredients garnered from the bottom of a vegetable basket and the corners of a half-empty fridge.

This urge arises from his early training. As a cook, Mum never wasted anything. Not a spoonful of dripping or a drop of stock. Even the greens liquid came to the table as soup. Though there is no need to be, Benny is still careful. He cannot change. Neither can

I. If a bread roll and a £10 note were to drop from the dinner-table at the same time, Benny would pick up the bread roll first. The Captain taught us that, in Germany in 1918, the bread roll could save a life – the bank note turned out to be worthless. In the last resort, food is more valuable than paper.

There is a revealing story, of which there are several apocryphal versions, that illustrates Benny's attitude to food. It is appropriate that Peter Charlesworth, who was present throughout the incident, should tell it: 'Soon after we met, Benny asked me to take him in my Ford Consul to a war disposal shop in Paddington. He had heard that tinned food was being sold off cheap. The tins, without labels, were Christmas fare for the troops, salvaged from a sunken ship, bombed in the Thames Estuary during World War II. When we arrived, we saw a notice board which explained that the contents of each tin could not be guaranteed, but among the complement was stewed steak, fruit salad and Christmas pudding.

'Well, at that time, such delicacies were in very short supply – so the gamble was made to measure for Benny. He hates shopping and intended to make a bulk buy that would save him trips to the grocer's for months. Though the tins were only threepence each, his excitement did not arise from miserliness. He was like a kid dipping into a bran tub. He was intrigued by what he might find. The outcome was that we lugged out two sacks of tins and dumped one on the bench seat of my car and the other in the back. Benny paid up and off we went with our prize.

'When we got back to his place, he opened up some of the cans, found all sorts of goodies, including stewed steak. He then cooked the best meal I'd eaten in years. I can't remember what we had for dessert, but it was part of my reward for helping him. He's a brilliant cook, the most remarkable that I've ever come across. He's perfectly happy in a kitchen. That day, with me, Benny enjoyed the sense of creating something out of nothing. After all, that's what he's always done with his shows. He starts the year with nothing but his thoughts. By the end of six months, he has produced a sparkling, amusing entertainment for millions. The money doesn't figure. The creation has nothing to do with meanness.'

'I guess it's significant,' says Ronnie Hazlehurst, the composer and arranger, 'that of my long association with Benny, my most vivid memories have to do with food. Just before Christmas a hamper two feet high arrived at my home from Fortnum and Mason. There was no indication of who had sent it, so I rang the firm to find out. They told me the price, a small fortune, which I had not requested, and finally revealed the sender. It was Benny. I rarely received gifts like that – and never from comedians. Few comedians ever took the whole cast out to dinner, either, as he did, at the end of a radio series. The celebration was held in the first Japanese restaurant in London. Benny paid for the entire meal and ordered for everybody, as he was the only one who understood the menu. A little old Japanese lady did the cooking in a corner. Unfortunately, most of the delicacies were raw, and had to be dipped with chopsticks into dark sauce. Once the sake was flowing, everybody looked as though they had been creosoted.'

Because he enjoys it so much himself, Benny likes to offer gifts of food whenever possible. He has a sweet tooth and many a girlfriend has been delighted when, at the beginning of an evening, my brother has arrived at her door with a huge box of chocolates, only to discover, hours later, that he has eaten most of them. He even described his television presentation in those terms to Kay Gardella of the New York *Daily News.* 'I compare the show to a box of chocolates; some are solid, some are filled with caramel, others with nuts, still others with cherries. It's an assortment. You like some bits; you don't like others. But you don't throw the whole box away!'

Chocolates are not the only treats that undo all Benny's efforts to get slim. He loves sausages and was recently overjoyed to find fatless bangers in his local supermarket. However, he was quite chopfallen when Dennis Kirkland told him that two at a time was top weight. Poor Benny. On one occasion he was comparing tins while shopping when he was spied by a reporter who alleged in a national newspaper the next morning that my brother was looking for the cheapest. 'I was only counting calories,' wailed Benny, plaintively.   Buying food is, by and large, the only shopping my brother ever does. He knows about that and is comfortable with it. Uneasy in hardware or furniture shops, he rarely enters them. He loves walking around Harrods in the same way that he enjoys visiting the National Gallery. He has no desire to possess things, no lust to collect. 'I can only wear one shirt at a time,' he says, 'eat one meal at a time.' He takes Wordsworth seriously.

> The world is too much with us: late and soon,
> Getting and spending, we lay waste our powers.

Benny was once peering at a piece of Chinese pottery in a shop window. 'Isn't that beautiful?' he remarked to his friend Peter Charlesworth.

'You can afford to buy that,' replied Peter.

'I don't want to own it,' said Benny. 'I just want to look at it.'

In a society so careless of resources, in which citizens are encouraged to consume and accumulate, such sanity may well be construed as subversive.

20

Funny is Difficult

Many years ago, soon after Benny began his television specials for the BBC, his director fell ill. The replacement was a younger man, to whom my brother gave the full script for the next hour-long show. On the morning of the first rehearsal, the young director swept into the studio, clapped his hands and cried to the assembled cast, 'Attention, boys and girls! Everything's been changed! The show's going to have a story-line and it all takes place on board ship!' Benny was appalled. He could see disaster staring at him in the faces of dissatisfied viewers. It took him over an hour to disengage the young turkey-cock from his folly.

Dennis Kirkland, who was then floor manager, first encountered Benny in 1966, when the funny man was improvising some comic ballet steps in a corner of the rehearsal hall. He burst out laughing at the sight. 'Book him! Sign him up!' ordered Benny at once. 'He's a good audience. We must have him!' Dennis has been the perfect foil and a tower of strength ever since, working in some capacity on every single entertainment that Benny Hill has presented for ITV. In 1978 he took over the show as director. By that time, Dennis knew his star well enough to be impressed by Benny's professionalism. He was aware of what Sue Upton discovered. 'My relationship with Benny changes slightly when we are working. It's suddenly professional again. He's employing me. I feel rather nervous, on my toes, just one of the girls. Of course, I realize that the show claims one hundred per cent of his thought, his time and his effort. And, if he gives me a word of praise, it makes my week. Then, once the show is finished, we slip back into our casual friendship again.'

The character actress Patricia Hayes, who remembers the early days, made her views known first to Benny and then to the radio audience. 'Benny was a joy to work with all through the weeks of preparation. He was great fun – and always a gentleman to the ladies. But, on the day of the show, his personality changed. He grew pernickety, and would find fault with your costume, your make-up or something.'

A slightly different attitude to my brother's behaviour was revealed by Nicholas Parsons, who was the straight man on many shows. 'I enjoyed working with Benny. He was always so disciplined, friendly and helpful. It's true that he was a trifle tense at the final recording, but that was to be expected. The man was carrying a tremendous weight of responsibility. The show had to be right. And Benny was at the centre of it, with complicated songs, quick changes, different characters, et cetera. He knew all our livelihoods were at stake. One duff show, one duff sketch, even, and the critics would pounce. No wonder he was tense.'

'In the early days,' Dennis Kirkland told me, 'Benny was so tense that people felt he was hard work. Some performers didn't like to join the Benny Hill Show because he expected a lot from them. He never lost his temper. He was never unpleasant. But he was difficult to please. Everything had to be exact, to be clear, to register. "This door won't open properly," he would say. "The tumbler's not big enough, the tablecloth's the wrong colour, a chocolate cake on a dark brown plate won't show up on the screen!" What is so galling to a director is that Benny always has good reasons for his comments. He is right. You can't fault the beggar! You see, most comedians are not so particular. They don't care so much. Benny's the best in the world because he cares most.'

'Somebody once said that genius is an infinite capacity for taking pains,' I said.

'If that's so,' replied Dennis, 'then Benny is a genius! And I was able to convince him that I thought so – or, at least, had great respect for him soon after I became director of the show. Benny was balking at a scene set in a hotel bar. The viewers would be unable to see his funny movements, he claimed, as his white suit would be lost against the silver-coloured bar. He wasn't happy with the set-up. The visual comedy wasn't working and some of the jokes were not strong enough. So I asked the designer to spray the bar a darker colour, and sat in a corner with Benny to talk things over. I had to win his trust – so I told him I could see that his heart wasn't in it and suggested that carrying on would just be a waste of time. "We'll scrub today," I said. "Let's just lose it. I'll have the bar re-designed and we'll try again another day." It was unheard of to waste a studio day and Benny knew that I was going out on a limb for him. But I meant it. And he knew I meant it. "No, no," he replied, "we can't lose a studio day. Let me try it out against the re-sprayed bar." He did – and the scene began to look good. His confidence returned and we solved each problem which had seemed insoluble before. After that, he realized that I was on his side and began to relax with me. "You're at the top. You've made it," I've told him countless times since. "It's not a matter of life and death!" He's much less tense these days and consequently performers fight to get on the show.'

Benny still writes much of his material when travelling abroad and sends it in pieces for Dennis to collate.

Currently, the hieroglyphic script, with its diagrams and drawings, is more likely to arrive on hotel notepaper than the beer-mats, paper napkins and laundry bags he quite happily despatched in the past. Most of the comedy will be based on observation, usually recent. When he returns home, he will top up the show with items based on comments and situations reported in newspaper cuttings. These will be culled from his cardboard boxes of priceless rubbish. Michael Billington did not call Benny 'a ramshackle archivist of humour' without good reason. Any holes in the script will then be filled by tried and tested material from The Dustbin. This is the imaginary receptacle that contains the traditional jokes and sight-gags that are at least fifty years old and known to every comedian of that age or older. No matter how well it fits the sketch, Benny will not include one of these if he knows that it has been used on British television in the last three years.

The Dustbin is not to be despised. 'A sixty-year-old joke that has been neglected,' says Benny, 'can, in the right setting, shine like a gem to the generations that have never heard it. On the other hand, there is nothing older than a new joke that has been used three times on television and five times on radio in the last month. A few years ago, an elderly comedian presented a remarkably successful one-man show in London, using material almost exclusively from The Dustbin. The modern audiences loved it. More recently, in the West End, an old-style revue very effectively featured nothing but surefire jokes – all Dustbin comedy. It is important to distinguish between a joke and a witticism or mildly amusing comment. I define a joke as a story or statement that provokes a rib-tickling, falling about, tears down to here response. Much of what passes for comedy nowadays is perceptive observation that I call "the humour of recognition", which does little more than stimulate "a hearty smile", in Dave Freeman's pithy phrase. Using my definition of a joke, I rarely hear or read a new one. Nowadays, I almost always admire only the order in which familiar jokes are presented, or the unusual alteration or juxtaposition of "old friends". It is an unexpected treat to hear a comedian get a big laugh with a joke which is not a version of something I have used myself.'

It is not only Dennis Kirkland's awards and trophies that mark him out as a remarkable talent, but the shrewdness with which he encourages my brother's creative efforts. 'When you have a world-beater like Benny,' he says, 'you let him run. You don't stand on his toes. I give him as much room as I can. Let him follow his fantasy. I never say, "No, we can't do that. We can't afford it!" or "You're crazy. It's just not possible." Let him dream. Let him play. Improvise, juggle with it, then, when he has perfected the crazy comedy notion, think about ways of bringing it to the screen. If we do this, it might work. It might be practicable. If we do that, it would be cheap enough to put on. And so on. Never cut him down. Never stifle his imagination.'

In his scripts, Benny takes care not to include references to topical events or interests that may have been forgotten by the time the show is broadcast, perhaps a year later. However, he still has 'the key of the street' and anticipates with a precision that is uncanny. Some time ago, he sensed that investigative television journalists were displaying a zeal in pursuing reluctant interviewees that would one day result in a public scandal. He wrote and performed in a sketch that depicted such harassment. Months later, the sketch was shown on British screens in the same week that, for the first time, an investigative television journalist was answering similar charges in a court of law.

Benny is so prolific a writer that he always provides scripts for more items than can be included in one show. Even when the decision has been made to produce two or three shows at a time, he will supply ample material for them all. The mass of comedy pieces is then sorted and arranged in order, with reference to the likely length of each sequence, its originality, the possibility of its further development, and the need for variety as an overall effect. The crucial factor around which the show assembles itself is the time required for location filming. The Benny Hill Show is unique in many ways, but one of the most obvious is the amount of time it spends in the open air. This is why it is probably the most expensive television comedy presentation in the world.

The choice of location is made as early as possible. According to the requirements of the playlets, the venue may be the grounds of a club, the gardens of an ancient manor, a farm, or a private park. Whether the outdoor filming takes place near London, in Australia or the US, the procedure is much the same. At the moment of writing, Burt Reynolds is trying to persuade Benny to use a Florida golf-course so that he can appear in the run-off chase.

Once the comedy segments have been chosen, and a running order established, auditioning and casting begin without delay. Benny prefers to employ performers he knows and trusts rather than newcomers. That is why members of his team stay with him for years before moving on. However, he is eager to see his colleagues prosper and will do what he can to help their careers. 'Never miss an opportunity,' he tells the younger players.

When Patricia Hayes asked Benny if she could leave to play the title role in Jeremy Sandford's 1971 television drama *Edna, the Inebriate Woman*, he released her from her contract without hesitation. No one was more delighted or less surprised than Benny when Pat turned in a stunning performance that won her international acclaim. He had recognized her quality years earlier, which is why he used her so much. Pat was kind enough to thank Benny for his help when accepting the BAFTA award for her outstanding performance.

The Benny Hill company is run like a first-class soccer team. Nobody is ever absolutely certain that he or she will be picked for the next game. Your last appearance may, in fact, be your last. The team carries no passengers. In this way, a high standard of general performance is maintained. Those seasoned players who do stay with the show for many years are so dedicated and skilled that it takes an extraordinarily gifted newcomer to oust them.

If a member of the cast is dropped from the team for any reason, Benny keeps in touch and does what he can to assist. When the bald-headed Irish leprechaun Jackie Wright became, at 82, too ill to work, Benny included every unused clip of his tiny chum in the shows, so that not only was Jackie receiving his cheques, but he could see himself still getting laughs on the show. Later, when the pint-sized comic was confined to bed, Benny offered to write a hospital sketch and film it around Jackie in his own home in Belfast.

After the show is cast, the players are fitted with their costumes. Benny once decked himself out as a Viking warrior at a well-known theatrical costumiers. Wearing a horned helmet far too small for his melon head, he suddenly bumped into Sir Laurence Olivier in a narrow alley between the racks of costumes.

The greatest actor in the world took a step back, cried, 'Oh, my God!' and tottered off down the alley, choking with laughter.

'You didn't get many laughs in *Richard III*, didja?' shouted Benny after the theatrical knight. 'Even with all that bloody nose-putty!' Unable to speak, Sir Laurence waved a hand in acknowledgement of the riposte.

After the costume fittings, outdoor filming starts at the location chosen earlier. As most of the scenes will be physical, visual comedy sequences with very little dialogue, the soundtrack is dubbed on later. Thus, the problems created for most movie-makers in the Home Counties by the non-stop cacophony of aircraft, motor-cars, crowds, machinery and radios do not arise. Sightseers may be a nuisance on rare occasions. One convenient location in Surrey is visited by residents from a mental hospital next door, but they often go undetected as their behaviour is less eccentric than that of old hands in the Benny Hill Show.

The most eccentric person on the park is always Benny himself. You can spot him a quarter of a mile away in Florida shirt and slacks, or any one of a thousand outlandish guises. He is a natural Bully Bottom and insists on playing everybody else's part first. After all, he has written it and remembers exactly how it all goes. And, as the scene is clearly established in his head, who knows better than he how to direct it? So it is he who cannot resist pointing the finger, setting out his field of players like a cricket captain, and his saucy blue eye that peeps many a time and oft through the eyepiece of the camera. The voice that booms across the greensward is also occasionally one familiar to millions. The next minute, the same voice is in earnest discussion with that of Dennis Kirkland, suggesting a sight-gag that will add another laugh to a sequence that is already top-heavy with hilarious surprises. A moment later it is quietly coaxing the lovely owner of two eyes of blue to come smiling through a sparkling spray from a garden hose.

'For the cast and crew,' explains stuntman Ken Sedd, 'filming the Benny Hill Show on location is hard work but great fun. Benny's into everything, miming, cajoling, ad libbing, demonstrating, reasoning, joking. Nothing happens on the set that he doesn't immediately pick up and use to make everyone laugh. He does it all the time. I remember once we needed a horse for one scene and the owner was explaining how calm the animal was. "He's making no sign of nervousness."

' "If he does," said Benny, quick as a flash, "I want it for my rhubarb!" '

My brother does not even need an excuse to raise a laugh. If he sees one of the cast looking glum, he may well stroll over and say, apropos of nothing, 'Thirty days hath September, April, June and November. All the rest have thirty-one. It just isn't *fair*!' or 'Roses are reddish, violets are bluish. If it weren't for Christmas, we'd all be Jewish!' Whatever tosh he recites, Benny never fails to turn a frown into a smile.

Dennis Kirkland and Benny Hill, with decades of television comedy experience between them, have evolved a kind of directorial telepathy. For most of the time, they know exactly what needs to be done next. So, usually without discussion, they share the responsibilities, each anticipating imminent needs and getting on with the job in hand. Thus, a day's shooting on location puts an impressive length of quality film in the can. What depresses Dennis is that so much of it is double-speeded on the show and edited so tightly that it takes only a fraction of its normal time on the screen.

The Benny Hill Show is, he claims, the most complex, technically, of all television comedy presentations.

The cast are expected to be equally dedicated to their work. The smallest, and perhaps the pluckiest, of the Angels, Sue Upton, whom Benny sometimes addresses as 'Uptonogood', is often called upon to make contributions beyond the call of duty. In her time, she has careered down a hill on a tricycle with no brakes, bruised her legs dropping into a pit from a jungle vine, and burned her breasts from the back-fire of an exploding bra. Sue remembers with particular vividness the occasion when, as the indestructible Wondergran, she beat off all attacks by Jekyll, Hyde and crony, who were disguised as Benny, Bob Todd and Henry McGee. She had to stand, nonchalantly humming, while being subjected to a barrage of huge missiles. Balsa-wood park benches, tables, chairs and polystyrene boulders were all hurled, she says, 'with conviction'. As they crashed into her, poor Sue conveyed the impression that she was impervious to pain. In fact, she was shaken and terrified, but she did not flinch. When Dennis shouted, 'Cut!' everybody cheered and clapped her courage. Sue was so relieved that she burst into tears.

Despite his age and weight, Benny still undertakes as many of his own stunts as he can manage. He hates heights but will practise falls of all kinds until he is black and blue all over. Over the years, Benny has suffered many minor injuries while filming, such as a sabre cut, a pulled thigh muscle, a strained back, a broken tibia and a strained ankle. Once he delayed a kidney operation in order to finish a show. When some of the crew went on strike, Benny took the chance to nip into hospital. After the strike was over, he returned to complete his entertainment. 'I've dropped many a clanger in my time,' he quips, 'but I'm the only comic to have dropped a kidney in the middle of a show!'

While making a television commercial for the campaign, 'There's a Humphrey About', which suggested that mysterious milk-snatchers were stealing pintas everywhere, Benny appeared in his familiar guise as a milkman in front of a milk-float. In the next shot, he was shown searching the area where the float had stood, suggesting that someone had nicked it. In fact, the heavy battery-driven vehicle was suspended by crane out of camera range, directly above him. Three times he looked about under the float and said his lines. 'Just one more take, Ben,' pleaded the director. Luckily, this time my brother went through the motions with less conviction. As he said his lines, the float suddenly fell with a cataclysmic crash right on the spot where he had stood for the first three takes. It missed him this time by inches. 'Gordon Bennett!' exclaimed Benny to the director. 'That was a close one! It would have been instant death. I wouldn't even have had time to give you Bob Monkhouse's phone number!'

Not all accidents on the set are quite so dangerous. Little Jackie Wright was the victim of one that left him in some disarray, nevertheless. He was playing a boy scout learning to scale a high wall. Scoutmaster Benny swung a large anchor hook, intending to catch it on the top. The sight-gag was that the anchor hook would goose Jackie right up the bum, he would leap a foot and scream 'Oooh!', thus evoking mirth among millions. Although the hook was made of rubber, Jackie nervously braced himself for a bump in the rump. According to Ken Sedd, 'As Benny swung the rope, Jackie let out the loudest, longest fart you have ever heard in your life. It echoed round the grounds. Everybody heard it – the girls, the crew, the cast – and they immediately exploded with laughter. They couldn't stop, bending over, holding their sides, even falling on the ground and waving their feet in the air. Benny was as convulsed as everybody else. The only exception was Jackie, who stood there looking rueful, trying to pretend that it wasn't him. Everybody knew it was, so, when people saw his face, they laughed twice as hard. The laughter went on for ten minutes, but, when all was calm at last, Benny said to me, "You have to admit – it's still the funniest sound in the world!" '

It is understood by those who work with him that there are times when Benny prefers to be left alone. This is when he retires to his van for a simple lunch, or when a scene is being shot to which he feels he cannot contribute. People say that he likes his privacy. In truth, it is rather more a matter of re-charging his batteries. Sometimes, he likes to find a companion and play. Ken Sedd says he was the only witness to one remarkable game when Benny ambled away from the filming for a few minutes. Everybody else was watching the scene being shot, including an interested by-stander who had wandered into the grounds with her small school-boy son.

The mother was concentrating on the action. Her son was concentrating on his ice-cream cornet a few yards away. Cap at an angle, he stood in short trousers, with his tiny legs crossed, and socks down round his ankles. Ken's attention was suddenly riveted by the interaction between Benny and the little boy. Without warning, Benny became a shy little boy, too. Everything about him altered as if by magic. He moved tentatively towards his new friend in slow, casual little-boy steps. 'I watched in amazement, totally enthralled by the transformation in Benny. It was incredibly child-like behaviour, perfect reproduction of hand, arm and head movements and body language. He kept looking shyly at the little boy and then looking away. He moved a little closer in so innocent a manner that the boy recognized a fellow-child. I could see the little lad responding. In a strange way, I could see him reaching for Benny. Without a word being said, they were establishing a friendship between equals. The little boy had absolute trust in this huge, strange, unlikely kid. They were enjoying each other's company. Just for a minute. Then, the filming ended and everybody was on the move again. But I've never seen anything in my life, before or since, like the rapport between Benny and that little boy.'

Benny's rapport with children has not always come to his aid. During the eighties he began to introduce the toddlers of his Angels and ex-Angels into the show. Jade Westbrook was the first, because she was a charmful little armful, to be followed by equally irresistible children. But Benny has found that the lovely, cuddly little darlings who win his heart soon get smart, grow up and have wills of their own. 'They won't take direction,' he moans plaintively. That means that they refuse to do as they are told. As directors, he and Dennis are stumped by the stubbornness of their cast of infants. The kids have found out that they are dealing with a couple of old softies. I find Benny's account of the difficulties hilarious.

'They're lovely children, really sweet, but such little beggars! Gordon Bennett, they drive you crazy. You say, "That's it, dear. Just pick up the boot, please."

' "Don't want to."

'Judas Priest! "All right, dear!" Then we start up the line in age. So I say to the next one, "You're a fine big girl. You'll pick up the boot for Uncle Ben, won't you? Please?"

' "No, I'm not going to pick it up. Louise didn't pick it up – so I'm not going to pick it up, either."

' "Oh, my sainted Aunt!" So we finally come to Richard. "You're a fine-looking lad, Richard. You'll be a big man some day. You'll pick up the boot for Uncle Ben, won't you?" Richard nods. "You'll pick up the boot?" He nods again. "Good boy, Richard." So he picks up the boot and slings it over the wall! Oh, I'll get hold of him one of these days! Everything we do with the children takes twice as long as it should. We had a great idea of doing "When Father Papers The Parlour" with the kids. It could be a great sketch – loads of paper, buckets of paste – a real riot! But Den said to me, "It's Don't Want To Time with the little beggars these days. They're getting so bolshie it'd take us three days to record it!" '

Despite his grumbles, Benny loves working with the children of his Angels. He is delighted when they get a big laugh at his expense. In this, as in so many matters, he turns accepted, conventional wisdom on its head. Every comic knows the adage, 'Never work with children or animals'. Benny works with both and thrives on it. 'Anything for a laugh' is his personal motto, and he does not mind who raises it. Those, on the other hand, who try to limit laughter are the objects of his withering scorn.

The Little Angels present Uncle Ben and Uncle Den with just as many problems indoors as on location. When two-year-old Louise Upton made her debut, she brought the entire studio to a standstill for half an hour. She had to take part in a throwaway sight-gag lasting only a few seconds. Benny was reluctant to lose it, as he sometimes likes to hit the viewing audience with one joey after another in quick succession. The more the merrier. In the scene, Benny played a long-haired rocker/greaser, who dumped his bike indoors and left his helmet upside-down on the floor. Louise was to mistake the helmet for a pottie and sit on it. However, being a well-brought-up little girl, she would have none of it. The adults tried everything to persuade her, even putting money under the helmet to bribe her, to no avail. In the end, Louise's mother, Sue, was reduced to squatting on the helmet herself. 'Look, Louise, watch Mummy. Mummy's sitting on the pottie. Now you do it.' The ruse worked. Louise sat on the helmet just long enough for Dennis, who had speeded up the shot, to obtain a take that, slowed down, would last the vital seconds to win a laugh. Sue's delight was cut short when the scene was played back. She was horrified to see herself sitting on the pottie. Dennis had kept the cameras rolling while Sue was crouched on the helmet. 'How would you like to view that on your home screen?' he chuckled.

'The rotten devils!' she grins. 'If they ever show me in that position, I'll sue them to within an inch of their lives!'

'The rotten devils', Ben and Den, know that people work best when they are enjoying what they do. So the lively pair are always clowning and jollying their cast along like a couple of Butlin's redcoats or Catskill toomlers. Den usually plays the straight man. An example of the kind of nonsense they employ occurred when a great, stuffed bear was being lined up for a shot. Giving the feed-line, Dennis shouted, 'Benny! Let's have the bear behind!'

'Righto!' replied Benny immediately, turning round and beginning to drop his trousers.

Bob Todd, the mature gent with the poached-egg eyes, whose lived-in face adapts itself perfectly to every kind of character, told me that, one day in the studio, Benny muttered confidentially, 'Jackie Wright just said – "Ay port on stondin auto proctiballay naze flock condimoniom!" I can't understand a word of it. Do you know what he's on about?'

'Search me,' replied Bob. Just then, he noticed Jackie talking to a stage carpenter. 'Why don't you ask the carpenter to translate for you?' he suggested. As my brother approached the workman, Jackie walked away and Bob noticed the fellow talking earnestly to Benny. When my brother came back, Bob asked, 'What did the carpenter say?'

'He said, "Ay port on stondin auto proctiballay naze flock condimoniom!" '

Bob Todd, who has been with the show for seventeen years, finds some scenes a terrible trial, as Benny makes him giggle. The more important the scene, the tenser Bob gets and the more likely he is to break up. He does not always need Benny to set him off. He is such a funny man that he often finds his own position ridiculous. Before one live show, to be recorded in front of an invited audience, Dennis told him, 'Don't you dare giggle, Bob. You'll kill the sketch stone dead if you do. This is one take – and it's got to be right. So I want a professional performance from you. I'll be very angry if you destroy it.' A little later, Bob found himself standing behind a flat, on the other side of which was the stage and a packed house. Waiting to make an entrance, he began to smile at the absurdity of it all. 'Look at you!' he said to himself. 'You, an ex-squadron leader in the Royal Air Force, a respected pillar of the Sussex yeomanry and a dignified father of children, standing there, with gigantic tits, wearing a blond wig with a star, and dressed in a ballerina skirt, white tights and cook's boots! What do you think you're doing, man? In a minute, you're going to be prancing out there, crying, "Whoops! I'm a Fairy Queen!" ' By this time, Bob was laughing with such abandon that he was afraid the front rows would hear him. There was only one thing to do. He bit his tongue so hard that the agony drove all thought of laughter from his mind. So that, when he danced on-stage, he was able to give his usual hilarious, disciplined performance.

What Bob does not realize is that Benny is just as susceptible to giggles. In order not to ruin sketches, my brother carries a tiny, sharp nail file that he can palm at will to drive into his fingers. Many a time he has finished a piece with blood on his hands. It would not do for him to appear so unprofessional as to spoil a valuable sequence. Bob says that, in this respect, Benny is like the first-rate captain of a crew. He sets an example of dedication and expects others to follow it. He never raises his voice but, if you are slacking, you are soon made aware of his disapproval.

Having created the script, Benny is always word-perfect. He assumes that the rest of the cast will know their lines, too, and deliver them as written. According to Henry McGee, his long-time straight man, my brother spots the tiniest deviation from the printed page. The only ad libbing to be heard is when Benny covers for a colleague who has forgotten or made a mistake. 'It's easy to learn a part that Benny has written,' explains Henry. 'He knows the rhythms and cadences of your speech and he creates the role for you with your abilities in mind. It just flows naturally.'

If you ever get a chance to join the studio audience for the Benny Hill Show, don't miss it. Anyone who has followed the story of my brother's life to this page, will be fascinated by the entertainment offered. The show is not two hours of undiluted hilarity, although there is plenty of that. It is a chance to see a record-breaking television presentation in the final stages of its assemblage. Just as each edition is different, so every concoction of this most popular of programmes is different, to some extent depending on whether it is made in Britain, Australia or the US. However, you are likely to be introduced first to Dennis Kirkland, the show's director and the evening's host. He is a jovial, friendly fellow, a comedian manqué, who makes his tour of the battery of cameras, hanging screens, microphones, booms and studio paraphernalia a source of instruction and entertainment. He will explain why you must never use the word 'monitor' and expect you to join the audience in shouting, 'Right!' to indicate that you have grasped each point. When he has everyone in a good humour, he presents the star for the evening (and many evenings), Benny Hill, who, dressed for a Western square dance, holds his wide-brimmed hat and advances to the edge of the stage. If he has had his way, my brother will be close to the audience and above the first row. As usual, he is embarrassed by the intensity of the thunderous welcome. It is a standing ovation! When the audience sits down at last, they burst into loud applause once more as he announces that another Eastern European state has joined the many countries showing the Benny Hill Show. 'That makes One Hundred and Thirty!' he says, like a darts commentator. Then he may welcome a coachload of fans from another city, or even a chartered planeload from another country. He never fails to make gentle fun at their expense, moving on to familiar music-hall material.

'I must apologize for the facilities here,' he says, with the corners of his mouth twitching. Some punters are already laughing. 'But I see there's still no light in the gents' loo. It's a disgrace, having to go in there with a lighted match in one hand and . . . ' His voice trails off and is lost in great gales of laughter. 'And there's no lock on the toilet door. You have to keep your foot up all the time. You feel such a fool. And the door opens outwards.' Pause. 'I shall never be able to look Thora Hird in the face again!'

Benny's saucy smile and the way his teeth and bright blue eyes sparkle under the lights will make older music-hall buffs imagine for a moment that he is the reincarnation of the Cheeky Chappie himself, the great Max Miller. But the opening sketch will remind them that this is the great Benny Hill, who is not only a master of patter but the doyen of visual comedy. Younger visitors will some day remember with advantage the night they saw the legendary comedian in one of his rare live performances.

The opening square dance, with its wicked lyrics triple-tongued by Benny, has to be re-taken a couple of times, but it gives him a chance to step forward and ad lib a routine that endears him even more to the studio audience. He appears happy and relaxed, leaving all directorial decisions to Dennis. Much of the evening's entertainment consists of loosely edited film and video of the location sketches, the studio quickies, the dance routines, all shown on twenty hanging screens, interspersed with sketches taking place on the stage to be recorded in front of the visiting fans. Benny is in and out of the proceedings all the time, never at a loss for a joke or a cheeky remark. It is always a stunning performance, as he never puts a foot wrong. At last, he sends his fans, smiling and excited, out into the night.

Now that the filmed pieces and final items have all been recorded to genuine audience laughter, a single Benny Hill Show, as it stands, will last for about one and a half hours. This has to be reduced to fifty-one minutes so that, with nine minutes of commercial breaks, the entertainment lasts one hour exactly. Dennis Kirkland is an excellent editor, but, as he has masses of paperwork to do, Benny volunteers to edit the mass of material down to the required length. I mislead you. 'Volunteers to edit' is wildly inadequate. Try and stop him! Benny loves it. He sits at home in front of his little machine watching the scenes fly by as he notes the numbers of the frames destined for the chop. He rips the show to ribbons. It is a good job Benny is not a surgeon or his patients would die the death of a thousand cuts. He is ruthless. Recently, he made eighty cuts in a seven-minute sketch. 'Eighty cuts!' screams Dennis. 'You're a butcher!'

'No, Den,' explains my brother gently. 'I'm shaping it – making it sharp. Look, each cut is only one and a half seconds.'

'Not worth the effort,' says Dennis.

'No, Den. Eighty times one and a half seconds is two minutes. I've taken two minutes of boredom out of a seven-minute sketch. Now we've got a five-minute sketch that goes like a bomb!'

By the time Benny has trimmed down the ninety minutes to fifty-one, the programme will look much like these two actual shows, whose running order is reproduced below. It will be seen immediately that each hour's entertainment is broken up into three segments, interrupted by two commercial breaks. In both cases, the longer segments begin and end the show, with the shortest sequence coming between the two breaks. Each comedy hour begins with a minute of quickies, a series of fast cameos, and ends with a run-off, in which credits are rolled over a hue and cry after the instigator of such unseemly mirth.

There are times when Benny is busy in his kitchen, but not cooking. He is not cleaning, either. An array of various kitchen receptacles will be standing on the table. He may be pouring water into some of them,

THE BENNY HILL SHOW – A		THE BENNY HILL SHOW – B	
Editing Order	*Minutes*	*Editing Order*	*Minutes*
QUICKIES	1.00	QUICKIES	1.00
BURLESQUE	8.00	ROCK'N'ROLL	4.00
EDITORS	7.00	HAUNTED	5.30
FUNNY OLD WORLD	8.00	HERD	8.30
	24.00		19.00
Commercial Break		Commercial break	
QUICKIES	1.30	QUICKIES	2.30
WEST COUNTRY		CAFE DE L'OPERA	7.30
MONOLOGUE	4.30		
WILLIE'S WHISTLE	7.00		
	13.00		10.00
Commercial Break		Commercial Break	
QUICKIES	1.30	MONOLOGUE AND	
WIFE SWAPPERS	8.30	FOREIGN SHOWS	15.00
HEEL – RUN OFF	4.00	JADE (ARTIST)	
		– RUN OFF	7.00
	14.00		22.00
TOTAL RUNNING TIME	51.00	TOTAL RUNNING TIME	51.00

tapping them with a little hammer, rattling them with a drumstick, or slapping them with a wire brush. He may even be knocking two together or moving round the kitchen clouting everything in sight with one of them. He has not finally taken leave of his senses: he is busy inventing new noises for his show. 'Benny is brilliant at producing sound effects,' reveals Dennis Kirkland. 'He'll come into the dubbing session with a plastic bag full of saucepans, tin cans, bags of coins or plastic bottles, and say, "Listen to this one! It's just the right sound effect for when Bob Todd bounces the rolling pin on my head." And it'll be a corker, spot on! That's the magic of the Benny Hill Show. All the Boing! Clonk! and Splat! You see, if you fall off a horse, it can look very funny. But if you fall off a horse with the right crunch, it'll look twice as funny. So we spend more time than anybody putting on sound effects and music. Four solid days' dubbing. It's unheard of. But Benny insists – and he's right. He says, "If I open the door and walk to the table to do a sight-gag with the coffee pot, that's shoe leather. Until I do the gag, nothing's happening!" '

'That's what Phyllis Diller calls "dead air",' I said. 'She won't have it. She says, "Either I'm talking or the audience is laughing!" '

'Exactly. She's a smart lady,' replied Dennis. 'So, to avoid "shoe leather" or "dead air" with the coffee-pot gag, you have to catch your sleeve on the door-handle and fall over the cat before you get to the table. And you have to work with a jolly, bouncy musical background. The music will carry you. Our show is full of it. Benny has taught them all how to do it. Before the Benny Hill Show, nobody used sound effects or musical backgrounds effectively in comedy. We've noticed show after show follow us. They just copy Benny. Do you know, even Marcel Marceau is using music in his act now?'

The fact that Benny has so often been ahead of his time, following his hunches with such persistence, has sometimes created pitfalls for him. One such was the unwarranted reputation for producing a show that was 'nothing but knickers and knockers'. Few viewers now remember that for nearly twenty years Benny was the star of a BBC comedy show that was a respectable family entertainment. It was extremely popular, but there were those who found it a trifle dull. Benny's cousin, Billy, was one of these. In the mid-sixties, Billy was invited to see my brother's BBC telecast from the Shepherd's Bush studio. After the broadcast, he complimented his cousin on a skilful performance. 'Your comedy is always intelligent,' he said, ' – sometimes brilliant.' This was a widely held view at the time.

'So they tell me,' grinned Benny. 'But?'

'Well, the rest of the show is dull.'

'Did you see it last week?' asked my brother.

'No,' said Billy. 'I was watching the other channel. They had can-can girls from the Pigalle in Paris. That's what you need. Did you realize that everybody on your show tonight was dressed right up to the neck? You need a lot more sex to give it more excitement. Let's see a troupe of sexy dancing girls.'

Benny, of course, had already considered that possibility and had decided against it. He knew that most of his letters came from women, mainly married women, and felt that they made up the majority of his fans. 'I didn't want to cause trouble between married couples at home. A troupe of sexy dancers might excite the old man into saying, "Cor, look at her!" But the wife

would soon put a stop to that by switching over to
the other channel. I felt I couldn't afford to lose the
women's vote. So I hired nice, healthy, next-door-
type girls for my shows. However, in the early seventies, I received an increasing number of letters from
wives saying what a smashing girl was in such and
such a show. So, gradually, the girls got prettier. One
evening in the mid-seventies, David Hamilton, introducing me, said, "Lucky Old Ben among all those
gorgeous girls" – and I thought, "Right, I'll go for
it!" So I hired Love Machine, one of the groups of
sexy dancers that were becoming fashionable. They
did my ratings, which were already at the top, no
harm at all. Then, soon after that, Kenny Everett hired
Hot Gossip, another raunchy team, for his comedy
show – and his ratings took off. He actually said,
in an interview, "Thank Heavens for Hot Gossip!" I
knew then that my hunch was paying off and so I
went to a lot of trouble to find the loveliest girls in
Britain, organized their training and introduced them
as "Hill's Angels".'

'A lot of trouble' means that Benny spent scores
of hours looking at thousands of photographs and
interviewing dozens of beautiful young girls in his
Queens Gate flat. This led to a great deal of misplaced winking and nudging in the profession. Nothing, but nothing, is more important to Benny than
the Benny Hill Show. Girls who thought that sexual
favours would get them anywhere professionally with
him have been in for a big surprise. Everyone possesses
sex: few have talent. Benny values his hand-picked
cast and has a high regard for them. But he is also
patient with the less gifted. Even if he could see at
a glance that a candidate was unsuitable, he would
give her ample time to impress. She would be put at

her ease, offered something to drink, and earnestly
quizzed. Benny had so often been hurt himself by
rejections in the past that he could never bring himself brusquely to dismiss an unlikely applicant. In any
case, an inadequate dancer might make a splendid
actress or a talented comedienne. Every girl, therefore, was thoroughly questioned and tested, firstly on
goals and ambitions, moves to achieve them, qualifications, strengths, weaknesses and future plans. Then
a googly that has bowled out many a smoodge artist
– 'What have you done in the last month to improve
your craft?'

Benny is very keen on determination, enthusiasm
and preparation for success. He is impressed by what
used to be called accomplishments – musical, physical, linguistic, theatrical, technical. He is even more
impressed if the girl is currently taking courses to
develop her talents. After a pleasant chat, he would
then test the girl's claims. Sing classical. Sing jazz.
How high? How low? Harmonize. Ballet dance. Tap-
dance. Musical instrument. Voice. Dialects. Imitate
this. Act a tragic scene. Play a funny sketch. The
whole audition might last two hours, rarely less than
one. During it, Benny would be chattering away, acting, singing and accompanying the girl on his guitar.
The time flew. Most girls loved it. But most girls never
made it.

Hill's Angels (originally to be called, believe it or not,
The Hornettes) were an instant success. They raised
the roof at the live show, they raised the ratings,
they raised the temperature, male blood-pressure and
eyebrows all over Britain, to name but a few. There
were rivals, if not imitators, on the box every evening
– fourteen or fifteen sexy dance routines each week –
Foxy Feeling, Legs and Co, Pan's People, and so on.

The Suspender Belt stretched from Cardigan Bay to the Wash.

The heat was on. Competition was intense. Ratings and correspondence showed that the sexier the dance, the more popular it was. It was obviously male reaction that generated all the applause. Or was it? Let us not forget the experience of the manager of the Crazy Horse in Paris, the foremost striptease theatre in the world, who asserted that his most enthusiastic customers were coachloads of English ladies.

Whoever was enjoying the reeling and writhing, was enjoying it a lot. Benny therefore decreed that, if they could work an Angel into a sketch, they would; better still, a host of Angels; better yet, a host of Angels in suspender belts and black stockings. It was his ambition to send his viewing millions to bed happy, heads filled with flights of Angels to sing them to their rest.

He always wanted a hand in the direction of the comedy, and was interested in the dances largely in so far as they could be used for humorous or whimsical effects. He asked a great deal of his choreographer, Libby Roberts, as he insisted on intelligent, unusual routines on a theme that he would suggest for each show. The dances had to be an integral part of the entertainment, with reasons for being where and how they were presented. 'A routine must not be just stuck in,' asserts Benny. 'It has to have a *raison d'être*.' Creating and producing what was often a minor masterpiece of performance art required very much more thought, imagination and effort from the choreographer than the viewing public realized.

Everybody wanted to see more of Hill's Angels. Dennis Kirkland did his best to oblige. In January 1981 he filmed the girls in bright, brief body-stockings

at their popmobility exercises in a gymnasium. Trying to please the physical jerks among those who
watch the show, he allowed the camera to linger
lovingly on quivering thigh and the desmesnes that
there adjacent lie. The filmed routine was in no way
indecent. However, in a country that might be dubbed
the Democracy of Hypocrisy, where nobody buys the
millions of gynaecophysiological magazines that are
sold every week, it was raunchy enough to arouse
the professional ire of the familiar self-appointed self-
publicists. Benny was not unduly upset. After all, only
three letters of complaint had been received out of a
viewing public of twenty million. Par for the course.
Of the three letters, one was from a man who inadvert-
ently admitted that he had taped the show for his VCR.
'Now,' said Benny, 'he can be offended as often as he
likes, at any time, in the privacy of his own home.'

Benny is used to the double standards that obtain in
the eccentric country of his birth. Within one month
in 1972, sketches that were condemned by the Festival of Light as having 'degrading moral overtones'
won the Society of Film and Television Arts awards
for the Best Light Entertainment Production and Best
Script.

Although only a handful of people ever took the
trouble to send a letter of complaint, the press began
to concoct a story of widespread indignation at my
brother's classic comedy. When the *Nursing Journal*
began to object to what Joe Orton once called 'medical
romps with Nursie', Benny acted. In the next can-can
sequence, he substituted meter maids, and, surprise,
surprise, there was not a single complaint. Although
just as much creamy thigh was exposed, the Angels
were dressed as the dreaded female traffic wardens and
nobody gave a damn what they did on the show. Dean

Martin, who weathered a storm in the US in 1966 over his scantily-clad Golddiggers, advised Benny, 'Hang in there, kid. It'll blow over!'

Creative comedians, like other artists, tend to re-work obsessional themes. Chaplin, for instance, was much exercised by the vulnerability of 'the little fellow'; Bob Hope is often preoccupied with physical cowardice; Woody Allen with the fear of death; Jackie Mason with the anxieties of a Jew in a Gentile world; Dave Allen with the terrors of a Catholic upbringing. Benny Hill explores the pangs of unrequited lust. Male sexual frustration has been a valid and a proper, not to say inevitable, subject for comedy since Aristophanes – and long before. In *Lysistrata*, women stop a war by refusing to sleep with their soldier husbands and lovers until they cease fighting. The play creates some very funny situations. When, after a period of enforced chastity, a soldier appears with a huge erection, the sergeant says, 'I see you have standing orders!' Anybody shocked? 'The fact that people are shocked is the best proof that they need shocking,' wrote Aldous Huxley. He also suggested that the sheer ridiculousness of many aspects of sex kept laughter alive during the long, dark night of human prehistoric development. Laughter has survival value, among other virtues, for our species. It is clear that the importance of sex in comedy has not escaped Benny's notice. His version of the Latin tag is 'Vita brevis, arse longa', which, roughly translated, means 'Life may be short, but someone is at it all the time!'

I have always been astonished by the responses of a few viewers of the Benny Hill Show, who are disturbed by the sexual aspects of the presentation. The comedy team are male grotesques, weak, incompetent and grossly unattractive, who suffer monstrously unfair

physical abuse and psychological humiliations while
the most delectable, clean, healthy girls, at the peak
of their beauty, pass on untouched, like Good Queen
Bess, in maiden meditation, fancy-free. If anyone is
demeaned or degraded, it is the unfortunate clowns.
The girls are never chased. Benny has not made a
show for years where a female is chased. On the
other hand, he is always chased – for at least three
minutes in every show for nearly ten years. But, of
course, nobody has noticed that. For an explanation
of the vociferous criticisms of a few, I asked the wisest
man I know on matters sexual – the writer Anthony
Burgess.

'Benny should pay no attention to that stupid sexist
legend,' he said. 'His comedy, like all good comedy, tells the truth. People are like that. There's no
hypocrisy there. People are genuinely as he portrays
them.'

'But why the criticism?' I asked.

'A good deal of it comes from people whose own
sexual lives are unhappy. All presentation of sex is
painful to them. Under accusations of bad taste or
sexism, they express their fear of it. Benny tells the
truth. A lot of people can't take that.'

Jack Lemmon tended to agree. 'They're whackos,
most of them,' he said. 'Any suggestion of a natural physical relation is dirty to them. If they ever
need to reproduce, those blue-noses keep their eyes
closed even when the lights are off. And they're so
wrong about Benny. There's nothing dirty at all in
his work. There's a total innocence about it. He uses
sex to make fun of it. It's all terribly overt, not las-
civious to the slightest extent. It's a tool to create
laughs on a high level of comedy. I'll tell you what's
funny. It's that people think Benny is dirty. Because

he is about as far away from that as an entertainer can be!'

'It's the bloody BEB, the British Envy Barrier. That's behind most of the criticism,' said Michael Caine confidently. 'Benny doesn't get much stick from the Americans, does he?'

'No,' I said.

'I know he doesn't. I lived in the US for nine years. He's massive over there, on the television every night. They're not envious. They say, "He's a success. I'm going to do what he does." Over here, it's "How can we pull him down? Or destroy him?" Benny's big failing is that he makes it look too easy; they all think they can do it.'

It was when Benny heard a comment from the veteran film-maker Hal Roach, who was associated with Harold Lloyd and Laurel and Hardy, that he began to think seriously about altering his television show once more. At a campus lecture, Roach was asked if any modern comic measured up to the great comedians of the past. 'I guess there's only one,' said the distinguished producer, ' – Benny Hill. But I wish he'd clean up his act!'

Benny has great respect for Hal Roach and did not take his opinion lightly. However, he felt that his own show was based on honest vulgarity in the McGill seaside postcard tradition. He was proud of an entertainment as British as Brighton Pier and saw himself as the successor to Fred Karno and Sid Field. His life's work has been to bring the touring revue to the small screen. In doing so, Benny had always been careful not to go too far, never using the foul and obscene language now in common usage on television, never employing topless models. But the times they were a-changing. The rival sexy dance teams had wriggled their way off-screen and into oblivion. A bevy of beautiful girls could no longer give an ailing show the kiss of life.

Benny made up his mind. In the early weeks of 1986, previous orders were countermanded and new ones introduced that were diametrically opposite to the ones he had issued in the late seventies. One – No Angels in sketches unless needed. Two – A minimum of cleavage and stocking-tops. Three – No more reeling and writhing. At the news, suspender beltomanes were fainting in coils.

All Benny's efforts to accommodate the wishes of his strident critics were of no avail. Thames Television repeated ancient editions and re-cast versions of older Benny Hill Shows so that he was castigated by a fickle public for sequences that had been immensely popular when they were first shown. No one is more censorious than a reformed rake. The viewers had little appreciation that the whole tenor of his hour-long entertainment was different, that everything he has made since 1985 has been sexually blander. His introduction of sketches with young children has been very successful, but he is still seen as the comedian who runs after young women, although that is something he has literally never shown on screen.

'My humour is, I believe, totally innocuous. Some of it is based on male disappointment. My would-be lovers never succeed. A man who succeeds is not funny. A man who fails is funny. At bottom, it is very sad. Chaplin knew that. Presented in the right way, failure can be very funny. Success never is. So although my male characters hope, dream and endure all manner of blows for their hearts' desire, they are always defeated. If my sketches teach anything, it is that, for the male, sex is a snare and a delusion. What's so corrupting about that?'

Benny was saddened recently when one of the most successful of the 'alternative comedy' generation, in a public interview, asserted that he could find nothing funny in Benny Hill's little old man chasing girls round the park when the incidence of rape was up 45 per cent. Benny was depressed on two counts. Firstly, because the comment revealed that the young man had not watched the show. Benny Hill's little man has *never* chased girls round the park. Secondly, because the statement is a nonsense. It has the same validity as the view that Basil Fawlty should not poke his finger in the Spanish waiter's eye because of the incidence of racist violence.

'Personally, I would never make a serious public statement criticizing another performer's work,' says Benny. 'I may make a joke about one in my acts – and I don't mind him doing that to me. But, God knows, there are enough critics out there already, without performers at one another's throats.' I know Benny's sincerity in this. Whenever an entertainer is criticized in his presence, my brother always shames the critic by saying, 'He always speaks well of you!' The only time I have ever seen Benny really angry at his parents was when they spoke disparagingly of a fellow-performer.

Benny has found watching the development of alternative comedy in Britain a somewhat dispiriting experience. Very little of the material has been genuinely funny; some of it unspeakably revolting; the presentation has too often been strident; the reactions of audiences violent. 'The alternative comedy movement in this country has succeeded only in changing the taboos,' he says. 'When I started in the business, I couldn't make jokes about politics and religion. Now, I can't make jokes about women and race. Big deal!'

Benny has overlooked one important change. It has

nothing to do with comedy. It has a lot to do with political demagoguery. The Scottish comedian Arnold Brown said it first, 'Don't cheer. That's how fascism started.' Those who taught the disaffected young to raise their right arms to shout, 'Right On! Right On! Right On!' may live to regret it. The Diceman Cometh!

In the film, *Let's Make Love*, Yves Montand played a would-be comedian insisting on fresh comedy material. 'New jokes!' he demanded. 'I must have new jokes!' Replied his scriptwriter, 'New is easy; funny is difficult.' Benny feels that way about alternative comedy.

21

Top Banana

1984 was a sad year for Benny. During it his sister Diana in Australia contracted leukaemia. Characteristically she made light of her illness. Benny did everything he could to help but by the time we realized how serious her condition was, it was too late to visit her. We received the news of our sister's death with disbelief as she had been so full of life and so much younger than us.

At about the same time Benny's irreplaceable stooge, Jackie Wright, became too ill to work. 'I wish I could have done more for Jackie,' says my brother. 'But he was such an independent little feller. I tried to get him to cut out chain-smoking, but he insisted on performing scenes with a lighted cigarette up his sleeve. As he was an old man, I told him to take it easy, but he fell off a chair at home and broke two ribs. When he was at St Thomas's Hospital, I took a couple of Angels with me every visit because I knew he wanted to show off his girlfriends to the other patients. Then he went back to Belfast to recuperate. Because he was 84 and unsteady, he was given a walking-frame and a stick, but I'm told he wouldn't use them. One day he fell over on his way to the corner shop and broke his hip. We sent flowers to the hospital and the next we heard, early in 1989, was that Jackie had been dead some days. We sent wreaths at once, hoping they were not too late for the funeral. I had missed him for years, a fantastic, loyal friend and a vital part of the show. He will be missed in the States, too. He had his own fan club over there. Women loved him. We all did.'

Another blow for Benny, and many others, in 1984, was the death of Eric Morecambe, whom my brother liked and admired. His respect for his fellow-comic was such that he not only sent a stunning flower arrangement to the funeral but returned to the stage for the first time in a quarter of a century to perform in the Eric Morecambe London Palladium 'Bring Me Sunshine' tribute show. This featured a host of stars and was attended by Prince Philip and many other notables.

Morecambe would have appreciated Benny's effort as, before the performance, my brother was shaking with stage fright, a condition to which Eric himself was no stranger. The great ones all shake. Although Benny is never less than word-perfect at any performance, for this one he chose to present a schoolteacher skit with the book of his script in front of him to give him confidence.

A crowd of British star comedians stood at the back of the Palladium auditorium to watch Benny's rehearsal. Dennis Kirkland was there, also, to hear his man run through the material. 'All the big comics were absolutely fascinated, gathered there to see Benny,' he says. 'They're in awe of him. Not just because he's the most popular comedian in the world. But because they can't understand him. They don't know him socially, because he doesn't play golf with them, go to Stringfellows or showbiz parties. He's a mystery man. They're all there, agog with excitement, when Jimmy Tarbuck says, in wonder, "This is the first time Benny has set foot on a stage for twenty-five years!" Mike Yarwood pipes up, "Then it's about time he got himself a better agent!" '

As you might expect, Benny's agent, Richard Stone, sees things rather differently. 'I hope I have helped him with his career. I think I have put together some good deals for him, from a business point of view. I have also looked after a lot of other stars – Dave Allen, Victoria Wood, Terry Scott and many more. But Benny was the only one that never needed my artistic guidance. He knows everything about show business. He always knew more than I did. He is one jump ahead of the game every time and makes the television medium work for him.'

Benny's mastery of television was the subject of some perceptive comments by young American stand-up comics on Jasper Carrott's radio and television shows featuring the comedy clubs of New York and Los Angeles. I wanted to hear more of them. Having undertaken to write my brother's biography, I thought the transatlantic viewpoint might be refreshing. Jasper was most helpful and encouraging so that it was not long before I discovered that all the stories were true and that a deck of Benny Hill photographs assured me a warm welcome into the US. Within hours of my arrival in New York, reporters were asking my opinion of Mayor Koch, chat show hosts were inviting me to talk to the citizens, and bathrobed ladies were bumping into me in the hotel corridor. Needless to say, I was too terrified to respond to any of the approaches.

The terror did not last long. I soon found that, in the US, whenever the subject of Benny Hill comes up in conversation, people smile. Every time. Everybody. Men, women, children, old-timers and the folks who live on the hill. Not just Wasps, but every kind of American – Blacks, Hispanics, Jews, Chinese, Arabs, everybody. They all smile at the thought of the chubby comedian. It is an involuntary response. At the mention of his name, even the ranks of his feminist critics can scarce forbear to cheer up. The millions without an axe to grind smile openly, grateful for his supreme contribution to the gaiety of nations. To them, Benny Hill means laughter, warmth, joy and the affectionate recognition of human weakness. He is a regular visitor to every American home, a familiar figure in the lounge, a cheery companion, a much-loved friend. As his brother, I was given a welcome so spontaneous and generous that it overwhelmed me.

The first invitation I accepted was from Chuck Horner, the comedy writer, who entertained me royally in his magnificent Riverside Drive apartment. He told me that he had recently attended a gathering of high-level television producers, who had about three hundred years' broadcasting experience between them, having produced many prestigious shows on the networks. When the subject of comedy came up, they all agreed that the funniest series on American television was the Benny Hill Show. Chuck said that, although he felt the same way, he was astonished that there was not a single dissenter among them.

My new friend was kind enough to help me with my enquiries so that, a few nights later, I was up front at Michael's Pub (where Woody Allen sometimes sits in with the jazz combo) to see the fabulous Joan Rivers. She was in great form – 'I got this dress from Benny Hill. But he looks better in it!' – and tore the place apart. Later, she told me: 'Sexual attraction is a fact of life. It's not going to go away – and Benny deals with that from the male point of view. I think sometimes that maybe he is an anachronism, but he is so unique, such a superb performer, that he has survived the permissive age, the feminist movement, and I believe he will steam through the new puritanism.'

The view that the Benny Hill Show is enjoyed only by the lower orders was given a knock when I met Joel Parker in the Museum of Broadcasting in New York. He told me that, as Chairman of the Board of Fire Commissioners, he held a three-way telephone conversation first thing each day with the Head Attorney and Chief of the Westchester Fire Department. Every morning, the object of the conference call was the same – to discuss and laugh about what they had all seen on the Benny Hill Show the night before.

A typically warm American welcome awaited me at the comedy club, Catch a Rising Star. Its enthusiastic creative director, Louis Faranda, a Benny Hill fan from way back, soon had me settled and enjoying the show. Of the sixteen or so stand-up comics, my favourite was Larry Amoros, a very sharp ad libber, whom I trapped as soon as he came off the stage.

'Congratulations,' I said. 'I'm Leonard Hill.'

'Thanks. And I'm Fanny Hill!' he quipped.

'I've read you before,' I essayed.

'Well, you must admit my page eighty-three is really exciting.'

'But you always fall open at it!'

'That's because I'm not an omnibus edition like you!'

That tore it. I should have known better than to mix it with a real pro. Larry had seen most of the Benny Hill Shows and was much taken with a gentle sketch in which a number of girls independently sit down on the grass in a half-circle to look up the kilts of three recumbent Scotsmen. I was able to explain to Larry that my brother had observed half a dozen men doing just that to three office girls in Hyde Park. Benny had successfully reversed the sexes. So much for the accusations of invariable stereotyping!

My night was so enjoyable that I visited a couple of other comedy clubs and found the entertainment more engaging and audience reaction much more civilized than in similar clubs in London. However, Louis Faranda had made such a fuss of me that I could not resist returning to his First Avenue club, where I was lucky enough to catch Patty Rosborough's act. A gorgeous brunette feminist, she takes no prisoners, attacking with a verve that wins as many gasps as laughs. 'I'm macrobiotic. That means I don't smoke, I don't drink and I don't take drugs . . . I do, however, sleep with large, black men!' She is enraged at the female condition. 'Even in the animal kingdom, it's the lioness that goes out, kills the prey, drags it back to the lion, who's lying in the sun licking his balls. It's the same thing for women – only worse. The woman goes out, buys the pot roast, drags it back to the man who's lying on the couch – *and* she has to lick his balls!' Whee! I just had to talk to a gal who could lay it on the line like that. Patty was equally frank off-stage. 'There are too many tits in the Benny Hill Show,' she asserted. 'He's funny in spite of them. I love his playfulness, his slapstick physical humour, his silly falls. He's so cute, open and full of himself. He doesn't give a damn. I like that. But I wish he'd ban the boobs. My feminist friends feel the same.'

'Tell your feminist friends that they've made their point,' I reassured her. 'The boobs are much less in evidence these days.'

Another memorable evening in New York, I enjoyed the hospitality of the sparkling television and musical star, Denise Lor, who cooked me a delicious shark steak. Over dinner, she expressed her admiration, in particular, for Benny's acts as a clown, working against a black background. These, she believed, would become comedy classics. Later, she confessed a weakness for my brother's breathtaking impersonation of Oliver Hardy. It is easy to guess why. I have heard that Denise herself is a brilliant impressionist, who creates a knock-out representation of her friend Phyllis Diller.

Within a week, I was on my way, flying to see the original First Lady of Comedy at her home in Brentwood, Hollywood. It is Chandler country and, as my cab rolled at a deferential pace through the expensive, residential parkland, I thought I caught a glimpse of General Sternwood in a distant conservatory. Arriving at a large, pristine villa, I was ushered through a lounge dominated by a huge portrait of Bob Hope to a terrace, where I discovered, to my astonishment, that Phyllis Diller is a frail, beautiful woman. After the formalities, she offered me a glass of cool nectar that had the body of wine and the taste of chocolate.

'I've never met him, you know,' she began. 'I'm crazy about him but we've never met. I think he's divine and I wanted to talk to him. We stayed at the same hotel in Australia, but he wouldn't come out of his room to see me.'

'I know Benny admires you tremendously,' I said.

'Oh, I understand. He's hypersensitive. Yet on screen he had such courage. He went and did what's funny. I became an instant, mad fan as soon as I saw him. I follow every show of his. As a performer, I like constant laughter. That's Benny's aim, too. When you watch him, you're hysterical, because he's out of his mind. But people don't understand the mechanics or philosophy of humour. If everything is within the confines of propriety, they're not going to laugh. They want to laugh, yet they criticize what makes them laugh. Comedy's comedy. It can't be pretty. Pretty is a royal wedding. We're not dealing with that here. Benny's

ensemble of ugly old men in drag are not pretty, but
they're a hoot! And Benny's a hoot because he's a
consummate actor. He's so intimate, he doesn't have
to say anything. They show a lot of close-ups of his
face. It's so expressive, so mobile, so constantly in
motion. He tells the story with it. That's why he's
superb on television. He's arch. His look is worth a
thousand words. Bob Hope says Benny has a face like
an open fire. He should have gone into pictures. He
would have made a great movie star.'

Several days later, a great movie star was on the telephone line from Florida. 'I've been a fan of Benny's for
ages,' said Burt Reynolds, 'long before he became so
tremendously popular over here. He reminds me a lot
of Jack Benny in his takes. Especially when he does his
female characters. When Jack Benny did it, he would
dress up and show off a kind of feminine walk. By
comparison, Benny Hill's campy stuff is very real. It's
not, for me, that far over the top. Only when he wants
it to be, but it's terribly funny. And also, Jack Benny, of
course, was always looking at the audience – whenever
he had a chance. He was famous for that. Benny Hill
does the same thing. That's what makes the show for
me – the absolutely uninhibited way it's presented. It's
like we're peeking in at a rehearsal. We see something
go wrong, or whatever, and Benny's there, winking at
the audience. I believe you can break the wall to the
audience any time you want to, if it's the right kind of
show. And Benny has the perfect show to break the
wall in, which he does, to let the audience in on what's
going on. I know that it's controlled and that it's part
of his repertoire, but when he does break up, I buy it
almost every damn time. I say, "Well, the sonofabitch
got me again!" When he gets you like that, you're mad
for him. I just love his work.'

On the other hand, in Santa Monica, there is a married woman who thinks Benny Hill is too funny. 'What do you mean, too funny?' I demanded.

'Well,' she replied, 'every time Benny's on the television, my husband laughs so hard, he spills his beer and peanuts all over the carpet. And I have to clean it all up!'

A few miles inland from Santa Monica is the Improv, a Hollywood comedy club, where one evening I spent six fascinating hours watching a non-stop parade of bright young entertainers. The one who caught my eye was the bubbling Warren Thomas, of San Francisco, who has a trick of getting a double laugh on his witticisms when he explains them for the slower patrons. After I had prised him loose from his admirers, he told me, 'Benny Hill is one of the roots of my comedy. That's where it comes from. I was in High School, growing up, when I first saw him. My friends and I would emulate the things we saw him do. We loved him because he was the antithesis of the political parody shows. The Benny Hill Show was pure fun, pure comedy, absolute wackiness. That's what I like to do on-stage. Comedy should be shameless. There are a lot of American performers who are afraid to put on a dress, to go nuts on-stage, because they are too cool. Benny doesn't mind being uncool. I love that uncool element.'

A great American performer who is not afraid to put on a dress kindly invited me into his luxurious office a few days later. 'Like other artists of talent,' said the erudite Jack Lemmon, 'Benny has a sense of rhythm. He's very musical, very sensitive in that way. In performance, Benny knows when to look and then give the line. He also knows when to come right in. He knows when to overlap. That's a sense of rhythm. Benny also has a sense of humour. We use the phrase of someone who enjoys a joke, meaning an appreciation of humour. But a true sense of humour is something more. It means an understanding of humour. Benny has it. Because he is not just a performer; he's a writer; he's a producer and a great director, because he understands what he should show and what he should leave to the imagination. He has to know, as a good writer like Neil Simon knows, what will be funny, if it is delivered correctly. Now, that is a sense of humour. And not all performers have that. Most of them have an instinctive talent for comedy. They can get up and do it. But they can't create it. They're not really in the top drawer, because they just don't have it. You're born with it. A sense of timing, a sense of delivery and a sense of humour, in the way that I define it, are gifts you have or don't have. You can't learn them. If you're lucky, you can sharpen them by using them, working with other people who are very talented – good writers, good fellow-actors. But Benny has it all. I get such a kick out of him that I don't know anybody working in his field that even comes close.'

I returned to Britain in December 1988 to find that Benny had recently made a video with Genesis, the world-famous rock group. It seems that Tony Banks, the keyboard player, had written a number called 'Anything She Does', with sexy Page Three girls in mind. Who more suitable, yet more unlikely, to add a touch of humour to the video than Benny Hill? He had never appeared on one before and would give the project the slightly tongue-in-cheek flavour that Genesis favour. Benny agreed, provided no girls were chased in the scenes. Phil Collins was delighted. 'I have a lot of love and respect for Benny,' he confesses. 'But he's an enigma that fascinates me. How can he have remained so successful without playing the publicity game? I was a little in awe of him when we met and astounded that he looked so youthful. Suddenly I was talking to one of my heroes. He was charming but very professional and we were all soon at ease.'

The video was made at Wembley Conference Centre. Benny played his Fred Scuttle character, in uniform as the Securititty guard, keeping girl fans away from the group. Unfortunately, when he arrived to give the lads a call, he found their dressing-room in a mess. With the aid of a little trick photography, he soon had it tidy. Then Fred Scuttle ushered the musical stars through the back-stage area and on to the stage.

On tour, Genesis opened their show with the video. The lights would go out and Benny, in characteristic Scuttle pose, would appear on two gigantic screens. In the huge American stadiums, with 50,000 fans assembled, Benny would get a fantastic reception.

'The audiences shouted and cheered him,' reports Phil. 'At the end of the video, we walked on-stage. Which is a great way to start the show. It may have seemed an odd combination to the Americans, but we wanted Benny to be part of our work because he was part of our past. We all grew up with him on television and have a lot of affection for him. I think he's a wonderful comedian. I could shout his praises from the rooftops. It was a feather in our cap, a major coup for us to get him on our video.'

In February 1988, the local section of the British Academy of Film and Television Arts organized a 'Hollywood Salute to British Comedy' celebration lunch at the Bel Age Hotel, Los Angeles, with Prince Andrew, Duke of York, as guest of honour, accompanied by the Duchess of York. Benny was invited but could not attend. In her speech of welcome, Anjelica Huston, who was escorted by Jack Nicholson, said, 'The British

exported comedy to America. The spirit of "That Was
The Week That Was" is alive and well and lives today
in "Saturday Night Live"; the British bigot Alf Garnett
begat the American bigot Archie Bunker; Benny Hill,
of course, begets himself!'

After Dudley Moore had replied, clips of British
comedy films and television programmes were shown.
Among them was my brother's brilliant sketch in
which, accompanied by his ugly old gimmer of a
wife, a defeated Benny Hill throws a coin into a
wishing well. Immediately, his wife disappears and,
to his delight, a beautiful girl appears from nowhere;
the beautiful girl, however, throws in a coin and gets
a handsome muscleman, who takes one look at her
and throws in a coin. The pretty girl disappears as
the muscleman grabs Benny by the arm and tries to
mince off with him. Just in time, Benny throws in a
coin to banish the muscleman and get back his safe,
ugly, old gimmer.

In May 1989, a month after audiences of 190 million
had given it a rapturous reception throughout the
Soviet Union, Thames Television announced that it
would no longer finance further editions of the Benny
Hill Show. There appeared to be three critical factors
that led to the decision. Firstly, over twenty-one years
the company had built up a huge stock of Benny Hill
programmes that could be earning money indefinitely
for the company, especially with the East European
countries clamouring for them. Secondly, the show is
probably the most expensive television comedy project
in the world and Thames wanted the money tied up in
it for other projects. Thirdly, the future of British television had become unclear, with deregulation looming,
and the company needed as much room for manoeuvre
as possible.

Benny took the news in his stride, as he is constantly fending off propositions and knew that finance would always be available to underpin his efforts.

Schnozzle Durante used to sing 'I can do widout Broadway, but can Broadway do widout me?' The world, apparently, cannot do widout Benny Hill. Offers flooded in to present the next Benny Hill Show – from Australia, France, Belgium and the US. My brother was charmed by 'some very nice people in America' – friends of Don Taffner – and flew over to scout locations. He got as far as Central Park, New York. 'Oh, this is great!' he enthused. 'Just think what I could do with those four-wheeled surreys (the little carriages that glide around the huge playground).'

It is clear that the attractions of the Big Apple kept him there. He saw a tearaway fight bill at the rumbustious Deacon Theatre. 'There's a whole lot of superlative boxing talent waiting in the wings,' he states. Benny had his photograph taken with the millionaire Donald Trump, both doing the Scuttle salute. Coming down in the lift with Trump, he was suddenly recognized by a black guy in uniform. 'Oh, my God!' cried the startled fellow. 'It's Benny Hill! You're great, man, you're great! I love you!' and pumped his hand. His greeting was so intense that my brother suspected a trick. 'Come on, Donald,' he said, 'you gave the man fifty dollars to put on that performance, didn't you?' But apparently the fan's joy at meeting his hero was quite genuine.

Benny was asked, with Audrey Hepburn, Walter Cronkite and Hal Holbrook, to present trophies at the International Emmy Awards ceremony. He was proud to play a part in honouring the British comedian Alexei Sayle, one of his own favourites, and delighted to meet Audrey Hepburn, whom he had tipped for stardom when she was dancing in the West End revue *Sauce Tartare* with Bob Monkhouse in 1949.

'I knew Audrey had star quality, even then, but that's not enough. You have to hone it. I so admire women who make it – Phyllis Diller, who started late, with five kids to support, having to struggle against prejudice all the way. What a woman! And Joan Rivers, who goes out like a lion-tamer, night after night, to win over audiences. And never fails. I won't do it. I'm too scared to try. I saw the lovely Petula Clark squashing hecklers in Marseilles, no bother. What courage! Those girls certainly have my respect.'

Contrary to all the premature valedictions of the British press, the slush about the broken-hearted clown stricken by the collapse of his career, the bilious good-riddance articles, Benny's routine lifestyle continued smoothly, without any kind of hiatus, or even a hiccup. Within months he was back again at the Teddington Studios of Thames Television, with all his old chums, making the next Benny Hill Show. Except that, this time, the party was being paid for by 'some very nice people in America'.

No doubt Benny will produce some surprises in the new show, as he usually does. 'I'm still amazed,' Anthony Burgess told me recently, 'by the extreme versatility and the unfailing sense of newness. It's quite incredible that you don't get any real repetition. He does not reveal the same things twice. Some of the same themes come up again, of course. I think he's quite remarkable. He has my homage and always will have.'

There have been many examples of Benny's originality in recent years. One of my favourites is 'Piped Music', a supermarket sequence that is so packed with sight-gags that it defies detailed description and must be seen to be appreciated. However, I outline it here to illustrate the complexity of some of my brother's creations. The sketch depicts the effects of muzak upon a man and a girl shopping in a supermarket. When tinkling musical-box sounds are played, the pair find themselves caught up in an involuntary ballet. The mood is broken when the man hurts his leg, but a jaunty Scottish jig emboldens them both into stepping out apart, on opposite sides of a tin-packed gondola. Caribbean music has Benny drumming on a biscuit tin, while the girl, basket of fruit on head, sways round him, Carmen Miranda-fashion. The sudden appearance of Jackie Wright as the manager stops the capering, but, once he has passed, Spanish music introduces a mock bullfight, in which a speeding horned trolley is slowed down by picador Benny with two baguettes. Attempting to make passes with a tablecloth, Benny is caught off balance and bundled into another aisle. To the strains of a striptease number, Benny sexily swings a string of sausages, languidly drops packages into a basket, and slowly doffs his gloves. Hospital theme music has Dr Benny in rubber gloves with the girl as nurse, gazing at him adoringly. He picks up a swaddled loaf to the strains of 'Rock-A-Bye Baby' and presents it to the girl/mother. Lush, movie-type music induces the pair to dance and twirl into a romantic embrace. However, a brass band heralds the arrival of the police, male and female. They are also enthralled by the music and join the miscreants in a maypole folk-dance. Suddenly, the police come to their senses and march Benny and the girl away, followed by the manager, Jackie, who executes a little jig of triumph to finish the scene.

While Benny would be the first to admit that there is little fundamentally new in comedy, most of the items he presents are very much his own invention.

He does not always rely on observations from life to give him humorous ideas. A few years ago, he was playing with pages of magazine pictures. He began to cut out faces. When he turned them upside-down, he realized that with eyes stuck on either side of the chin, a strange fish-like head appeared. He used the illusion in a short sketch featuring these strange creatures in a tank. It was a popular novelty – so popular that it was immediately employed by others.

One of Benny's recent bulls-eyes depicts the outdoor scene on the lawn of a nursing-home with many patients in wheelchairs, in plaster and on crutches. Benny, wearing a suit and an ill-fitting hair-piece, walks across the lawn with a disobedient little dog. 'Heel!' he orders. The little dog takes no notice. 'Heel!' shouts Benny. As the camera moves directly close in on him, 'Heal!' he cries, 'Heeawl!' and puts out a hand of splayed fingers towards us. Suddenly, Benny is that appalling American television evangelist, he of the false hair-piece and soapy smile. 'Heeawl,' he bleats again. And, all at once, the patients leap from their wheelchairs, kick off their plasters and throw their crutches up in the air – CURED! I think this sketch is hilarious, relevant and does more to unmask religious hypocrisy than a raft of newspaper articles.

That particular sketch attains all of Benny's immediate aims. 'I see it as my function to be interesting, funny, and to make a certain amount of social comment, in that order,' he says. He achieves a great deal more than that. Benny is a remarkably successful ambassador for Britain, the living proof that the inhabitants of these islands are not all upper-class twits and illiterate hooligans. He is so widely loved that there are rumours in the respective countries that he is of German extraction, partly Spanish, or has some Chinese blood. He regards himself as a citizen of the world. 'We are all brothers under the skin,' is a favourite saying of his. He responds openly to people of all races and has respect for all.

Twenty years ago, when he first joined Thames, he made a live broadcast to Yugoslavia via the BBC Eurovision link. After a recording of the Benny Hill Show, the programme continued with questions from a Yugoslav audience in London with translations of Benny's answers into Serbo-Croat. He finished the broadcast by making a warm and friendly speech in impeccable Serbo-Croat that had taken him four days to learn from a cassette specially made for the purpose. The Yugoslavs attending the show in London applauded him wildly: no other Western entertainer had ever bothered to say much to them in their own language. Benny has tried, where possible, to continue that courtesy and recently made a short speech of best wishes in Russian to open his series of shows in the Soviet Union.

Benny's international fame is suggested by travellers' reports of innumerable cafés, bars, tavernas, restaurants, petrol stations and hot-dog stands all over the world that are named after him. To assess his popularity, I went to Madame Tussaud's to talk to some of the tourist fans who have their photographs taken alongside the wax Benny Hill look-alike. The interviews revealed various responses.

Rungien of Mauritius watches the show with his family and friends.

Asrat and Ahmet from Cairo play Benny Hill videos (sent by an uncle from Houston) in the intervals of the dances they organize.

Liza from New York finds Benny 'dashing'.

Isabelle of Aveiro, Portugal, cannot get enough of the show.

Costas of Crete likes it because it is funnier than most
Greek comedy.

Miriam from Tel-Aviv, Israel, loves Benny and wants
his telephone number.

Andrei of Dortmund, Germany, and his young friends
hold Benny Hill parties.

Tim of Zambia knows a man who left his wife because
she preferred watching Benny Hill to making love.

Maria of Pila, Argentina, is embarrassed because her
neighbours hear her laughing at Benny.

There is no need for Maria to feel embarrassed. After
all, even at the height of the Falklands War, millions
in Argentina were still enjoying the Benny Hill Show
regularly, every week.

Hostilities did not prevent an Argentinian television
magazine from displaying the Saucy Boy and his Angels
on the front cover. There was greater official disapproval in Iran, where an Iranian traveller risked and
suffered a jail sentence to smuggle Benny Hill videos
into the country. There is no ban on the show in
Nicaragua, however, where there was a noticeable
lull in the fighting when both sides in the civil war
withdrew to see Benny at play. As for the Lebanon,
Bob Saget of CBS reported, 'When Benny Hill comes
on Syrian television, every antenna in the Middle East
turns towards Damascus, and there is a *de facto* ceasefire
along the Green Line. Having Benny Hill on twenty-four
hours a day might keep the world laughing instead of
fighting.'

Every country that broadcasts the Benny Hill Show
has its own way of expressing its enthusiasm for the
blue-eyed British comic. In Spain, Benny is regularly
followed by lines of marching children shouting, *Ah,
que sava SABA!'*, the slogan of Benny's commercial for
the Saba television set. It is based on the Spanish saw,

'one who knows, knows'. In Turkey, Benny has many imitators, according to Turkish comedian Levent Kazak in a BBC Television travel show – and in China, because he is chubby, Benny's appearance on the television in a home is said to bring good luck.

A few years ago, my brother was ringside at a boxing show at the Stade Coubertin, Paris. Lucien Rodriguez, the European heavyweight champion, seated nearby, came over between the bouts to say hello. Benny took to the burly fellow immediately. As they were chatting, the crowd recognized my brother and began to chant, 'Benny Eel! Benny Eel!' The chants got louder and a great mob gathered round the pair, trying to push Benny up into the ring. Everyone expressed good-will towards the English funny man, but the efforts of the mob were making the situation unpredictable. Suddenly, my brother was shoved into Rodriguez, who fell, with Benny on top of him. After a long moment, Benny was able to disentangle himself and help the big man to his feet. The pair fought their way through the crowd, with the stadium now resounding to the thunder of 'Benny Eel! Benny Eel!' As Rodriguez hustled my brother to safety, he grunted, 'You've just done what the heavyweight champion of the world, Larry Holmes, couldn't do.' 'What's that?' asked Benny. 'Knocked me down!' grinned Rodriguez.

When Ben and Den went to Greece to promote the new home videos of the show, a press call had been arranged upon arrival in the lounge at Athens Airport. As their plane taxied to a halt, Den looked out of his window to see fifty cameramen and television crews already on the runway. He immediately rushed up front and returned with the captain's cap, which Benny put on sideways to stand saluting on the top of the steps. At the sight of their hero, everyone cheered. More

photographers ran over from the lounge and they all
began to fight one another for advantage. When Greeks
joined Greeks, there was the tug-of-war. At last, Ben
and Den tottered down the stairway and into the airport
bus with all the other passengers. Mistake! A Mafia-
type Cadillac with black windows had been provided
to take them the full fifty yards to the lounge. Once
there, an active press conference took place which
frightened our heroes more than somewhat. Calling
upon their police escort for protection, they asked
for safe conduct to their hotel. 'Just get us away from
the press, please!' they pleaded. The police were most
obliging. Sirens howling, they rushed the precious pair
across town, cutting corners, thumping curbs, rock-
ing and squealing, with outriders sweeping traffic out
of the way. The parade finally screeched to a halt at the
hotel. Out stepped the odd couple, green and shaken.

'Well, we've lost the press,' said Den.

'That's not all we've lost,' said Ben, retching into a
potted plant.

An hour later, Ben and Den sneaked out of the hotel
to find a quiet pavement table in a tranquil square.
Watching the world go by, round the square, they
saw it winding down. Horns blared. Drivers waved,
laughed and shouted. 'Benny Eel! Benny Eel!' Traffic
jammed to dead slow. Stop. People on foot filled in the
spaces between the cars. The square was packed! Total
chaos and cacophony! 'Benny Eel! Benny Eel!' Benny
Eel and partner paid up, left the table and crept, oh so
casually, out of the snarl-up they had created.

Next day, Benny, dressed as a Greek Tsolias soldier,
in white, flared skirt and pom-pom shoes, was driven
up the hill for a photo call at the Acropolis. Once again,
as soon as he appeared, chaos reigned supreme. Five
hundred tourists mobbed him.

'We can't have this,' cried the curator. 'The Acropolis is a sacred site. You must go. Take your pictures on the hill across the way.'

'Sorry for all the fuss, mate,' said my brother.

'Benny Hill,' grins Dennis, 'must be the only person to have been thrown off the Acropolis since the invasion of the Turks!'

In Europe, the Benny Hill Show is a delight shared by people of all countries. Alf Scrimgour, Tours Director of the travel company Snow World, finds it gives him a common interest with clients over the entire Continent. This was brought home to him vividly when, in West Berlin, he was helping a friend to park his car in a quiet square. As there was little traffic about, Alf was clowning, pretending to be drunk as he waved his arms and shouted instructions. A passing middle-aged German – cropped hair, impassive face – suddenly broke into peals of loud laughter, stopped, slapped his thighs and pointed at Alf. 'Benny Heel, ja? Benny Heel! Benny Heel! Ha-ha-ha!' It was the ultimate accolade in a language they both understood.

Early in 1990 Scrimgour was on the first plane from London into Bucharest after the revolution. He had been invited, with members of the press, by the Romanian tourist authorities for a first-hand inspection to assure the world that the new regime was stable and open for business. Alf was interested in a luxurious hotel, the Alpin, at Sinaia, a small skiing village in the mountains to the north of Bucharest. Upon arrival at the Alpin, he and his twelve associates were ushered into a magnificent banqueting hall where a table, sparkling with crystal and silver, had been laid for the party. Round the only other occupied table, an obviously important family of ten were already at lunch. In a corner of the hall was a large television set showing Western videos, which were generally being ignored.

Suddenly, the group's guide ceased talking. His eyes lit up. 'Benny Hill! Benny Hill!' he shouted. Everybody in the hall stopped and turned towards the television set, where Benny was starting the beach sketch with the bouncing ice-cream cones.

'Immediately, everyone was shrieking with laughter,' says Alf. 'The atmosphere was electric. The family left their meal to watch, and the grandfather was beside himself. He laughed so hard I was afraid he was going to have a seizure. I've never seen people having such a good time. So I asked the guide about it. "There was an official ban on the Benny Hill Show in the old days," said the guide, "but, since the revolution, everyone all over the country is talking of Benny Hill. We think he is wonderful. He has become the most popular star in Romania in the space of three weeks!" '

The news that he has brought laughter to yet another country that badly needs it will please Benny. 'It has never been my aim to be clever for six of my friends,' he says. 'I have always sought the largest possible audience. That is why my work is so varied, including the complex and the simple. And that is why my comedy is visual – so that it may transcend boundaries of language and culture. When I started on television, comedians were talking heads. Many of those young comedians, who feel they are bringing about fundamental changes in comedy today, are still just talking heads. There is room for them, room for us all. Laughter is a valuable commodity and any laugh is better than none. I don't believe in the comedy of hate. There is no such thing. Hatred can create excitement – not true comedy. Look at the Nazi attempts to make fun of the Jews. It's all sour – there's not a laugh in it. But listen to Jackie

Mason and you will laugh non-stop for two hours at jokes about the Jews. Because it's presented with a love and understanding that evokes those sentiments in the listener. It is significant that likely victims are advised by the psychologists, "Make your kidnapper laugh. Laughter will breed love." '

Laughter also heals. 'I'm eternally grateful to Benny,' says Michael Bentine, 'because, when I was at rock bottom and the hour was at its darkest, I could always turn to him and get a good laugh. A number of people in hospital, and a lot of them in great pain, have told me that, despite everything, they always got a laugh out of the Benny Hill Show. Now that's a great gift to be able to offer another human being in pain.' Herbert Kretzmer made a similar point when he described his hospital experiences in the *Daily Mail*, ' . . . the high-light of the week was undoubtedly Benny Hill. I am not likely soon to forget the sight of pyjama-clad men, most suffering some degree of physical pain or discomfort, literally holding their sides and shaking in their beds at the drolleries of the outrageous Mr Hill. The effect was instant and medicinal, and gave a new meaning to the phrase, "had us all in stitches" . . . laughter is one of the greatest healing forces in the world. Benny Hill would have been proud to have seen the effect of his handiwork.'

Benny was proud to learn from a member of the Chaplin family that Charlie admired his work. In the year that my brother first starred in his own BBC tele-vision show, he watched Chaplin shooting *Limelight* in London. At that time, Laurel and Hardy were making their last film, Abbott and Costello were top box-office attractions. On the small screen, Arthur Askey was Britain's favourite comedian, while Milton Berle and Arthur Godfrey battled it out in the States.

During the ensuing forty years, during which he has won scores of awards, Benny has never left the top. He began by introducing satire of television itself on television, developed female impersonation, dropped that and created warm, family shows, moved on to raunchier humour and provocative dance routines, and changed again with the introduction of children and the exploitation of male stupidity without offence to the ladies. He has always kept ahead of public taste, though many commentators have been slow to catch on.

In a medium ravenous for fresh faces, new shows, innovative ideas, Benny has achieved the summit and stayed there by talent and dedication alone. Family influence was minimal. There was no financial backing. There was no support from any group with an interest in helping him. As Bob Monkhouse has remarked, 'Benny has always refused to dance to anybody else's tune.' My brother is not a Freemason, a Catholic, a Jew, a homosexual, a member of the Oxbridge mafia, a public-school boy, a regimental-tie man, or an adherent of any religious, political or social organization. Like Oscar Wilde, he has nothing to declare but his genius.

Throughout four decades, he has reached wider and wider audiences. Aged sixty-six, he is working hard on his present show with two more planned and others expected. If any entertainer has earned the right to sing Stephen Sondheim's song, 'I'm Still Here!' it is Benny Hill.

If you consider for a moment the lives of great men – the artists, whose masterpieces lie in cellars and bank vaults, the scientists, whose discoveries have been used for destruction and carnage, the prophets and holy men, whose followers have left a centuries-old trail of bloodshed and torture, the political idealists, whose revolutions have led to oppression and mass homicide – you may be persuaded by this proposition. It is that there would be few of the aforementioned who would not envy the epitaph that my brother has already carved for himself: 'Benny Hill made more people laugh longer than any entertainer in history.'

He was profoundly satisfied when *Variety* recently confirmed his supremacy by describing him in a headline as 'Global TV's Top Banana'. The face that launched a thousand quips is now the most famous face in the world. From it, as Dick Van Dyke has observed, 'shines a boundless love of all humanity'. Humanity returns that love. Benny Hill is held in affection and respect from China to Peru – a tribute to the kid from Southampton who began with the catch-phrase, 'Bless Your Hearts' and finally found a place in millions of them.

Index

Freemasonry, 95, 97, 98
imitative ability, 24-5
learning from strangers, 40
life and career: wandering
childhood, 27; life with
Fossett's circus, 27-9; period
as cheapjack, 29-30; service
in First World War, 31-3;
prisoner of Germans, 31-3;
success in rubber goods
business, 34-5; marriage,
1920, 35-6; birth of children,
36; family life, 36-7; tricks
younger son over nuts, 83-4;
teaches sons grafters' slang,
100-101; boxes with sons, 108;
wartime bungalow at
Hounsdown, New Forest,
121, 128, 174; sums up
Second World War, 193-4; trip
to Australia, 1955, 284; holiday
in Spain with BH, 382-3;
illness and death, 383-5
office, 98-9
one-string fiddles, 37
pleasure in baseball, 47-9
scornful about BH's trumpet,
174-5
Hill, Benny (Alfred Hawthorn)
account of touring
comedians, 1930s, 114
admiration for Danny
Thomas, 215-16
artistic ability, 93-4
attitude to clothes, 426-7
BH at home, 309-11
combating myth of
homosexuality, 338-9
conservatism, 332-3
correspondence, 376
dislike of cars, 426
dispirited by alternative
comedy, 479
'Dustbin' of old jokes, 451
effigy in Madame Tussaud's
497
enjoyment of food

and cooking, 443-6
entertains during blitz, 1-2
experience with Spanish
child, 431-2
experience with Spanish
pickpockets, 430
explores male disappointment
in sketches, 475, 478
expresses criticism of
father, 213-14
faithfulness to show team, 454
film buffdom, 443
friendship with brother
Leonard, 108-9, 196, 198
friendship with women, 434-7
generosity, 437-8
giggling problem, 464
girlfriends, 262-3, 264-6, 267
house in Southampton, 425
impersonations of film stars,
95-7, 292
invention of sound effects,
468-9
lack of concern over money,
332-3, 438-9
life and career: birth, 1924,
5-6, 7, 36; family background
6-7, 15-23; infancy and
boyhood, 2-6, 7-13, 21-2,
40-42; entertains as a child,
37-8; way of dealing with
father's domination, 43-4;
encounter with hornet, 46-7;
early sexual awareness, 51-3;
pushes marble up nose, 53-4;
'collides with motor car', 54;
encounters 'nasty, dangerous
man', 54-6; favourite
playground, 56; learns to read,
56-7; first visit to theatre, 58;
recollections of family
Sundays, 58-9; leaves Infants'
School for 'Big Boys', 60-61;
problem of petit-bourgeois
at working-class school,
61-2; enjoyment of cards,
62-4; tonsils removed, 64-5;